AMERICAN PHOTOGRAPHERS
Capturing the Image

The Collective Biographies Series

Collective Biographies

AMERICAN PHOTOGRAPHERS
Capturing the Image

Ann Graham Gaines

Enslow Publishers, Inc.

40 Industrial Road	PO Box 38
Box 398	Aldershot
Berkeley Heights, NJ 07922	Hants GU12 6BP
USA	UK

http://www.enslow.com

Copyright © 2002 by Ann Graham Gaines

Library of Congress Cataloging-in-Publication Data

Gaines, Ann.
    American photographers : capturing the image / Ann Graham Gaines.
       p. cm. — (Collective biographies)
    Includes bibliographical references and index.
    Summary: Discusses the lives and influences of Mathew B. Brady, Jacob A. Riis,
    Alfred Stieglitz, Lewis Wickes Hine, Man Ray, Dorothea Lange, Ansel Adams,
    Margaret Bourke-White, Diane Arbus, and Gordon Parks.
    ISBN 0-7660-1833-4
    1. Photographers—United States—Biography—Juvenile literature.
    2. Photography—United States—History—Juvenile literature.
    [1. Photographers. 2. Photography.] I. Title. II. Series.
    TR139 .G35 2002
    770'.92'273—dc21   2001002363

Printed in the United States of America

10 9 8 7 6 5 4 3 2

Illustration Credits: AP Photo, 76; Associated Press, AP. Photographer–Jeff
Chiu, Staff., pp. 86, 89; Dover Publication, Inc. p. 16; Jacob A. Riis
Collection, p. 31; Library of Congress, pp. 22, 26, 34, 38, 47, 50, 55, 60,
63, 81, 94, 97; Courtesy of the Estate of Sol Libsohn, p. 42; Nancy R.
Schiff/Getty Images, p. 70; National Archives, p. 73.

Cover Illustration: AP Photo (photo of Margaret Bourke-White); Library of
Congress (photos of Gordon Parks, Jacob A. Riis, Alfred Stieglitz).

Contents

Preface

Photography is one of the most popular hobbies in the United States today. Millions of Americans own cameras. They take billions of pictures each year. People record personal events in their lives through snapshots and videos.

There are also many professional photographers. We see their work everywhere, in books and magazines, in advertising, in television and movies, and on the Internet.

However, photography has only been around since the 1830s. Before that time, people had to rely on drawings, paintings, or engravings for visual images. And only the wealthy could afford them.

The Beginnings of Photography

Since the days of ancient Greece, artists had been using a device called a camera obscure, which means "dark room." They knew that when light passes through a small opening into a darkened room, an image of the scene outside forms on the opposite wall.

Artists used a camera obscure to trace images onto paper or metal plates for engravings. Over time, the camera obscure was made smaller and smaller, until it became the size of a portable box.[1]

In the early nineteenth century, scientists and inventors worked to find a process that would make camera obscure images permanent. They included William Henry Fox Talbot of Great Britain, and Joseph-Nicéphore Niepce and Louis Daguerre of France.[2]

Louis-Jacques-Mandé Daguerre was a stage designer in the French theater. For years he experimented with different materials to discover how to make lasting photographic images. His success, however, came about by chance.

One day Daguerre had a copperplate coated with silver in his camera obscure. He exposed the copperplate to light. But the impression he got was not dark enough. Daguerre decided to have the plate repolished to use at another time.

He put the copperplate in a cupboard where he also stored bottles of acid. The next day, when he opened the cupboard, there was a tiny picture on the copperplate. When Daguerre found that he could repeat this process, he was very excited. He told his wife, "I have seized the light, I have arrested its flight."[3]

In August 1839, Daguerre gave a speech at the French Academy of Sciences. He explained how he made his daguerreotypes. People were very interested in his discovery. Every seat in the room was filled when he spoke.

Francois Arago, a scientist, had made arrangements for Daguerre's speech. In exchange for

Daguerre agreeing to explain about his discovery, Arago had asked the French government to give Daguerre an annuity, a yearly payment.

Photography Arrives in America

Within weeks, the story appeared in American newspapers. American scientists and inventors began to experiment with photography, too.

Alexander Wolcott, an American, took out a patent for a camera. Daguerreotypists set up studios all over the United States. Americans were eager to have portraits made.

Among the first American photographers were Albert Sands Southworth, a pharmacist, and Josiah Johnson Hawes, a painter. Southworth and Hawes became business partners and moved to Boston. Celebrities came to have their portrait taken.[4]

Within fourteen years, 3 million daguerreotypes were being produced in the United States every year.[5]

New Processes Develop

Scientists and inventors continued to experiment to improve the photographic process. A daguerreotype had limitations. The picture was not always easy to see—the viewer had to tip the copperplate for a clear image. To make a daguerreotype the sitter had to hold still for more than ten minutes. Sometimes daguerreotypists became ill from breathing in the fumes from the mercury and chemicals used to develop the plates. But the most serious problem was that a daguerreotype's plate could not be reproduced.[6]

A process was needed to create a negative from which positive images could be made. William Fox Talbot discovered a way to print a photograph on paper. But his so-called calotypes were blurry.

In 1851, Frederick Scott Archer of Great Britain discovered he could coat a wet plate of glass with collodion, a thick chemical solution. The wet-plate process produced beautiful, sharp images, but it was inconvenient. A photograph had to be developed before the glass plate dried. This was not a problem in a studio, but it was for the photographer who took a picture out of doors.[7]

New Uses for Photography

In the beginning, photography was used almost entirely for portraits or posed pictures of people. But over time, American photographers found new subjects to photograph.

As early as 1842, antique dealers made photographs of their wares. Detectives used hidden cameras to take secret photos of criminals or crimes in progress.

Photographers took pictures of landscapes and streetscapes, at home and while traveling.[8] Although daguerreotypists had taken the first travel "photographs" in Egypt in 1839, these could not be directly reproduced. Engravers had to trace the daguerreotypes and reproduce them as copperplate engravings to print them.

In 1855, Roger Fenton, an English landscape photographer, became the first photojournalist. He photographed the Crimean War, a war involving Russia, Turkey, Great Britain, and France. But the four hundred photographs Fenton took were posed and showed none of the real horrors of war.[9]

Mathew Brady was the first American photojournalist. He was famous in the 1840s as a portrait photographer. When the U.S. Civil War began, Brady and his team of photographers captured the images of battle and its aftermath.

After the war, photographers took pictures of the American West, many on government-sponsored expeditions. They showed Americans exciting places like Yosemite and the Grand Canyon.

Some photographers served as anthropologists. Artists had often shown Native Americans as "noble savages." Photographers like Jack Hillers showed that the lives of Native Americans were often miserable. They had to compete with white people for land and resources.[10]

As the century progressed, stereographs, cardboard cards that featured two nearly identical photographs, became very popular. They were viewed through a stereoscope, an instrument that combined the images of the two photographs to appear as a three-dimensional picture.[11]

Photography Becomes a Hobby

For years photography remained mainly the work of professionals. The process of producing photographs was considered too complicated and inconvenient for the average person.

George Eastman, an amateur photographer, was frustrated by having to use the huge wet-plate cameras of his day. "It seemed that one ought to be able to carry less than a pack-horse load," he said.[12]

Eastman developed a roll film that could be produced in mass quantities. Then, he invented the Kodak, a camera that was small enough to carry around and easy to use. It became a sensation. Americans bought his inexpensive Kodak Brownie camera to take snapshots anytime, anywhere.

Photography as Social Commentary

The period from the 1900s to World War I is referred to as the Progressive Era, when reforms were popular. Politicians and others worked to clean up corrupt local governments and to correct problems in society.

Jacob Riis was one of the first photographers to document social problems. His photographs showed the terrible living conditions of the poor in slums. Another photographer, Lewis Hine, brought attention to the children who worked in American factories and coal mines.

In the 1930s other photographers worked for the federal government. They recorded the effects of the Great Depression, when many businesses failed and people lost their jobs. They made photographs of the Dust Bowl, the Great Plains region where drought changed farmland to dust.

Photography as Art

During the nineteenth century, photography was generally regarded as a scientific process rather than an art. Its purpose was to record real life.

In 1902 photographer Alfred Stieglitz started a campaign to change attitudes toward photography. He and his fellow photographers wanted photography to be acknowledged as a fine-art form. In the 1920s, photographer Man Ray experimented with photographic images. He combined elements of fantasy with those from real life.

Photographer Ansel Adams bridged the gap between photography as an art form and photography used for social causes. His nature photographs were artistic and contributed to the growing interest in preserving the environment.

Some photographers' work combined elements of both art and social commentary. Gordon Parks photographed gangs in Harlem and life in the African-American community. Diane Arbus used her camera to show people she called freaks, often outcasts in society.

In this book, the lives of a few of the individuals who contributed to the development of photography are highlighted. Their creativity and willingness to explore and experiment with the photographic process are noteworthy. They helped to make photography a part of Americans' everyday lives.

Mathew B. Brady

(1823-1896)

Mathew B. Brady was the most well-known photographer in the United States before the Civil War. He owned studios and galleries where famous people sat for their portrait.

But during the Civil War, Brady took entirely different kinds of pictures. Brady and a group of photographers he hired traveled all over the battlegrounds as the war was being fought. Working together, the Brady photographers "produced the greatest pictorial essay of [the] time."[1]

When their photographs went on exhibit, the grim realities and horrors of war shocked and fascinated Americans. The photographs were also copied as engravings and widely published.

Mathew B. Brady

Today, historians and history buffs alike still express great interest in these compelling photographs.

Mathew B. Brady was born in Warren County near Lake George, New York. He was never absolutely sure of the date of his birth, but he thought it was 1823. The only record of his parents' names, Julia and Andrew, is on Brady's own death certificate. It says his parents were born in the United States.[2] However, newspaper articles from that time state that both of Brady's parents were born in Ireland and had immigrated to the United States.

When Mathew was born, his family owned a farm on the frontier. Nothing is known about Brady's childhood, not even if he went to school.

At about age fifteen, Brady left home to seek his fortune. When he reached Saratoga, New York, he decided to stay. Saratoga seemed a large city to a farm boy. It may have been easy for him to find a job, since he was a strong young man accustomed to hard work.

In Saratoga, Brady met William Page and they became friends. They shared an interest in art. Page was a struggling artist who owned a portrait studio. Unfortunately, not too many people in Saratoga could afford to have their portrait painted.

When Page decided to move to Albany, a bigger city and the capital of New York state, Brady went along with his friend. In 1839 they both moved to New York City and Page opened a new studio. Brady became a clerk in a store. One day Page took Brady to visit a friend, inventor Samuel F. B. Morse.

Earlier in the year, Morse had been in Paris applying for a French patent for his telegraph invention. When Morse heard about Daguerre's discovery, he asked to meet him. Daguerre explained to Morse all about the process of making daguerreotypes. Before Morse returned home to America, he bought one of the first cameras, which had just begun to be manufactured for sale.

Brady was very interested in learning how to make daguerreotypes. When they met, Morse explained Daguerre's process to Brady. Morse decided to open a photography school and Brady became one of the first students to enroll.

Americans began to open photography studios less than a year after Daguerre's process was made public. In 1839, J. W. Draper took a picture of his sister. This portrait still survives and is the oldest photographic portrait in existence.

In 1840, John Plumbe opened the first of his chain of daguerreotype parlors. Then it was not easy to sit for a photographic portrait. People had to sit still so long that photographers built special chairs with a prop for the head.

By 1844, Mathew Brady had his own photography studio in New York City. He displayed some of his photographs at an exhibition. He won first honors. This was one of many he would receive in his lifetime.

A year later Brady announced his plan to photograph the important people of the time. He said, "From the first, I regarded myself as under obligation to my country to preserve the faces of its historic men and mothers."[3]

To save the photographs, Brady copied all his daguerreotypes onto glass plates. In 1850 he published a book, *The Gallery of Illustrious Americans*, with C. Edwards Lester. The book included engravings of twelve of Brady's famous portraits. It did not sell very well, however, probably because of its high cost of $30.

Brady's fame became nationwide after Jenny Lind, a famous singer, sat for her portrait. Thousands of copies of her picture were sold all over the country. Some were the size of calling cards, which were popular at the time. These were called *cartes de visite.*

In 1858, Mathew Brady had to stop taking most of the photographs himself. His eyesight had become poor.[4] That same year Brady became known internationally after showing his daguerreotypes in London. They were displayed at a world's fair, the Industrial Exhibition. He won a medal there.[5]

Back home, Brady continued to direct and train a staff of photographers. He supervised them when they took portraits. While he depended on their eyes for focusing the camera, Brady composed the photographs, deciding how people should be posed.

By 1858, Brady owned a second studio in Washington, D.C., where photographs of politicians and government officials were made. Brady was responsible for taking many photographs of Abraham Lincoln throughout Lincoln's presidency. The first photograph was taken on February 27, 1860, the day Lincoln made a speech at the Cooper Institute.

The photograph became famous. Thousands of copies of it were sold. Currier & Ives, publishers of prints of American scenes, sold copies of it as a lithograph. Lincoln once said, "Brady and the Cooper Institute made me president."[6]

Many of Brady's portraits were displayed in his studio for people to see. The public walked through elegant rooms, whose walls were filled from floor to ceiling with huge daguerreotypes in gilt frames.[7]

Brady's pictures were not exclusive. He made duplicates of his subjects and other photographers copied them. "Brady was the forerunner of today's gigantic news photo services. The subjects of his photographs also had prints made for themselves."[8]

Brady worked long hours, virtually every day at his photographic business. At night he went home to the National Hotel, where he lived with his wife, Julia. Although the date of their marriage is unknown, newspaper articles from the period say they married in the late 1840s. Julia's nephew, however, said he thought they married in 1860.[9]

When the American Civil War began in 1861, Brady sought permission from Abraham Lincoln to photograph the war. He received a note on which

Lincoln had scrawled "Pass Brady" and his signature.[10] That was enough to get Brady into army camps and through battle lines.

To photograph the war, Brady increased his staff to twenty photographers. He invested $10,000 of his own money in equipment. He hoped that the United States government would support his venture.

The wet plates used to print photographs had to be developed immediately, so Brady had portable darkrooms built. His photographers carried them in wagons along with their heavy camera equipment.

Brady's men took thousands of photographs. Many were used to make engravings. These were published from 1860 to 1865 in *Leslie's Illustrated Newspaper* and *Harper's Week*. They showed people in both the Union and the Confederacy the horrors of war.

In the fall of 1862, Brady was at the Battle of Antietam, one of the bloodiest of all Civil War battles. He and one of his photographers, Alexander Gardner, worked together. They took many photographs from the outbreak of the battle to its end.

The photographs of battle were both poignant and heartbreaking. When they were displayed and copied as engravings, they "did much to bring the grim reality of war into the American home."[11]

After the Battle of Gettysburg, Brady and several of his photographers arrived on the scene. They took many photographs of the dead soldiers. In some cases

Mathew Brady took this photograph of President Abraham Lincoln
(left) during the Civil War.

Brady's assistants actually moved the corpses in order to make the photographs more dramatic.[12]

It is difficult to determine which Civil War photographs Brady actually took himself. He took credit for all the photographs taken by his staff. At times, this angered the men who worked for him.

Alexander Gardner, for example, left Brady's employment and went to work for the Army of the Potomac. He published his own book of Civil War photographs.[13]

Throughout the war, Brady hoped that one day the government would buy the negatives of his Civil War photographs. In 1871 the Joint Committee of the Library of Congress voted to buy two thousand of Brady's portraits of celebrities for $5,000. But the deal didn't go through. The government never bought any of Brady's Civil War pictures either.

Brady was now deeply in debt. He had spent a lot of money on the photographic equipment he had bought. He had also given up his regular portrait business during the war. To settle his bills, he gave one set of negatives to a company he owed money.

Soon Brady was forced to sell his equipment and his New York galleries. In the 1870s, Brady declared bankruptcy. He could not pay his bills. The following years were difficult. Although Brady remained famous, he worked only from time to time.

To Brady's great sorrow, his wife died of heart problems in 1884. After her death, Brady had to depend on his relatives for financial support. He also needed their help getting around because of his poor eyesight.

When Brady died in poverty in 1896, his vast collection of wet plates was split up. Some went to the National Archives and the Library of Congress, others to the New York Historical Society. Some were also given to Levin Handy, a photographer who had married Brady's niece.

At his death Brady left behind virtually no personal papers, no diary, or letters. This has made it hard for historians to learn much about him. For a time his biographer James Horan wondered if "perhaps Brady, the greatest photographer of them all, could not write, though there seemed to be no doubt that he could and did read."[14]

Eventually Horan found one letter of recommendation that Brady had signed. Other letters written for him by assistants or clerks have also been located. Only one letter that Brady actually wrote has been discovered. It dates from 1843, before his eyesight failed.

Brady's work documents the people and important events of his time. It is an invaluable pictorial record of American history. His amazing photographs are his legacy.

Jacob A. Riis

(1849-1914)

Jacob A. Riis, an immigrant, came to the United States in the hopes of finding his fortune. But like many other immigrants, he found instead a life of poverty and hardship. By chance, however, he was offered a job as a newspaper reporter.

Riis's life changed as he rose to fame as a muckraking journalist, a reporter whose articles exposed the awful conditions of immigrant life in the slums. Riis used his writing to stir up public concern for the need for social reforms. He used his camera to help document the misery he saw in the poor neighborhoods in New York City.

In choosing Jacob Riis as an all-time American hero, *Life* magazine said that when Riis came to the United States, he "made his way into a growing immigrant population he would change forever."[1]

Jacob A. Riis

Jacob Riis was born in Ribe, Denmark, in 1849. His father was the town's schoolmaster, an important and respected person in their town. Although a schoolmaster's pay was good, it was not enough to support a large family of fifteen children. In addition, Jacob's cousin also lived with the family after her parents died. Later in life, Jacob Riis found out that to support his family his father had taken a second job—writing and editing the town newspaper.

Jacob's father hoped that his son would also become a teacher. But "I hated the school from the day I first saw it," Jacob remembered.[2] The work was not interesting and the discipline was severe. However, Jacob liked to learn in his free time. When Jacob was young, his father taught him English. Jacob practiced by reading novels written by Charles Dickens.[3]

By age fifteen, Jacob left school. His father let him become an apprentice to a local carpenter. The carpenter had a big contract doing repairs on the home of the wealthy owner of a cotton mill. On the job Riis learned carpentry, but he often hurt himself. The sight of the owner's daughter, Elizabeth, constantly distracted him. He loved her, but she paid no attention to him.

After a year Riis went to the city of Copenhagen, the capital of Denmark. There he trained for four more years as a carpenter. He received a certificate and joined the Danish carpenter's guild. He returned home to Ribe and proposed to Elizabeth. She was only sixteen years old and refused to marry him. It was at this point that he decided to go to America because "the farther I went from her the better."[4]

Riis's friends and neighbors took up a collection of money to help pay for his travel expenses. He went to Glasgow, Scotland, where he boarded the *Iowa* and sailed for New York. He traveled in steerage, the lowest-paying fare, and slept in a huge room below decks with hundreds of other people. It was a long and stormy voyage.

In April 1870 the ship anchored off New York City's Castle Garden, the place of entry for immigrants. Customs officials interviewed those who wanted to become American citizens. Later, Ellis Island would be the place where immigrants were admitted to the United States.[5]

New York City amazed Riis. At home in Denmark, he had heard stories of America from a man who had gone to California during the gold rush. Riis had pictured America as a wild land populated by buffalo and Native Americans. He was amazed to discover that New York was just as civilized as Copenhagen![6]

Riis had spent all his money on his voyage, so he signed up to work at an ironworks on the Allegheny River. There he helped build huts for miners. He tried his hand at coal mining but hated it.

One day Riis read in a newspaper that Germany had attacked Denmark and France. Determined to go home and help fight, he went to New York City. He arrived with only one cent to his name. At the consul's office, he joined the Danish Army's reserves. But he found out that no one was interested in paying passage for volunteer soldiers.

Like many immigrants, Riis had thought America was the land of opportunity. But life in New York was difficult for Riis. He took what work he could find, but he was often homeless and hungry.

One night when Riis had only a few cents left, he slept in a lodging room run by the police. The next morning he awoke to find both his last memento of home—a locket—had been stolen and his dog killed. It was at that point, Riis later wrote, that he decided to stop dreaming and start being useful.[7]

Riis found a job with a newspaper, the *New York Tribune*. From 1877 to 1888 he was the Tribune's police reporter, covering crime. While writing for the *Tribune*, he also did a series on poverty in New York City, which he later expanded into several books. The most famous is *How the Other Half Lives*.[8]

Riis's work became critically acclaimed and very popular. Theodore Roosevelt, then New York City's police commissioner, went out at night with Riis to see firsthand the conditions that Riis wrote about.[9]

Riis's articles on life in the crowded tenements helped to create the Tenement House Commission in 1884. This commission worked to initiate reforms to improve the terrible conditions in the slums.

In 1888, Riis left the *New York Tribune* to work for the *Evening Sun*. He bought a camera with a flash to take photographs inside the dark tenements and at night on the streets. He wanted to document his articles on slum condition with photographs.

Immigrants let him take pictures of the squalor in which they were forced to live. He showed how crowded the tenements were, the windowless rooms many slept in, the lack of sanitation, the filth.

Riis also visited Ellis Island, prisons, and sweatshops, where immigrants worked long hours for little money. Many of Riis's most heart-wrenching photographs were of immigrant children, who worked to help their families survive.

Riis was not an artist. He never studied photography and paid little attention to the artistic quality of his photographs. Photographer Cecil Beaton wrote: "[It] is astonishing that out of so many thousands of pictures only one or two have even a 'picturesque' quality."[10]

Riis used a "detective" camera, a handheld box camera adapted to take instant pictures, unlike large studio cameras. He used a huge flash to light up dark places he photographed inside tenements and on the streets and alleys of the slums at night. He lit his flash from a fire he kept going in a frying pan. When the flash was still not bright enough inside, he fired a revolver and took the photograph in the brilliant light it created.

Jacob Riis used a "detective" camera to show the poor living conditions of immigrants to New York City.

Several times Riis started fires while taking photographs. Once he set his own clothes on fire, and twice he set buildings on fire. Another time he almost blinded himself when a flash went off too close to his eyes.

Years later famous photographer Ansel Adams wrote about Riis's photos: "Many of the people shown in Riis's work looked at the camera and the photographer at the moment of exposure. They did not realize that they were looking at you and me and all humanity for ages of time."[11]

Riis's photographs appeared as illustrations in his books. He also used his pictures when he lectured. He had the photographs made into lantern slides, which were pictures on transparent slides.

Riis's work helped to bring about new child labor laws, the building of parks and playgrounds, and improvements in housing and education for the poor.

Most of Riis's work focused on New York City. But his articles and photographs caused other reformers to look at slum conditions in their cities, too. Riis became a very powerful force in what is known as the Progressive Era, a time when public concern led to significant social reforms.

Theodore Roosevelt offered Riis public office many times. Roosevelt thought Riis should lead government investigations into living conditions of the poor. But Riis replied, "To represent is not my business. To write is; I can do it much better and back up the other, so we are two for one."[12]

Riis wrote five books. In addition to *How the Other Half Lives,* he wrote *The Children of the Poor, Out of Mulberry Street, The Making of an American* (Riis's autobiography), and *Children of the Tenements.*

A seemingly tireless man, Jacob Riis was often out working during the day and night in all kinds of weather. He was also a devoted family man. Eventually, Elizabeth, the girl he had proposed to in Denmark, immigrated to the United States. She and Jacob married. When their daughter married, Theodore Roosevelt was one of the guests at the wedding.

After 1904, Riis developed a heart condition. He remained, however, an energetic writer and lecturer until he died in 1914.

Alfred Stieglitz

3

Alfred Stieglitz
(1864-1946)

Alfred Stieglitz was one of photography's most influential men. He spent much of his adult life working to have photography recognized as an art form. But "it was only after the turn of the [twentieth] century that photography began to breach the walls of gallery and museum world in America . . ."[1]

Stieglitz was one of the first photographers to be recognized as an artist. In addition to receiving recognition for his own work, Stieglitz also influenced the lives of other artists. He was a pioneer in introducing and promoting modern art in America.

Alfred Stieglitz was born in Hoboken, New Jersey, on January 1, 1864. At the time, most Americans lived in small towns or in the country. During his lifetime, Stieglitz would witness tremendous change, as the United States transformed itself from a rural nation into an "industrialized and cultural superpower."[2]

Alfred Stieglitz's parents, Edward and Hedwig Stieglitz, had immigrated to the United States from Germany. Hedwig Stieglitz was just nineteen when Alfred was born. He was the first of the family's six children.

As a child, Alfred went first to school at the Charlier Institute and then to a public grammar school in Hoboken. When Alfred was nine years old, he became interested in photography. He entered a photography contest in Boston and won a ribbon. He continued to take photographs for pleasure all through his childhood.

One summer, while on vacation with his family at Lake George in the Adirondack Mountains, he met a professional photographer. The man let him watch while he developed prints in the darkroom.[3]

In 1881, at the age of seventeen, Stieglitz moved to Germany with his family to further his studies. He attended a Realgymnasium (an advanced high school) in Karlsruhe. A year later he enrolled in technical college in Berlin to study mechanical engineering.

Stieglitz took a class in photochemistry. From that point on, photography was his main interest. He studied darkroom techniques at school and practiced taking photographs in his free time.

While touring in Europe, Stieglitz used his camera to capture a variety of landscapes and street scenes. He was interested in the composition of a picture. He experimented with light and shadow and practiced how to "frame" a photograph. His goal was to make his photographs works of art rather than just records of what he saw.

In 1886, Stieglitz entered his first photographic competition as an adult. A year later he received recognition after he won the top prize in a photographic competition sponsored by *The Amateur Photographer*, a magazine published in London. Soon periodicals began to buy Stieglitz's photographs for publication.

In 1890, Stieglitz returned to the United States and moved to New York City. He used a gift of a large sum of money from his father to start his own business as a photoengraver. Photoengravers used a photographic process to transfer an image (like a drawing) to a plate. The image was etched into the plate, which was then used for printing.

This was not a job that required much creativity, but it gave Stieglitz an income. While working as a photoengraver, Stieglitz also took on a volunteer position and became editor of the American *Amateur Photographer*.

However, it was through his work as a photoengraver that he met his wife, Emmeline Obermeyer. They married in 1893. Their only child, a daughter named Katherine, was born in 1898.[4]

In 1895, Stieglitz closed his photoengraving business in order to concentrate fulltime on his own photography work. He continued to work to make

Alfred Stieglitz liked to take photographs in all types of weather.
Here, he photographed a snow scene in New York City.

his photographs artistic and tried new ideas and techniques. But he refused to manipulate his negatives or prints, to add special effects, or to retouch the photographs. He preferred to work on technical problems using his camera to achieve an effect.

Stieglitz went out in all kinds of weather to take photographs. He experimented with different lighting conditions. He was the first professional photographer known to have taken successful photographs outside in the snow and rain. Stieglitz also experimented with a flash to take streetscapes at night. He wanted his photographs to express a mood as paintings did.

Later Stieglitz wrote: "Artists who saw my earlier photographs began to tell me they envied me, that they felt my photographs were superior to their paintings, but that unfortunately photography was not an art."[5] Stieglitz thought they felt this way because photography was created by a machine—a camera. The artists did not recognize the role the photographer played in creating photographs.

In 1897, Stieglitz started a new magazine for photographers called *Camera Notes*. Stieglitz was a member of the Camera Club of New York, which sponsored the magazine. However, Stieglitz soon had a falling-out with the other more conservative members of the club who were more traditional in their thinking. Stieglitz wanted very much to help photography win recognition as art.

In 1902, Stieglitz resigned from *Camera Notes* to found the Photo-Secession movement. The goal of Photo-Secessionists was to advance photography as it applied to pictorial expression, to make photography an art form. Other photographers joined the movement, including Clarence White, Edward Steichen, Alvin Langdon Coburn, and Gertrude Kasebier. Stieglitz was the leader of the group.

From 1903 to 1917, Stieglitz published and edited *Camera Work*, the Photo-Secessionists' magazine. It was a publication filled with artistic photographs.

Stieglitz opened his first art gallery in 1905 in New York City. It was called the Little Galleries of the Photo-Secession. It became known as 291, because of its address, 291 Fifth Avenue. The gallery was open from 1905 to 1917 and exhibited the works of modern artists and sculptors as well as photographers.

World War I brought *Camera Work*, the Photo-Secession galleries, and the 291 group to an end. Stieglitz was anti-American and pro-German during the war. This was a very unpopular stance to take.[6]

During World War I, Stieglitz concentrated on his own photography. He took a series of photographs of clouds and another of New York skyscrapers. But he missed the interaction with other people interested in the creative arts.

After the war, Stieglitz ran the Intimate Gallery, from 1925 to 1929, and An American Place, from 1929 to 1946. Through his galleries, "he [Stieglitz] introduced modern European art to [the United

States]."[7] He organized the first American exhibitions of works by Pablo Picasso, Henri Matisse, George Braque, and Paul Cezanne. They are all well-known artists today, but then they were just beginning to gain recognition in the art world.

Stieglitz also championed American modern artists like Arthur Dove, John Marin, and Georgia O'Keefe. O'Keefe became one of the most famous American painters. She did huge paintings of flowers. Later in her career she produced landscape scenes of New Mexico. Stieglitz was one of the first gallery owners to recognize her talent and display her work.

Stieglitz and O'Keefe often fought over many things, including the nature of art. Nevertheless, they became romantically involved and married. After their relationship began, Stieglitz's photographs were mostly of O'Keefe. Over a period of time, he took some three hundred portraits of her.

Stieglitz was very interested in the relationship between various art forms and predicted that photography would change them all. In 1937, when he became ill, he stopped taking photographs. But his influence remained. "From 1902 until the time of his death, Stieglitz was the very centre [sic] of photographical [sic] activity in the United States."[8] Stieglitz died on July 13, 1946.

After his death, Stieglitz's large personal collection of photographs went to the Metropolitan Museum of Art in New York City. The photographs are a lasting record of his tremendous talent and creativity.

Lewis Wickes Hine

Lewis Wickes Hine
(1874-1940)

Lewis Wickes Hine, was a photographer who used his camera to promote social reform. Like Jacob Riis, Hine hoped his work would draw attention to the needs of the underprivileged in America. He focused his work particularly on the children working in factories and mines at the beginning of the twentieth century.

Hine succeeded in creating great sympathy for their plight. "His work . . . was the driving force behind changing the public's attitude and was instrumental in the fight for stricter child labor laws."[1]

Lewis Hine was born in Oshkosh, Wisconsin, on September 26, 1874. Even though his family was poor, Lewis did not have to work. But after school and in his free time, he helped his mother and father with many chores.

After he graduated from high school, Hine got a job as a laborer, working in construction. Hine's parents could not afford to send him to college, and his grades were not good enough to earn him a scholarship. But he started to think about college after he took some art courses.

When Hine was twenty-four, he enrolled at the University of Chicago. There he met Frank E. Manny, a professor at the State Normal School, the teacher-training institute at the university. Manny had just been appointed superintendent of the Ethical Culture School, an experimental school in New York City. Manny inspired Hine to study education and become a teacher.[2]

After Hine graduated, Manny hired him to teach at the Ethical Culture School. Hine taught there from 1901 until 1908. During this period, Hine married Sara Ann Rich. He also decided to go to graduate school at New York University and study education. In 1907, Hine went to Columbia University to study sociology.

While teaching at the Ethical Culture School, Hine took up photography as a hobby. He took pictures of the classes and events at the school. He also started a photography club there. It was as the result of the club that he met photographer Paul Strand, who later helped organize an exhibit of Hine's work.

In 1905, Hine began a series of photographs showing immigrants arriving at Ellis Island, the entry point for the United States. At the time, many Americans expressed hostility toward the immigrants. Manny encouraged Hine to show dignity and respect for them in his photographs.

In 1907, Hine got his first freelance job with the National Child Labor Committee (NCLC).[3] This nonprofit group hired him as an "investigative photographer."[4] This meant that Hine was to use his camera to collect information about child labor in America.

In the early days of the twentieth century, there were no laws that required children to go to school. Many poor families needed their children to work to help earn money for the family. In some cases, the children worked only after school. But thousands upon thousands of children worked fulltime, every day. They worked right beside adults, in places like factories.

Many of the children worked at jobs that required hard physical labor and placed them in danger. Children operated dangerous machinery in textile mills and factories. The NCLC wanted to gather evidence to convince the public and politicians that child labor laws were needed to protect children.[5]

In 1908 the NCLC started to pay Hine a monthly salary to document the plight of child laborers. Hine visited mines, factories, textile mills, canneries, and farms. He photographed the children and their working conditions. He visited their homes and the schools, which were sparsely attended because so many children were at work.

Hine took photographs of children picking cranberries in New Jersey, berries in Delaware, and cotton in Texas. He photographed children growing tobacco in Kentucky, topping beets in Colorado, and herding cows. He photographed the shacks where migrant workers lived. He took photographs of children working in the middle of the night and of children arriving at work before dawn.

Many of the photographs Hine took when he visited mines focused on children's injuries. In at least one case, he photographed a child's working documents to show how the parents lied about the age of their child so the child could work. Hine attached his photographs to reports he made to the committee. The committee also published his photos in their publications and exhibits.

The same year, Hine published an article on social conditions, which he illustrated with his photographs. An editor of a magazine called *Charities and the Commons* saw it and hired Hine as a staff photographer. To illustrate articles for the magazine, Hine continued to take photographs to show where social reforms were needed.

Hine's photographs directly affected the public's social conscience. They helped bring about child labor laws designed to protect children. Hine's photographs clearly illustrated how work affected children's health, education, and safety. Hine's work

When Lewis Hine took this photograph, he was trying to capture images that showed there was a need for social reform.

appeared in many publications and exhibits. He often used his photographs to illustrate his lectures.

In 1912 the Hines had a son they named Corydon. They also bought land in rural New York, hoping one day to build a house there.

After working for the NCLC for a number of years, Hine's salary was cut in 1917. Hine then worked for the American Red Cross, recording the effects of World War I in Europe. He focused not on the soldiers or battlefields, but on the plight of the refugees.[6]

When Hine returned to the United States, he worked for many different agencies and publications. He also started to do some commercial photography. In 1921 he saw an exhibit of Alfred Stieglitz's photographs. He was affected by Stieglitz's work as an art form. Hine was encouraged to try to give more attention to the artistic aspects of his work. In turn, he received good reviews from art critics.

Even though Hine had become famous, he sometimes had trouble financially. In 1930 his situation eased for a time when he was hired to photograph the construction of the Empire State Building. A year later, the Yonkers Art Museum had a large exhibit of Hine's work. In 1932 his book *Men at Work* was published. The photographs in this book included many he took of the construction workers on the Empire State Building. These photographs celebrated American labor.

During the remainder of the decade, Hine put together portfolios of his work, which were acquired by museums such as the Metropolitan Museum of Art and the Museum of Modern Art.

In 1936, Hine began work as the head photographer for the National Research Project of the Works Progress Administration (WPA). He wanted to work for the Farm Security Administration (FSA) but was not chosen because "Roy Stryker [head of FSA's historical section] considered Hine unfashionable and difficult to work with."[7]

In 1939, Paul Strand and Alfred Stieglitz organized a retrospective of Hine's work. By the time Hine died in 1940, his work was owned by museums all over the nation. But his grown son could not find a museum interested in taking the family's collection of his father's work. It was years before the collection ended up at the George Eastman International Museum of Photography.

The Library of Congress owns five thousand of Hine's labor photographs. These are of interest to researchers studying the history of labor conditions in America.

Through the use of photography, Lewis Hine helped the public develop a social conscience and become aware of the need for social reforms. Hine summed it up when he wrote: "I wanted to show the things that had to be corrected. I wanted to show the things that had to be appreciated."[8]

Man Ray (self-portrait)

Man Ray

(1890-1976)

As a young man, Man Ray became famous as a Surrealist artist. Surrealism was an art movement that developed in the 1920s. Surrealist artists, photographers, sculptors, and writers explored dreams and the subconscious. They created fantastic and sometimes unusual combinations of images in their work.

Man Ray was an artist, a sculptor, and a photographer. However, art historians admire him most for his photographic work. He was the first Surrealist photographer. When he died in 1976, he was still experimenting and creating new, imaginative art.

When Man Ray was born in Philadelphia, Pennsylvania, on August 27, 1890, his name was Emmanuel Radnitsky. Later, when his family moved to Brooklyn, New York, they shortened their last name to Ray and their son shortened his first name to Man.

In high school Man Ray studied freehand drawing and industrial draftsmanship. Industrial draftsmanship required the precise, detailed drawings needed to build a machine or construct a building. But Ray did not want to become an architect. He said, "I'm not interested in the exterior aspect. I'm interested in a building's inside."[1] Ray was not interested in interior design either, though he liked decorating his own places.

After graduating from high school, Man Ray enrolled in New York's Academy of Art, a school for artists. He studied there from 1908 to 1912. Then he got a job as a graphic designer, planning and designing advertising, books, and magazines. Later on he also drew maps for a map and atlas publisher.

In his spare time, Ray liked to visit art galleries and museums. New York City was then, as it is now, one of the nation's cultural centers. Many people in the creative arts, such as painters, sculptors, composers, and writers, lived and worked there.

At photographer Alfred Stieglitz's gallery, known as 291, Man Ray saw examples of the newest modern art. Although Stieglitz was a photographer, he also exhibited paintings and sculptures in his gallery. Man Ray was amazed by the work of the Cubists artists, particularly Pablo Picasso.

Cubism was a new style of painting. The subject was broken up into geometric shapes that flattened and simplified form. These shapes overlapped to create a different sense of space from that in conventional art. It was as if the subject was viewed from many different angles. In 1913, Ray painted a portrait of Alfred Stieglitz in the Cubist style.

Ray married writer Adon Lacroix in 1914. They collaborated on her books—he lettered her texts by hand and created drawings and lithographs for them. The marriage did not last, however.

Man Ray became friendly with other avant-garde artists, artists who experimented with new concepts. In studios and over meals and drinks, Ray and his friends discussed their art and what art meant. Conventional artists continued to paint traditional pictures. But this was not the type of art that captured the imagination of Ray and his friends.

One artist with whom Man Ray formed a close friendship was Marcel Duchamp. Ray, Duchamp, and the Spanish painter Francis Picabia formed New York's "proto-Dada group."[2] The Dadaists were artists who rejected traditional art forms. They regarded modern life as absurd. They often included an out-of-place object in what appeared to be an ordinary scene, such as a pair of giant lips floating in the sky instead of clouds.

In 1920, Man Ray contributed to the magazine *New York Dada*. Only one issue of this magazine was ever published. The average American did not care for avant-garde art. Man Ray said, "Dada cannot live in New York."[3] This comment reflected the criticism he and his fellow Dadaists received from even sophisticated New Yorkers.

In the 1920s, society was changing. Young people wanted greater freedom in everything from clothing and hairstyles to a loosening up of the traditions of their parents' generation. At the same time, the economy prospered. This meant that people had time to devote to recreation and entertainment.

Artists, writers, and musicians flourished.[4] But some of them began to feel that Europeans appreciated their work more than Americans did. Many artists became expatriates and moved to Paris. There they rented cheap apartments in picturesque neighborhoods. When they weren't writing or painting or composing, they spent their time in cafés or at parties. The expatriates formed a community in Paris and encouraged one another's search for creative expression.

Ray moved to Paris where he devoted himself fulltime to his art. At first, he only painted. But then he decided to make prints of his artwork. To do so, he needed to photograph his paintings. Eventually Ray became interested in photography as an art form for its own sake. Over time, Ray "revolutionized the art of photography."[5]

In Paris, Ray was part of the literary and artistic movement known as Surrealism. The Surrealist writers and artists explored new techniques and art forms. They used dreams and myths as the subjects of their works, often in unusual combinations with

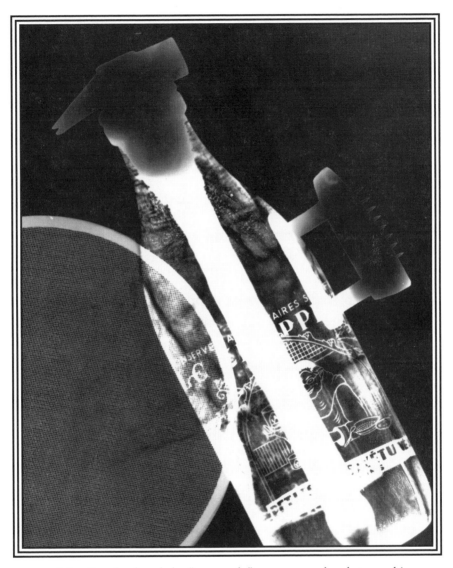

Man Ray developed the "rayograph," a way to make photographic images without a camera. He would place objects on photographic paper and expose them to light to develop the images like he did here.

familiar objects. They wanted to capture impressions rather than realistic representations of the world around them.

Ray used a camera to take photographs of his friends and fellow Surrealists.[6] He took photographs and did graphic design for French publishers who were printing the expatriates' work in English. He worked on magazine covers and took photographs of models for fashion magazines and advertisements.

Ray was always experimenting with photographic techniques. He discovered a way to make photographic images without using a camera. He called them rayographs, or photograms.

He placed objects on photographic paper and exposed them to light to develop the images. Ray experimented with the arrangements of the objects, often overlapping them to express a particular idea or achieve a special effect. Sometimes he used more than one exposure on a single work, adding more objects to the rayograph.

Some people who looked at his rayographs saw just shapes and shades of color. Others read more into them, seeing, for example, a silhouette of a man dreaming—the dream symbolized by a strip of movie film.[7]

Ray experimented with other techniques, too. He made prints of negatives. These photographs looked like blown-up negatives. He deliberately distorted and blurred scenes with his camera to create a new and interesting effect. He used solarization, a technique in which film is overexposed to light so that a photograph's color tones change.[8]

Although Ray liked to pretend that he was not interested in craftsmanship, actually the opposite was true. Ray "let us believe that his photographs were the result of chance. This presentation of his work [an exhibition in Paris] proves that they were rather the product of careful reflection and diligent labor."[9]

Ray lived and worked in a studio in Montparnasse where many other artists and writers came to see him. Sometimes they collaborated on creative projects. He and his friends also traveled together, going to the south of France every summer, for example. His friends included other photographers, such as Eugène Atget, Berenice Abbott, Bill Brandt, and Lee Miller.

Miller and Ray became romantically involved. They also worked together as artists. She helped him with his solarization experiments. Sometimes in public they discussed their work. But they often misled others as to the techniques they used. They wanted to keep them secret.

In 1930, Georges Ribemont-Dessaignes wrote the first biography of Man Ray. That same year a friend, Maurice Tabard, betrayed some of Ray's secrets. He revealed how Ray produced some of his work. Other American photographers experimented with solarization. But German artists and designers influenced them more than Ray had.

In 1934 a retrospective book of Ray's photographs was published. His photographs also appeared in exhibitions and in magazines like *Harper's Bazaar.*

Ray returned to the United States in 1940 and met Juliet Browner, whom he later married. They lived in Hollywood for ten years. Their home was a center of artistic activity for creative people. They came for dinner and stayed to discuss art and the meaning of life. In addition to doing more fashion photography, Ray also painted and taught art classes.[10]

In 1950, Ray went back to Paris with Juliet. There he continued to experiment with art and color photography for more than twenty-five years. In 1967 the American Center in Paris had an exhibit called a "Salute to Man Ray."[11] In 1974, Andy Warhol, a member of the younger generation of modern artists, made a series of paintings and prints influenced by Man Ray.[12]

Man Ray, an artist of many talents, died on November 18, 1976. After his death, his works were donated to the Centre Georges Pompidou in Paris, the world's most famous avant-garde art museum.

6

Dorothea Lange
(1895-1965)

Dorothea Lange was born around the same time as Man Ray. Like Ray, she also became a world-famous photographer. But her work is very different from his. Lange wanted to record exactly what she saw. She went out of her way to make sure that no artistic touches were added to her photographs.

Many of her most famous pictures are of farm families in the depths of the Great Depression. Her photographs recorded a level of suffering that still affects the viewer today, more than fifty years later.

Dorothea Lange was born Dorothea Nutzhorn on May 25, 1895. Her parents, Joan Lange and Henry Martin Nutzhorn, lived in Hoboken, New Jersey.

When she was seven, Dorothea became ill with poliomyelitis (polio). The disease, which causes paralysis, left one of her legs shorter than the other.

Dorothea Lange

Other children teased her dreadfully because she walked with a limp, and she became very shy. In 1907, when Dorothea was twelve, her father abandoned the family. Dorothea missed him very much.

Dorothea and her brother and mother moved in with Dorothea's grandmother, Sophie, who lived in New York City. Dorothea's mother supported the family by working as a librarian. Life at her grandmother's house was hard for Dorothea. Her grandmother was a heavy drinker, who hit her grandchildren. To escape, Dorothea spent many days with a friend walking the streets and in museums.

In 1913, Dorothea graduated from high school. By this time, she called herself Dorothea Lange, using her mother's maiden name as her last name.[1]

Lange grew up during a time when more job opportunities were opening up for women. However, they remained largely limited to what were called genteel, or respectable, positions.

Dorothea's mother knew how important it was for a woman to be able to support herself. She pushed Dorothea to enroll in a teachers college in New York. But Lange never wanted to be a teacher. Despite the fact that she did not own a camera, had never taken a photograph, and that the field did not welcome women, she dreamed of becoming a photographer.

One day while still in college, Lange visited a photography studio owned by photographer Arnold Genthe. She talked him into giving her a job. In the San Francisco earthquake, Genthe had lost all his possessions. Somehow he had managed to borrow a camera and he had taken remarkable photographs of the disaster.

In 1911, Genthe moved to New York City. He took photographs of many of the celebrities of the day. He taught Lange how to take portraits.[2]

While working for Genthe, Lange also studied with photographer Clarence White at Columbia University in 1917 and 1918. White taught Lange several very important lessons. He taught her to plan her photographs and to take time to look at her subject before she shot film. He also encouraged her to take many photographs of the same people, to "come to a deeper understanding of their intrinsic emotions."[3]

White despised artifice, anything artificial. Despite the fact that he took very pretty photographs, he did not create these scenes by adding props or rearranging people. He simply looked for the beautiful in life.

In January 1918, Lange moved to San Francisco, where she opened her own portrait studio. She also joined a camera club. One of its members was Maynard Dixon, a painter of western scenes.

On March 21, 1920, Lange and Dixon married. They began traveling together all over the West. Dixon painted and Lange photographed the wilderness. In 1925, Dorothea gave birth to their first child, a son they named Daniel. Four years later, they had a second son, John.[4]

This haunting image, by Dorothea Lange, helped get food supplies
for the 2,500 pea pickers, who had no way of earning any money.

In 1929 the Great Depression began. Lange and Dixon were affected like most other Americans. There were fewer people who could afford to buy paintings and photographs. So they moved to Taos, New Mexico, where they pooled their resources with other artists.

In 1933, Willard Van Dyke displayed some of Lange's photographs at his studio in Oakland, California. One of the people who visited the exhibit was a professor named Paul Taylor. He asked Lange to take photographs for studies he was making of how the Depression was affecting Californians.

A drought had begun that would have a terrible effect on the farmers in the Great Plains. What became known as the Dust Bowl lasted for several years. During this period, many farmers were unable to harvest any crops. They went bankrupt and lost their farms. Farm families became homeless. Thousands of "Okies," people who lived in the region, left home to migrate elsewhere. They hoped to find a less harsh climate and an easier way of life. Many settled in California.

In 1935, Taylor and Lange collected information for a report on migrant workers for California's State Emergency Relief Administration.[5] By this time, Lange and Dixon had divorced and Lange and Taylor married.

Thanks in part to the work Lange and Taylor had done, the federal government established in 1935 the Resettlement Administration. It evolved into the

Farm Security Administration (FSA) in 1937.[6] Its purpose was to help poor farmers.

Under both titles, the agency included a special division of photographers. Working for the FSA, Lange and other photographers traveled all over the country, documenting the plight of American farmers. As a group they became known as the Compassionate Photographers.[7]

The work made Lange's name known throughout the United States. It succeeded, too, in creating sympathy for the farmers. The public supported Congress when it voted to spend money to help the farmers. This was due largely to the efforts of the photographers.

One of the most striking examples of this occurred in 1936. In March, Lange visited a pea farm in Nipomo, California. Migrant laborers had arrived to pick the early crop, but bad weather ruined it. Twenty-five hundred people, already destitute, had no hope of earning any money.

Lange took many photographs at the migrant laborers' camp. One in particular remains famous to this day. It was titled "Migrant Mother." It showed a married woman with her seven children. All of the children are huddled in a makeshift tent on a freezing cold day. In 1960, Lange wrote about how she took the picture:

> I saw and approached the hungry and desperate mother, as if drawn by a magnet. I do not remember how I explained my presence or my

camera to her, but I do remember she asked me no questions. I made five exposures, working closer and closer from the same direction. I did not ask her name or her history. She told me her age, that she was thirty-two. She said that they had been living on frozen vegetables from the surrounding fields, and birds that the children killed. She had just sold the tires from her car to buy food. There she sat in that lean-to tent with her children huddled around her, and seemed to know that my pictures might help her, and so she helped me. There was a sort of equality about it.[8]

Two San Francisco newspapers first ran the photograph. As a result of its publication across the country, Americans made a tremendous effort to help the pea pickers. They collected twenty-two thousand pounds of food to send to the migrant laborers' camp.

The woman and her family, along with hundreds of other people, were brought back from the brink of starvation. The migrant mother lived for almost fifty more years. Lange continued to work for the FSA until 1942.

In 1940, Americans began to think about the possibility that war would soon break out in Europe. The federal government started to prepare. A new agency was established, named the War Relocation Authority (WRA). In 1941, Lange began to work for the WRA as well as the FSA.

When Japan attacked Pearl Harbor, Hawaii, Japanese Americans living in America were moved into internment camps. The government had ordered the camps to be opened. Lange photographed the forced relocation of the Japanese Americans.

She took photographs as the WRA requested. Her pictures, however, recorded something different from what government officials had expected. Her photographs showed the Japanese Americans as victims, people suffering unfairly. The WRA censored her work. They refused to publish most of her photographs.[9]

Some officials in other governmental agencies also did not like the idea of the internment camps. This helped Lange find employment with other agencies of the federal government. She continued working with the WRA until 1943, when she moved to the Office of War Information. After the war ended, she took photographs for the State Department when the United Nations was established in 1945.

In the 1950s, Lange finally went back to work as a commercial photographer. She cooperated on some projects with her son, Daniel, who had become a writer.

Between 1958 and 1962, Lange and her husband traveled to Asia, South America, and, in Africa, to Egypt. Many of her photographs from their travels appeared in *Life* magazine. She also worked on a book, *The American Country Woman*. In 1961 her photographs were featured in an exhibition in Milan, Italy.

In August 1965, Dorothea Lange was diagnosed with cancer. She died just two months later, on

October 11, 1965. The Museum of Modern Art had an exhibit of her photographs in 1966. Huge collections of her work are at the Library of Congress and the Oakland Museum of California.[10]

Dorothea Lange's photographs continue to be included in many books and exhibits. To this day her work remains famous. "America is proud of . . .[her] achievements and has made Dorothea Lange a national heroine," photographer Cecil Beaton wrote.[11]

7

Ansel Adams

(1902-1984)

Ansel Adams became world famous as a nature photographer. But he did more than just take pretty pictures of landscapes. He showed the beauty of the natural environment in his black-and-white photographs. Adams's work helped to create an interest in preserving the natural environment and conserving its natural resources.[1]

Ansel Adams was born on February 20, 1902, in San Francisco, California, to Olive and Charles Adams. He was their only child. His family lived in a big house with a spectacular view overlooking the San Francisco Bay.[2] Ansel Adams's ancestors had come to the United States from Ireland in the 1700s. His grandfather owned a very successful lumber company. In 1906 a massive earthquake rocked California. It destroyed much of San Francisco,

Ansel Adams

killing thousands of people.³ The Adams family was lucky to survive. None of them were hurt except for Ansel. He fell down during an aftershock and broke his nose.⁴

By the time Grandfather Adams died, the lumber business had gone bankrupt. But the loss of the family business did not change their lifestyle too much. The family continued to live in a large house and pay for luxuries like vacations and piano lessons for Ansel.

As a child, Ansel did not do well at school despite the fact that he was very intelligent. He excelled, however, at his piano lessons. He was musically gifted and studied the piano for years. From an early age, he planned to become a concert pianist.

In 1915 his family let him drop out of public school. Private tutors and his parents educated him at home. To broaden his education, his father bought him a season's pass to the Panama Pacific Exposition. This was a world's fair held that year in San Francisco.⁵

In 1916, when he was fourteen, Ansel's family vacationed at Yosemite National Park, one of the first national parks. It is a spectacular area of river canyon and redwood forest in northern California. Today, many thousands of people visit it every year. But in the early 1900s there were relatively few automobiles and, therefore, fewer visitors.⁶

In Yosemite, Ansel Adams took his first photograph, a landscape. After that vacation, he pursued his growing interests in both nature and photography. But photography would remain just a hobby for him for years.

In 1920, Adams got a summer job as the custodian of the Sierra Club's headquarters. The Sierra Club is an organization that was founded by John Muir. A Scotsman by birth, Muir had grown up in Wisconsin. As a young man, Muir had traveled to California, where he fell in love with Yosemite. Muir developed an overwhelming desire to preserve it. He started a conservation campaign. It attracted the attention of President Theodore Roosevelt.

The campaign was successful and resulted in the creation of many national parks and federal forests.[7] Today the Sierra Club remains a huge force in the United States' environmental movement.

Adams liked his job with the Sierra Club because it gave him time to explore. The next year he made his first trip into the Sierra Nevada mountain range. The year after that he had his first photograph published, in the Sierra Club's bulletin.[8]

In 1925, Adams decided he wanted to be a concert pianist. But he pursued this career for only a short time. Photography seemed to demand more and more of his attention.

In 1932, Adams was one of the founders of an avant-garde group of photographers. They called themselves Group f/64. The f/64 refers to a camera setting for light exposure. One year later Adams opened his own gallery in San Francisco. He

Ansel Adams loved to take pictures of beautiful landscapes, especially in New Mexico and Arizona. Adams took this picture of Taos Pueblo, New Mexico.

displayed his work as well as that of other photographers and artists.[9]

Ansel Adams was asked to join the board of directors of San Francisco's Sierra Club in 1934. He remained on the board for thirty-seven years. His interests in photography and nature dovetailed very well. He was a man who loved the outdoors.

Photographs Adams took in the 1930s helped influence the federal government's decision to establish Kings Canyon National Park.[10] Dozens of exhibitions of Adams's work followed his first important one, which opened at the Smithsonian Institution in Washington D.C., in 1931.

In 1940, Adams helped establish the first department of photography at New York City's Museum of Modern Art. MoMA, as it is known, was one of the world's first museums to concentrate on collecting contemporary art. Its collection includes some of the greatest abstract art. At first, the museum collected just paintings and sculpture. Adams helped its curators become interested in photography as modern art, too.

A year later Adams went to work for the government. He agreed to do photomurals for the Department of the Interior, which oversees the National Parks. In 1946, Adams founded the department of photography at the California School of Fine Arts. Over the years he continued his own photography and taught and lectured on the subject.

In 1975, Ansel Adams began a correspondence with David Hume Kennerly. Kennerly was then the official White House photographer. He invited Adams to visit the White House and meet President Gerald Ford. Adams discovered that he and Ford shared the same interest in national parks. Ford had been a national park ranger in the mid–1930s. Adams suggested that more needed to be done to preserve the parks.

When Adams returned home, he wrote President Ford a strong letter. He outlined ways in which he thought the federal government was shortchanging the national parks. Adams pointed out how the situation might be improved. Ford listened to Adams's suggestions.

As a result, "on August 29, 1976, against the backdrop of Yellowstone National Park, Republican President Gerald R. Ford stunned the environmental world. He announced that he would be submitting to Congress the 'Bicentennial Land Heritage Act,' a ten-year, $1.5 billion commitment to double the present acreage for national parks, recreation areas, and wildlife sanctuaries."[11]

Ansel Adams continued to work for almost ten years after this. Over his career, he would make some thirteen thousand photographs. That is an amazing number when one considers that Adams was a perfectionist. Sometimes he took an entire day to produce a single print from a negative.

Adams died in 1984. During his lifetime, he received many awards and honors for his photography and his work to protect the natural environment. Mount Ansel Adams on the southeast boundary of the Yosemite National Park was named for him.

Today, Ansel Adams's work continues to be reproduced in very popular cards and posters as well as in books. Most major museums in the United States own some of his photographs.[12]

Margaret Bourke-White

8

Margaret Bourke-White
(1904-1971)

Margaret Bourke-White was the first important American female news photographer. She was not only a photojournalist, but a war correspondent, a photographer of industry, and an author as well.

She was fearless and hardworking and would go anywhere there was a story to photograph. She became well known for her photo-essays for magazines such as *Life* and *Fortune.* She was also the author of a number of books.

Margaret Bourke-White was born on June 14, 1904, to Minnie and Joseph White, on their sixth wedding anniversary. The family lived in the Bronx, New York. As a child, her parents referred to Margaret as Margaret Bourke White. Bourke was her mother's maiden name. As an adult, Margaret added the hyphen to her name.

When her parents married, they vowed to create for their family "a perfect mental and moral home."[1] Margaret and her older sister, Ruth, were encouraged to set high standards for themselves in whatever they did. The children were discouraged from wasting time. Their parents were strict. They did not allow their children to read comic books, use slang, play card games, or chew gum. They tried to help their children learn by setting good examples.

The White family moved from the Bronx to Bound Brook, New Jersey, around 1908. That was also the year their third child, Roger, was born. Margaret's father, Joseph, was an engineer who worked in a factory that manufactured printing presses. She doted on him. They shared an avid interest in nature.

At the age of seventeen, Margaret graduated from high school and enrolled in Columbia University in New York City. In 1922 her father suffered a stroke and died. She mourned him and missed him terribly.

When Margaret was back at college, she signed up for a photography class. She studied photography with Clarence White, a well-known photographer. Her mother bought her a used camera. Margaret liked photography, but her goal in life was to become a herpetologist, a scientist who studies reptiles and amphibians.

In the summer of 1922, Bourke-White worked at a photography camp to earn money for college. She sold photographs on the side. When her father died, he had not left the family with much money. That fall, Bourke-White went back to college, but to another school, the University of Michigan. Neighbors helped pay her tuition.

At Michigan, Bourke-White studied herpetology with Dr. Alexander G. Ruthven. After some time, they both agreed that herpetology was not the field for her, although she was a good student.[2]

Bourke-White then decided that she wanted to be a news photographer. Dr. Ruthven asked her to take photographs for the Museum of Zoology at the university for an article he was writing.

That year, 1923, Bourke-White fell in love with a student named Everett Chapman. He was studying electrical engineering. They became engaged in the fall and married in June of 1924.

From the beginning, the marriage was a disaster, however. Things were difficult for the young couple. Chapman's mother spent a great deal of time with them. In the fall the couple moved to Indiana. Everett had landed a teaching job at Purdue University.

Then they moved again, this time to Cleveland. Bourke-White had a job teaching at the Cleveland Museum of Natural History. At night she took classes at Case Western University.

In the fall of 1926, Bourke-White announced the marriage over. She had decided she wanted an "independent life centered on her work."[3] She enrolled at Cornell University where she gained some fame for the photographs she took of the university's buildings.

In 1927, Bourke-White earned her diploma from Cornell University. She decided to move to Cleveland where her mother and brother lived. There she started a photography business.

Bourke-White began to get assignments from architects, and a magazine bought one of her photographs. She made friends with fellow photographer Alfred Hall Bemis. He helped her and gave her a camera and built a special enlarger for her prints.

Bourke-White became interested in taking pictures of industry. She started photographing factories, smokestacks, bridges, and trains. Inside steel mills, she took photographs of molten steel. She used magnesium flares to light up the interior of the mills. Her black-and-white photographs made industrial machines and structures look like pieces of modern sculpture. She had found a photographic style that suited her.

One of Bourke-White's photographs of a steel mill won her first prize in an exhibit of work in Cleveland. Soon other photographs of hers appeared in national magazines. Henry Luce, the publisher of *Time* magazine, saw them. He hired her as the first staff photographer for his new magazine, *Fortune.* Bourke-White wrote the first photo-essay ever published for *Fortune.*[4] It was on a meatpacking plant.

In 1927, Margaret Bourke-White moved back to Cleveland. She became interested in taking pictures of the industrial sections of the city. This is a photograph she took of the skyline of Cleveland.

Bourke-White decided to move to New York City. She hired a staff, which grew from a printer and a secretary to include eight people. With their assistance, she took on advertising jobs. She took photographs for companies such as Buick.

In 1930, Bourke-White was sent on an assignment to the Soviet Union. She was the first American photojournalist allowed in the country. She photographed the mills, quarries, factories, and farms of the country. Most people outside the Soviet Union had never seen them. The pictures appeared in her first book, *Eyes on Russia.*

Back in the United States, Bourke-White photographed the devastating effects of a severe drought on farmland, in what became known as the Dust Bowl. Farms were destroyed and families were forced to leave to find work elsewhere.

Bourke-White met the author Erskine Caldwell. His book, *Tobacco Road,* about poor families in the South, had just been published. In the summer of 1936, after her mother died, Bourke-White went to the South to meet Caldwell. There they documented the living conditions of tenant farmers.

They collaborated on a book about their experiences. When the book, *You Have Seen Their Faces,* was published, it helped legislation pass that aided the sharecroppers.

In the fall of 1936, Bourke-White started to work for *Life,* another new Luce magazine. Luce hired her and several other well-known photojournalists—Alfred

Eisenstaedt, Peter Stackpole, and Tom McAvoy. As the first female photojournalist, Bourke-White was given her own darkroom, a printer, and a secretary. Her photographs helped make *Life* magazine a huge success.

In the late 1930s, war loomed in Europe. Bourke-White traveled to Europe with Caldwell to record what was happening in countries like Czechoslovakia. In 1939 their book about their experiences, *North of the Danube*, was published.

When they returned to the United States, they married in February 1939. They moved into a house in Connecticut. But Bourke-White stayed there only eight months. In October, *Life* magazine sent Bourke-White to Europe to cover the events of World War II.

Bourke-White stayed at *Life* just a year, however, and then resigned from the magazine. She felt that *Life* was not using enough of her photographs. She also was concerned that sometimes her photographs did not receive proper credit when they appeared in the magazine.

In 1940, Bourke-White went to work for *PM*, a newspaper. She took mostly nature photos, which she found unrewarding. She discovered she missed working as a photojournalist and went back to work for *Life*.

In 1941, Bourke-White and Caldwell were sent on an assignment to Russia. They were both in Moscow when the Germans bombed the city.

Although the situation was dangerous, Bourke-White photographed the attack as it was happening. This was an amazing scoop, as Bourke-White was the only foreign photographer there at the time of the attack.

After the United States went to war, Bourke-White also became a photographer for the United States Air Force. She was the first female war correspondent allowed in combat areas during the war.

By 1942, Caldwell was unhappy that Bourke-White's work took her all over the world covering the war. They decided to divorce. Bourke-White never married again.

Bourke-White was kept very busy as a photojournalist. She seemed to have no fear and thrived on danger and adventure. She flew on bombing missions and went to North Africa and Italy to photograph the war there.

In 1945 she was at Buchenwald, the German concentration camp, when the prisoners were liberated. A year later she went to India and photographed Mahatma Gandhi, the nationalist leader of India, just before he was assassinated. In 1949 she photographed racial segregation in South Africa. Wherever there was a story tell, Bourke-White was there with her camera.

During the Korean War, Bourke-White was diagnosed with Parkinson's disease. She was unable to control her hands from shaking. Even after several operations and physical rehabilitation, the disease continued to worsen.

In 1963 her autobiography, *Portrait of Myself,* was published. In 1969, she retired from *Life* magazine. She had almost lost the power of speech, although she still thought and wrote clearly. Two years later she had to communicate by blinking her eyes when she helped put together an exhibit of her work in Boston.

That summer Margaret Bourke-White died at the age of sixty-seven. A eulogy published in *Life* magazine began: "Her pictures were her life."[5]

In the beginning of photographing I used to
make very grainy things. I'd be fascinated by
what the grain did because it would make a kind
of tapestry of all these little dots and everything

Diane Arbus' Nikon F camera on display as part of the
photographic exhibit "Diane Arbus: Revelations," at the San
Francisco MOMA in October 2003.

Diane Arbus
(1923-1971)

When Diane Arbus committed suicide at the age of forty-eight, she was already a legend among photographers. Arbus was regarded as a tremendous talent. Today her photographs are easily recognized, not because of their beauty, but because of their bizarre quality.

Toward the end of her life, Arbus had developed a fascination with people she described as freaks. She said they interested her because "most people go through life dreading they'll have a traumatic experience. Freaks were born with this trauma; they've already passed their test in life." Arbus seemed to regard it almost as her duty to focus on people at their worst, when they were most vulnerable. She explained it by saying, "I really believe there are things which nobody would see unless I photographed them."[1]

Diane Nemerov was born in New York City on March 14, 1923, to Gertrude Russek and David Nemerov. David Nemerov's grandfather had come to the United States from Russia as a young man. Diane's father was born in the United States. Her mother had immigrated to the United States with her family when she was still a child. Gertrude Russek's family had opened Russek's Fur Store, which sold fur coats and, later, women's clothing.

After Gertrude married David Nemerov, he ran the Russek's store. By the time Diane was born, her family was well-to-do. They grew up in a large, luxurious apartment that overlooked Central Park West. Diane attended the Ethical Culture School and then the Fieldston School, both prestigious, progressive private schools. Her art teacher said she had exceptional talent as a painter. As a teenager, Diane worked as a fashion artist for her family's store.

Although the Nemerov children received an excellent education and were well-off, in some ways they had a sad childhood. Their father was a very busy businessman. Their mother suffered from depression. Servants and nannies rather than their parents often took care of the children.

At the age of fourteen, Diane fell in love with one of her father's employees, a young man named Allan

This image was included in the "Diana Arbus: Revelations" exhibit at the San Francisco MOMA in October 2003.

Arbus. When she was eighteen, Diane married Arbus, against the wishes of her parents.

When they were first married, Allan Arbus introduced his wife to photography. During World War II he was assigned to the Army Signal Corps photography school in New Jersey. He set up a darkroom in their bathroom. When he came home at night, he showed his wife what he had learned. When she was about twenty, Diane Arbus became a photographer, too.[2]

In 1945, Diane Arbus gave birth to their first child, a daughter they named Doon. Later, they had a second child, a daughter, Amy.

After the war, Allan and Diane Arbus opened their own photography studio. They worked together as fashion photographers for magazines such as *Harper's Bazaar*. Diane did not particularly like fashion photography, although she worked at it for more than ten years.

In the late 1950s, Diane Arbus wanted to develop her own photographic style. She took a photography class from Berenice Abbott, who had lived in Paris in the 1920s and took portraits of other expatriates. When Abbott returned to the United States, she photographed street scenes in New York City, a subject that interested Arbus.

At the same time, several other successful photographers also influenced Arbus. One was Richard Avedon. Avedon had dropped out of school to work at a photography studio when he was seventeen.

During World War II, Avedon had joined the Marines and was assigned to their photography unit. After the war, he was hired as a fashion photographer on the staff of *Harper's Bazaar*. He quickly developed a reputation in the field. "His photographs could be relied upon to make an impression of enthusiasm and delight."[3]

Diane Arbus continued to study with other photographers. From 1958 to 1960, she took classes with Lisette Model, a documentary photographer at New York's New School for Social Research. Model encouraged Arbus to stop working as a commercial photographer in a studio. She suggested that Arbus work freelance as an independent photographer and develop her interest in documentary photography.

Arbus sold some of her photographs to magazines for publication. Others she added to her own collection. Eventually, Arbus also taught photography.

Diane Arbus began to take the kind of photographs that were considered unusual. She took photographs of people with deformities, the elderly, and those that were mentally ill. She photographed them in the bright glare of direct flash, exposing their flaws. She was interested in capturing private lives rather social realities.[4]

People were always surprised that Arbus's subjects readily agreed to pose and looked directly at her lens. Critics disagreed as to the emotion her photos evoked. Some critics said she was merciless. Others thought she gave her subjects dignity.

As the 1960s progressed, American society was changing. In keeping up with changes, Arbus became more and more liberated in her thinking and speaking. She said less and less of what was expected and more and more that was shocking.

Arbus's first photo-essay appeared in *Esquire* magazine in 1960. She worked very hard over the next ten years. Twice she was awarded a Guggenheim Fellowship, in 1963 and 1966. The fellowships paid her enough money so she did not have to worry about getting freelance assignments. In fact, they provided enough money for her to travel all over the United States.

In 1965, Arbus began to teach at the Parsons School of Design in New York City. The Museum of Modern Art held an exhibition of her work. "When Diane Nemerov Arbus's stark photographs were shown at the Museum of Modern Art in New York, the queue [line] for admission was as if for a popular . . . new movie," wrote photographer Cecil Beaton.[5]

Arbus's daughter, Doon, wrote that the purpose of her mother's work was not to shock but to make viewers look at all of life. She said, "This is how it is . . . an assault on all polite, habitual blindness to what's really there."[6] In 1967, MoMA had a second exhibit of Arbus's work.

In the next two years, Arbus taught at the Cooper Union, a college for students interested in art, architecture, and engineering.

In 1969, Diane and Allan Arbus divorced, after having led separate lives for close to ten years.

Diane Arbus died by her own hand on July 26, 1971. Historians still debate why. Arbus's biographer, Patricia Bosworth, says simply that Arbus was depressed.

Photography critic Elsa Dorfman regards this as an unanswered question. Dorfman speculates that Arbus was embarrassed by her talent and afraid of her success.[7] Dorfman suggests that Arbus had been sick with hepatitis and she may have been physically and mentally exhausted.

At the time of her suicide, Allan, her former husband, had moved to California; her daughter Doon had her own apartment; and her daughter Amy was away at boarding school. Arbus was alone.

Diane Arbus's death focused more attention on her name and her photographs. The year after her death, MoMA had an exhibit that reviewed Arbus's work. The exhibit toured for three years in the United States, Canada, Europe, Asia, Australia, and New Zealand. It met with enthusiasm everywhere.

Today, more than thirty years after her death, Diane Arbus and her photographs continue to be of interest to people. Her life is the subject of a video titled *Going Where I've Never Been.*[8]

Today Diane Arbus's family still owns most of her photographs. There are some in the collections of the Museum of Modern Art and the International Museum of Photography in Rochester, New York.

Gordon Parks

Gordon Parks

(1912-)

Gordon Parks is the first black photographer to have gained worldwide fame. But this is just one of his achievements. He is also a poet, the author of a number of books, a musician, a composer, and the first African American to direct a major Hollywood film.

Gordon Roger Alexander Buchanan Parks was born in Fort Scott, Kansas, on November 30, 1912, to Andrew Jackson and Sarah Ross Parks. Gordon was the youngest of their fifteen children. Gordon's parents were hardworking, religious, loving people who did their best to provide for their large family.

As a child, Gordon went to a segregated elementary school. Then he went on to an integrated high school. Although the black students attended classes, they were banned from all social activities with the other students.

When Gordon was fifteen his mother died and he had to drop out of school. He moved to Minnesota when he was sixteen to live with one of his sisters. But he fought with his sister's husband and Gordon was thrown out of the house in the middle of winter. He spent every night for a week sleeping on trolley cars.

From that time on, Gordon supported himself. Between 1928 and 1937, he worked at a number of different jobs. He was a busboy, a piano player, a lumberjack, a waiter in a railroad dining car, and a professional basketball player.

Gordon had a tremendous curiosity and the desire to succeed at whatever he did. He wanted to fulfill all his parents' wishes and make his family proud of him. To educate himself, Gordon became an avid reader and read books on many subjects.

In the 1930s most people traveled by train. Trains were equipped with special dining and sleeping cars. Many black men worked for the railroads as baggage handlers and waiters. Parks landed a job as a waiter on the Northern Pacific Railroad, which ran between Minneapolis and Chicago.

One day while cleaning up tables, Parks found a magazine featuring photographs taken by Farm Security Administration (FSA) photographers. The FSA was a government agency created by Congress in 1937. The FSA hired photographers to record the

Gordon Parks joined the Standard Oil Company's photography project with his colleague Ron Stryker. Photographs, like this one by Parks, were taken of industrial areas and small towns in the United States.

lives of farmers, including those forced off their land by the effects of a severe drought.

The FSA photographs affected Parks. He said later, recalling them, "They were photographing poverty, and I knew poverty so well."[1] Parks also

97

became interested in photography after he saw a World War II documentary made by photographer Norman Alley.

Parks bought a camera, a Voightlander Brilliant, for $7.50 at a pawnshop. He had a chance to take photographs during layovers in Chicago. He took photographs of life in the Chicago tenements.

During this same period, Parks wanted to try fashion photography. Still living in Minnesota, he talked the owner of a dress shop in St. Paul into letting him photograph the women's fashions. Parks also asked if he could display his photographs in the store.

Marva Louis, the wife of heavyweight boxer Joe Louis, saw Parks's fashion photographs. She suggested he move to Chicago. She helped him get started taking photographs of black society women in Chicago.

Parks also continued to take photographs of tenements and the people who lived there, which was a favorite subject of his. A representative of the Eastman Kodak Company saw Parks's photographs and arranged for them to be exhibited in the company's windows.

In 1941, as a result of the Kodak exhibition, Parks became the first photographer to win a fellowship from the Julius Rosenwald Foundation. Parks used the fellowship money to study under Roy Stryker, head of the historical section of the Farm Security Administration (FSA).

Parks joined the FSA and moved his family, his wife, Sally Alvis, whom he married in 1933, and his three children to Washington, D.C., in early 1942. Parks was shocked to find the city severely divided by race and class.

Parks spent almost two years training as a photojournalist with Stryker. In late 1943, the FSA shut down. Stryker was offered a new position at the Office of War Information (OWI). He arranged for Parks to work for the same agency. Parks was appointed the war correspondent for the first black air corps, the 332nd Fighter Group. He photographed their training, but he was not sent with them when they went to Europe.

Roy Stryker then joined the Standard Oil Company's photography project. Photographs were taken of industrial areas and small towns in the United States. Parks joined Stryker on the project.

In addition to working with Stryker, Parks also took pictures of celebrities such as Duke Ellington playing the piano at a New York City nightclub. For the Shell Oil Company, Parks took documentary photographs from the Arctic to Saudi Arabia.

In 1944, Parks looked for a job in fashion photography.[2] *Harper's Bazaar,* a women's fashion magazine, refused to hire him because he was black. But Parks got freelance work from *Vogue,* another important fashion magazine. Parks also completed two manuals on photography, *Flash Photography* in

1947 and *Camera Portraits:Techniques and Principles of Documentary Portraiture* in 1948.[3]

In 1948, Parks went to *Life*, then a brand-new magazine. He had two proposals for them, one a photo-essay on gang wars in Harlem and another on fashion in Paris. He got both assignments. Two years later he went back to Europe as a correspondent. There he photographed a wide range of subjects, from street urchins to movie stars like Ingrid Bergman.

Parks did a project for *Life* in 1961 that is now considered a classic example of photojournalism. He photographed the life of a Brazilian child, Flavio Da Silva, and his desperately poor family. The story created such public interest that enough money was raised to move the family to the United States.

In 1963, *The Learning Tree*, an autobiographical novel by Parks, was published. Parks made history as the first black director when he wrote and directed the movie version of his book for Warner Brothers.

Through photography, Parks developed connections that gave him access to the black community and its leaders. In the mid-1960s, Parks was permitted by black Muslims to photograph them. He made eloquent photographs of Malcolm X, one of their leaders.

Parks worked for *Life* until 1972. In the twenty-four years he worked for the magazine, he had undertaken three hundred assignments. At *Life* his work included photographs to illustrate other journalists' work and his own photo-essays. Some photo-essays recorded poverty in places like Harlem and Latin America. In others, he documented the lives of African Americans and the civil rights movement.

In 2000 Gordon Parks's exhibit "Half Past Autumn" went on tour. It opened at the Corcoran Art Gallery in Washington, D.C. The exhibit will travel to seventeen different cities. In the exhibit there are over two hundred photographs representing Parks's work over a period of more than fifty years.

Throughout his lifetime, Parks has received numerous honors for his creative visions. His work has inspired many, particularly young people. He offers them this advice on how to begin a career in photography: "Start with a camera and have something to say."[4]

Another piece of advice Parks offers is "[reach] out beyond your own community. Don't just concentrate on black artists or white artists. I read Richard Wright and Ernest Hemingway; listened to Duke Ellington and Rachmaninoff; looked at Degas and Picasso as well as Charlie White and Romare Bearden"[5]

As of 2001, Parks continues to work as a photographer.

Chapter Notes

Preface

1. Barbara London Upton with John Upton, *Photography* (Boston: Little, Brown and Company, 1985), p. 410.

2. Cecil Beaton and Gail Buckland, *The Magic Image: The Genius of Photography* (London: Pavilion Books Ltd., 1989), pp. 9–11.

3. Ibid., p. 10.

4. I. N. Stokes, *The Hawes-Stokes Collection of American Daguerreotypes by Albert Sands Southworth and Josiah Johnson Hawes* (New York: n.p., 1939), pp. 8–12.

5. Upton and Upton, p. 352.

6. Daguerreotypes Home Page. Library of Congress American Memory Web site <http://lcweb2.loc.gov/ammem/daghtml/dagdag.html> n.d. (November 23, 2000).

7. William Crawford, *The Keepers of Light: A History and Working Guide to Early Photographic Processes* (New York: Morgan & Morgan, 1979), passim.

8. Beaton and Buckland, pp. 12–13, 16.

9. Pat Hodgson, *Early War Photographs* (Boston: New York Graphic Society, 1974), p. 7.

10. William H. Goetzmann, *Exploration and Empire* (New York: Alfred A. Knopf, 1967), pp. 603–606.

11. Edward W. Earle, ed., *Points of View: The Stereograph in America* (New York: Visual Studies Workshop Press, 1979), p. i.

12. Upton and Upton, p. 364.

Chapter 1. Mathew B. Brady

1. James D. Horan, *Mathew Brady: Historian with a Camera* (New York: Bonanza Books, 1955), p. xiii.

2. Ibid., p. 4.

3. Mathew B. Brady Biographical Note Web page Library of Congress Civil War Photographs Home Page, September 22, 1997, <http://lcweb2.loc.gov/ammem/cwbrady.html> (November 8, 2000).

4. Horan, pp. xiv, 25.

5. Ibid., plate 29.

6. Ibid., plate 93.

7. Mathew Brady's National Portrait Gallery: A Virtual Tour Web page, National Portrait Gallery Web site <www.npg.si.edu/exh/brady/gallery/gallery.html> n. d., (November 8, 2000).

8. Horan, p. xvii.

9. Horan, p. 13.

10. Carl Sandburg, *Abraham Lincoln* (New York: Harcourt Brace and Co., 1954), p. 596.

11. Horan, p. 42.

12. Geoffrey C. Ward, *The Civil War: An Illustrated History* (New York: Alfred A. Knopf, 1990), p. 223.

13. Cecil Beaton and Gail Buckland, *The Magic Image: The Genius of Photography* (London: Pavilion Books Ltd., 1989), p. 61.

14. Horan, p. xiv.

Chapter 2. Jacob A. Riis

1. "Jacob A. Riis, *Muckraker*, LIFE Hero of the Week Profile" Life Magazine Web site <www.lifemag.com/Life/heroes/newsletters/nIriis.html> June 9, 1997, (November 11, 2000).

2. Jacob A. Riis, *The Making of an American* (1901), ch. 1, <www.bartleby.com/207/1.html> (November 11, 2000).

3. Ibid.

4. Ibid.

5. Paul S. Boyer, et al., *The Enduring Vision* (Lexington, Mass.: DC Heath, 1996), p. 610.

6. Riis, *The Making of an American*, ch. 2, <www.bartleby.com/207/2.html>.

7. Ibid., ch. 3, <www.bartleby.com/207/3.html>.

8. Jacob Riis, *How the Other Half Lives* (New York: n.p., 1890).

9. Jacob Riis Web page, Richmond Hill Historical Society Web site <www.richmondhillhistory.org/jriis.html> (November 11, 2000).

10. Cecil Beaton and Gail Buckland, *The Magic Image: The Genius of Photography* (London: Pavilion Books Ltd., 1989), p. 87.

11. Jacob A. Riis, *Muckraker,* "LIFE Hero of the Week Profile" Life Magazine Web site.

12. Web page, Richmond Hill Historical Society Web site.

Chapter 3. Alfred Stieglitz

1. [Photography as Art essay] Web page, American Photography: A Century of Images, <www.pbs.org/ktca/american photograpy/features/ art_essay.html> (November 11, 2000).

2. Alfred Stieglitz biography Web page <www.nga.gov/ feature/stieglitz/4biography.htm> National Gallery Web site, n.d., (November 11, 2000).

3. John Szarkowski, *Alfred Stieglitz at Lake George* (New York: Museum of Modern Art, 1995), p. 11.

4. Sue Davidson Lowe, *Stieglitz: A Memoir/Biography* (New York: Farrar Straus Giroux, 1983), p. 105.

5. Robert Delphire, *Alfred Stieglitz* (New York: Aperture, 1976), p. 7.

6. Lowe, p. 151.

7. Alfred Stieglitz biography Web page.

8. Cecil Beaton and Gail Buckland, *The Magic Image: The Genius of Photography* (London: Pavilion Books Ltd., 1989), p. 101.

Chapter 4. Lewis Wickes Hine

1. Lewis Hine Web page, American Photographers Web site <www.photocollect.com/bios/hine.html> n.d., (November 22, 2000).

2. Cecil Beaton and Gail Buckland, *The Magic Image: The Genius of Photography* (London: Pavilion Books Ltd., 1989), p. 104.

3. Verna Posever Curtis and Stanley Mallach, *Photography and Reform: Lewis Hine & the National Child Labor Committee* (Milwaukee, Wisc.: Milwaukee Art Museum, 1984), passim.

4. The Hine Collection Web page, Library of Congress Prints and Photographs Collections' Web site <http://lcweb.loc.gov/rr/print/coll/207_hine.html> n.d., (November 22, 2000).

5. Paul S. Boyer, et al., *The Enduring Vision* (Lexington, Mass.: DC Heath, 1996), p. 604.

6. Daile Kaplan, *Lewis Hine in Europe: The Lost Photographs* (New York: Abbeville Press, 1988), p. 1.

7. Lewis Hine Web page, American Photographers Web site.

8. Beaton and Buckland, p. 105.

Chapter 5. Man Ray

1. Man Ray Chronology Web page, Man Ray Photographer Web site at <www.manrayphoto.com/html/bio/setbio_gb.html> n.d., (November 22, 2000).

2. Cecil Beaton and Gail Buckland, *The Magic Image: The Genius of Photography* (London: Pavilion Books Ltd., 1989), p. 144.

3. Man Ray Web page, International Center of Photography Web site <www.icp.org/exhibitions/man_ray/mr_bio.html> translated by Molly Stevens, (November 13, 2000).

4. Paul S. Boyer, et al., *The Enduring Vision* (Lexington, Mass.: DC Heath, 1996), pp. 788–793.

5. Man Ray Web page posted on the International Center of Photography Web site.

6. Man Ray Chronology Web page posted on the Man Ray Photographer Web site.

7. Barbara London Upton with John Upton, *Photography* (Boston: Little, Brown and Company, 1985), pp. 204–205.

8. Ibid., pp. 378, 415.

9. Man Ray Web page posted on the International Center of Photography Web site.

10. Pilar Perez, *Man-Ray: Paris-LA* (Santa Monica, Calif.: Smart Art Press, 1996), passim.

11. Man Ray Chronology Web page posted on the Man Ray Photographer Web site.

12. Ibid.

Chapter 6. Dorothea Lange

1. Robyn Montana Turner, *Dorothea Lange* (Boston: Little Brown and Company, 1994), p. 7.

2. Cecil Beaton and Gail Buckland, *The Magic Image: The Genius of Photography* (London: Pavilion Books Ltd., 1989), p. 139.

3. Ibid., p. 103.

4. Famous Person: Dorothea Lange Web page, TeacherLINK Web site, authored by Molly Buck, <http://www.teacherlink.usu.edu/TLresources/longterm/Lesson Plans/famous/Dorothea.html> Winter 1997, (January 23, 2001).

5. Paul Taylor and Dorothea Lange, *Migration of Drought Refugees to California* (n.p.: California State Emergency Relief Administration, April 1935), p. 12.

6. The Farm Security Administration Web page, Library of Congress American Memory Web site, <http://memory.loc.gov/ammem/fsahtml/fasinfo.html> n.d., (November 22, 2000).

7. Beaton and Buckland, p. 169.

8. Dorothea Lange's "Migrant Mother" Photographs in the Farm Security Administration Collection: An Overview, Web page, Library of Congress Prints and Photographs Division Web site <http://lcweb.loc.gov/ rr/print/128_migm.html> (November 22, 2000).

9. Dorothea Lange Web page, Women Come to the Front: Journalists, Photographers, and Broadcasters During World War II, Web site authored by the Library of Congress, <http://lcweb.loc.gov/exhibits/wcf/wcf0013.html> (January 23, 2001).

10. Dorothea Lange Collections, Web page, Oakland Museum of California Web site <www.museumca.org/global/art/collections_dorothea_lange.html> (January 23, 2001).

11. Beaton and Buckland, p. 169.

Chapter 7. Ansel Adams

1. The Environment, a Global Challenge: Ansel Adams Web page, ThinkQuest Web site <http://library.thinkquest.org/26026/People/ansel_adams.html> n.d., (November 24, 2000).

2. Ansel Adams: A Chronology Web page, <http://web.singnet.com.sg/~kianyew/aa_chronology.html>, (November 24, 2000).

3. Gladys Hansen, *Denial of Disaster: The Untold Story and Photographs of the San Francisco Earthquake and Fire of 1906* (San Francisco: Cameron & Co., 1989), p. 1.

4. Ansel Adams: A Chronology Web page.

5. Burton Benedict, *The Anthropology of World's Fairs: San Francisco's Panama Pacific International Exposition of 1915* (Berkeley: Scolar Press, 1983), p. 66.

6. Ansel Adams, *Yosemite* (Boston: Little, Brown & Co., 1995), passim.

7. Paul S. Boyer, et al., *The Enduring Vision* (Lexington, Mass.: DC Heath, 1996), p. 725.

8. Ansel Adams: A Chronology Web page.

9. Cecil Beaton and Gail Buckland, *The Magic Image: The Genius of Photography* (London: Pavilion Books Ltd., 1989), p. 195.

10. The Environment, a Global Challenge: Ansel Adams Web page.

11. David Hume Kennerly, Ansel Adams: An American Icon, a Environmental News Network's Web <http://www.enn.com/enn-featuresarchive/1999/11/110299/ansel_5302.asp> (January 23, 2001).

12. Cecil Beaton and Gail Buckland, *The Magic Image: The Genius of Photography* (London: Pavilion Books Ltd., 1989), p. 194.

Chapter 8. Margaret Bourke-White

1. Susan Goldman Rubin, *Margaret Bourke White: Her Pictures Were Her Life* (New York: Harry N. Abrams, 1999), p. 13.

2. Ibid., p. 20.

3. Ibid., p. 21.

4. Ibid., p. 36.

5. Ibid., p. 89, quoted from *Life* magazine, September 10, 1971, p. 34.

Chapter 9. Diane Arbus

1. Cecil Beaton and Gail Buckland, *The Magic Image: The Genius of Photography* (London: Pavilion Books Ltd., 1989), p. 244.

2. *Diane Arbus: A Biography* by Patricia Bosworth, Web page <http://www.elsa.photo.net/arbus2.htm> on Elsa Dorfman's Photography Reviews Web site, n.d., (November 18, 2000.)

3. Beaton and Buckland, p. 252.

4. "Diane Arbus Took Photography into a New Realm" Dark Web, n.d., <http://www.netspace.net.au/vision-wk/dark4a.htm> (November 24, 2000).

5. Beaton and Buckland, p. 244.

6. *Diane Arbus* (New York: Aperture, 1972), passim.

7. *Diane Arbus: A Biography*, Elsa Dorfman's Photography Reviews Web site.

8. *Going Where I've Never Been* (New York: Camera Three Productions, 1989).

Chapter 10. Gordon Parks

1. Gordon Parks Biography Web page, <http://www.ftscott.cc.ks.us/parksweb/parksbio.html> (November 19, 2000).

2. Ibid.

3. Celebrating Black History Month: Gordon Parks, Gale Group Web page at <http://www.galegroup.com/freresrc/blkhstry/parksg.htm> n.d., (March 26, 2000).

4. "Gordon Parks's Images Inspire a New Generation," *Detroit News,* January 30, 1999.

5. Ibid.

Further Reading

Berry, Skip. *Gordon Parks.* New York: Chelsea House Publishers, 1991.

Dunlap, Julie. *Eye on the Wild: A Story About Ansel Adams.* Minneapolis: Carolrhoda Books, 1995.

Freedman, Russell. *Kids at Work: Lewis Hine and the Crusade Against Child Labor.* New York: Clarion Books, 1994.

Gleason, Roger. *Seeing for Yourself: Techniques and Projects for Beginning Photographers.* Chicago: Chicago Review Press, 1992.

Horwitz, Margaret F. *A Female Focus: Great Women Photographers.* New York: Franklin Watts, 1996.

Keller, Emily. *Margaret Bourke-White: A Photographer's Life.* Minneapolis: Lerner, 1996.

Partridge, Elizabeth. *Restless Spirit: The Life and Work of Dorothea Lange.* New York: Viking, 1998.

Sufrin, Mark. *Focus on America: Profiles of Nine Photographers.* New York: Scribner, 1987.

Sullivan, George. *Mathew Brady: His Life and Photographs.* New York: Cobblehill Books, 1994.

Internet Addresses

American Masters: Alfred Stieglitz
<http://www.pbs.org/wnet/americanmasters/database/stieglitz _a.html>

Women Come to the Front: Dorothea Lange
<http://www.loc.gov/exhibits/wcf/wcf0013.html>

"Half Past Autumn," *Newshour* **Transcript of Interview with Gordon Parks**
<http://www.pbs.org/newshour/bb/entertainment/ jan-june98/gordon_1-6.html>

Index

COUNTERTRANSFERENCE IN PSYCHOTHERAPY WITH CHILDREN AND ADOLESCENTS

COUNTERTRANSFERENCE IN PSYCHOTHERAPY WITH CHILDREN AND ADOLESCENTS

Edited by

JERROLD R. BRANDELL, PH.D.

Jason Aronson Inc.
Northvale, New Jersey
London

Production Editors: *Adelle Krauser* and *Judith D. Cohen*
Editorial Director: *Muriel Jorgensen*

This book was set in 11 point Bembo by Books of Deatsville, Alabama and printed and bound by Haddon Craftsmen of Scranton, Pennsylvania.

Library of Congress Cataloging-in-Publication Data

Countertransference in psychotherapy with children and adolescents / edited by Jerrold R. Brandell.
   p.   cm.
   Includes bibliographical references and index.
   ISBN 0-87668-481-9
   1. Countertransference (Psychology)—Therapeutic use. 2. Child psychotherapy. 3. Adolescent psychotherapy. I. Brandell, Jerrold R.
   RJ505.C68C68   1992
   618.92'8914—dc20   91-32229
                                                                          CIP

Manufactured in the United States of America. Jason Aronson Inc. offers books and cassettes. For information and catalog write to Jason Aronson Inc., 230 Livingston Street, Northvale, New Jersey 07647.

This book is dedicated to
child psychotherapist and child patient alike
and to their mutual subjectivity,
which transforms and so often enriches
the relational discourse that evolves between them

CONTENTS

PART II
COUNTERTRANSFERENCE IN
SPECIFIC SITUATIONS

CONTRIBUTORS

Maryann Amodeo, M.S.W., Ph.D., is the director of the Alcohol and Drug Institute for Policy, Training, and Research at Boston University, and Associate Clinical Professor in the School of Social Work. She also directs a postgraduate certificate program in Advanced Clinical Diagnosis, Intervention, and Treatment of Alcoholism and Drug Abuse. Dr. Amodeo was recently recognized by the Massachusetts Chapter of the National Association of Social Workers for her contributions to social work education in the area of alcoholism and drug abuse. She has written and lectured extensively on such issues as denial, countertransference, and stages of recovery.

Jules Bemporad, M.D., is Director of Education at New York Hospital–Cornell Medical Center, Westchester Division, and Professor of Clinical Psychiatry, Cornell University Medical College. He is on the editorial boards of both the *Harvard Medical School Mental Health Letter* and *Development and Psychopathology,* and he is Editor-in-Chief of the *Journal of the American Academy of Psychoanalysis.* He is the co-author or editor of several books and has written numerous articles and chapters on the psychotherapeutic treatment of children, adolescents, and adults.

Jerrold R. Brandell, Ph.D., is an Associate Professor at the Boston University School of Social Work, where he teaches clinical practice in the graduate program and directs the postgraduate certificate program in Advanced Child and Adolescent Psychotherapy. Dr. Brandell is Editor of *The Journal of Analytic Social Work,* and has published a number of articles and book chapters in the areas of child psychotherapy and research on therapeutic process. He is actively involved in private clinical practice and in providing clinical consultation to schools and to mental health and public welfare agencies in the Boston area.

Nancy Burke, Ph.D., recently received her doctorate from the Committee on Human Development at the University of Chicago, and is currently a post-doctoral fellow at the Institute of Psychiatry at Northwestern Memorial Hospital in Chicago. She has interests in psychoanalytic theory and in the psychology of women, and has presented and published in both of these areas. Her most recent published work is entitled, "Starved for words: On the anorexia of language."

Bertram J. Cohler, Ph.D., is William Rainey Harper Professor of Social Sciences and Professor, Departments of Psychology, Education, and Psychiatry at the University of Chicago, and faculty member, Chicago Institute for Psychoanalysis. Dr. Cohler is editor of *Psychoanalytic Psychology*, and the author, co-author, or editor of numerous books, book chapters, and articles in the areas of clinical and theoretical psychoanalysis and psychoanalytic developmental psychology. He was recently elected President of the American Orthopsychiatric Association.

Ann Drouilhet, M.A., is a social worker with extensive clinical experience in the treatment of children, adolescents, and families. She is clinical supervisor and faculty member of the Kantor Family Institute in Cambridge, Massachusetts, and an associate of the Alcohol and Drug Institute at Boston University, where she has provided training and consultation to a variety of social service and mental health organizations. She is actively involved in private clinical practice in the Boston area.

Rudolf Ekstein, M.S.S., Ph.D., is a training analyst and senior faculty member of the Los Angeles Institute for Psychoanalytic Studies. He is also Clinical Professor of Medical Psychology at the University of California at Los Angeles and Visiting Professor at the University of Austria. Dr. Ekstein is the author of over 500 papers and book chapters, as well as a number of books in the field of psychoanalysis. His major publications include *The Teaching and Learning of Psychotherapy* (with Robert S. Wallerstein), *Children of Time and Space, of Action and Impulse*, and *The Language of Psychotherapy*. He was formerly a training analyst and therapist at the Menninger Foundation, Topeka, Kansas, and the coordinator of research and training and director of the childhood psychosis project at the Reiss-Davis Child Study Center in Los Angeles.

Stewart Gabel, M.D., completed his general and child and adolescent psychiatry residency at Western Psychiatric Institute and Clinic of the University of Pittsburgh School of Medicine. He is currently the unit chief of Bard House, the children's day hospital at the New York Hospital–Cornell Medical Center, Westchester Division, and Associate Professor of Clinical Psychiatry at Cornell University Medical College. Dr. Gabel is an author of books, chapters, and articles, including *Difficult Moments in Child Psychotherapy* with Gerald Oster, Ph.D. and Cynthia Pfeffer, M.D.

Benjamin Garber, M.D., is director of the Barr-Harris Center for the Study of Parent Loss, and a training and supervising analyst at the Chicago Institute for Psychoanalysis, where he serves on both the psychoanalytic and child therapy teaching faculties. Dr. Garber is the author of a number of articles and book chapters on childhood bereavement, learning disabilities, and transference–countertransference issues in child treatment. He is engaged in the private practice of adult and child psychoanalysis in the Chicago area, where he also provides clinical consultation to several agencies serving children.

Peter Giovacchini, M.D., is Clinical Professor in the Department of Psychiatry, University of Illinois College of Medicine, and a faculty member of the Psychoanalytic Center of California, Los Angeles. Dr. Giovacchini is also a consultant to the Boyer-Marin Lodge in Marin County, California, and to the Mario Martin Institute for Psychotherapy and Psychoanalysis in Porto Allegre, Brazil. He has published approximately 200 papers and is the author or coauthor of twenty-two books, including *Tactics and Techniques in Psycho-analytic Treatment*, vol. 3, which emphasizes the contributions of D. W. Winnicott. Dr. Giovacchini is engaged in the private practice of psychoanalysis.

Arthur Mandelbaum, M.S.W., is currently senior consultant to the Family Therapy Training Program of the Menninger Foundation, a program that he previously directed. He has also served as Chief Psychiatric Social Worker of Menninger's Children's Division, and later as Director of Social Services. Mr. Mandelbaum holds part-time faculty appointments at both the Kansas State University School of Social Welfare and the George Warren Brown School of Social Work of Washington University. He has served on the editorial advisory boards of the *American Journal of Family Therapy* and *Family Process*, among others. Mr. Mandelbaum is the author or co-author of some forty articles and book chapters on such topics as family therapy, residential treatment, and the psychotherapy of emotionally disturbed and developmentally disabled children.

Jamshid A. Marvasti, M.D., is a child psychiatrist and the director of the Sexual Trauma Center in Manchester, Connecticut. He is on the faculty of the St. Joseph College Institute for Child Abuse Intervention in West Hartford, Connecticut, was formerly an assistant clinical professor at the University of Connecticut, and is a fellow of the American College of Forensic Psychiatry. Dr. Marvasti also maintains a private practice specializing in the psychotherapy of trauma victims/survivors and is an attending physician in the Department of Psychiatry at Manchester Memorial Hospital in Connecticut. He has presented numerous papers on the topic of child sexual abuse at national and international meetings and has written articles and book chapters on this subject as well.

Judith Mishne, D.S.W., is Professor in the New York University School of Social Work, where she teaches in the master's and doctoral programs. Dr. Mishne also serves as coordinator of the new specialization in the treatment of children and adolescents in the Ph.D. program. She received her doctorate from the Hunter College School of Social Work and a postgraduate certificate from the Child Therapy Program of the Chicago Institute for Psychoanalysis. She has frequently presented papers at professional conferences and has published extensively. Dr. Mishne is also the editor or co-editor of several books and the author of two: *Clinical Work with Children* and *Clinical Work with Adolescents*.

Donna M. Norris, M.D., is a child psychiatrist and senior associate in Psychiatry, Children's Hospital Medical Center and Judge Baker Children's Center, Harvard Medical School. She is actively involved in teaching first year medical students and residents training in child psychiatry. Dr. Norris is also engaged in the clinical practice of psychiatry with an emphasis on child forensic issues and serves as a consultant to various courts throughout Massachusetts. She has recently published an article on the impact of race and culture on the development of African-Americans.

Barbara M. Sourkes, Ph.D., is a clinical psychologist who specializes in psychotherapy for children and adults with life-threatening illnesses. She is currently a staff psychologist at the Montreal Children's Hospital, and clinical supervisor in the Department of Psychology at McGill University. Dr. Sourkes was instrumental in developing psychological consultation in the Division of Pediatric Oncology at the Dana-Farber Cancer Institute and The Children's Hospital in Boston, where she was formerly Chief Psychologist in Pediatric Oncology. She has published a number of articles and book chapters and is the author of *The Deepening Shade: Psychological Aspects of Life-Threatening Illness.* Dr. Sourkes is currently writing a book about psychotherapy with children facing life-threatening illness.

Jeanne Spurlock, M.D., is deputy medical director of the American Psychiatric Association, and Clinical Professor of Psychiatry at the George Washington University and Howard University Schools of Medicine. She serves on the editorial boards of *The Journal of Psychotherapy Practice and Research* and *Psychiatry: Interpersonal and Biological Processes.* Dr. Spurlock has published extensively and is the co-editor of two recent books: *Women's Progress: Promises and Problems* (with Carolyn B. Robinowitz) and *Black Families in Crisis: The Middle Class* (with Alice Coner Edwards).

Judith S. Wallerstein, Ph.D., is Executive Director of the Center for the Family in Transition in Corte Madera, California, and has been a lecturer in the School of Social Welfare at the University of California, Berkeley. Formerly a member of the clinical social work staff at the Menninger Foundation during the 1950s, Dr. Wallerstein was the principal investigator of the *Children of Divorce Project*, a landmark study of sixty families during the first five years after divorce. She has published a number of papers on such topics as divorce and its effects on children, child psychopathology and therapy, and the impact of therapeutic abortion on young unmarried women. Dr. Wallerstein is co-author (with Joan Kelly, Ph.D.) of *Surviving the Breakup*, based on her experience with the *Children of Divorce Project*. She is also author of *Second Chances*, a follow-up study of the same families originally discussed in her first book ten years post-divorce.

Donald W. Winnicott, M.D. (1896–1971), was a British pediatrician and child psychoanalyst who made a number of important contributions to the literature on psychoanalytic developmental psychology and the psychoanalytic treatment of children. He was a President of the British Psycho-Analytical Society, and a consultant to Paddington Green Children's Hospital for nearly forty years. Among his more well-known published works are *Collected Papers: From Pediatrics to Psycho-Analysis, The Maturational Processes and the Facilitating Environment: Studies in the Theory of Emotional Development*, and *Therapeutic Consultations in Child Psychiatry*.

Barry M. Wright, Ph.D., is a clinical psychologist with adjunct faculty appointments in the Department of Psychiatry and that of Pediatrics and Human Development at Michigan State University. Dr. Wright has specialized in the treatment of infant–parent pairs and has been a consultant in this area for the Michigan Department of Mental Health since 1986. He has also published and presented at professional conferences in the area of infant–parent psychotherapy. Dr. Wright is currently engaged in the private practice of psychotherapy in East Lansing, Michigan.

PREFACE

Countertransference is a phenomenon that can be traced back to the early years of the psychoanalytic movement, although it is only in recent years that is has gained respectability. Originally viewed as only a manifestation of the therapist's own conflicts and pathology, countertransference reactions were believed to interfere with the progress of the patient's therapy, even to the point of placing the treatment in jeopardy. Accordingly, therapists were advised to arrive at an understanding of their subjective reactions as expeditiously as possible, generally through further analysis. Countertransference reactions were to be understood, but only as a vehicle through which the therapist could remove them from the therapeutic equation. Once this excision was accomplished, then the real work of therapy might continue.

This early understanding of the countertransference, often referred to as the classical viewpoint, has gradually been replaced by a totalistic approach. In this contemporary view, countertransference emerges as much more than the subjective reaction of a therapist whose own unresolved conflicts have been reactivated by a patient's transference. An understanding of the totality of the therapist's attitudes, fantasies, and emotional reactions to the patient provides the therapist with essential clinical information and influences the course of treatment in a most meaningful and powerful way.

Clearly, there is much more interest in countertransference today than there was a generation ago. It is a topic that has come of age, and the clinical journals abound with articles on various countertransference themes and issues. Unfortunately, most of this literature is on adult treatment, with comparatively less attention to countertransference encountered in work with child or adolescent patients.

In this multidisciplinary collection, countertransference in the psychotherapy of children and adolescents is examined in detail. Much of the volume has been organized along clinical diagnostic lines, the premise being that specific countertransference attitudes, reactions, and responses seem to be associated with certain disorders and can be more meaningfully explored and understood in this way. Each contributing author was asked to review briefly the major theoretical and clinical issues for his or her particular clinical area, to examine relevant treatment literature, to provide a concise review of any literature on countertransference with such patients, and to present clinical case material for discussion. The volume as a whole has been further guided by the basic principle or supposition that countertransference is a ubiquitous factor in child and adolescent treatment, and that its recognition, understanding, and management are essential to effective psychotherapy. Finally, factors of race and culture may contribute to, intensify, and otherwise influence the form and content of countertransference reactions in work with children and adolescents, and these issues have been addressed separately.

The first chapter reviews the concept of countertransference and its evolution in both the adult and child/adolescent psychotherapy literature from Freud's early contributions to the present. Possible explanations are provided for the paucity of clinical writings, in general, on countertransference in work with children. Important contributions to the understanding and management of countertransference reactions in clinical work with children and adolescents are reviewed and discussed. Various models for conceptualizing countertransference (object-relations, self psychological, and so on) are also presented.

Although the literature on countertransference in work with children and adolescents is relatively modest in volume, several historically important papers address both clinical and theoretical aspects of this theme. In this volume, two such influential works are included. The first, entitled "Hate in the Counter-transference," was originally published in 1949 by the eminent British psychoanalyst and pediatrician D. W. Winnicott. The second article, "Countertransference in the Residential Treatment of Children," was originally published in 1959 by Rudolf Ekstein, Judith Wallerstein, and Arthur Mandelbaum. (The reader is referred to Chapter 1 for a more extensive discussion of these and other classic papers.)

Perhaps it is a given that in a multiracial and ethnically diverse society, the same tensions, stereotypic distortions, and prejudices that occur on a society-wide basis are also frequently distilled and expressed in the therapeutic discourse. Norris and Spurlock examine such racial and cultural issues within the framework of countertransference theory. Through the use of clinical vignettes derived from transcultural and transracial treatment situations, they illustrate some of the more commonly encountered countertransference themes and configurations.

Clinicians have long recognized that depressed and suicidal children and adolescents evoke powerful reactions in their therapists. Nevertheless, this subject has remained relatively neglected in the literature. In their chapter, Bemporad and Gabel discuss typical countertransference responses, the relationship of these responses to such factors as the patient's developmental age, and the nature of the depressive disorder, as well as to more idiosyncratic features of the patient's or therapist's personality. They also present a detailed case illustration of a suicidal latency-aged boy and his parents to demonstrate specific strategies for both understanding and using countertransference reactions.

In his chapter on clinical work with infants and parents, Wright begins with the observation that the clinician's understanding of countertransference is linked both to effective treatment and to the therapist's own psychological survival. Such treatment situations, frequently involving highly dysfunctional parent–infant relationships, often have extraordinary affective intensity; typically, parents employ psychologically primitive defenses or processes such as projective identification. Using an object relations framework, Wright describes a totalistic model for understanding countertransference that emphasizes the parent's internalized relationships, the enacted parent–infant relationship, and the therapeutic relationship.

In his chapter on the severely disturbed adolescent, Giovacchini describes patients whose structural defects determine not only the nature and content of the therapeutic discourse, but also the particular reactions and responses they typically elicit from therapists. Giovacchini begins with the assumption that countertransference may represent either a "homogeneous" response (that is, a reaction that any clinician in a similar situation would have) or an "idiosyncratic" one (that is, a reaction determined by specific personality features, characterological structure, or unresolved infantile conflicts of the therapist). He focuses also on those patients whose behavior in the consulting room becomes so challenging to the therapist's typical way of conducting himself professionally that special countertransference perils are created.

In their chapter on the psychodynamic psychotherapy of eating disorders, Burke and Cohler describe the range of feelings, wishes, and fantasies that emerge in the therapist in response to the anorectic's psychological distress. Reactions often include rage, hopelessness, and despair, and to the extent that the therapist is capable of recognizing such reactions as an experience parallel to that of the patient, empathic resonance or counterresonance with the patient's distress is possible. Burke and Cohler prefer the use of the concept counterresonance rather than countertransference to describe the process through which the patient's transferential enactments are absorbed, subject to analytic reflection, and finally made available to the patient as the therapist's empathic resonance. At the same time, they observe that intense and sometimes extraordinary countertransference pressures are a common feature in work with the anorectic patient and may become a powerful force that undermines and ultimately destroys the treatment relationship.

Psychotherapy with childhood victims of incest, physical abuse, and profound neglect—a challenging enterprise even under the most optimal conditions—is often further complicated by the strong countertransference reactions that clinicians tend to develop in such clinical situations. Marvasti describes a variety of countertransference reactions and responses in clinical scenarios involving abused and neglected children and their families. He emphasizes the importance of considering such reactions in light of the therapist's own unresolved issues as well as those that the patient's transference may evoke. Marvasti suggests that countertransference is not restricted to the treatment proper, but may also be involved in the reporting of suspected abuse or even in the selection of the treatment modality. The notion of countertransference as vicarious traumatization in the psychotherapy of abused and profoundly neglected children is also explored.

In the clinical encounter with a child whose parent has died, therapists are often quite eager to recommend treatment not only to alleviate the suffering caused by the loss, but also as a compensation for it. Garber observes that countertransference appears in a variety of guises: children who may not be developmentally capable of mourning are expected to mourn as adults do; therapists may make unwarranted assumptions about the intactness of the surviving child and parent; and there may be disapproval when the child does not oblige the therapist by talking enough about the lost parent, with whom the therapist may have become identified. In the case of parental divorce, reactions may be of a somewhat different nature. Children of divorce are often—whether due to loyalty conflicts, difficulty in trusting adults, or other reasons—difficult to engage in treatment. The therapist may grow impatient or angry at them or at the parents, whose battles disrupt or even derail their child's therapy. Garber also reviews research examining the differing sequelae of loss of a parent by separation or divorce in contrast to loss through death, and the implications that the findings have for our understanding of treatment issues.

Beginning with a series of seminal papers published in the early and mid-1950s by authors such as Mahler, Ekstein, and Weil, increasing interest was demonstrated in a group of child patients who appeared to exhibit fundamental similarities to the adult borderline. These children, Mishne observes, also posed special clinical management issues and, not too surprisingly, tended to elicit powerful and often disjunctive countertransference responses in the clinicians who treated them. After reviewing transference themes and configurations associated with such disorders in children and adolescents, Mishne proceeds to examine the various countertransference reactions and responses such patients are apt to evoke in the child therapist. The importance of counterreactions, counteridentifications, and countertransferential phenomena experienced toward the child's parents are also discussed.

The ubiquity of countertransference in the psychotherapy of children with life-threatening illness should ensure a prominent place for this subject in the clinical literature, but according to Sourkes, such discussion is virtually nonexistent. Children who suffer from life-threatening conditions often evoke very powerful countertransference reactions from caregivers, and Sourkes examines these in detail. Such reactions range from the discrete and highly specific, such as the use of denial, withdrawal, and other defensive maneuvers, to the more generalized or global, as in the case of "burn-out." Themes such as attachment and loss, guilt over one's own good health, and difficulty in witnessing the child's pain, disfigurement, and other physical aspects of the illness pervade the therapeutic field. Sourkes uses a number of clinical vignettes and treatment scenarios both to illustrate these and other countertransference dilemmas and to explore various strategies for minimizing their disruptive impact.

Clinical work with the substance-abusing adolescent patient, according to Amodeo and Drouilhet, poses unique countertransference difficulties that may further undermine an already tenuous therapeutic alliance. They describe four major sources of countertransference response, including the effect of drugs on the adolescent's functioning, the therapeutic context in which the treatment occurs, the attitudinal and emotional "filters" or prisms of the therapist, the adolescent's personality, and the nature of the transference. The relationship between the sources of the therapist's countertransference and the patient's stage of recovery is also explored.

Countertransference is not easy to discuss, nor have there been rewards in the past for clinicians whose natural inclination toward introspection and self-awareness led them to disclose their countertransference reactions. On the one hand, there was almost universal agreement that countertransference was an undeniably important element of the clinical work. On the other, many supervisors would decline to discuss countertransference in supervision, preferring instead that such discussions take place within the framework of the supervisee's personal therapy. This perspective on countertransference, of course, served only to further entrench the prevailing classical view that countertransference is an essentially pathological reaction. In the chapters that follow, countertransference will be defined in a variety of ways, and authors will sometimes differ as to how countertransference knowledge can or should be used. However, there may be nearly complete consensus on the significance of countertransference knowledge to the clinical enterprise, and of the need for such reactions and responses to become normalized in the treatment of children and adolescents.

1

Countertransference Phenomena in the Psychotherapy of Children and Adolescents

Jerrold R. Brandell, Ph.D.

HISTORY OF AN IDEA

Countertransference in child psychotherapy, a topic that should evoke intense clinical and research curiosity, has historically been relegated to a role of relative insignificance in the child psychotherapy literature (Christ 1964, Kohrman et al. 1971, Marshall 1979). To some extent, this state of affairs bears analogy with that of the adult psychotherapy literature, in which, until the 1970s, countertransference was also a comparatively rare and esoteric topic.

Before reviewing the literature on countertransference in the psychotherapy of children and adolescents, it may prove useful to review the concept of countertransference itself as it has evolved since the time of Freud. Accordingly, this chapter will be organized in the following manner: Countertransference: A review of the concept in psychoanalytic psychology from Freud's time to the present; the neglect of countertransference in the child treatment literature; Early

---

Author's note: In order to maintain nonsexist language as well as to ensure the readability of this chapter, the masculine and feminine pronouns have been used interchangeably in most instances (rather than "he/she" or "the therapist/the patient").

contributions to the child psychotherapy literature; contemporary views on countertransference in the child psychotherapy literature; differences between adult and child psychotherapy in regard to countertransference phenomena and conclusion.

Many of the articles reviewed in the following pages are derived from both the child psychoanalytic and the child psychotherapy literature. The important differences between these two approaches to child treatment have been well documented elsewhere (Sandler et al. 1980) and are beyond the scope of this chapter. Despite such differences, it is my contention that countertransference reactions and responses are not easily differentiated according to which of the two treatment methods is employed. While it may be said that historically speaking, child analysts have been more aware of these phenomena, countertransference appears to be as ubiquitous, as intense, and as potentially disruptive in child psychotherapy as it is in child psychoanalysis. Accordingly, there will be no effort here to draw artificial distinctions between the treatment method and the intensity, scope, or character of the countertransference experience. Rather, my premise will be that differences in the experience of countertransference are more often associated with such factors as the patient's and the therapist's personalities and the unique quality of the intersubjective discourse that develops in a particular treatment situation (Brandell 1988).

ORIGINS OF THE CONCEPT IN PSYCHOANALYTIC THEORY

The first reference to the topic of countertransference in the psychoanalytic literature appears in a brief essay of Freud's, first published in 1910 and entitled "The Future Prospects of Psychoanalytic Therapy" (Freud 1910c). In it, Freud refers to awareness of "the 'countertransference' which arises in [the physician] as a result of the patient's influence on his unconscious feelings" (1910c, p. 144) as an innovation in technique. The therapist is exhorted not simply to recognize the manifestations of countertransference, but to overcome this potential obstacle to analytic neutrality and, hence, to effective psychoanalytic treatment.

Freud returns to the topic of countertransference in a 1915 publication entitled "Observations on Transference-Love" (Freud 1915b). In this essay, he again characterizes countertransference as a hindrance or obstacle to effective psychoanalytic treatment, although the link between the patient's transference attachment and the counter-transference reaction of the analyst is more clearly made here. Several years earlier (1912b) Freud had prescribed a "fundamental role" for the analyst: that "he must turn his unconscious like a receptive organ towards the transmitting unconscious of the patient" (1912b, p. 115). He rather forcefully makes the additional point that any psychological "defects" of the analyst that "hold back from his consciousness what has been perceived by his unconscious," any "unresolved repression(s)," constitute a "blind spot" in the analyst's perception of the patient (1912b, p. 116). The interweaving of Freud's two schemas—that of the analyst's use of his own unconscious as an organ of reception, and of countertransference as an obstacle to treatment—appears as a "double helix throughout the historical development of psychoanalytic conceptions of countertransference," according to Epstein and Feiner (1979a, p. 282).

It is of some interest that erotic countertransference is the only specific countertransference reaction to which Freud (1915b) appears to refer (in "Observations on Transference-Love"). Although Freud had already written careful descriptions of the hostile–aggressive components associated with "negative" transference (1912a), none of his brief excursions into the clinical realm of countertransference specifically addresses hostile-aggressive features in the countertransference. One possible explanation for this would be the close relationship in time between Freud's (1905b) publication of "Dora" and the publication of the three essays just named. Dora's powerful and at times highly erotized transference to Freud has been identified as a factor of potential significance in an effort to understand Freud's mishandling of her treatment (Gay 1988, p. 253). That Freud may have experienced an induced countertransference to his patient's erotic transference, and attempted to defend against such feelings through the use of an aggressive, imperious interpretive style, has been suggested as one explanation (Gay 1988, Glenn 1986). It is of additional significance that Freud's understanding of transference received an early and critical impetus from his work with hysterics, for whom the transference invariably contained powerful erotic components that, in themselves, may have given rise to erotically fixed countertransference reactions. He also struggled with the professional behavior of his close friend and analytic disciple Sandor Ferenczi, whose tendency to become erotically involved with his female analysands was greatly disturbing to Freud (Gay 1988, pp. 578–579). Such behavior, by Freud's (1915b) own description, constitutes an enactment of (induced) countertransference, which he implored analysts to scrupulously avoid through a combination of self-analysis and thorough training.

Unfortunately, Freud never actually published a separate essay on countertransference, so it is difficult to extrapolate much beyond the content of the passages from the essays just described. It is possible to conjecture, however, that Freud would have reacted with skepticism, if not alarm, to the view of countertransference advocated by many contemporary psychoanalysts. That view, which will be described in detail in the next portion of this chapter, purports that there is much to be learned from the analyst's countertransference to his patient, and further, that such information is critical to the success of the therapy.

Although Freud's treatment of the topic of countertransference never underwent the elaborate theoretical development that his theory of transference did, other exponents of classical psychoanalysis, such as Annie Reich, have elaborated on this theme. Reich's contribution consists of three papers, written between 1951 and 1966 (Reich 1951, 1960, 1966). Her position is that countertransference neither constitutes a source of data for enhancing the therapist's understanding of the patient nor can it be employed as the basis for making therapeutic communications. Reich argues that such attempts to use the analyst's emotional responses or other reactions that are of a countertransferential nature are no more than theoretically and clinically indefensible "substitutes for empathy" (Epstein and Feiner 1979a, Reich 1960). Reich is quite critical of the work of Racker, Little, and Heimann (which will be discussed in the next section) for their "attempts to work directly with the id and exert immediate influence upon the object relations" (Reich 1960, pp. 393–394). For Reich, as for Freud 45 years earlier, countertransference represented a departure from the desideratum of analytic neutrality. The therapist should not experience intense emotional reactions to the patient, which he described as the pathological residuum of the therapist's incompletely resolved conflicts.

Reich's view has been characterized as the "classical conception" of countertransference, "in which countertransference is viewed as the unconscious resistive reaction of the analyst to the transference of the patient, or parts of the patient, and as containing both neurotic and nonneurotic elements" (Epstein and Feiner 1979a, p. 293). Reich's principal argument, however, is that countertransference is first and foremost a problem or obstacle in the therapy. Other classicists, most notably Glover (1955) and Fliess (1953), have presented views that bear much likeness to Reich's.

AN OVERVIEW OF OTHER IMPORTANT WORKS ON COUNTERTRANSFERENCE

A number of writers have contributed to the literature on countertransference since Freud's first statements on the topic appeared in the essays cited earlier. Fromm-Reichmann (1950), Cohen (1952), Thompson and colleagues (1952), Searles (1958), Kohut (1971), Epstein and Feiner (1979a, b), Sandler (1976), Langs (1976), and Goldberg (1977) have all addressed aspects of countertransference from a variety of theoretical and clinical perspectives. A comprehensive review of the literature on countertransference is beyond the scope of this chapter, which is fundamentally concerned with the historical development of the countertransference theme in the psychotherapy of children and adolescents. The reader who is interested in a detailed review of the countertransference literature should consult Langs (1976) and Epstein and Feiner (1979b) in particular. This portion of the chapter focuses on the work of the following writers, whose contributions have exerted both an important general influence on the conceptual development of the idea of countertransference, and a more specific influence on the evolution of the concept in the child treatment literature: Heinrich Racker, Donald Winnicott, Paula Heimann and Margaret Little, Peter Giovacchini, and Morton Shane.

Heinrich Racker

Racker's contribution to the literature consists of two seminal papers, "The Countertransference Neurosis" (1953) and "The Meanings and Uses of Countertransference" (1957), both of which later appeared in a book of essays entitled *Transference and Countertransference* (Racker 1968). Racker has been called a "totalist" because of his assertion that countertransference phenomena are ubiquitous and that all of the therapist's emotional reactions are necessarily born of countertransference:

> It is precisely this fusion of present and past, the continuous and intimate connection of reality and fantasy, of external and internal, conscious and unconscious, that demands a concept embracing the totality of the analyst's psychological response, and renders it advisable, at the same time, to keep for this totality of response the accustomed term *counter-transference*. [Racker 1957, p. 163]

Racker maintains that the therapist's countertransference, in analogy to the patient's transference, is both the "greatest danger" and "an important tool for understanding," an assistance to therapists in their efforts to decodify and interpret the meaning of patients' dilemmas (1957, p. 158). It is through the experience of countertransference that the therapist gains important data about the patient's self-experience and, further, is able to identify those aspects of the patient's communications or behavior that require a therapeutic response (Epstein and Feiner 1979a).

Racker differentiates two basic kinds of countertransference: *direct* and *indirect*. *Direct* countertransference occurs in response to the patient, whereas indirect countertransference occurs in response to any psychologically important third person outside the therapy situation, such as a supervisor or other colleague, a friend or relative of the patient's, or "anyone whose good opinion . . . the therapist might be concerned about" (Racker 1957, p. 289). Racker suggests that there are two basic processes that, together, constituted direct countertransference; these he calls *concordant identifications* and *complementary identifications*. The concordant identification is fundamentally the same as what others have termed *empathy,* although Racker specifically understood such empathic experiences to represent a reverberation of the therapist's ego or id with that of the patient. Palombo (1985) has described concordant identifications as arising from the therapist's efforts "to remain in empathic contact with the patient. That is, they represent the therapist's efforts at understanding the patient's psychic reality. . . . The therapist tries to become immersed in that view of the world and thus to merge with the patient in experiencing what the patient thinks, feels, and remembers" (pp. 37–38).

Complementary identifications, according to Racker, constitute the other major variety of direct countertransference. In a clinical situation that involves a complementary countertransference reaction, the therapist feels that she is being treated as an *internalized object* of the patient, with whom the therapist subsequently becomes partially identified. Racker relies upon Klein's construct of projective identification to explain the emergence of such reactions in the therapist. In effect, it is through the efforts of the patient to rid himself of either malevolent introjects or unwanted parts of the self that the therapist comes to experience these split-off and projected parts of the patient's personality as affects, impulses, or attitudes of her own. If, for example, the therapist experiences both feelings of loathing and paranoid fears and fantasies in the course of treating a patient suffering from a paranoid personality disorder, it could be explained in the following manner. In effect, the patient has regressively recreated a childhood milieu by splitting off and projecting a hostile-paranoid parental introject onto the therapist, who then begins to feel pressured to respond with counterprojective attitudes, impulses, or affects. (Epstein and Feiner 1979a, p. 289, Palombo 1985, p. 38).

Racker observes that such counterprojective reactions in the complementary countertransference are governed by the law of talion ("an eye for an eye, a tooth for a tooth"). Positive transference gives rise to positively valenced countertransference, while negative transference evokes negatively valenced countertransference (Racker 1957, p. 167). The therapist must be able to recognize the transference situation that has induced a particular countertransference in her; contain the patient's projected attitudes, thoughts, and feelings; and then attempt to arrive at an analytic understanding of the intersubjective phenomena involved in this transference-countertransference matrix. Only then will the therapist be in a position to formulate useful interpretive interventions (Epstein and Feiner 1979a, p. 289).

Racker's ideas, while radical for his time, adumbrated more contemporary views on countertransference phenomena. However, Racker presented his ideas in a Freudian–Kleinian metapsychological framework that has been criticized by several authors (Epstein and Feiner 1979a, Hunt and Issacharoff 1977) for its complexity and use of experience-distant terminology.

Paula Heimann and Margaret Little

Heimann and Little were both English psychoanalysts writing in the 1950s. In rather different ways, they each introduced ideas about the countertransference and its role in analytic treatment that have attained an enduring status in the psychoanalytic literature.

Heimann, like Racker, defines countertransference to include the totality of the therapist's feelings toward the patient, rather than simply adhering to the classical position, which restricted countertransference to the neurotic or otherwise pathological aspects of the therapist's response (Epstein and Feiner 1979a, Heimann 1950). Heimann (1950) advocates the countertransference as "an instrument of research into the patient's unconscious" (p. 81) and rejects the idea that countertransference reactions are of necessity "bad," or negatively valenced, or that they are inevitably an obstacle to analytic understanding. Heimann states that "our basic assumption is that the analyst's unconscious understands that of his patient," a view that has been identified both with Freud (Epstein and Feiner 1979a) and with Reik (1948), and is expressed so poignantly in the phrase "listening with the third ear," which is attributed to Reik.

Heimann seems to suggest that empathic rapport is, in itself, a

countertransference phenomenon, and that the analytic attitude, consisting of evenly hovering attention directed to the patient's free
associations, be extended to include the therapist's own emotional
reactions (Epstein and Feiner 1979a, p. 284). She goes somewhat
further, however, in concluding that the therapist's countertransference
is a "creation" of the patient, a "part of [his] personality (Heimann
1950, p. 83)." Other authors have suggested that although the generalizability of such a conclusion remains in question, it is applicable to
work with certain kinds of patients. For example, Epstein and Feiner
(1979a), in quoting Spotnitz (1979), contend that patients who are
narcissistically overinvested in themselves may induce an analogous
self-preoccupation in their therapists. The schizophrenic patient who
verbalizes feelings of depersonalization, confusion, or a loss of hope
may create analogous feelings of despair, alienation, or confusion in the
therapist (Epstein and Feiner 1979a, p. 284).

Little (1951, 1957) felt that countertransference had a central role in
understanding and working effectively with the severely disturbed
patient. She maintains that patients may develop awareness of the
therapist's "real" feelings before the therapist himself has such awareness.

In this sense, the patient holds up an analytic "mirror" to the
therapist in much the same fashion as the therapist holds up a mirror to
the patient (Epstein and Feiner 1979a). Little (1951) advances the view
that the patient is subject not only to the influence of the therapist's
consciously intentional interventions, but also to the therapist's unconscious, countertransferential attitudes and emotional reactions. She
advocates the idea that the therapist deploy countertransference reactions as an internal instrument to aid in analytic understanding, but she
also promotes a far more radical notion—that the therapist openly and
frankly admit to countertransference reactions and explain their significance to the patient. Little maintains that such explanations are
essential in promoting a therapeutic discourse and, more specifically, in
contributing to the patient's ability to feel confidence and trust in the
integrity and benevolence of a therapist "who is also seen as having the
right to make mistakes" (Epstein and Feiner 1979a, p. 285).

Little, who worked extensively with severely disturbed patients,
felt that such patients constantly scrutinize the therapist to determine
whether he is able to successfully manage his own instinct tensions.
Should it be revealed that the therapist does not have the requisite ego
strength to do this, the patient will become profoundly distressed.
Epstein and Feiner (1979a) have suggested that Little's work adumbrated that of Bion, who felt that the therapist optimally functions as
"an active container and metabolizer of the patient's projective identi-

fications and projected inner contents" (Epstein and Feiner 1979a, p. 286). Others, including Kernberg (1965), Issacharoff (1979), Langs (1976), and Grinberg (1979) have been influenced by this aspect of Little's work.

In Little's (1957) paper, "'R'—The Analyst's Response to His Patient's Needs," she emphasizes the need of the severely disturbed patient to experience meaningful human contact with the therapist. For Little, this means not only that it should be apparent to the patient that the therapist can accommodate or tolerate the expression of the patient's instinctual tensions, but also that the therapist, too, has limitations when it comes to truly noxious stimuli. Others who have worked with borderline, schizophrenic, or other severely disturbed patients (Searles 1958) have arrived at a similar perspective regarding the value of such communications to the patient.

D. W. Winnicott

Winnicott's status as a pre-eminent figure in the British object-relations school has been assured through such highly original contributions to developmental theory as the holding environment, transitional objects, and the true and false self. He has also made a brief though notable contribution to the clinical literature on countertransference entitled "Hate in the Counter-transference" (reprinted in Chapter 2 of this volume). In this essay Winnicott asserts that countertransference should be viewed as a therapeutically useful source of information about the intersubjective field, in addition to its significance as an instrument for understanding various aspects of the patient's personality. He contends that countertransference is, in effect, a sort of process measure of the therapy itself. He also suggests that there are two major varieties of countertransference, one of which conforms to a more or less traditional view of countertransference as a pathological response on the part of the therapist that requires further analysis to resolve. The second variety Winnicott refers to as "objective countertransference," defined as "the analyst's love and hate in reaction to the actual personality and behavior of the patient based on objective observation" (Winnicott 1949, p. 195).

Winnicott emphasizes that certain kinds of patients—those who tend to evoke feelings of hatred in the therapist—have a *maturational need* for direct feedback from the therapist about countertransference reactions. He uses the example of a young boy whom he took on as a foster child. The boy's behavior served to arouse intense feelings of hatred in Winnicott. Winnicott (1949) stresses that before such an individual is able to experience "objective love," he must first "be able to reach . . . objective or justified hate" (p. 199). Feedback from the therapist regarding his "objective hatred" for the patient then becomes essential for the therapy, according to Winnicott.

Winnicott also notes that the therapist must be able to "detoxify" powerful countertransference reactions in order to remain available to do the other work of the therapy. In this recommendation, he again seems to be saying that not *all* countertransference reactions are helpful to reveal to the patient, although a particularly intense countertransference configuration must always be carefully examined and understood for what it may contribute to the therapist's understanding of the patient's personality and to the therapy itself.

Peter Giovacchini

Giovacchini is an American psychoanalyst whose contributions to the literature of countertransference are unique in that they are derived from his extensive clinical experience both with severely disturbed adults and with adolescents (1975, 1981a). In his article on "Countertransference and Therapeutic Turmoil" (1981a), Giovacchini observes that the "acknowledgment and discussion of countertransference responses has become respectable" (p. 565). Giovacchini, while conceding, after Freud, that unrecognized countertransference can have a powerful and deleterious impact upon treatment, subscribes to the broad definition of countertransference associated with Little, Heimann, and Racker. He notes that "countertransference is ubiquitous" and that is to be "found in every analytic interaction in the same way transference is" (1981a, p. 567).

Giovacchini also differentiates between two basic varieties of countertransference, which he terms (1) homogeneous and (2) idiosyncratic. A *homogeneous* countertransference reaction is regarded as a reaction that is somewhat predictable given a particular transferential stimulus. In other words, most therapists, given a certain state of affairs in the therapy, might be expected to react in a certain way. If a patient reveals homicidal fantasies and then behaves threateningly, most clinicians would feel fearful. A patient who reacts to the intercurrent loss of a close relationship by retreating into despair may activate a wish in the therapist to rescue him, even if such a wish is not actually enacted behaviorally. Giovacchini asserts that such situations are commonplace, and that so long as the analytic perspective is not surrendered, they remain manageable.

Idiosyncratic countertransference reactions are defined as reactions that arise from the "unique qualities" of the background of the therapist or from his or her "particular character make-up" (1981a, p. 569). Such reactions can be particularly distressing and are sometimes the result of unresolved conflicts or other psychopathology present in the therapist. At the same time, certain "idiosyncratic orientations" may make a therapist uniquely suited to provide treatment to patients whom other therapists would find difficult to tolerate. For example, one therapist reported during a staff conference that an adolescent boy with whom he had worked on a twice-weekly basis for over 8 months had reached a stage of the therapy in which he could finally offer an invitation to his therapist to join him in a game of pinball. The therapist's colleagues expressed both surprise and curiosity that the therapist had been able to function for so long as a sort of mirroring selfobject for this primitive adolescent without experiencing either boredom or narcissistic rage, in light of the fact that the boy treated the therapist as if he were simply "not there" much of the time. The therapist responded that this boy's narcissism, on the contrary, had made him both clinically challenging and appealing in a peculiar sort of way, and that the boy's newly acquired capacity to engage in cooperative play made the therapy more like working with a pre-latency–aged child. It seems clear that the therapist's ability to understand his patient as a developmentally arrested child rather than a highly narcissistic adolescent contributed to his success in the management of the case.

Giovacchini (1975) also discusses special countertransference problems that are frequently experienced in psychotherapy with adolescents. Aside from the more common countertransference problem of the therapist's guilt and inadequacy for failing to help the patient, clinicians who treat adolescents may react from "the other side of their ambivalence," by wishing "that the patient remain as he is" (1975, p. 368). Such a countertransference reaction may be understood as the therapist's resistance to change, a factor that is clearly associated with treatment failure. Giovacchini observes that the very process of adolescent development, characterized as it is by continual and often dramatic change, poses a threat to the therapist's inherent inertia. For this reason, Giovacchini asserts, some therapists may view the treatment of adolescents with trepidation, and most therapists who work with adolescent patients will need to acknowledge and work through their own ambivalence so that it does not interfere with treatment efforts.

Morton Shane

Although he writes from a developmental self psychology orientation, Shane (1980) also appears to have been influenced by the "totalist" tradition of Racker, Heimann and Little (Shane 1980). Shane views countertransference as possessing a potential diagnostic and therapeutic utility and in this regard seems to echo the prevailing psychoanalytic view represented in the work of authors such as Giovacchini (1975, 1981a), Kernberg (1965), and Sandler (1976). Shane's unique contribution consists of both his use of the developmental orientation as a frame of reference and his efforts to "apply concepts of ongoing development to the other partner in the analytic situation—the analyst" (1980, p. 196).

Shane, after Kohut (1971, 1977), asserts that simply providing patients with an opportunity for insight is unlikely to enable them to achieve resolution of neurotic conflicts. Patients must have the additional opportunity for the completion of a developmental process that is arrested, delayed, or otherwise prematurely hypertrophied (Shane 1979, 1980). Shane (1980) goes further in declaring that the *therapist* may discern neurotic conflicts in her countertransference reactions that, similarly, reflect developmental arrests, lags, or premature hypertrophies. As these are recognized and worked through, "unanticipated developmental gain may thus accrue to the analyst" (p. 179). Shane emphasizes the circularity in the process by which the therapist's interpretations to the patient are linked with self-knowledge. Freud, Shane maintains, "learned from his patients about himself at the same time he learned from himself about his patients" (1980, p. 198). Interpretations, to paraphrase Loewald (1979), *arise from* the therapist's self-understanding, and insights about the therapist's self *are restimulated through* this same process of interpretation. Shane observes that a developmental approach to the understanding of countertransference phenomena relies to a considerable extent upon "global and less time-bound reactions rather than particularized, moment-to-moment countertransference exchanges" (1980, p. 210). In consequence of this focus on more global or pervasive countertransference reactions, Shane holds that the "working-through" process needs to be more extensive or thorough than a "single act of self-analysis" (p. 210).

Kohut (1971) has also addressed in some measure the mobilization of therapist countertransference in the treatment of patients suffering from narcissistic or selfobject disorders, although he has not written any papers specifically on this topic. Kohut advances the view that particular selfobject transferences, the idealizing and mirror transferences, respectively, are likely to elicit particular countertransference responses. In the case of the idealizing transference, Kohut notes that the analyst who has not yet "come to terms" with his own grandiosity may respond to a patient's idealization with an intensification of his own defenses out of acute discomfiture with the remobilization of his own grandiosity. This, in turn, may lead the analyst to reject the idealizing transference altogether, and cause him instead to focus on interpretations of the patient's underlying hostility and oedipal competitiveness (Kohut 1971). If this analytic posture becomes chronic and rigidified in consequence of the analyst's countertransference reaction, the patient, Kohut warns, will be prevented from establishing the idealizing transference. This, in turn, will interfere with the patient's developmental need to achieve enduring transmuting internalizations of the idealized (parental) selfobjects and result in an incomplete (or failed) analysis.

In the case of the mirror transference, the therapist becomes a focus of transferential demands for approval, affirmation, and admiration of the patient's exhibitionism and greatness. These demands, according to Kohut, may impose emotional hardships upon the therapist, who may find it intolerable to function in the "passive role of being the mirror of the patient's infantile narcissism" (1971, p. 272). If the therapist's own narcissistic needs are considerable, the likelihood of such a reaction increases accordingly, as does the potential for disruption of the emerging mirror transference.

THE NEGLECT OF CONTERTRANSFERENCE IN THE CHILD TREATMENT LITERATURE

As I mentioned at the beginning of this chapter, relatively little attention has been devoted to the development of theoretical or clinical understanding of countertransference in child psychotherapy, to judge from a careful survey of the literature. Other authors who have reviewed this literature have arrived at essentially the same conclusion (Berlin 1987, Christ 1964, Kohrman et al. 1971, Marshall 1979, Palombo 1985, Schowalter 1986). Several reasons for the paucity of contributions in this critical area of clinical practice have been suggested.

Schowalter has recently addressed the "neglect" of this concept, concluding that the "most important motive for eschewing the concept of countertransference is . . . a powerful resistance" that "arises from the difficulty and discomfort . . . involved . . . in any serious act of self-examination" (1986, p. 40). This, of course, speaks to the psychotherapy experience in general, without specifically attempting to explain why there are even fewer contributions in the child psychotherapy literature than in the adult literature.

Kohrman and colleagues have also discussed the problems that contribute to the dearth of literature on countertransference in child treatment, which they feel is closely linked with the difficulties that child therapists have in acknowledging emotional reactions evoked by child patients, generally speaking. Palombo has summed these up nicely:

1. Children may arouse intense infantile longings in the therapist.
2. Therapists come to be considered by children as substitute parents, which induces in therapists a parenting response rather than a purely therapeutic response.
3. Children's communications are often primitive and action-oriented; these forms of communication may evoke defensive reactions in the therapist, which cloud the perception of the child's transference.
4. Children's regressions may lead the therapist to identify with the child patient and therefore not deal therapeutically with the regression.
5. The fact that contact with parents is often obligatory in work with children adds to the complications of the treatment process. [Palombo 1985, p. 40]

Kohrman and associates (1971), Wolf (1972), and Marshall (1979) also suggest that other factors may have contributed to the failure of early child therapists to develop the concept of countertransference. Anna Freud, a leading authority on child analysis and therapy, maintained for many years that children were incapable of developing a "transference neurosis" (A. Freud 1926). Although she amended this declaration somewhat in later years (A. Freud 1965), she did continue to insist that there are important qualitative differences in the transferences formed by children as compared with those formed by adults in treatment. It is possible to adduce from Anna Freud's work on transference that countertransference reactions, therefore, would also be of a somewhat different nature owing to the diminished scope and intensity of the transference relationship. In any event, neither she nor Melanie Klein ever addressed countertransference issues directly in their writings, a situation that may have "deterred less courageous therapists from formal exploration" (Marshall 1979, p. 596). Anna Freud (1926) also observes that "negative impulses toward the analyst . . . are essentially inconvenient, and should be dealt with as soon as possible. The really fruitful work always takes place with a positive attachment" (Marshall 1979, p. 596). Marshall makes the compelling observation that such pronouncements could easily have engendered anxiety or guilt in child therapists who might otherwise be willing to discuss their "negative" countertransference reactions to a child.

A final point in attempting to explain the neglect of this concept resides in our cultural value in protecting, helping, and giving love to young children. Marshall (1979) observes that formidable defenses protect us from awareness of destructive and sexualized impulses, fantasies, and feelings toward children. Such taboos have been no less powerful for many therapists than they are for the rest of the culture. Kohrman and colleagues, in an anecdotal remark, refer to an experience that one of the authors once had while participating in a clinical discussion of a child analysis case at a national conference. This therapist suggested at an appropriate moment that a puzzling aspect of the case under discussion might be illuminated by examining the therapist's contributions to the clinical situation, which signaled a possible countertransference problem. At this point, the moderator intervened, declaring emphatically, "We don't talk about such things" (1971, p. 488).

EARLY (PRE-1970) CONTRIBUTIONS TO THE CHILD PSYCHOTHERAPY LITERATURE

The Work of Berta Bornstein

Bornstein is generally credited with having made the earliest major contribution to our understanding of countertransference in child treatment (Berlin 1987, Kohrman et al. 1971, Marshall 1979, Palombo 1985). Her paper, published in 1948, is entitled "Emotional Barriers in the Understanding and Treatment of Young Children."[1]

Bornstein's paper is noteworthy as a pioneering effort for several reasons. She observes that therapists are frightened by children because of their unpredictable nature, their tendency toward narcissism, their comparatively greater difficulty (than adults) in modulating affects, and their closeness to the primary process (Bornstein 1948). Bornstein also

---

[1]Kohrman et al. (1971) note that this important paper was not even indexed under the heading of countertransference in 1971, although that error appears to have been corrected at some point in the intervening 20 years.

states that a feeling of helplessness or powerlessness may be engendered in the therapist when she has the realization that it is not possible to make predictions of the future course of the child's illness, and that this may generate countertransference difficulties.

Another argument that Bornstein makes is in regard to what she terms the "regressive pull" of the child's continuous sexual and aggressive provocations, a phenomenon that she believes is ubiquitous. As Kabcenell (1974) notes, the therapist does not have a "therapeutically oriented 'healthy' ego to join him in antiregressive moves when engaged in therapeutic work with a child" (p. 31). The problem of the child's regressive pull is compounded by the therapist's need to remain a participant in the treatment. Bornstein suggests that some child therapists become "educative" as a means of providing themselves with insulation from the unceasing provocations and deprecatory remarks of their child patients. Bornstein writes that such an instructive posture will give rise to increased aggression or withdrawal on the child's part, neither of which serves the therapy in a beneficial way (Bornstein 1948, Kabcenell 1974).

Bornstein also discusses the child therapist's reactions to the parents of the child patient. She recommends that the child therapist be careful in titrating both the nature and the frequency of her involvement with parents and not succumb to temptations to treat the child's parents. She clearly states, however, that when the parents and their problems remain outside of the therapist's empathy, it will likely have a destructive impact on the child's treatment. If the therapist is able to understand the disturbing influence of the parents as part of the child's treatment in a manner analogous to the periodic occurrence of resistance in the treatment of adults, the therapist's capacity to tolerate parental interference will be enhanced (Bornstein 1948, p. 693). If the therapist is unable to do this, the likelihood of her becoming resentful of the parental parameters in the child's treatment is greatly increased. The consequence, according to Bornstein, of the accumulation of this "unexpressed counteraggression" may be the erecting of "insurmountable emotional barriers to the treatment of the child" (p. 693).

Kohrman and colleagues (1971) note that Bornstein's paper, while seminal, suffered from two related difficulties. First, she described various phenomena that constitute either direct or implicit manifestations of countertransference, and yet she "used the word rarely, casually, and vaguely" (p. 489). A further problem inheres in Bornstein's failure in satisfactorily differentiating countertransference from the other responses described in her article.

The Work of Rudolph Ekstein

Ekstein's major contribution to the countertransference literature consists of two articles, published in 1959 and 1964. In the first article, entitled "Countertransference in the Residential Treatment of Children," Ekstein and colleagues became the first authors to refine existing conceptions of countertransference and to apply them systematically to the arena of residential treatment. This article is an important one for several reasons. Ekstein and his colleagues (1959) suggest that in the treatment of children, the "countertransference potential . . . embraces the parent–child unit as well" and includes reactions and responses both to the child's contemporary parental milieu as well as "to the transferences and displacements that occur in treatment" (p. 188). Relying upon an object-relations framework, Ekstein and associates make the further observation that the clinical necessity of including a child's parents in the treatment effort mirrors the intersubjective reality of the parent–child unit as it unfolds within the transference-countertransference relationship in the child's psychotherapy.

Ekstein and his colleagues also make the argument that there is an intensification of countertransference potential and response in the residential setting owing to the fact that the residence assumes the function of the parent in providing care for the child:

> It follows that whatever unconscious guilt would attach to fantasies elaborated around the replacement of the child's parents would be correspondingly magnified. Out of this unconscious guilt comes support for the counter-fantasy that the staff represent the "good" parents who replace the "bad" parents of the child. And it will be found that the categorizations of good and bad, loving and rejecting, eager to help and uncooperative, which are used subtly to dichotomize treatment staff and parents, are current in some measure in all settings where children are treated. . . . Some of the many insuperable difficulties which frequently beset the relationship between the real parents and the residential center can be linked to these feelings [e.g., that the child has been a helpless victim of psychological traumata inflicted by the parent]. Generally children who have endured a particularly unhappy life experience or whose condition calls forth immediate pity are more likely to evoke rescue fantasies and concomitant rage against the parents. [1959, pp. 188–189]

One of the factors contributing to the complexity of countertransference within an inpatient milieu versus the outpatient psychotherapy setting is that the psychotherapist tends to project countertransference feelings onto the child-care staff as well as the child. Ekstein and associates refer to both this phenomenon and its counterpart, in which the child-care staff experience powerful emotional reactions toward the therapist–child unit. The latter is characterized through the concept of "peripheral spread," a process that causes individuals not directly involved in the treatment of a child to become "emotionally involved and contribute their own anxieties to the countertransference problem" (Ekstein et al. 1959, p. 210).

Ekstein and co-workers, after Winnicott (1949), make the argument that countertransference, when associated with the manifestations of psychotic transference, increases exponentially in force and complexity. Taking this point a bit further, they state that countertransference reactions to borderline and psychotic children appear to be different in both nature and degree than reactions to neurotic children. Aside from the anxiety and hate that primitively functioning children characteristically evoke in therapists, such children "call forth an extraordinary investment of love, infinite patience, tenderness, skill and devotion" (Ekstein et al. 1959, pp. 190–191). Treatment disruption with such patients seems always to involve feelings of sadness and personal failure, Ekstein's group observes, precisely because of the presence of both love and hate in the therapist. This, they assert, remains incontrovertibly true even when such feelings are partly covered over by anger, which at such times is a more readily experienced reaction (p. 191).

Ekstein's second article on countertransference (Ekstein and Cauruth 1964), like the article just discussed, is an effort to extrapolate countertransference theory from the clinical data of an intensive case study. Ekstein continues his effort to understand the linkage between the client's transference distortion, affects, and behavior and what they give rise to in the therapist's subjective experience. There is a somewhat more modest effort in this second article, however, to move beyond the clinical data. Again, countertransference is presented as being indissolubly linked with the transference, and both are viewed within the framework of object-relations theory. Ekstein actually presents a technique here for using insights derived from countertransference reactions as a means of moving treatment along. In describing the treatment of a 16-year-old schizophrenic boy, Ekstein remarks that if the therapist is to be effective, he must help his patient to perceive him less as an extroject and more as an introject. In the case discussed, this meant that the therapist needed to provide his patient with an "echo" (what Kohut would refer to as "mirroring"), and yet alter the "nature of this echo sufficiently so that the patient can gradually permit him (the therapist) to become himself," thus greatly enhancing the nature of the therapeutic discourse (Ekstein and Cauruth 1964, pp. 84–85).

Ekstein does not make any clear attempt in either of these two important publications to define exactly what is meant by "countertransference" and "countertransference phenomena," although it is possible to infer a totalistic conception of countertransference from the manner in which case material is presented and discussed (Ekstein et al. 1959, Ekstein and Cauruth 1964).

Such a view seems also to be reflected in the closing section of Ekstein's 1959 article, in which the authors make the following observation:

> Children who are constantly threatened by catastrophic continuity from within and without, and who therefore need our assurances the most, are those whose treatment is most likely to be disrupted. For they successfully assail in us that which they need most desparately—our sustained capacity for treatment continuity. [Ekstein et al. 1959, p. 217]

Other Early (pre-1970) Contributions to the Child Psychotherapy Literature

In addition to those articles discussed in the preceding section, a small number of others appeared in the child treatment literature during the late 1950s and 1960s.

Colm made an interesting attempt to apply field theory to the arena of transference and countertransference in work with children (Colm 1955). She maintains, however, that in the field experience, there can be only a sort of "spontaneous acting and reacting to the situation" (p. 339). In such a milieu, countertransference is simply one aspect of the field, of the common experience of child patient and therapist. Colm also argues that "every countertransference has in it a grain of reality in terms of the current situation with the patient" (p. 343). Although she suggests that the therapist initially come to an understanding of her countertransference reaction independently of the patient, she advocates that later, such a process should be a collaborative endeavor with the patient. Such a recommendation goes well beyond the view of both countertransference and therapist self-revelation that prevailed in the 1950s, although Colm's work bears an interesting resemblance to the work of Racker, Little, and Heimann, who were writing about countertransference in adult treatment during the same period.

Proctor (1959) was another early contributor to the countertransference literature. In his article on countertransference in work with character-disordered children, he observes that such children and adolescents tend to evoke powerful countertransference reactions in therapists. This he attributed to their comparatively greater impulsivity and the associated tendency toward "acting out," and also to their "narcissism." Proctor defines countertransference as ". . . the reverse of transference, those grossly regressive, relatively fixed patterns determined by infantile object relations which are transferred or projected on the therapist and, consequently, lead to the therapist being reacted to as the past object rather than as a real person. In countertransference the therapist transfers to the patient in the same regressive way . . ." and furthermore, demonstrates "a striking tendency . . . to react to or identify with the patient as a part-object" (pp. 294–295). Although Proctor's effort to understand countertransference here suggests a conception that calls to mind classicists such as Reich and Glover, he quickly abandons this definition in favor of a much more totalistic one that "includes all emotional responses and reactions of the therapist toward or about the patient," contending that the two conceptions "blend inextricably" (p. 295). The effect is somewhat confusing, however, and leaves the reader wondering why Proctor felt compelled to provide the first definition at all. Proctor advocates careful, partial interpretation of countertransference reactions to the patient, and also suggests that the therapist provide confirmation of correct interpretations that the patient has made of the therapist's countertransference reactions. In this Proctor also seems to be closely allied with the totalists, although his tendency to use the language of drive psychology in both the theoretical and the clinical portions of his article marks this contribution as something of a bridge between the classical and the totalistic conceptions.

Yandell (1962) and Christ (1964) both contributed early papers on erotized or sexualized countertransference in work with children. As with Proctor's article, the clinical focus of these works is borderline and psychotic children. Such children, according to Palombo (1985), seem to arouse disjunctive countertransference responses in therapists more often than less severely disturbed children do. Perhaps for this reason, and because it is possible to achieve clinical distance more easily when discussing severely disturbed children, this focus was a more acceptable one in the 1950s and '60s. Christ defines countertransference as "those reactions of the therapist to the patient which are motivated by defenses against the therapist's pregenital impulses and which affect the therapist's technique or understanding of the patient" (Christ 1964, pp. 301–302). In offering such a definition, he avoids entering the center of the controversy as to whether a child with living parents can develop a full-fledged transference in the treatment situation. Yandell (1962) was possibly the first author in this clinical area to describe the connection between the sexual drive derivatives of psychotic children and the responses such provocations are apt to evoke in therapists. He observes that therapists tend to defend against awareness of the erotized material with denial or disavowal and at times to react with (retaliatory) anger when the patient evokes a sexual feeling in them.

Weiss (1964) briefly mentions countertransference as a possible factor in the use of "parameters" (p. 590) in the psychoanalytic treatment of children, and Weiss and colleagues (1966) also advise that "the child analyst must constantly examine his own countertransference reactions and deal with them in the same fashion as he does with the child's transference reactions" (p. 660). Brief mention of countertransference is also made in the report of a panel on "Indications and Goals of Child Analysis" (Bernstein 1957), specifically in regard to the part played by the therapist's personality in deciding between child analysis and child psychotherapy.

Barchilon (1958), in an article on countertransference cures, cautions child therapists that fantasies or desires to parent a child patient may arise out of unconscious conflicts and should not, therefore, be dismissed as "normal." Furthermore, such countertransference reactions place the child in the position of needing to act out solutions to the therapist's conflicts (Barchilon 1958, Kohrman et al. 1971).

In a panel report entitled "Child Analysis at Different Developmental Stages" (Abbate 1964), countertransference is discussed at greater length than in previous panels on child treatment, leading Kohrman and associates (1971) to refer to it as a "milestone in our field." Some of the more important points made by panelists included the contribution that the child analyst's status as a "real object" makes to issues of countertransference; the difficulty of remaining an analytic observer while engaged in play with preschoolers; the transparent nature of the therapist's countertransference as viewed by the child patient (in contradistinction to what is typical with adults); and, echoing Weiss (1964), the tendency to use parameters without a carefully developed rationale as a manifestation of countertransference. The final point, that of the countertransference meaning of the use of parameters, was enlarged upon in a panel discussion on "The Relationship Between Child Analysis and the Theory and Practice of Adult Psychoanalysis", held the following year (Casuso 1965). This position, which is similar to that of Coppolillo (1969) and Kohrman and colleagues (1971), essentially holds that it is in consequence of an uneasiness of the analyst's own that certain deviations from the "basic model technique" (that is, from a technique requiring that interpretation be used as the exclusive mode of therapeutic communication) are introduced.

A panel report on the "Problems of Transference in Child Analysis" (van Dam 1966) makes some mention of countertransference as well. Anthony is quoted as noting that problems of countertransference seem to be more ubiquitous in work with children than in work with adults, and further, that such difficulties serve to disguise the child's transference neurosis. Countertransference is also implicated as a factor in the therapist's overstimulation of the child's dependency needs, and in the therapist's reactions to the child's parents.

CONTEMPORARY VIEWS OF COUNTERTRANSFERENCE IN THE CHILD PSYCHOTHERAPY LITERATURE

Although countertransference remains a neglected topic in the child treatment literature, there have been far more publications with this focus since 1970 than prior to that time. Authors have also begun to focus on various clinical populations, such as suicidally depressed patients, parent-loss cases, and anorectic girls, to name several. In addition, papers on countertransference in child treatment now appear in a variety of publications, whereas prior to the 1970s most were published in psychoanalytic or child psychiatry journals.

Countertransference Issues in Milieu Treatment Settings

A number of authors have begun to explore the fertile terrain of countertransference phenomena associated with residential treatment (first discussed by Ekstein and colleagues in 1959), although more than a decade separates Ekstein's work from later contributions.

Borowitz, writing in 1970, observes that countertransference is a complex and multifaceted phenomenon in the residential setting. He notes that "a staff member's attitudes towards a child arise both from elements of his own personality and [from] his interactions with the child," although he believes that the latter is of greater etiological significance (p. 132). Borowitz, who makes his observations out of an object-relations framework, emphasizes the role played by the child patient's perceptions of the adult staff member. Because such perceptions evince significant distortions owing to the primitivity of many children in residential settings, the child may tend to evoke correspondingly more primitive countertransference reactions in the caregiver. The attitudes of staff members, Borowitz declares, "are determined to a considerable extent by the disturbed child's perceptions." Since these perceptions are, in turn, "determined by the nature and quality" of the child's self and object representations, changing staff attitudes over periods of time "may signal alterations in the nature and quality of the child's self and object representations" (Borowitz 1970, pp. 132–133). Having already acknowledged his debt to Ekstein and colleagues, Borowitz concludes that an important aspect of milieu treatment involves the child's efforts to recreate real or fantasied aspects of his past life, including the pathological relationships that have contributed to his misery. This repetition invariably provokes environmental compliance, so that the emotions and attitudes of the caregivers around the child coincide with the child's regressed expectation. It then becomes the responsibility of the staff members to recognize and understand exactly what the child is endeavoring to recreate from his real or fantasied past, in order to accomplish two interrelated therapeutic aims: (1) to avoid an enactment of the induced countertransference, and (2) to continue to view the child as an unhappy and disturbed individual who both needs and wants to receive the staff's help, despite behavior or attitudes that may suggest the contrary.

The work of Halperin and colleagues (1981) bears an essential similarity to that of Borowitz and others who have written about countertransference in the residential treatment setting, insofar as they also operate out of an object-relations framework. They observe that such phenomena as splitting, projective identification, and displacement are commonly experienced by staff who work closely with disturbed youth in a long-term residential setting. Halperin and associates examine both negative and positive countertransference reactions and responses and the impact that such reactions and responses exert on the treatment effort. They subscribe to a totalistic orientation, although they also note that countertransference can often be countertherapeutic and must always be understood. In support of this, Halperin and colleagues (1981) assert that staff turnover is far greater when countertransference problems are not addressed collectively, and further, that individual management of the worker's countertransference "often becomes the essential ingredient in therapeutic payoff" in an interdisciplinary residential treatment setting (p. 576).

King (1976) examines countertransference reactions that child-care workers are likely to experience in working with violence-prone youth in correctional settings. He identifies several kinds of typical reactions, including (1) *rejection*, characterized by rage, anxiety, and a subjective experience of helplessness; (2) *appeasement/identification*, characterized by the reluctance of the worker to pursue important issues that require confrontation and by the worker's unconscious identification with the adolescent's flaunting of rules, acting out, and so on; and (3) the *wish to punish*.

Perkins and Hornsby (1984) discuss countertransference from a Sullivanian-interpersonal perspective in a paper on common counter-transference issues in inpatient and residential work with children. In their article they make certain observations that Colm (1955) had made nearly 30 years earlier, particularly in reference to field theory, although her work is not cited. Perkins and Hornsby also make use of Marshall's (1979) typology of countertransference reactions and discuss the impli-cations of their model as an inservice training vehicle for promoting "staff understanding and therapeutic management of countertransfer-ence."

Reeves (1979) discusses countertransference briefly in an article entitled "Transference in the Residential Treatment of Children." Citing Heimann (1950), he draws a distinction between the therapist's countertransference and the therapist's transference onto the patient. Reeves explains his use of countertransference here to mean feelings, fantasies, and behavior that are induced in the therapist in consequence of the child's transference. He contrasts this with the therapist's transference onto the child, which emanates from the therapist's unresolved conflicts or complexes. Reeves suggests that both of these phenomena can be identified in the residential treatment situation, although he emphasizes countertransference proper to a greater extent. Reeves makes the additional and useful point that the residential setting must allow for the taking on of parental roles in the transference, which he deems essential for effective therapy with severely disturbed chil-dren. At the same time, Reeves cautions that the danger of (uncon-scious) induced countertransference reenactment is thereby increased, which may result only in a repetition of the patient's past rather than in the therapeutic sequence of repeating, remembering, and working through.

In a recent article, Bonier (1982) focuses upon the effect of disturbed adolescent in-patients on relationships between staff mem-bers. He suggests that character-disordered and borderline patients can elicit unresolved or repressed staff conflicts and cause these conflicts to be enacted. Should these enactments remain unexamined, or should certain reactions to a patient be dismissed because that patient evokes a similar feeling in a number of staff members, a disruption in staff relations will result. Bonier observes that the stressors unique to adolescent milieu treatment require supportive staff structures that can be used to contain and correct countertransference problems, and he proposes several such structures in his article.

Bettelheim pursues a somewhat different path than others who have addressed countertransference issues in residential treatment in a 1975 publication based on his work at the Sonia Shankman Orthogenic School. Bettelheim (1975) argues that countertransference reactions and responses always contain a highly personal and idiosyncratic meaning that must be unravelled, worked through, and understood. Failure to do so will invariably interfere with the clinician's ability to remain empathically attuned to severely disturbed children.

Bettelheim observes that the provocative, primary-process behavior of severely disturbed patients awakens profound anxieties and fears in inexperienced clinicians who are otherwise well-adjusted and highly functioning young adults. In order for the clinician to work effectively with severely disturbed children, a restructuring of the therapist's personality must occur. This requires a period of from six months to two years, according to Bettelheim, and "a familiarity with and much greater acceptance of one's own and other persons' unconscious and primitive mental life than is required for almost any other activity in society" (Bettelheim 1975, p. 259). Although Bettelheim does state that countertransference reactions are "normal reactions to particular stress situations" in which the individual's ego integration has been threatened, his view of countertransference seems to have more in common with that of Reich and the classicists than with the views of the other authors whose work is reviewed in this section. For Bettelheim, countertransference may well be induced by the patient, but it is the personal meaning, the reverberation within the clinician, that is of greatest significance to him.

Countertransference Issues Pertaining to Patient and Therapist Narcissism

As the language and concepts associated with psychoanalytic self psychology have gradually filtered through to the child treatment literature, several writers have begun to address transference and countertransference issues within this new theoretical framework. Tylim (1978) observes that adolescent patients, like narcissistic personalities and patients suffering from other character disorders, tend to develop narcissistic or selfobject transferences in treatment. The adolescent may wish to restore a "lost narcissistic attachment to an idealized, powerful object" (p. 289) in an effort to compensate for missing or incomplete self-structure in the idealizing sphere. Tylim suggests that such idealization within the transference may lead to narcissistic tensions in the therapist, which may take the following forms: (1) verbal and/or nonverbal efforts to reject the patient's idealization, or (2) premature interpretation of aggressive and libidinal drive (particularly the former). In the mirror transference, the therapist is "cast in the role of a passive reflector"—a role that leads to boredom, aloofness, or inattentiveness due to the patient's inability to relate to the therapist except as a mirroring selfobject (pp. 289–290). Tylim (1978) and Bleiberg (1987) both note that the principal feature of these transference configurations is the reliance of the adolescent patient on the therapist as a selfobject who can both provide external regulation of the adolescent's self-esteem and ensure the stability of his/her narcissistic homeostasis. "The ultimate challenge to the therapist's empathy is to accept (instead of confront or interpret) that the patient experiences and treats the therapist as an extension, a substitute for missing pieces of psychic structure, rather than as an independent person . . ." (Bleiberg 1987, p. 297). It is only through the patient's comfort in fully expressing the thwarted narcissistic needs, and the therapist's acceptance of them, that the process of transmuting internalization can resume. Once reactivated, this structure-building process allows the adolescent to become gradually less reliant on external (selfobject) sources of self-esteem and for "arrested narcissism to transform into more mature forms" (p. 297).

Palombo (1985) also discusses countertransference in work with children from the viewpoint of psychoanalytic self psychology. He makes the critical point that countertransference is not only unavoidable in the psychotherapeutic endeavor, but in a sense constitutes a practically necessary ingredient for successful treatment outcomes. Palombo seems to use countertransference interchangeably with the concept of empathic breach or rupture. Such breaches in empathy, he argues, "will invariably occur. The issue is not whether it is therapeutic or untherapeutic that they occur, but rather that, once having occurred, how they are managed determines the course of the treatment" (Palombo 1985, p. 46). Palombo, after Racker, also differentiates among varieties of countertransference reactions. In addition to Racker's complementary and concordant types, he includes "disjunctive attitudes and responses," under which are subsumed the various kinds of empathic breaches that arise out of therapist vulnerabilities.[2]

Touhy (1987) uses the concept of "narcissistic depletion" or

---

[2]This same typology of countertransference reactions and responses is used in another article on countertransference issues in confidential adoption (see Kraft et al. 1986).

"narcissistic exhaustion" to describe specific kinds of countertransference reactions encountered in work with abusing families. She describes the state of narcissistic depletion as one that exists when the therapist is providing prodigious inputs to the family but receiving little, if anything, in return. "The extreme dependency needs encountered in abusing families, in combination with the frequent crises and intense negative transference reactions, often lead to workers feeling 'drained,' 'used up,' and 'burned out'" (Touhy 1987, p. 38). Touhy cites denial and conscious or unconscious identification with the child as the two major countertransferential responses to abuse. Denial is usually of the abusive act itself and enables the therapist to "see only the pleasant side of the parent" (Holmes et al. 1976). According to Touhy, the impulse to rescue the child or be a better parent than the child's own parents also frequently portends countertransference difficulties.

Countertransference Issues in the Treatment of Adolescents

In a recent review of the literature on countertransference phenomena encountered in the psychotherapy of adolescents, Gartner (1985) observes that although there appears to be consensus on the difficulties that inhere in treating this population, there are nevertheless relatively few references to countertransference per se. In addition to the explanations already discussed to account for this phenomenon in the child psychotherapy literature, Gartner suggests that adolescent psychotherapy has always been something of a "stepchild" to child psychotherapy. "Conceptual trends in adolescent psychotherapy, such as the studied use of countertransference, have tended to be somewhat delayed in their appearance because of resistances among child therapists" to addressing issues pertaining to adolescents (Gartner 1985, p. 195).

Gartner points to the adolescent's unique ability to arouse a recrudescence of the therapist's own adolescent conflicts, which she feels has partly to do with the existence of powerful cultural stereotypes about adolescent aggression, sexual feelings, and impulse life. Countertransference reactions involving narcissistic injuries are also felt to be frequently activated by the adolescent's undisguised boredom, incessant complaints of not being helped, and devaluation of the therapist's technique or person. Giovacchini observes that, while "countertransference problems are as complex and varied as are the personalities of different therapists," there may nonetheless be "some homogeneous features to our reactions which go beyond personal idiosyncracies" (1975, p. 356). He observes that countertransference issues with adolescents may involve a range of reactions, including therapist guilt and/or inadequacy for failing to help the patient; the wish for the patient to remain as he is; and the therapist's resistance to change, which becomes especially problematic in light of the rapid change and growth that characterize adolescent development.

In a 1970 paper on adolescent depression, Anthony describes two contrasting types of depression in this group and the countertransference phenomena associated with both. His first type is a predominantly preoedipal depression, consisting of marked orality and extreme dependency, and rooted in a pronounced symbiotic attachment with an omnipotent, need-satisfying mother. Such patients demonstrate object relationships of the narcissistic type, and an inability to maintain clear boundaries between self and other. The countertransference in such a case may consist of induced feelings of helplessness or gloom, reflecting the patient's inner psychological state; or it may be characterized by feelings of uselessness or fantasies of reciprocal interchange, which are closely related to the patient's narcissistic mode of relating (Anthony 1970, p. 854). Anthony's second type of adolescent depression is oedipal in nature, and typically consists of excessive guilt and moral masochism, which are in turn linked to a punitive superego. The adolescent's hostility, originally intended for the parents, is turned against the self, "and the self-depreciating trends are ultimately related to the wish to destroy the idealized image of the parents, by whom the child feels betrayed." Self-disgust is also related to this phenomenon, and leads ultimately to an "aggression against the self in which both self and hated incorporated objects are annihilated, and death is the punishment for the wish to kill" (Anthony 1970, pp. 849–850). He contends that the countertransference to this kind of depression is more libidinal in type, although it is just as likely to induce depressive contagion in the therapist.

Countertransference issues in working with the suicidal adolescent are explored in a 1981 publication by Mintz. Mintz lists four critical issues that must be confronted by therapists working with suicidal youngsters:

1. The therapist's fears that a patient might commit suicide can inhibit the therapist from exploring the issue, and thereby add to the patient's feelings of isolation and explosiveness; such therapist anxiety can also lead to a dangerous denial.
2. The therapist may experience the patient as burdensome, particularly when the patient fails to improve. This is compounded by hostile attacks (in effect the harsh attacks that such patients themselves experience from harsh, punitive superegos) that the patient makes on the therapist, and can lead to

counteraggressions that jeopardize the therapy and perhaps the patient's life (as, for example, when the therapist challenges the patient to "Go ahead. Why *don't* you kill yourself?").

3. The therapist may be unable to recognize the patient's fear of change, or the anguish that he is endeavoring to avoid through death, or that suicide represents an effort to control his life and destiny.

4. The therapist's feeling of loss of control and his wish to heal all wounds may create insurmountable problems for the therapy; inability to achieve success may lead to helplessness, a sense of impotence, and, finally, hopelessness. [Mintz 1981, pp. 495–496]

Countertransference issues in the psychotherapy of anorectic adolescents are also complex and quite powerful. Cohler characterizes the emotional reactions to such patients as "perhaps the most intense encountered in a therapeutic relationship" (1976, p. 353), although he also observes that the therapist's anger and hopelessness in such cases is a "genuine and intrinsic part of the treatment process" and not an aspect of countertransference (p. 354). Countertransference, he notes, consists of "affective reactions to the patient that interfere with the therapist's objectivity and, therefore, are harmful to treatment . . ." and, that invariably arise from "the therapist's own prior life history and relationships with significant figures in his own parental family" (Cohler 1976, p. 354). Cohler describes other emotional reactions, even very intense ones, as constituting attempts to become or remain empathically attuned to patients. "Such feelings . . . arise from the therapist's sensitivity to the patient's self and to the patient's characteristic relations with others" (pp. 354–355).

Cohler claims that in the treatment of the anoretic patient, it is only via such empathic sharing in the patient's feelings and perceptions that the therapist can begin to arrive at an understanding of the patient's "particular perceptions of self and others" and their significance for the patient's survival (1976, p. 372). This is held to be of inestimable value in the treatment of anorexia nervosa, the pathogenesis of which can be fully understood only in light of the significance of self–other boundaries and the issue of loss of control. Cohler concludes his argument by advising that it is important in the therapy of anorectic patients to allow the opportunity "to reexperience the original mother–daughter symbiosis in the transference." As the therapy moves forward and the patient makes beginning efforts to achieve a resolution of this symbiosis, the therapist must submit to being placed in a "helpless position of being controlled by the patient" (1976, p. 378). It is only through the therapist's acceptance of this part of the treatment process that the patient will gradually achieve individuation, a sense of autonomy, and consolidation of identity (See Chapter 8).

Zerbe (1986) has also addressed relational issues in work with anorectic adolescents. Unlike Cohler, she prefers a broad definition of countertransference that includes the range of emotional reactions to the patient. Zerbe, however, does seem to be in basic agreement with the position that autonomy, separation, and control constitute the predominant relational themes. Zerbe describes the case of a 15-year-old anorectic patient who had requested to switch appointment times with her mother (who was also in treatment with the author) in order to participate in an after-school activity. Although the author felt uncomfortable with this request, she nevertheless agreed to it. In so doing, the author observes, she was repeating the pathology of the symbiotic relationship between this girl and her mother, for she became aware that she feared that she would lose them as patients if she denied the patient's request. In essence, the countertransference here paralleled her patient's fear that she would disrupt or damage the symbiosis with her mother if she did not consent to her mother's intrusions.

Countertransference in Work With Children: Contemporary Efforts to Achieve Conceptual Clarity

It is probably quite clear by now that many of the authors whose works I have examined are not in basic agreement as to the nature of countertransference, its scope, or even its specific manifestations. A paper written by Bernstein and Glenn (1988) has provided a carefully devised typology for differentiating countertransference phenomena from other varieties of emotional reaction and epitomizes the classicist position of Freud, Reich, and others.

Bernstein and Glenn make the following categorical distinctions in trying to differentiate countertransference from other emotional reactions:

1. *Countertransference:* The therapist's response to a patient's transference with his own transference, which may involve aggressive as well as libidinal drive derivatives.
2. *Transference to patients or their parents:* Differs from countertransference in that there is *no transferential stimulus*; the therapist may be reacting to nontransferential aspects of the patient's appearance or behavior, or to fantasies about the patient that are rooted in the therapist's own unresolved conflicts or issues.

3. *Relating to patients or parents based on character traits:* Differs from transference inasmuch as it is a variety of transference that is "incorporated into rigidly frozen character traits with stereotyped behavior and attitudes"; it is a habitual relational mode.

4. *Identification:* Differs from countertransference in that there is no specific transferential stimulus on the child's part, although identification with the child "may occur concomitant with the development of transferences to the child's parents," who are equated with the therapist's own parents.

5. *Counteridentification:* A response in which the therapist reacts to the child's identification with him by identifying with the child; it involves regression to a primitive mode of relating in which there is a blurring of self and object representations.

6. *Narcissistic attachments to the patient:* Occurs when the therapist experiences the child as an extension of himself or feels fused with the child as if he were the parent.

7. *Responses to the patient or parents as real people:* These responses consist of empathy, which is typically a less intense and shorter-lived emotional reaction than countertransference; failures of empathy, which signal reactions or affects that are also based upon an attunement process with the child; and "failures to understand the patient due to differences in the developmental level" of the child and the therapist. [Bernstein and Glenn 1978, pp. 375–378, 1988, pp. 225–228]

Bernstein and Glenn (1988) also examine some of the special countertransference issues and other emotional reactions associated with the treatment of children at different developmental stages. In a concluding section, they focus upon therapists' reactions to the termination phase of treatment.

Other authors have also recommended delimiting the broad conceptual scope that countertransference has assumed in the past twenty-five to thirty years. Piene and colleagues "find it most appropriate to use the term *countertransference* in a restricted sense as an emotionally based blocking" in the therapist, and "take Freud's (1912b) definition as our point of departure" (1983, pp. 50–51). Marcus states that it is "untenable to view countertransference as all of the analyst's [therapist's] emotional responses . . . and as a general reaction which includes all unconscious and conscious attitudes, feelings, and actions" (1980, p. 288). He prefers to think of countertransference as a complex phenomenon with origins in the therapist's unconscious or preconscious processes that "has specificity to the patient, to the transference, or to other components of the patient's material." Furthermore, like

Cohler, Marcus believes that countertransference is by definition a defensive development that interrupts or disrupts the therapist's conduct of the treatment (1980, pp. 286–287), and he therefore differentiates it from such phenomena as the character traits of the therapist or her concordant identifications with the child.

COUNTERTRANSFERENCE AND THE ENGLISH OBJECT RELATIONS SCHOOL: CONTEMPORARY VIEWS

Recent publications by English and South American authors attest to the enduring influence that writers such as Winnicott, Bick, Heimann, Bion, Little, Racker, and Meltzer have had on conceptions of countertransference in the English object-relations school.

Waksman considers various meanings of the term *countertransference* in a review of the concept as it applies to child analysis, before proposing that countertransference be "understood as the overall response of the analyst" to the child patient in the treatment situation (1986, p. 414). Alvarez also tends to be quite global in her use of the term, which, she observes, should "include all the feelings the therapist may have toward his patient"—which might consist of the therapist's "own unanalyzed transference to the patient or a displacement onto the patient from outside" as well as "feelings put into him by the patient" (Alvarez 1983, p. 11). Judd, too, seems to subscribe to a totalistic view of countertransference, making references to the role of the patient's projective identifications in the development of countertransference reactions and fantasies in the therapist (Judd 1986).

Dresser (1987) asserts that early countertransference reactions to children, including those present in the diagnostic interview, can prove vital for understanding both conscious and unconscious communications of young patients. Dresser feels that many questions as to the child's intrapsychic and object-relational development are, in fact, answerable only through the perception of transferential and countertransferential phenomena. Alvarez, in addressing herself more to the domain of treatment rather than to assessment, advises that receptive containment in the countertransference is a fundamental aspect of effective child therapy. She further states that it is only "when the therapist is honest with himself about his countertransference" that he will be able to "make interpretations which can be experienced and heard by the patient as meaningful" (Alvarez 1983, pp. 21–22).

Countertransference Issues in Specialized Clinical Situations

Several authors have addressed themselves to varieties of countertransference encountered in specialized or unusual clinical situations not already discussed. Garber (1988) provides a thoughtful discussion of countertransference complications in work with children who have experienced the loss of a parent. He suggests that many therapists, owing to adultomorphic errors in empathy, assume that therapy for any child who has lost a parent must include "mourning." This assumption is often held irrespective of the child's cognitive skills or object-relations development; hence it constitutes a perceptual distortion on the therapist's part. Many clinicians also experience a great degree of difficulty in tolerating the child's expression of anger toward the deceased parent. They are generally far more comfortable and empathically attuned to the "child's longings and feelings of sadness and loss" (Garber 1988, pp. 154–155). Yet another countertransference complication is reflected in the tendency to use treatment parameters such as changes in the appointment time or frequency of sessions. Various rationalizations that have to do with the hardships encountered by children who have lost parents are then invoked. In addition, therapists may be too readily inclined to provide realistic responses to questions about their private lives so that they do not "deprive and frustrate the child by withholding" (p. 158) (See Chapter 10).

Buirski and Buirski (1980) have commented on the phenomenon of split transference in the simultaneous treatment of mother and child, with particular attention to the countertransference response. They focus on the effect of the mother's split transference when the mother's split-off hostile affects are displaced onto the child's therapist. In each of the cases they discuss, the mother's analyst, for reasons related to countertransference activation, became "embroiled in the mother's criticism of the child's treatment" (Buirski and Buirski 1980, p. 644). They emphatically recommend that the split transference in such cases be thoroughly understood and interpreted to the mother lest both the mother's and the child's treatment be imperiled.

Blotcky and Looney (1980) have addressed the countertransference dilemmas associated with the treatment of silent, nonproductive children. Such children, they observe, make therapists feel awkward if not clinically "impotent" and are "experienced at best as tedious and, at worst, as untreatable" (p. 493). The therapist's emotional response to such children may include management errors, anger and frustration, breaches in confidentiality, and despair. Although the authors seem to use a totalistic framework in their depiction of countertransference, they also note that the therapist's ability to face his or her own narcissistic needs may prevent a complete derailment of the treatment. Furthermore, their clinical data strongly suggest that silent, nonproductive children who are able to continue in treatment are often able to improve.

DIFFERENCES BETWEEN ADULT AND CHILD PSYCHO-THERAPY IN REGARD TO COUNTERTRANSFERENCE PHENOMENA

Although the psychotherapy literature abounds with theoretical and clinical-anecdotal comparisons between the treatment of children and that of adults, there have been notably few efforts to examine differences in the realm of countertransference.

Anthony (1986) suggests that countertransference reactions in child treatment are more intense and ubiquitous than those encountered in the treatment of adults. This is especially true in the treatment of borderline and psychotic children, where countertransference reactions and disjunctive responses occur with perhaps greater frequency and greater intensity. Anthony observes that the child therapist may, paradoxically, be less prone to disruptive countertransference responses precisely because the likelihood of induced countertransference is so predictably high.

A panel held at a national conference in the mid-1970s (Feigelson 1974a) also addressed this theme. Four significant differences in child versus adult treatment were identified:

1. The presence of the parents as a "third party" is a potential pitfall for countertransference.
2. The child lacks conscious motivation for treatment, whereas the adult provides active and informed consent.
3. The fundamental "action orientation" of the child in combination with poor frustration tolerance and poorly developed capacity for delay requires more active participation of child therapist, and leaves less room for self-monitoring than in the typical case of adult patient and therapist.
4. The regressive impact of the child patient on the therapist causes both qualitative and quantitative differences in the therapist's countertransference response as compared to the response to the adult patient. [Feigelson 1974a, pp. 603–604].

One of the only research investigations to address this (or any other) aspect of countertransference in work with children is reported by Beiser (1971). In a comparative examination of the personality characteristics of child analyst students and adult analyst students using data obtained by the Q-sort method, Beiser made an interesting discovery. Child analyst students appeared to be somewhat better able than their adult analyst student peers to monitor their own feelings and to describe the effect of their feelings on their patients. On the other hand, they seemed to have difficulty in recognizing the countertransference aspects of these feelings and demonstrated "countertransference blindspots in evaluating themselves," according to Beiser. The generalizability of this investigation to a nonanalyst child therapist population remains, of course, unclear.

Table 1–1 is intended to provide a concise summary of articles that were published from 1948 through 1988 on the subject of countertransference with children and adolescents. For each article in this table I have attempted to extract the author's theoretical conception or definition of transference, as well as to specify whether the author's views are predominantly classical/traditional or totalistic. Also included are brief descriptions of the clinical subjects whose cases illustrate these articles.

Table 1–1: Journal Articles That Have Focused Exclusively or Partially on Countertransference in the Treatment of Children and Adolescents, 1948–1988

Author	Predominant Theoretical Orientation			Conception or Definition of Countertransference	Characteristics of Clinical Illustrations Used
	Totalistic	Classicist	Other		
Bornstein (1948)	–	–		Not defined	Not applicable
Colm (1955)	X			A "facet of the common humanity of patient and analyst" that consists of parataxic distortions and reality	Psychoneurotic and character-disordered, although not clearly described
Barchilon (1958)		X		Viewed in classical terms as an unconscious response to the patient that must be understood lest it interfere with the therapeutic process	Analytic cases, although no child cases are presented

Author	Predominant Theoretical Orientation			Conception or Definition of Countertransference	Characteristics of Clinical Illustrations Used
	Totalistic	Classicist	Other		
Ekstein et. al. (1959)	X			"Countertransference potential in work with children embraces the parent–child unit . . . and includes the therapist's responses to the contemporary parents of the child as well as to the child's transferences and displacements" (p. 189)	Borderline and psychotic children in residential setting
Proctor (1959)	X			Defined both as "the reverse of transference" and "to include all emotional reactions and responses of the therapist towards or about the patient"	"Severely character-disordered children and adolescents"
Christ (1964)	X			Defined as "those reactions of the therapist to the patient which are motivated by defenses against the therapist's pregenital impulses and which affect the therapist's technique or understanding of the patient"	Schizophrenic adolescent with an erotized transference
Ekstein and Cauruth (1964)	X			Not defined	Schizophrenic children
Weiss (1964)		X[†]		Not defined	Psychoneurotic
Weiss et al. (1966)		X[†]		Not defined	Not applicable

Author	Predominant Theoretical Orientation			Conception or Definition of Countertransference	Characteristics of Clinical Illustrations Used
	Totalistic	Classicist	Other		
Coppolillo (1969)	X			Not defined	Borderline and psychoneurotic
Borowitz (1970)	X			Consists of emotions and attitudes that either are evoked by interaction of the therapist with a particular child or arise from elements of the therapist's own personality	Children in residential treatment
Anthony (1970)	X			Not defined as such, but understood as a product of the therapist's interaction with a child	Psychoneurotic and character-disordered adolescents
Kohrman et al. (1971)	Contains elements of both totalistic and classicist orientations			*Universal Countertransference* equals total response of the child analyst to the patient, the parents, and the therapeutic situation; *countertransference proper* equals unconscious reaction to the patient's transference, originating in therapist's unresolved conflicts	Not applicable
Yandell (1962, 1973)		X		Not defined	Schizophrenic and severely disturbed children
Kabcenell (1974)		X		Defined as the "reactivation of early emotional states and relationships under the impact of the transference"	Psychoneurotic

Author	Predominant Theoretical Orientation			Conception or Definition of Countertransference	Characteristics of Clinical Illustrations Used
	Totalistic	Classicist	Other		
Bettelheim (1975)				Not defined	Autistic and psychotic
Giovacchini (1975)	X			Not defined	Moderate and more severely disturbed adolescent outpatients
King (1976)	X			Suggests that "countertransference . . . in therapy with violent youths" has "infinite parameters of expression" and is linked not so much with the therapist's unresolved issues as it is with other aspects of experience with violence-prone patients	Violent, including homicidal children and adolescents described in several case vignettes
Cohler (1976)		X		Defined as "feelings toward the patient [that are] based on the therapist's own prior life history and relationships with significant figures in his own parental family"; such reactions interfere with the therapist's objectivity and are therefore potentially harmful to treatment; differs from empathic understanding	Anorectic adolescents
Tylim (1978)	X			Not defined	Adolescent outpatients

Author	Predominant Theoretical Orientation			Conception or Definition of Countertransference	Characteristics of Clinical Illustrations Used
	Totalistic	Classicist	Other		
Bernstein and Glenn (1978)		X		Defined as the specific unconscious response of the analyst to the child patient's transference	Child and adolescent analytic patients
Marshall (1979)			X[§]	Defined to include four types; Type I: Unconscious and derived from the therapist's side; Type II: Conscious and therapist-derived; Type III: Unconscious and induced by the patient; Type IV: Conscious and induced	Outpatient child and adolescent cases; e.g., depressed, acting-out, obsessive-compulsive
Reeves (1979)	X			Defined as "counter feelings invoked in the therapist by the child's transference activity" in accord with Heimann's definition	"Maladjusted" (character-disordered) children in residential treatment
Marcus (1980)		X		Defined as a complex phenomenon that has its origins in the unconscious or preconscious processes of the analyst; has specificity to the patient, to the transference, or to other components of the patient's material; and defensively interrupts or disrupts the analyzing function	Analytic cases involving children ranging in age from 3½ to 15 years

Author	Predominant Theoretical Orientation			Conception or Definition of Countertransference	Characteristics of Clinical Illustrations Used
	Totalistic	Classicist	Other		
Blotcky and Looney (1980)	X			Not defined	Character-disordered, schizophrenic, and anorectic children
Mintz (1981)			X	Certain countertransference reactions are regarded as commonplace in work with the suicidally depressed adolescent but are still believed to constitute blind spots that should be removed	Not applicable
Halperin et al. (1981)	X			Emphasis on the positive and negative manifestations of countertransference and how it is influenced by staff role delineations, staff diversity (in terms of background), and therapist personality attributes	Adolescents with substance abuse problems, sexual identity issues, and chronic schizophrenia in transitional residential care
Bonier (1982)	X			Believed to be inevitable and of potential usefulness to the therapy; defined as the arousal of repressed feelings as they are stimulated in the milieu treatment setting, especially (but not always) in response to the transference made onto staff by the patient	Not applicable

Author	Predominant Theoretical Orientation			Conception or Definition of Countertransference	Characteristics of Clinical Illustrations Used
	Totalistic	Classicist	Other		
Alvarez (1983)	X			Used "to include all the feeling the therapist may have toward the patient" with the exception of empathically perceived feelings; also influenced by Bion's notion of "containment"	Ranging from phobic to "borderline schizophrenic" children
Piene et al. (1983)		X		Used "in a restricted sense" to refer to emotional reactions and emotionally based blocking in the analyst, although also includes notion of containment	Child analytic cases
Perkins and Hornsby (1984)			X	Viewed as "a natural, role-responsive, necessary complement or counterpart to the transference of the patient or to his style of relatedness"	Child and adolescent inpatients: cases involve depressed, over anxious-oppositional, suicidal, and anorectic children
Palombo (1985)	X			Consists of concordant and complementary positions and responses, and disjunctive responses	Child and adolescent outpatients presenting with behavioral problems
Gartner (1985)	X			Consists of therapist's unconscious response to the patient's transference and the reactions to nontransference factors in the therapy, as well as the internal promptings of the therapist	Clinical anecdotes from secondary sources

Author	Predominant Theoretical Orientation			Conception or Definition of Countertransference	Characteristics of Clinical Illustrations Used
	Totalistic	Classicist	Other		
Zerbe (1986)	X			Linked to Lang's notion of management of the therapeutic frame, the concept of projective identification, and Bion's schema of containment	Adolescent anorectic patient in long-term out-patient treatment
Judd (1986)	X			Linked to Bion's schema of containment, projective and introjective identification, and two-dimensionality (Meltzer)	10-year-old girl referred for intensive outpatient therapy; presented with impoverished social relations, nervous tics, and marked immaturity
Anthony (1986)	X			Includes transference reactions to the child, identifications with the parents, and reactions to the child's transference	Not applicable
Waksman (1986)	X			Viewed as the "overall response of the analyst, including vocational factors," and linked with the work of Bion, Bick, Meltzer, and Racker.	Not applicable
Schowalter (1986)			X‡	Differentiates countertransference from counter-reaction: countertransference reactions are transference reactions that occur in response to the clinical situation;	Anecdotal remarks on outpatient therapy of latency-aged children; special issues vis-à-vis countertransference as a theme in clinical supervision

Author	Predominant Theoretical Orientation			Conception or Definition of Countertransference	Characteristics of Clinical Illustrations Used
	Totalistic	Classicist	Other		
				a counterreaction is *any* reaction stimulated by the clinical situation; always a relation between the therapist's past needs, conflicts, and countertransference	
Berlin (1987)	X			Refers to "feelings and thoughts evoked in the therapist" that are stimulated by the patient's behavior or attitudes, and that lead to a revival of experiences that the therapist has had with past significant objects	Child and adolescent outpatients presenting with depression, school refusal, and generalized anxiety
Bleiberg (1987)	X			Includes self-aspects or self-experiences the child is attempting to disown (and project onto the therapist); also includes empathic perceptions	Extensive discussion of three cases involving inpatient treatment of two latency-aged boys and an adolescent boy, all suffering from narcissistic or selfobject disorders
Touhy (1987)	X			Linked with the collective societal use of denial, minimization, and projection in regard to abuse; broadly defined to include reactions to whole families	Not applicable

Author	Predominant Theoretical Orientation			Conception or Definition of Countertransference	Characteristics of Clinical Illustrations Used
	Totalistic	Classicist	Other		
Dresser (1987)	X			Includes projected material both within and outside of the transference that is experienced countertransferentially by the therapist; "vital . . . for understanding communications and especially the unconscious communications of the patient"	Diagnostic interviews with two children, aged 5 3/4 and 4 years
Bernstein and Glenn (1988)		X		Defined very narrowly as "the analyst's response to a patient's transference with his own transference" (see also Bernstein and Glenn, 1978)	A number of clinical vignettes derived from analytic work with prelatency, latency, preadolescent, and adolescent cases
Garber (1988)	X			Not defined	One or two brief clinical anecdotes

*Contains elements of this orientation.
†Inferred.
‡Also contains elements of the totalistic orientation.
§See definition.

PART I

CLASSIC PAPERS ON COUNTERTRANSFERENCE

2

Hate in the Counter-transference

D. W. Winnicott, M.D.[1]

In this paper I wish to examine one aspect of the whole subject of ambivalency, namely, hate in the counter-transference. I believe that the task of the analyst (call him a research analyst) who undertakes the analysis of a psychotic is seriously weighted by this phenomenon, and that analysis of psychotics becomes impossible unless the analyst's own hate is extremely well sorted-out and conscious. This is tantamount to saying that an analyst needs to be himself analysed, but it also asserts that the analysis of a psychotic is irksome as compared with that of a neurotic, and inherently so.

Apart from psycho-analytic treatment, the management of a psychotic is bound to be irksome. From time to time [2,3] I have made acutely critical remarks about the modern trends in psychiatry, with the too easy electric shocks and the too drastic leucotomies. Because of these criticisms that I have expressed I would like to be foremost in

---

[1]Based on a paper read to the British Psycho-Analytical Society on February 5, 1947.

[2]*British Medical Journal* correspondence (1947) and "Physical Therapy of Mental Disorder." *British Medical Journal*, May 17, 1947, pp. i., 688.

[3]"Leucotomy," *British Medical Students'Journal*, Spring 1949, pp. 3, 2, 35.

recognition of the extreme difficulty inherent in the task of the psychiatrist, and of the mental nurse in particular. Insane patients must always be a heavy emotional burden on those who care for them. One can forgive those who do this work if they do awful things. This does not mean, however, that we have to accept whatever is done by psychiatrists and neuro-surgeons as sound according to principles of science.

Therefore although what follows is about psycho-analysis, it really has value to the psychiatrist, even to one whose work does not in any way take him into the analytic type of relationship to patients.

To help the general psychiatrist the psycho-analyst must not only study for him the primitive stages of the emotional development of the ill individual, but also must study the nature of the emotional burden which the psychiatrist bears in doing his work. What we as analysts call the counter-transference needs to be understood by the psychiatrist too. However much he loves his patients he cannot avoid hating them, and fearing them, and the better he knows this the less will hate and fear be the motive determining what he does to his patients.

STATEMENT OF THEME

One could classify counter-transference phenomena thus:

1. Abnormality in counter-transference feelings, and set relationships and identifications that are under repression in the analyst. The comment on this is that the analyst needs more analysis, and we believe this is less of an issue among psychoanalysts than among psycho-therapists in general.
2. The identifications and tendencies belonging to an analyst's personal experiences and personal development which provide the positive setting for his analytic work and make his work different in quality from that of any other analyst.
3. From these two I distinguish the truly objective countertransference, or if this is difficult, the analyst's love and hate in reaction to the actual personality and behaviour of the patient, based on objective observation.

I suggest that if an analyst is to analyse psychotics or anti-socials he must be able to be so thoroughly aware of the counter-transference that he can sort out and study his *objective* reactions to the patient. These will include hate. Counter-transference phenomena will at times be the important things in the analysis.

The Motive Imputed to the Analyst by the Patient

I wish to suggest that the patient can only appreciate in the analyst what he himself is capable of feeling. In the matter of motive, the *obsessional* will tend to be thinking of the analyst as doing his work in a futile obsessional way. A *hypo-manic* patient who is incapable of being depressed, except in a severe mood swing, and in whose emotional development the depressive position has not been securely won, who cannot feel guilt in a deep way, or a sense of concern or responsibility, is unable to see the analyst's work as an attempt on the part of the analyst to make reparation in respect of his own (the analyst's) guilt feelings. A *neurotic* patient tends to see the analyst as ambivalent towards the patient, and to expect the analyst to show a splitting of love and hate; this patient, when in luck, gets the love, because someone else is getting the analyst's hate. Would it not follow that if a *psychotic* is in a "coincident love-hate" state of feeling he experiences a deep conviction that the analyst is also only capable of the same crude and dangerous state of coincident love–hate relationship? Should the analyst show love he will surely at the same moment kill the patient.

This coincidence of love and hate is something that characteristically recurs in the analysis of psychotics, giving rise to problems of management which can easily take the analyst beyond his resources. This coincidence of love and hate to which I am referring is something which is distinct from the aggressive component complicating the primitive love impulse and implies that in the history of the patient there was an environmental failure at the time of the first object-finding instinctual impulses.

If the analyst is going to have crude feelings imputed to him he is best forewarned and so forearmed, for he must tolerate being placed in that position. Above all he must not deny hate that really exists in himself. Hate *that is justified* in the present setting has to be sorted out and kept in storage and available for eventual interpretation.

If we are to become able to be the analysts of psychotic patients we must have reached down to very primitive things in ourselves, and this is but another example of the fact that the answer to many obscure problems of psycho-analytic practice lies in further analysis of the analyst. (Psycho-analytic research is perhaps always to some extent an attempt on the part of an analyst to carry the work of his own analysis further than the point to which his own analyst could get him.)

A main task of the analyst of any patient is to maintain objectivity in regard to all that the patient brings, and a special case of this is the analyst's need to be able to hate the patient objectively.

Are there not many situations in our ordinary analytic work in which the analyst's hate is justified? A patient of mine, a very bad obsessional, was almost loathsome to me for some years. I felt bad about this until the analysis turned a corner and the patient became lovable, and then I realized that his unlikeableness had been an active symptom, unconsciously determined. It was indeed a wonderful day for me (much later on) when I could actually tell the patient that I and his friends had felt repelled by him, but that he had been too ill for us to let him know. This was also an important day for him, a tremendous advance in his adjustment to reality.

In the ordinary analysis the analyst has no difficulty with the management of his own hate. This hate remains latent. The main thing, of course, is that through his own analysis he has become free from vast reservoirs of unconscious hate belonging to the past and to inner conflicts. There are other reasons why hate remains unexpressed and even unfelt as such:

1. Analysis is my chosen job, the way I feel I will best deal with my own guilt, the way I can express myself in a constructive way.
2. I get paid, or I am in training to gain a place in society by psycho-analytic work.
3. I am discovering things.
4. I get immediate rewards through identification with the patient, who is making progress, and I can see still greater rewards some way ahead, after the end of the treatment.
5. Moreover, as an analyst I have ways of expressing hate. Hate is expressed by the existence of the end of the "hour." I think this is true even when there is no difficulty whatever, and when the patient is pleased to go. In many analyses these things can be taken for granted, so that they are scarcely mentioned, and the analytic work is done through verbal interpretations of the patient's emerging unconscious transference. The analyst takes over the role of one or other of the helpful figures of the patient's childhood. He cashes in on the success of those who did the dirty work when the patient was an infant.

These things are part of the description of ordinary psycho-analytic work, which is mostly concerned with patients whose symptoms have a neurotic quality.

In the analysis of psychotics, however, quite a different type and degree of strain is taken by the analyst, and it is precisely this different strain that I am trying to describe.

Illustration of Counter-transference Anxiety

Recently for a period of a few days I found I was doing bad work. I made mistakes in respect of each one of my patients. The difficulty was in myself and it was partly personal but chiefly associated with a climax that I had reached in my relation to one particular psychotic (research) patient. The difficulty cleared up when I had what is sometimes called a "healing" dream. (Incidentally I would add that during my analysis and in the years since the end of my analysis I have had a long series of these healing dreams which, although in many cases unpleasant, have each one of them marked my arrival at a new stage in emotional development.)

On this particular occasion I was aware of the meaning of the dream as I woke or even before I woke. The dream had two phases. In the first I was in the gods in a theatre and looking down on the people a long way below in the stalls. I felt severe anxiety as if I might lose a limb. This was associated with the feeling I have had at the top of the Eiffel Tower that if I put my hand over the edge it would fall off on to the ground below. This would be ordinary castration anxiety.

In the next phase of the dream I was aware that the people in the stalls were watching a play and I was now related to what was going on on the stage through them. A new kind of anxiety now developed. What I knew was that I had no right side of my body at all. This was not a castration dream. It was a sense of not having that part of the body.

As I woke I was aware of having understood at a very deep level what was my difficulty at that particular time. The first part of the dream represented the ordinary anxieties that might develop in respect of unconscious fantasies of my neurotic patients. I would be in danger of losing my hand or my fingers if these patients should become interested in them. With this kind of anxiety I was familiar, and it was comparatively tolerable.

The second part of the dream, however, referred to my relation to the psychotic patient. This patient was requiring of me that I should have no relation to her body at all, not even an imaginative one; there was no body that she recognized as hers and if she existed at all she could only feel herself to be a mind. Any reference to her body produced paranoid anxieties because to claim that she had a body was to persecute her. What she needed of me was that I should have only a mind speaking to her mind. At the culmination of my difficulties on the evening before the dream I had become irritated and had said that what she was needing of me was little better than hair-splitting. This had had a disastrous effect and it took many weeks for the analysis to recover from my lapse. The essential thing, however, was that I should understand my own anxiety and this was represented in the dream by the absence of the right side of my body when I tried to get into relation to the play that the people in the stalls were watching. This right side of my body was the side related to this particular patient and was therefore affected by her need to deny absolutely even an imaginative relationship of our bodies. This denial was producing in me this psychotic type of anxiety, much less tolerable than ordinary castration anxiety. Whatever other interpretations might be made in respect of this dream the result of my having dreamed it and remembered it was that I was able to take up this analysis again and even to heal the harm done to it by my irritability which had its origin in a reactive anxiety of a quality that was appropriate to my contact with a patient with no body.

Postponement of Interpretation

The analyst must be prepared to bear strain without expecting the patient to know anything about what he is doing, perhaps over a long period of time. To do this he must be easily aware of his own fear and hate. He is in the position of the mother of an infant unborn or newly born. Eventually, he ought to be able to tell his patient what he has been through on the patient's behalf, but an analysis may never get as far as this. There may be too little good experience in the patient's past to work on. What if there be no satisfactory relationship of early infancy of the analyst to exploit in the transference?

There is a vast difference between those patients who have had satisfactory early experiences which can be discovered in the transference, and those whose very early experiences have been so deficient or distorted that the analyst has to be the first in the patient's life to supply certain environmental essentials. In the treatment of the patient of the latter kind all sorts of things in analytic technique become vitally important that can be taken for granted in the treatment of patients of the former type.

I asked an analyst who confines his attention to neurotics whether he does analysis in the dark, and he said, "Why, no! Surely our job is to provide an ordinary environment, and the dark would be extraordinary." He was surprised at my question. He was orientated towards analysis of neurotics. But this provision and maintenance of an ordinary environment can be in itself a vitally important thing in the analysis of a psychotic, in fact it can be, at times, even more important than the verbal interpretations which also have to be given. For the neurotic the couch and warmth and comfort can be *symbolical* of the mother's love;

for the psychotic it would be more true to say that these things *are* the analyst's physical expression of love. The couch *is* the analyst's lap or womb, and the warmth *is* the live warmth of the analyst's body. And so on.

Objective Hate Under Test

There is, I hope, a progression in my statement of my subject. The analyst's hate is ordinarily latent and is easily kept latent. In analysis of psychotics the analyst is under greater strain to keep his hate latent, and he can only do this by being thoroughly aware of it. Now I want to add that in certain stages of certain analyses the analyst's hate is actually sought by the patient, and what is then needed is hate that is objective. If the patient seeks objective or justified hate he must be able to reach it, else he cannot feel he can reach objective love.

It is perhaps relevant here to cite the case of the child of the broken home, or the child without parents. Such a child spends his time unconsciously looking for his parents. It is notoriously inadequate to take such a child into one's home and to love him. What happens is that after a while a child so adopted gains hope, and then he starts to test out the environment he has found, and to seek proof of his guardians' ability to hate objectively. It seems that he can believe in being loved only after reaching being hated.

During the second world war a boy of nine came to a hostel for evacuated children, sent from London not because of bombs but because of truancy. I hoped to give him some treatment during his stay in the hostel, but his symptom won and he ran away as he had always done from everywhere since the age of six when he first ran away from home. However, I had established contact with him in one interview in which I could see and interpret through a drawing of his that in running away he was unconsciously saving the inside of his home and preserving his mother from assault, as well as trying to get away from his own inner world which was full of persecutors.

I was not very surprised when he turned up in the police station very near my home. This was one of the few police stations that did not know him intimately. My wife very generously took him in and kept him for three months, three months of hell. He was the most lovable and most maddening of children, often stark staring mad. But fortunately we knew what to expect. We dealt with the first phase by giving him complete freedom and a shilling whenever he went out. He had only to ring up and we fetched him from whatever police station had taken charge of him.

Soon the expected change-over occurred, the truancy symptom turned round, and the boy started dramatizing the assault on the inside. It was really a whole-time job for the two of us together, and when I was out the worst episodes took place.

Interpretation had to be made at any minute of day or night, and often the only solution in a crisis was to make the correct interpretation, as if the boy were in analysis. It was the correct interpretation that he valued above everything.

The important thing for the purpose of this paper is the way in which the evolution of the boy's personality engendered hate in me, and what I did about it.

Did I hit him? The answer is no, I never hit. But I should have had to have done so if I had not known all about my hate and if I had not let him know about it too. At crises I would take him by bodily strength, and without anger or blame, and put him outside the front door, whatever the weather or the time of day or night. There was a special bell he could ring, and he knew that if he rang it he would be readmitted and no word said about the past. He used this bell as soon as he had recovered from his maniacal attack.

The important thing is that each time, just as I put him outside the door, I told him something; I said that what had happened had made me hate him. This was easy because it was so true.

I think these words were important from the point of view of his progress, but they were mainly important in enabling me to tolerate the situation without letting out, without losing my temper and every now and again murdering him.

This boy's full story cannot be told here. He went to an Approved School. His deeply rooted relation to us has remained one of the few stable things in his life. This episode from ordinary life can be used to illustrate the general topic of hate justified in the present; this is to be distinguished from hate that is only justified in another setting but which is tapped by some action of a patient (child).

A Mother's Love and Hate

Out of all the complexity of the problem of hate and its roots I want to rescue one thing, because I believe it has an importance for the analyst of psychotic patients. I suggest that the mother hates the baby before the baby hates the mother, and before the baby can know this mother hates him.

Before developing this theme I want to refer to Freud's remarks. In "Instincts and their Vicissitudes" [1915d] (where he says so much that is original and illuminating about hate), Freud says: "we might at a pinch say of an instinct that it 'loves' the objects after which it strives for purposes of satisfaction, but to say that it 'hates' an object strikes us as odd, so we become aware that the attitudes of love and hate cannot be said to characterize the relation of instincts to their objects, but are reserved for the relations of the ego as a whole to objects. . . (1915d, p. 137). This I feel is true and important. Does this not mean that the personality must be integrated before an infant can be said to hate? However early integration may be achieved—perhaps integration occurs earliest at the height of excitement or rage—there is a theoretical earlier stage in which whatever the infant does that hurts is not done in hate. I have used the word "ruthless love" in describing this stage. Is this acceptable? As the infant becomes able to feel a whole person, so does the word "hate" develop meaning as a description of a certain group of his feelings.

The mother, however, hates her infant from the word go. I believe Freud thought it possible that a mother may under certain circumstances have only love for her boy baby; but we may doubt this. We know about a mother's love and we appreciate its reality and power. Let me give some of the reasons why a mother hates her baby, even a boy.

A. The baby is not her own (mental) conception.
B. The baby is not the one of childhood play, father's child, brother's child, etc.
C. The baby is not magically produced.
D. The baby is a danger to her body in pregnancy and at birth.
E. The baby is an interference with her private life, a challenge to preoccupation.
F. To a greater or lesser extent a mother feels that her own mother demands a baby, so that her baby is produced to placate her mother.
G. The baby hurts her nipples even by suckling, which is at first a chewing activity.
H. He is ruthless, treats her as scum, an unpaid servant, a slave.
I. She has to love him, excretions and all, at any rate at the beginning, till he has doubts about himself.
J. He tries to hurt her, periodically bites her, all in love.
K. He shows disillusionment about her.
L. His excited love is cupboard love, so that having got what he wants he throws her away like orange peel.
M. The baby at first must dominate, he must be protected from coincidences, life must unfold at the baby's rate and all this

needs his mother's continuous and detailed study. For instance, she must not be anxious when holding him, etc.

N. At first he does not know at all what she does or what she sacrifices for him. Especially he cannot allow for her hate.

O. He is suspicious, refuses her good food, and makes her doubt herself, but eats well with his aunt.

P. After an awful morning with him she goes out, and he smiles at a stranger, who says: "Isn't he sweet!"

Q. If she fails him at the start she knows he will pay her out for ever.

R. He excites her but frustrates—she mustn't eat him or trade in sex with him.

I think that in the analysis of psychotics, and in the ultimate stages of the analysis, even of a normal person, the analyst must find himself in a position comparable to that of the mother of a new-born baby. When deeply regressed the patient cannot identify with the analyst or appreciate his point of view any more than the fetus or newly born infant can sympathize with the mother.

A mother has to be able to tolerate hating her baby without doing anything about it. She cannot express it to him. If, for fear of what she may do, she cannot hate appropriately when hurt by her child she must fall back on masochism, and I think it is this that gives rise to the false theory of a natural masochism in women. The most remarkable thing about a mother is her ability to be hurt so much by her baby and to hate so much without paying the child out, and her ability to wait for rewards that may or may not come at a later date. Perhaps she is helped by some of the nursery rhymes she sings, which her baby enjoys but fortunately does not understand?

> Rockabye Baby, on the tree top,
> When the wind blows the cradle will rock,
> When the bough breaks the cradle will fall,
> Down will come baby, cradle and all.

I think of a mother (or father) playing with a small infant; the infant enjoying the play and not knowing that the parent is expressing hate in the words, perhaps in birth symbolism. This is not a sentimental rhyme. Sentimentality is useless for parents, as it contains a denial of hate, and sentimentality in a mother is no good at all from the infant's point of view.

It seems to me doubtful whether a human child as he develops is capable of tolerating the full extent of his own hate in a sentimental environment. He needs hate to hate.

If this is true, a psychotic patient in analysis cannot be expected to tolerate his hate of the analyst unless the analyst can hate him.

Practical Problem of Interpretation

If all this is accepted there remains for discussion the question of the interpretation of the analyst's hate to the patient. This is obviously a matter fraught with danger, and it needs the most careful timing. But I believe an analysis is incomplete if even towards the end it has not been possible for the analyst to tell the patient what he, the analyst, did unbeknown for the patient whilst he was ill, in the early stages. Until the interpretation is made the patient is kept to some extent in the position of infant, one who cannot understand what he owes to his mother.

SUMMARY

An analyst has to display all the patience and tolerance and reliability of a mother devoted to her infant, has to recognize the patient's wishes as needs, has to put aside other interests in order to be available and to be punctual, and objective, and has to seem to want to give what is really only given because of the patient's needs.

There may be a long initial period in which the analyst's point of view cannot be (even unconsciously) appreciated by the patient. Acknowledgment cannot be expected because at the primitive root of the patient that is being looked for there is no capacity for identification with the analyst, and certainly the patient cannot see that the analyst's hate is often engendered by the very things the patient does in his crude way of loving.

In the analysis (research analysis) or in ordinary management of the more psychotic type of patient, a great strain is put on the analyst (psychiatrist, mental nurse) and it is important to study the ways in which anxiety of psychotic quality and also hate are produced in those who work with severely ill psychiatric patients. Only in this way can there be any hope of the avoidance of therapy that is adapted to the needs of the therapist rather than to the needs of the patient.

3

Countertransference in the Residential Treatment of Children

Rudolf Ekstein, Ph.D., Judith Wallerstein, Ph.D., and Arthur Mandelbaum, M.S.W.[1]

In order to understand the complexities of countertransference in residential treatment, one must be willing to study treatment failure. That this represents an unwelcome undertaking is not primarily because our vanity disallows failure, or because it is painful to be reminded of suffering which has gone unrelieved, but in large measure because residuals of the experience persist long after the patient's discharge. The would-be observer feeling still somewhat involved is reluctant to look back. In this way, countertransference raises a barrier to its own examination.

It is well known that treatability is a function of the conjoined answer to two sets of questions, namely: (1) what is our expectable influence on the patient? And, (2) what is his expectable influence upon us? Yet, within the residential treatment center for children, the complex interrelationship of these two sides of the treatment coin needs further study. In particular, the growing proportion of borderline and psychotic children among the patients has added many new and relatively

---

[1]Read to the Topeka Psychoanalytic Society, September 1957, and before the Los Angeles Psychoanalytic Society in December 1957.

obscure factors to the delicately balanced, intense, and oftentimes disequilibrious interaction between the treatment staff and the child.

The essence of the residential treatment process is that as each child projects his inner world against the macrocosm of the residence, by and large the staff will find within itself the strength to resist stepping into the projected transference roles. For clearly, to the extent that the child succeeds in evoking from the residence or hospital staff the response which he evoked within his own family, the treatment will founder. Generally we know that the greater the child's disturbance, the more difficult it becomes to restrain the push of counterfantasies and counterbehavior and to resist entanglements.

Our interest in this paper is to bring under scrutiny some of the elusive psychological processes which characterize these entanglements and which appear to be inherent in the experience of prolonged exposure to very disturbed children. Specifically, we are concerned with understanding reactions evoked within a residential setting by a child with a symbiotic psychosis.[2] We propose to follow the preadmission history and residential experience of an 8-year-old boy who was discharged after seven months because, despite his encouraging response to intensive psychotherapy, he was found to be untreatable within the structure of a residential setting. Unquestionably many weighty factors dictated this particular child's discharge and he was, in fact, maintained as long as seven months in the face of formidable difficulties. Our interest is not with the rightness or wrongness of decisions but rather with the psychological underpinnings which were, in this instance, revealed with unusual clarity. Our experience emphasizes that while the countertransference responses which we propose to examine may at times be contained or counterbalanced by factors making for more stability and a different outcome, in one or another guise such responses are always present and inevitably threaten the continuity of all residential treatment of children in these clinical groups.

We begin with some general theoretical formulations regarding countertransference in the treatment of children. Within the established confines of the standard psychoanalytic situation, transference and countertransference in the treatment of children are distinguishable

---

[2]This project was carried out in Topeka, Kansas. The function of the authors during this patient's experience at Southard School was as follows: Dr. Rudolf Ekstein, Training Consultant; Judith Wallerstein, Child Psychotherapist; Arthur Mandelbaum, Chief Residential Worker.

Dr. Ekstein was Coordinator of Training and Research at the Reiss–Davis Clinic, Los Angeles.

from their counterparts in the treatment of adults. It has been understood for some time that transference manifestations of children include not only the projection of early repressed relationships but also displacements of the crucial relationships with the living contemporary parents. We suggest that corollary to this, the countertransference potential in work with children embraces the parent–child unit as well, and includes the therapist's responses to the contemporary parents of the child, as well as to the child's transferences and displacements. The child therapist faces countertransferences in relation to the parents which are just as complex as those which involve the child and which can best be understood when considered as part of a unit response to the child and his parents of today and yesterday. Thus the reality recognition that work with children necessarily includes the parents is the clinical reflection of the psychological reality of the parent–child unit within the transference and countertransference. This position is supported by the observation regarding the extent to which beginning workers with children commonly invoke fantasies of magically rescuing the child from the wickedness of his parents. Such fantasies can be said to reflect the defense against archaic guilt and anxiety generated in reaction to the fantasied replacement of the child's parents, and "parents" more generically.

The potential intensity of reactions to the parent–child unit is magnified many times within the residential setting because the residence actually assumes the parental function in taking over care of the child. It follows that whatever unconscious guilt would attach to fantasies elaborated around the replacement of the child's parents would be correspondingly magnified. Out of this unconscious guilt comes support for the counterfantasy that the staff represent the "good" parents who replace the "bad" parents of the child. And it will be found that categorizations of good and bad, loving and rejecting, eager to help and uncooperative, which are used subtly to dichotomize treatment staff and parents, are current in some measure in all settings where children are treated. These displacements have been given theoretical underpinnings over the years by the orientation which views the sick child as the helpless victim of psychological traumata inflicted by the parent. Fully extended, this is the concept of the "schizophrenogenic mother." And while these concepts may be theoretically outmoded, their emotional roots remain and continue to find expression within the countertransference. Some of the many seemingly insuperable difficulties which frequently beset the relationship between the real parents and the residential center can be linked to these feelings. Generally children who have endured a particularly unhappy life experience or whose condition calls forth immediate pity are more likely to evoke rescue fantasies and concomitant rage against the parents. Sometimes, as in the case we describe, the impact of a particular child can evoke these fantasies and feelings in a total staff with extraordinary swiftness and intensity.

This kind of identification with the loving mother and the living out of the magical helping fantasy may represent a useful point of departure in residential treatment. Surely, it makes for therapeutic optimism and a willingness to undertake treatment situations under very difficult conditions. When the expected change in the child does not appear, however, bewilderment and anxiety may ensue and the helplessness which every magical rescue fantasy obscures will show through. The anger and disappointment caused by the child can at this time only with difficulty be displaced onto the parents who are no longer in immediate contact with the child. Therefore, new displacement objects may be sought. This, we suggest, is one of the continuing problems of residential treatment of very disturbed children because of the inevitable disappointments encountered during the course of their treatment.

It may be observed generally that the close relationship between psychotherapist and child represents a specific emotional constellation within the residential setting. We have already suggested that in the familiar outpatient treatment of children, the parent–child unit often becomes the object of countertransference projections of the psycho-therapist. Within the residential treatment center and in the continued absence of the real parent, the particular constellation of therapist and child can be said to fulfill a similar psychological function for the remainder of the treatment staff. Corollary to this, the psychotherapist, also in the absence of the real parent, tends to project countertransfer-ence feelings upon that unit consisting of child care staff and child. Clearly, psychological phenomena such as transference and counter-transference within this multi-group setting are more complex and varied than those described within the one-to-one relationship of psychoanalyst and patient. Many aspects of the responses to children which occur within the shifting tensions and harmonies of the residen-tial setting require the refinement of concepts and the development of new concepts. At this point in our knowledge we may say, however, that the relationship between the residential staff and the psychothera-pist, by virtue of crisscrossing countertransference responses, repre-sents one of the major seams of the treatment community, a seam which is never completely invisible in that it tends to show almost immediately the effects of the conflicting tugs and strains upon it.

The kind of unity which is seen to exist between psychotherapist and psychotic child and which is particularly evident in the treatment of a child with a symbiotic psychosis imposes a special strain upon this seam. Frequently with such children, the treatment strategy, as in the case described, renders the therapist a magical extension of the child in accord with the dominant transference. In this psychological role vis-à-vis the child, the psychotherapist and those directly occupied with the psychotherapy come almost inevitably to share in the intense love and hate feelings aroused by the child.

In general, countertransference gains immeasurably in force and complexity as it is linked to psychotic transference manifestations. Winnicott (1949) described some of the fears and angers which attach to therapeutic work with psychotic patients which have, in his view, no counterpart in the treatment of the neurotic. He distinguished between the reawakening of infantile anxiety in the therapist and the objective hate which must necessarily arise in the therapist because of the demands placed upon him by the patient. And he stressed his conviction that unless the therapist can appreciate both the depth of the response stirred up within him and the objective basis of a considerable part of his anger, these feelings will insidiously immobilize the therapist's capacity to understand the patient and to help the patient to disentangle his feelings and relationships. Thus, borderline and psychotic children invite a countertransference potential, in relation both to themselves and to the child–parent unit, of an entirely different kind and magnitude than that which obtains in work with their neurotic peers.

It is important that besides the anxiety and hate which they stimulate, these children call forth an extraordinary investment of love, infinite patience, tenderness, skill, and devotion. It is, in fact, because of the presence of both love and hate that treatment disruption when it occurs always reflects feelings of sadness and personal failure, however covered these may be by the anger which more frequently finds forceful expression at these times.

In the treatment of psychotic children, whatever his treatment framework or function, the residential worker will find many times that his understanding fails. Unlike the parent who, as Money-Kyrle (1956) suggests, has a variety of ways which he can employ to reach and comfort the child, each worker is bound by his single avenue of approach and clinical understanding, by his particular set of skills and by the limits imposed by the nature of his helping effort. When these seem inadequate to his task, he will feel distressed and anxious. Although individual supervision, group meetings, and other familiar devices are unquestionably useful at such times, the residential staff generally does not have the safeguards provided by personal analysis or extensive training to draw upon. Consequently the residential worker becomes more susceptible to the push of a child's projections. And while the group offers help to its members in providing the camaraderie and relief of shared feelings, it also makes for a contagion and spread of countertransference responses which can rapidly become crystallized and which are undone with difficulty. Moreover, the group itself often makes for less reflectiveness and more proneness to take action. Therefore, one of the distinguishing attributes of countertransference in residential treatment may well be its capacity to erupt precipitously into what Gitelson (1952) has called "acting out in the countertransference."

In the case which we have selected, a schizophrenic child cast his psychological shadow against the background of the treatment center. The psychotic transference consisted of a continual re-enactment of his attempted murder by the mother which had in reality occurred several years prior to his admission. In this enactment the child alternately and simultaneously symbolically assumed the fragmented roles of murderer and victim, assigning the complementary roles to the psychotherapist, the residential setting, and its various representatives.

We suggest that the staff was able to maintain its helping role and separateness in the face of the child's onslaught and to support the psychotherapeutic relationship and the residential experience with extraordinary persistence until the time when the child finally succeeded in evoking a response from the staff parallel to that which he had evoked in his own family. At this time the treatment came to an end.

Ken was brought to Southard School at the age of eight. He was a skinny, undersized little boy whose face most frequently appeared drawn, tense and impassive, in marked contrast to his hands and especially his feet which were engaged in a rapid, unremitting activity, usually of a destructive nature, and which in this endeavor seemed to operate with a strength and vitality all their own. This contrast, coupled with a heightened alertness to distant auditory stimuli, lent an odd, simian quality to the child's appearance, which became especially striking when he was engaged in climbing trees and buildings, an activity which he undertook frequently with extraordinary daring, grace, and agility. When in repose his taut bodily stance expressed a constant expectation of attack from every quarter. He seemed poised, first for rapid flight and in lieu of this for counterattack by means of savage, random, and essentially uncontrollable destructiveness. Sometimes, the rigidity of the child's facial mask would give way to what appeared to be wild glee in anticipation of mischief or in satisfaction at having bested the adult. At other times, the child curled upon the floor, sucking and smelling, hands and toes together, eyes glazed, rhythmically rocking and inaccessible to immediate stimuli; yet still acutely attuned to the sounds in the distance and especially to distant music. On rare occasions he would approach the adult with a pitiable expression of whimpering, panting, and smelling of the person approached. These positions defined the range of relationships available to him at the time of the initial examination.

The parents complained of obstreperousness, wanton destructiveness, and obscene language, of open masturbation, sucking and rocking, nonconformity to the simplest family routines except in the face of severe punishment (among which the most effective was ignoring the child), of need for constant attendance and attention and entertainment, and of many irksome demands upon the family of the kind described by Kanner (1949) which seemed aimed at preventing any kind of change in the environment.

The disturbance was described as extending back to infancy and pervading all aspects of the personality so that retardation and disturbance were evident in thought, language, all modes of behavior, habit training and all relationships. More recently the child had shown some signs of capacity for more integrated behavior and curiosity for knowledge of mechanical objects. He had acquired for himself some of the rudiments of written language and numbers and had made some tentative moves toward imitative play with other children.

The parents had apparently been able to manage and control the boy during the past two and a half years which he had spent in the home by a combination of extraordinary large doses of sedatives and tranquilizing drugs, various punishments, and by submitting to his tyranny over the family life. They were desperate for a solution short of lifelong hospitalization in a mental hospital.

Ken was an unplanned and unwanted addition to a family already sorely beset with a chronic and severe addictive illness of the mother, the self-absorption and cold detachment of the father, and three older children who were showing sufficient neurotic difficulties to occupy fully whatever emotional reserves the parents still had available. The mother's addiction began shortly before this, her second marriage, and the marriage itself had been replete with stress and misery from the start, interspersed with many moves, opposition from both families, repeated psychotic episodes and hospitalizations for the mother and an increasingly constricted life for the father who more and more concentrated on his business activities and withdrew interest from other aspects of his life.

The mother was sick and unhappy and used large doses of sedatives during Ken's pregnancy, yet steadfastly refused a therapeutic abortion although this was strongly recommended by the physician who attended her. The child was delivered healthy and was described as healthy and happy for the first few months of his life. Very early, however, within a few months he began to look "ugly" to the parents who, when they returned from a vacation of a few weeks, felt there was something "missing" from his face. By two years and ten months he was brought for psychiatric examination and diagnosed as an autistic child. At that time he did not speak, was uninterested in his surroundings, did not smile, was unwilling to look up, and refused to eat unless his mouth was pried open by the mother and the food poured into it. Furthermore, destructiveness ensued when he was taken from the crib. The psychiatric recommendation was for immediate long-term placement which could offer "love therapy." These recommendations were undertaken in the face of the mother's enormous hurt and rage which may have gone largely without expression at the time.

During the two and a half years that followed, the child lived with a foster mother who apparently with infinite patience, tenderness, and sensitivity, and with some psychiatric direction, gradually nursed the child to the point that he fed himself, slept well, mastered language, gave up tantrums, established toilet training, began to imitate the play of other children, and seemed happy and demonstrably affectionate. Yet each time the child was returned home for a visit, this precipitated a severe setback, wiping out entirely the newfound gains. For instance, during his third year the child was left for a few days with the mother. When found, both mother and child required emergency hospitalization: the child was described as emaciated, dehydrated, suffering severe cold, and behaving like a wild animal; the mother was stuporous.

At the age of five and a half, Ken was returned to his home by the foster mother who no longer could keep him. A few weeks following his arrival, the mother, again stuporous, attacked the child in his bed at night, attempting to kill him. She was intercepted, whereupon she retreated to her room and tried to commit suicide. She stated of this episode, "I thought if I did away with the two sickest members of the family the rest would be better off." She was admitted to a hospital with a diagnosis of acute depressive psychosis and remained there for several months.[3]

---

[3]The psychological report on the mother during this hospitalization by a psychologist who was not informed of the mother–child relationship or of the episode preceding hospitalization contains the following excerpt: "The test material indicates great stress and involvement in her relationship to her son (or sons) and what the son (sons) means to her unconsciously. The content of the Rorschach response which is most revealing of her break with reality and her delusional thinking is tied up with concern about proper conduct and with a son. One wonders if her son represents to her the worst part in her personality and thus is mixed up with her superego conflict." These observations are of special interest in view of the clinical finding of a symbiotic psychosis in the child.

There was general concurrence at the final evaluation conference in a diagnosis of "schizophrenia of childhood in a child of at least average and probably superior intelligence." The recommendation was for long-term residential treatment together with individual intensive psychotherapy for the child and casework or psychotherapy for the parents. The suggestion was that outpatient psychotherapy be instituted immediately on a once-a-week basis during the few weeks' waiting period although this was not a common practice of the treatment center. The hope was that the child could begin to establish a relationship with the psychotherapist which would facilitate his separation from the mother and his transition into the school. Similarly, it was thought that the mother might make use of the casework during this period in order to help separate from the child. Considerable note was taken of the relationship between mother and child and of the mother's repeated attempts to destroy herself and the child together. It was feared that although the child himself might be treatable, the mother–child unity, i.e., the hostile symbiosis which characterized the relationship between Ken and his mother, might prevent treatment in that the mother would probably repeatedly attempt to disrupt the treatment experience. Conspicuously absent were doubts regarding the child's treatability or any extended consideration of his impact upon the residential setting or his needs within the setting, although his extraordinary destructiveness and need for constant surveillance had been abundantly clear during the two-week examination period.

From a close examination of this intake conference, one can discern at the outset those conflicts which later assumed major proportions. For instance, it appears that two contradictory frames of reference were simultaneously in operation; namely, that which viewed the child and his mother as caught within a mesh of mutually interacting psychoses; and that which viewed the child as capable of forming a relationship with the psychotherapist on a once-a-week basis sufficient to alleviate his anxiety regarding separation from the mother.

If we take such confusions in an experienced staff as symptomatic of conflict, then we may add as symptoms the significant omission from consideration of the additional staff time which the child would require; the limited consideration of the physical and psychological toll upon staff and children which his presence could be expected to exact; and, central for our thesis, the relative absence of doubts and misgivings about the child's treatability which is particularly striking in view of the degree of emotional crippling and the long-standing nature of his illness. Corollary to these omissions was the considerable concern with the mother's role in threatening the treatment continuity, as if whatever recognition there was of threat to treatment could only be relegated to and experienced as coming from the outside, i.e., from the mother–child unit.

When the figure of the child is placed between the figure of the mother, of whom it was feared that she might disrupt the treatment, and the figure of the psychotherapist, of whom it was thought that in a short time she would establish a meaningful and comforting relationship with the child, then the emotional response becomes clearer. In accord with the view which we have stated, the three figures together reflect the countertransference response. We surmise that what happened was a very quick identification with the child, perhaps because of the extent of his disturbance and some pathetic appealing quality in his chronic terror, or perhaps because of his extraordinary history of an attempted murder by the mother. Hand in hand with this identification went the taking over of the positive aspects of the healing mother who will save the child. And, inseparable from this fantasy of the "good" mother, we find the projection of the cause for illness and possibilities for treatment rupture upon the "bad" mother. The taking over of the role of the "good" mother found expression in the magical overevaluation of the psychotherapist as the representative of the rescue fantasy; in the magical overestimation of the influence and power of the residential experience; and in the failure to estimate correctly the serious degree of the child's psychopathology.

This kind of identification with the child with its concomitant fantasies is by no means unusual in work with disturbed children. In fact, it can be argued that the capacity for quick identification with the child is of pivotal importance in therapeutic work with children. Particularly in work with schizophrenic children, it may be that one must believe in one's own omnipotence and find therapeutic failure unacceptable as Eissler (1951) has suggested. It appears rather that the attitude of identifying with the "good" parent and projecting the blame upon the "bad" parent who "abandoned" the child to residential treatment is the beginning bias of the residential worker. Such a bias may facilitate work with a disturbed child where the child care worker sees himself as the "good" parent who has been given the responsibility for therapeutic care of the child after the real parent has found it necessary to give him to others. This attitude surely assists the worker in becoming that "good" parent, but it may cause considerable irritation when he discovers that being a "good" parent is not the only requirement for therapeutic care and can lead to serious frustrations when the satisfactions reasonably expected by all "good" parents are not forthcoming.[4]

At about the time that Ken began treatment, a research project was initiated at the treatment center in which an effort was to be made to predict expected developments in the psychotherapy. Specifically, the project was designed to make use of the evaluation material, therapy hours, and control hours in order to make explicit the treatment strategy and to extrapolate expected transference developments and expected changes in behavior in the residence school. In this way, we hoped to consider more systematically some of the theoretical formulations which had evolved in recent years in our work with borderline and psychotic children. We present here the second and third psychotherapy hours with Ken which, together with several others and the evaluation material, led us to guarded encouragement regarding the child's accessibility to intensive psychotherapy and enabled us to arrive at some formulations regarding expectable developments in the psychotherapeutic process.

My second hour with Ken began by his recognizing me immediately and coming with a marked lack of hesitancy. He grinned mischievously with a little of a private grin and mumbled he was going to crash things around today as we went upstairs together. He ran into the playroom, threw his shoes and socks toward the ceiling with a vigorous gesture, scrambled into the sandpile and started to throw great quantities of sand around with wild gestures, accompanying this throwing with an entirely masklike face and a set grin. I said that I was beginning to understand why he crashed things around. In response to this, Ken threw more wildly. I said we would have "holding time" and as I held him I said very slowly and softly that I thought he was afraid to stop throwing and that he threw because he was really too afraid to stop. He answered by sitting quietly for a while and for the first time he did not become limp with terror as I held him. He then asked me whether I had gotten him some toys. I said that I had and showed him some little trucks in his cupboard. He explored these with what looked like a brief moment of genuine pleasure, but this could not last as he returned to throwing sand and toys. Again I restrained him by holding him. I repeated what I had said, adding that I doubted if he could stop throwing things alone even if he should want to and that he needed help in this.

---

[4]It may be argued that the essential mistake made was to accept the child for treatment. The validity of this argument is in itself an indication of strong countertransference responses at the time of the initial evaluation. For in view of the knowledge of the child, his history, and his behavior, which was entirely available to the staff at the time of the evaluation, a mistake can only be understood as reflecting countertransference response.

At this point Ken saw a baby bottle and ran excitedly to fill it with water. He started to spill water all around the room and said something about being naughty rather gleefully. I agreed he was having an awfully hard time being naughty and he couldn't play with any of the toys or have any fun. He then took one of the puppets and started to fill it with water with savagery from below the puppet's skirt. I asked whether he was Mama Ken and he said vigorously and laughingly that he was. (This play was interspersed with considerable throwing of the dolls, the bottles, the sand, and every toy within reach, and was by no means really continuous although it makes up some kind of a complete unit.) I asked whether he was mama Ken feeding the baby, and he agreed and said that it was a hungry baby. I asked whether it would get enough to eat and surely hoped it would. "The water is poison," he yelled at me, "and I am killing the baby." I asked why and he said because the baby was naughty and mean. I said that I understood that because I knew a little boy who was very frightened. He thought his mother had tried to hurt him very much and would try to hurt him very much and he was so terribly frightened that he threw things all the time. As if in direct confirmation of this, Ken started to throw, but this time there was some real feeling and excitement that came through in the throwing in that his hands were no longer divorced from the child. I held him again for "holding time" and he sat quietly but not limply and as I held him I said over and over again that I would never hurt him, that I knew it frightened him when I held him, and I knew it frightened him when he threw things, and sometimes it frightened him more when I held him than when he threw things, but I would never hurt him and I wanted him to know that. He mounted then with lightning rapidity to the window and attempted to pry it open. I pulled him back and repeated that I would not hurt him nor would I let him hurt himself.

Ken ran wildly in and out of the room several times and finally said he wanted to play with the phonograph. I offered him the pretend phonograph of the crate with building blocks in it and he asked me quietly whether I would help him remove the blocks. I said that what I wanted to do most was to help him. Together we removed the blocks and this time he did so without throwing the blocks, but when he came across pieces of chalk in the box he picked them up and ground them under his feet as if just seeing something that could be ground stimulated the activity which seemed isolated from the rest of his attention and behavior. He finally got into the box, telling me he was a long-playing record. I said I wanted so much to hear a long-playing record. He directed me to the imaginary controls of the phonograph and told me to shut and open the top of the box like in a real phonograph while he got inside and that I should turn the record on. I did as he directed and he started to kick wildly inside of the box. I asked him what that was and he said, "That's the record." I agreed that it was and stated that it sounded like an angry and frightened little record kicking around in the box and trying to get out. He continued to kick for some time, opening the box and shutting it down on himself and almost catching his fingers dangerously under the very heavy lid, with complete lack of concern about this. I said that I very much liked long-playing records and I was pretty sure there were many tunes this particular record could play and I would like to hear them when the time came. On this note the hour ended and I took him back to his mother. As he saw her, he dismissed me from the landscape.

In the third interview which was the last interview before he came into the school, Ken was very agitated, ran wildly and terror-stricken around the room, round and round like a hunted animal, throwing everything he could get hold of. He urinated all over the room and seemed most of the time oblivious of my presence. Twice he approached me crying pitifully and wringing his hands, saying he would never see me again because he was going to come to Southard School. It was quite clear he had fused me with the mother and felt himself in great danger, but my attempts to get through to him in anything I did or said went unheard and unnoticed.

The original evaluation material and the early interviews as noted provided the basis for a long and detailed analysis of the case from which we have taken the following excerpts. It is relevant that all of this thinking was discussed in detail with the entire staff at the time the child entered the residence school and was shared with the team members throughout the child's stay.

Ken's basic relationship position is that of a hostile symbiosis with the mother and his core conflict is his struggle toward and away from this position. The symbiotic arrangement with the mother is experienced as hostile and destructive, threatening to engulf him and bringing with it the loss of even the precursors of self. He attempts to escape from the symbiotic position by returning to an autistic world which shuts out the mother figure, expressing itself in total self-preoccupation and/or loss of contact. Alternately he attempts to find another more advanced independent solution which consists for him of blind impulsivity, wild destructiveness, seeming lack of control eventuating in ego fragmentation, and the return to the autistic position.

The "Jack-in-the-box" fantasy which dominated the first hours of psychotherapy reflects the core conflict. Hiding in different boxes, Ken stated that he was a long-playing record and requested the psychotherapist to manipulate the knobs which control the record machine. As the long-playing record, the child kicked violently against the walls of the box while remaining inside the box. As the child emerged from the box, he threw different objects violently and wildly and seemingly without control.

His dilemma as expressed in this fantasy is his wish for and dread of being contained in the "mother box." For this problem he envisages two possible solutions, both of which end disastrously. One solution is that of a violent kicking struggle for independence which eventuates in castration, ego fragmentation, destruction, and self-destruction. The other solution is that of autistic isolation and death. In reality, for this patient, kicking within the confines of the symbiotic relationship (kicking inside the mother box) signifies to be alive.

Ken has no integrated self-image and no clearly cathected ego boundaries; his perception of himself is fragmented and fluid. At times he thinks of himself as an armless and lifeless "big turnip." At other times, various objects such as spinning toys are grafted onto his body image. Feet particularly are experienced alternately as enemies and love objects, alternately included and ejected from his ego boundaries. Thus the outside world shifts its boundaries and it consists at times of those parts of his body which are used for motoric activity. At such times his self-concept is characterized by an effort to conquer feet and arms which are experienced as external enemies and do not wish to become part of the self-organization.

Transference paradigm: It is expected that during the many months of initial treatment the transference will primarily reflect the dominant symbiotic relationship, showing both its hostile and positive compo-nents, and be accompanied by escape into the autistic position as his symbiosis becomes too threatening and by thrusts toward independent separate activity as the symbiosis offers assurance. Specifically the patient will utilize the therapist as an extension of himself and as a means toward achieving various primitive gratifications. When the hostile aspects of the symbiosis become dominant, the patient will in identification with the fantasied aggressor *play act* murder of the therapist and self-destruction in various ways. He will also escape into autism via hiding, primitive self-preoccupations, and periodic loss of contact.

The loving aspect of the symbiosis may give rise to erotic feelings which will, in becoming too threatening, also lead to withdrawal, hostile acting out, primitive erotic rituals (of a masturbatory nature), and contact loss. At the same time the patient may attempt to utilize the grafted strength of this symbiotic relationship to live out magical fantasies of omnipotence and phallic concepts of masculine strength, which will probably lead him to act out what will seem like delinquent manifestations.

If the child is enabled to stabilize his symbiotic relationship and to find it not as fearful as expected, then we may expect a cumbersome attempt to introject certain aspects of the therapist via imitation and cue-taking. We may begin to see some beginning emergence of the precursors of neurotic mechanisms, particularly the precursors of obsessive-compulsive mechanisms.

The *therapeutic strategy* is to facilitate the development of a positive symbiotic transference since we are of the opinion that only out of the consolidation of a positive symbiotic relationship with the mother substitute can the precursors of identification, i.e., imitation and introjection, emerge. The first goal is therefore to help the child establish this kind of positive symbiosis by diminishing his fear of annihilation at the hands of the symbiotic mother equal therapist. This may perhaps be achieved by accepting the magical role of an all-powerful extension of the child, by repeated assurances of protection, by imitation of the child in offering oneself as a partner in his endeavors, and by interpretation of his fears of being destroyed.

Among the many foreseeable technical problems are those which relate to setting limits on the behavior as it swings from antisocial to very regressed behavior, the extent to which such limits are necessary, therapeutic, etc., and, of course, the primary problem of doing therapy with a child unable to reflect upon his own behavior.

One of the interesting aspects of this report is that despite the fact that there was considerable coincidence between developments in the therapy and in the residence school and those predicted in this case analysis, there is here too little recognition of the countertransference problem. Thus while the analyzed data all pointed to the deep well of primitive responses which could reasonably be expected to be stirred up by the entrance of the child upon the scene of the residence, yet this detailed spelling out of the child's psychosis remained separate from a recognition of the countertransference potential. And it may be that this omission prevented these formulations from being as useful as they might have been in helping to maintain the continuity of the child's treatment.

In the residence Ken's behavior made it possible to begin to make plans for the treatment in the living situation. When Ken entered the school, his behavior was that of a child in a desperate struggle for survival who was in mortal danger and had lost all of his physical strength as a result of separation from his parents. He insisted upon being fed, complaining of the lack of strength in his arms, and he confined his eating to dry cereal and milk. Initially at mealtime, while being fed, his entire body expressed a complete total passivity except for masturbatory activity. His mouth was kept wide open to receive the food as if he were an automaton. Within a few days, Ken began to attack the walls of his room, breaking off large pieces of plaster with great strength. He repeated over and over again the play of enclosing himself in a box, closet, or any dark place, only to burst out again using his feet vigorously. On occasion he would crawl out of his window onto the roof of the house into a precarious position. When the windows were closed, he broke through and smashed the outer screen as if he always needed an escape route. His toilet habits were regressed. He made no use of bathroom facilities. He defecated and urinated in his room, in drawers and closets. Sometimes he would consent to go outside, but generally he expressed fear of using the bathroom. His most integrated behavior in these early weeks was a game of tying a weight to a piece of string and while seated on the top of the stairs, lowering the string up and down in seemingly endless repetition. (This, of course, calls immediately to mind the play of the eighteen-month-old child as classically described by Freud, 1920b.)

The structure of the therapeutic care which Ken required in the residence was designed to provide Ken with safety against his own swift destructive attacks against himself, other children, adults and property, as well as to meet his most regressed infantile needs, such as requiring to be fed and clothed. Three workers were assigned to his individual care, and because of Ken's difficulty in maintaining a constant image and memory of persons coming and going, each worker kept the same shift so as to provide the most constancy and stability.

As in the psychotherapy, the aim of the child care worker's relationship with Ken was to assist in the development of a relationship designed to diminish his fear of annihilation by protecting him from attacks by the other children and from attacking them when they came too close. His relationships with the adults in the residence also offered him nurturing care, feeding him as he wished to be fed, bathing him so he did not experience terror and panic, allowing him to urinate and defecate in places of safety, until he might gradually learn to use the bathroom.

As the child care staff became familiar with Ken's interests, especially with his intense love of music, his preoccupations with radios, phonographs, batteries, odd bits of machinery, activities became structured for him which had play and educational value, and which gave him the feeling that he was doing as the other children were when they attended their school. There is no doubt that Ken was one of the sickest children ever accepted by the residence in the sense that his needs were expressed in most infantile and primitive ways, so that any excellent care which met his most basic needs also tended to get too close to the child and resulted in fusion fantasies followed by panic and swift physical attack. At the same time too much distance from Ken also brought panic and fears of being abandoned, neglected, and left to be destroyed, and this too was followed instantaneously by swift rage attacks. The child care workers assigned to Ken needed to learn and test constantly that optimum distance, neither too close nor too far, which gave to Ken his greatest feeling of comfort and security. The three workers assigned directly to him required more frequent supervision than other child care staff, for much needed to be quickly understood about Ken's behavior, i.e., his fascination with entering closets and boxes, enclosing himself and then bursting out furiously, his curiosity about electrical motors and wiring of the residence, his intense desire for a radio and then his wild attacks on it. Constantly the child care staff explored together with their supervisor and the psychotherapist ways in which protection and care could be afforded Ken, meeting his savage attacks with firm, nonretaliatory limits and encouraging him to relinquish his autistic withdrawal by their availability and by providing Ken in a most imaginative way with objects he greatly desired and which had great emotional significance to him, and helping him to play with them. This was the philosophy underlying the residential treatment for the child.

In response to Ken's behavior, the entire staff was able to take an attitude of extraordinary patience and interest. Their observations were acute and perceptive as evidenced in the detailed notes kept by the child care staff on the child's frequently incoherent rambling in the hope that the psychotherapist might be able to use this material in the therapy. The sensitivity and interest of the entire staff are perhaps epitomized in the remark of one of the cooks who said that Ken wanted to be fed and not use his hands because otherwise he might throw food.

Gradually the tolerance gave way and by the time several weeks had gone by feelings of anger and retaliation were aroused. This the staff experienced and expressed by seeing the child's aggression as deliberately designed to control and provoke them. They began to make use of the concept of "testing" as applied to Ken's destructive activity, implying willful and conscious behavior, particularly in regard to his toilet habits. The fact that at times the child seemed able to make a real effort to conform when limits were placed on his behavior emphasized and reinforced this opinion. Also, there was considerable jealousy, disturbance, and regressive behavior among the other children which undoubtedly contributed greatly to the child care staff's discomfort. Nevertheless, the dominant attitude in this initial period was a sober recognition of the serious nature of the child's disturbance coupled with many feelings of sympathy and a wish to protect him from the other children. And in general, the first few weeks of the child's stay reflect the intent of the total staff to master feelings of repugnance, anxiety, anger, and frustration, and with great devotion to make the child's treatment possible by providing a total change in his milieu and facilitating his individual psychotherapy.

The first indication of the emergence of the kind of countertransference which threatens treatment continuity occurred vis-à-vis the psychotherapy in a particular incident. In the seventh week of Ken's stay in the residence, he and the psychotherapist were playing with mud on a little wooden porch in back of the office building. Ken was engaged in making mud pies with considerable pleasure, and his usual primitiveness and untidiness soon made for a mud-smeared porch. An experienced staff member, who assumed no direct psychotherapeutic responsibility but had considerable understanding of the privacy of psychotherapy by virtue of his semiprofessional and administrative position, passed by and apparently unable to restrain himself, said directly to the child, "Do you know what happens to little boys who make a mess of the director's nice clean porch?" After a slight pause, he added, "They have to clean it up." After making several similar remarks, and continuing to ignore the therapist who was standing by the child, he then quickly left the scene. There followed a precipitous regression in the child from the advance of the mud playing to wild defecating coupled with psychotic incoherences while running wide-eyed with terror in circles around the yard.

It is of central importance in understanding this episode that the staff member was evidently in intense conflict regarding this intervention. Since he acted in the face of his unquestioned knowledge that such intervention was not acceptable, we infer the extraordinary push of anxiety which could not be contained. Furthermore, it is relevant that this particular staff member had the confidence of the custodial and kitchen staff and expressed in his behavior a ground swell of opinion which had not yet reached the ears of the professional staff.

We present this incident in detail for several reasons. At the beginning of the child's admission into the school, we described a magical overvaluation of psychotherapy. It had been fully expected that the therapist would in a few weeks establish a relationship with Ken which would have considerable influence in alleviating his anxiety. Here one can see the opposite: an intervention into the therapy hour with a disregard of its privacy; a shunting of therapy and therapist aside; in effect, a devaluation of psychotherapy. Parenthetically, we note that we do not consider this incident either unique or extraordinary, but rather that such incidents are more numerous than many have been willing to believe.

This particular incident heralded the gradual emergence of a pattern in which the therapist, the therapist's supervisor, and the special child care workers who were assigned to work with Ken were pushed, as it were, into being viewed as the partners of the child's illness, as party to his destructiveness, in effect, as symbiotic partners of the child. It was as if the projection of wickedness onto the departed mother had been moved and was now reprojected onto the psychotherapist and the other workers engaged in direct work with the child. Especially the psychotherapist in her inability to fulfill the magical expectations that she would contain the child and curb his impulses became a partner, a stimulus, and in its final extension, a "schizophrenogenic" mother. This was borne out in various ways. When on occasion Ken attacked one of the children at the school who was brought for evaluation and the therapist was standing nearby, the therapist was blamed for "permitting" Ken to attack the other child. When property was damaged, similar statements were made. Gradually, incidents such as these began to multiply and their emotional charge became increasingly intense.

This incident is important also because of its impact upon the therapist in leading to an abrupt and uncomfortable recognition that in achieving her goal of being included in the child's psychological orbit, she had come as well to share responsibility for his misbehavior and destructiveness. Beyond this, the incident, in precipitating a psychotic regression and undermining the child's concept of the psychotherapist as a magical protector, had particular repercussions which undoubtedly magnified its immediate importance, namely that it collided directly with the therapeutic strategy. It was at this time that the seam between therapist and the remainder of the staff, which we have mentioned before, began to show the strain of conflicting tugs and to require reinforcement.

Within both a practical and a psychological framework, psychotherapy with Ken depended in considerable measure upon the active support of those administratively and directly responsible for the child. In practical terms, during many weeks of therapy, Ken was unable to remain in the playroom without panics which occurred without discernible warning and which were marked by destructiveness which was heedless of the value of the object attacked. For many successive hours in the initial phase of treatment, Ken and the therapist crawled together in the subbasement of the residence looking for underground hiding places and subterranean passages where they could remain for a brief respite away from the rest of the world. Several weeks were spent in therapy in water play with a hose in which the attempt was to channel the "nasty nasty" (the child's term for water) in order to avoid the "flood" which threatened to break through the dikes which he and the therapist built and rebuilt. Sometimes, the "flood" occurred despite the dikes and the efforts to contain it. At times, Ken climbed ten to fifteen trees in rapid, breathless succession in order to distinguish "loving" trees from "angry" trees, and needed to be forcibly restrained from going up telegraph poles. He discovered a stagnant pool on a neighboring property and would return to it at intervals to ask plaintively and despairingly of the therapist whether it could ever be cleared, how it got that way, and whether he could be protected from rats and mosquitoes. Sometimes he demanded to be carried to therapy and he rarely arrived except accompanied by his radio from which he was inseparable and sometimes requesting that big motors and other equipment which he had salvaged from the junkyard be carried to therapy along with him. All of this behavior placed heavy demands upon the staff and represented at the very least a chronic nuisance about which the therapist could not help but feel concerned.

The therapeutic decision to attempt to join the child to the extent possible at the level of his regression, within this nightmare in which every reality stimulus was either potentially or actually dangerous, in which the child's hope was to stay ahead of the terror but never to escape it completely, depended upon the actual help or at the very least upon the tacit support of the environment. Practically speaking, the attitudes of the surrounding staff, whether expressed or inexpressed, have particular relevance to this kind of therapeutic effort since they combine to create a psychological climate which ultimately determines whether this kind of therapy can or cannot develop. For, regardless of the extent to which the child therapist is able to identify with the primary-process world of the psychotic child, as an adult she faces within herself the demands of adult society. This double foothold in the psychotic world of the patient and the reality world of everyday living must be maintained at an even balance which permits free motion and spontaneity. In order to deal with the kind and degree of anxiety and physical exhaustion induced by this kind of patient, the therapist needs to rely upon the structure of the setting and its essential friendliness toward what she is attempting to accomplish. Naturally she is made anxious and angry by the patient and by her own reawakened opposition to parental images. The approval or disapproval of the surrounding staff represents in this a reinforcement of either permissions or prohibitions within the therapist herself. And it becomes then difficult to maintain the necessary psychological balance in the face of a living out of inner prohibitions by the surrounding environment. Moreover, the attitude of the staff, which came to view the psychotherapist as responsible for the child's destructive and deviate behavior, converging with the psychotic transferences of the child which also held mother-therapist responsible for illness, together placed a heavy burden upon the maintenance of the spontaneity in the therapeutic process.

It is interesting that hand in hand with the view of the psycho-therapist as a partner to the child in his illness was the constancy of the surprise expressed by the staff when the child made clear repeatedly the significance of his relationship to the therapist. Over and over again the daily notes reflected the amazement of the child care staff when Ken mentioned his "therapy" in many contexts throughout the day. Much of his behavior during the entire day represented seemingly endless repetitions of activities begun in his therapy hours, as if in some very primitive way he was trying to remember, to retain, or to continue the experience, much like sucking continues the nursing experience. Frequently he addressed himself to his radio, promising that he would take his radio to see his "therapy." He called his turtle a "therapy turtle" and he tenderly clipped pictures of hoses from magazines and pinned them to the wall of his room during the period of water play in therapy. It is interesting that the other children in the residence learned quickly that they could reduce Ken to terror by taunting him with the threat that they were going to take his psycho-therapist away. Yet it is almost as if the psychological need to make a symbiotic unit out of therapist–child generated so much anxiety that at one and the same time the intimacy and significance of the therapeutic relationship needed to be denied by a large part of the staff.

In actuality, the child could play out little else but variations of the central conflict, whether in his psychotherapy hours or in the residence. We infer that the fact of the staff's continued amazement about the significance of the therapeutic relationship to Ken was their need to displace their own anger and anxiety from the child onto the therapist. In defense against their own unacceptable anger against the child, they could see her as the hostile symbiotic parent and remain themselves as the loving parents.

It soon became apparent that Ken evoked a wide and various spectrum of fearful and angry feelings. In part, resentment derived from the continual rebuffs which the adults received from this child in response to good intentions, kindness and love generously proffered. These rebuffs coupled with physical and verbal abuse gradually gener-ated latent disappointment and anger which could not find an accept-able place in the training and orientation of the total staff. These feelings, always on the verge of breaking through, exacerbated anxiety and unconscious guilt and required the stiffening of characteristic defenses. One worker referred to Ken as being like an old model car, an antique for which no parts could be obtained. He described Ken as the original primitive car, and no other prototype seemed to exist so that one could know how to fix and care for him. In its uppermost meaning, the worker's statement conveys his feeling that Ken was beyond repair, with no spare parts available to make him function well and ready, therefore, only for the junk heap. Of considerable interest, however, is the "distance" of the example (removed in space and time from current car models almost beyond recognition) and the gross denial of the child's impact which was surely as high-powered as the most up-to-date car.

Beyond this, however, one approached what Winnicott (1949) referred to as "the anxiety of psychotic quality and . . . hate produced in those who work with severely ill psychiatric patients." The strange and intense preoccupations which characterized Ken's behavior, the fading in and out of people and objects, the fluidity of ego boundaries, the primitive animism alongside of the devitalization and fragmentation of living things combined to create a great stress. For, inevitably, they called forth counterfantasies against which normal defensive operations in the external devices of individual supervision and group meetings seemed to be of little avail. Thus, in order to defend against the fusion impact of the child, the ego boundaries of those who worked with him were necessarily overcathected.

Much of Ken's behavior appeared like action in a dream accompanied by the kind of reality testing which the sleepwalker retains. He utilized himself and his many extensions, namely, his turtle, his motors, his radios, to represent at different times the all-powerful destructive mother and the impotent anxiety-ridden mother; the all-powerful pseudo-phallic boy and the helpless whimpering infant. In each of these rapidly shifting identities, his capacity to mobilize anxiety in the people around him was tremendous since each identity seemed total, all-engulfing, and unmodified by other identities. On one occasion he savagely stomped a dead turtle to pieces with his bare feet and while the onlookers were still recovering from the shock, he calmly and efficiently picked up the remains and flushed them away. At such times we were tempted to hazard that the fluctuation itself—namely, the fact that each identity did not endure indefinitely—made it possible to withstand anxieties which he called forth.

An additional problem in the work with Ken was the seeming separation between impulsive behavior and feeling. It was shocking to observe that the link between impulsive behavior and affect did not obtain and that destruction could occur without anger or panic. Gradually one realized that the surrealistic movies which make use of dream symbols—the man being pursued by the hostile eyes, and the uppraised fist—were all reasonably close to portraying the inner life of this child in its lack of full-dimensioned introjects and inability to make connections. A child who behaves in this way evokes stark fear comparable to the panic experience in a nightmare.

One of the most interesting aspects of the total experience was what we have called its peripheral spread. It was striking that people not directly involved with the patient, the psychotherapy, or the management of the child became emotionally involved and contributed their own anxieties to the countertransference problem. Somehow, gradually and insidiously, the child began to dominate the entire structure of the residence. His ubiquitousness was extraordinary and he seemed to be everywhere at the same time, disturbing each function of the setting. Those most concerned with the administrative responsibility became increasingly troubled about the safety and physical well-being of the child as well as about the high cost of his care and his destructiveness. The kitchen staff felt aggrieved and put out because of his refusal to eat the food that they had prepared and the fact that he confined his eating to dry cereal and milk. The custodial staff was greatly troubled by the wanton destruction of property which recurred. The child care staff resented the special rest periods and the special privileges accorded those staff members who were employed to take care of Ken for whom special rest arrangements were necessary. In short, the disturbance reverberated through every aspect of the residence.

In the face of all of these difficulties the treatment was sustained. Few would question that cogent reality reasons for discharge could surely be derived from the occurrences up to this point. Yet, it is germane to our thesis that only as the child finally entered upon an activity which evoked intense rage and despair coupled with feelings of utter helplessness that the treatment was abruptly brought to a close. Thus the treatment end can be linked to a particular psychological constellation vis-à-vis the child.

It is not within the scope nor purpose of this presentation to delineate all of the complex factors which led to the administrative decision to discharge the child. Our purpose is to describe the psychological impact Ken had on the residence and the ways in which countertransference powerfully influenced the decision to accept the child for inpatient treatment and how the countertransference also dictated his discharge. Ken had within him the capacity to arouse the generosity of people to rescue him, and also the opposing capacity to activate great amounts of hostility. These fed each other back and forth, with wider and more intense fluctuations to the negative side. It may be said that the sympathy created by the child and his tragic life made it possible for him to be accepted for treatment and the rising negative feelings he could arouse caused him to leave it.

Ken had begun to climb out on the roof of the residence and the therapy building when he entered the school. But it was only in the fourth month of his stay that this gradually became his most frequent symptomatic activity. On snowy days when the roof was icy, on rainy days when the roof was slippery, he would mount the fire escape and remain up on the roof, tearing off large pieces of shingle and hurling them to the utter distraction of the workers below. There were several attempts to work out various plans to prevent this roof climbing but these proved abortive, as if some lack of conviction surrounding each plan rendered it unworkable. The fact that he undertook this activity in therapy as well increased the discouragement. Primarily, there seemed no way to get past the discouragement and feelings of helpless rage caused by the fact that instead of experiencing limits as protective, these were viewed as forces of destruction which engendered wild panic. Thus, if the child care worker was stationed on the fire escape to block the climb, Ken reacted terrified, like a dreamer who in his dream encounters a figure from the outside. It is relevant to add here that Ken never hurt himself throughout his entire stay in the residence although he constantly undertook grave risks which might well have been fatal to other children his age. As the roof climbing became his most frequent activity, the decision to discharge was made with the recommendation to the parents that the child was in need of closed hospital treatment. In the psychological climate surrounding the discharge, the silences, the sadness, the anger, the blame, the difficulties in discussing or communicating the decision, the haste that went into the discharge planning, we may find the counterpart to those feelings which had welcomed Ken into the residential setting.

Theoretically we may conceptualize treatment disruption as analogous to play disruption in that it serves the same purpose of keeping the unconscious conflict from coming into conscious awareness. With no attempt to depreciate the reality considerations, we suggest that the treatment disruption here served to prevent certain unconscious conflicts in the treatment staff from coming into consciousness, namely, to keep from consciousness that potential for behaving like the real mother which the child had so deftly aroused. From the very beginning of Ken's residential experience those who worked directly with him and were able in such an exceptional way to tolerate his behavior reported in their notes and their supervisory conferences that the most upsetting aspect of his behavior was his open and desperate pleading to be destroyed which sometimes followed his breaking out of bounds. Thus from the outset, the child's provocation of the adult to step into the role of the murdering mother was that which needed to be warded off most strongly. And we suggest that it was this fantasy that was warded off in the striking omission of misgivings and practical difficulties from the intake process. For in this way the staff was able to avoid the question,

"What is my potential for acting like the mother?" And as the child at long last found a way to reduce the staff to a position of helpless rage without seeming psychological or practical recourse, the accumulated anxieties and angers led to a symbolic re-enactment of the mother's role. Thus in his final activity of roof climbing and its consequent discharge, Ken succeeded in casting himself again as a helpless victimized child vis-à-vis the anxious, destructive mother.

There is a particular aspect to the convergence of psychological events which occurred at the point of discharge which may have implications for the future, namely, that the discharge coincided with a change in the clinical picture in the direction which had been predicted, i.e., the beginning emergence of the precursors of compulsive-obsessive defenses. Unfortunately these changes cannot be evaluated since they did not sustain the shock of the discharge. Nevertheless it may be that just as the depressed patient is most dangerous to himself as the depression begins to lift, similarly the threat of treatment rupture out of hate, fear, and anxiety in the countertransference is greatest with these clinical groups as the child becomes less sick, begins to give up his autistic preoccupations and begins increasingly to intrude into relationships around him. What is clear from this material, however, is that there were no indications that the child was less treatable at the time the discharge decision was made and several indications to the contrary.

An excerpt from the child's last hour in therapy before the decision to discharge was made follows. We suggest that in this we see the beginning emergence of the precursors of obsessive-compulsive defenses in the play around "do not touch."

Ken arrived accompanied by his companion. He bounded into the inner office and asked whether I had gotten the toy which he had requested (a little wind-up washing machine, which I had). He took hold of it excitedly, started to wind it up and led the way outside. I went to get my coat while he as usual waited patiently, and suddenly as I joined him, he noticed John, the child care worker, who was remaining in order to stay on the fire escape and who was still talking to the receptionist. Ken, realizing John's purpose in being there, pushed his way quickly through the two heavy doors and was off for the roof, getting there, of course, well ahead of John or anyone else. He was, however, sufficiently aware of me to realize that I had not followed him. I returned to the upstairs playroom and after a few minutes I heard Ken calling plaintively, "Where is my therapy, where is my therapy?" He arrived on the second floor, took my hand and pulled me toward the staircase in a dazed and bewildered way, saying plaintively, "Where did you go?" I answered that I thought that he had run away from me so I was waiting for him in the hope that when he was ready he would come back, since I never, never chased people. Ken listened to me in his characteristic expressionless way, his quivering nostrils providing the only indication of his having heard me. He pulled me out the door and toward the water faucet, where he proceeded to play with the washing machine by sucking water out of the little pipes while keeping the mechanism whirling. His investment in this activity was intense, his eyes were partially closed, and though he was by no means out of contact, the distance between us was very great. I said softly and in a recitative kind of way which I had found helpful before with this child that now Ken could feed himself all by himself. He doesn't have to worry about not getting enough food or the wrong kind of food, he doesn't have to worry about people not being there, and so on. Ken continued this activity for just another minute after I spoke with him and then he put the toy down and started to lead the way to the basement. On the way down the steps he looked up and saw John sitting on the fire escape and he asked blankly, "What's he there for?" I said that John was there so that when Ken got frightened in therapy he wouldn't have to go up on the roof. "I'm going to throw water on him," announced Ken menacingly, getting his hose ready. I said, "John is not going to throw water on you Ken or hurt you in any way." Ken then relinquished his awareness of John and proceeded into the basement. He began to inspect the furnace and asked about the various parts with a competence that seemed to reflect some experience and I asked whether he had a furnace like it at home. Yes, he said that he had one in the basement. I asked whether his mother let him look at it there. No, he said, she didn't. I asked why not, and Ken said it was because she said he might get hurt. "I see," I stated, "I understand now Ken, that when somebody tells you something is dangerous you think maybe that they are going to hurt you and that's what makes it dangerous. And that's also why you try to do dangerous things to show that you're stronger and that you won't get hurt." As expected, for one long minute there was no direct response to what I said. Then he went directly over and looked at the fire extinguisher. He looked at it long and searchingly. I said nothing but what I did was to softly and slowly move closer toward him. He then was able to pass the fire extinguisher without touching it and went outside toward the Sterling Building.

As he led the way into the Sterling Building he stopped off briefly at Mrs. W.'s office where the door was open and asked her what the different objects in her room were, especially a table tied to the wall. I explained that it was tied there because some children didn't know how to play with it and would destroy it. He listened soberly and led the way into the furnace room. He pointed gleefully to the fire and identified different parts of the furnace. He then started to open different steel boxes which enclosed equipment and fuse boxes and other boxes whose function I did not know and therefore told him I thought we ought to find out what they were before we played with them; that I did not think he ought to touch them until we found out whether or not they were dangerous. Ken's activity consisted of his opening the boxes or getting me to open them, or getting me to hold him so that he could open the boxes. He would open the door of the box, look at the inside intently and then say each time, "That's dangerous. You can't touch it." I would respond that it was a relief to know that some things were dangerous and some things were not dangerous and what was and what wasn't. This same activity with the boxes was repeated ten or twelve times in each building of the school. He would repeat his part and I would repeat mine.

Finally it was the end of the hour and I told this to Ken and he left with considerable reluctance since we had not finished looking at all the boxes in the basement. I assured him that we would have lots of time to do so. He finally agreed to come across the street with me. Once there, we ran into difficulty since there was nobody there to leave him with and the one person who was in charge was not eager to receive him at the moment. Ken sat down and started to kick a hole in the wall. I restrained him and told him I would surely not leave him until I found someone who would take very good care of him. By this time John had arrived. As I said good-bye to Ken I noticed that this was the first time in my entire contact with the child that he did not need to shut me out as I left him. Instead, to my considerable surprise, he turned to me and asked me whether I would bring him another little toy washing machine to our next therapy hour. I said that I would be happy to and patted his cheek and left him holding John's hand.

During this same period the child care staff routed the chief residential worker out of his bed early one Sunday morning to tell him, in great excitement and pleasure that could hardly be contained, that Ken was playing football according to regulations with the other children. This represented the first time that Ken had been able to engage in any play in its usual sense or had been able to establish any contact of a nondestructive kind with the other children. It was also of importance that the other children were apparently pleased to have him in their game. Also at this time he remarked to his child care worker that he was a butterfly coming out of a cocoon; and, in beginning recognition of the world around him, he painstakingly wrote the names of all the children in the residence on his arms and legs. This, incidentally, was our first indication that the child could write since he had had no formal schooling at all.

All of these observations and particularly the football incident reflect the love and interest in the child which were sustained until the very end. It may well be that as a child begins to improve, the staff is most vulnerable to the threat of the hate and anxiety countertransference in that their investment in the child may be at its height.

The résumé of the interview between the chief residential worker and Ken, in which the child was informed of the discharge and the transfer, now follows.

When I entered Ken's room to tell him the news of his transfer to the X school, he was lying on his bed listening to the radio, his foot up to his nose, sucking his finger. After some interchange, I told him that next week his parents were coming to take him to another school. He began to smile after I reached the words that his parents were coming and then it dawned on him that he was being taken by them to another school rather than home. The smile immediately changed. He came close to me, throwing his arms around my neck. He began to quiver throughout his whole body and to whimper and I reassuringly patted him as I would an infant in distress and spoke to him about the fact that he would be transferred to this new school. He asked immediately why his parents were taking him to the new school and I told him that after some discussion with his parents it was the decision of the staff here that he would do better in a different kind of school where he would have a chance to be with children like himself and there would be additional protection and care. He gazed several times intensely into my eyes as he asked these questions and as I began answering them, he backed up onto the bed, stating with glee that in the other school he would also climb into the closet, move the bed, and when they attempted to bolt it down, he would make it impossible for them to do so and he would destroy things and he would surely go up on the roof. Several times he lay back on the bed, rolling from side to side with his foot up to his nose and his fingers in his mouth making small quaking noises. He asked if the school would have psychotherapy. He also asked if his favorite child care worker would be able to accompany him. As I was beginning to leave, he began to get more restless, hyperactive, and started to run in and out of the hall saying he was going to kill one of the little boys. Later he was reported saying to several people, "But I still have my problems, how can you send me away?"

To come again full circle, the child's discharge was followed by a depressive mood which prevented the staff for many months from discussing what had occurred.

One cannot help, of course, but be struck by the coherence of this psychotic child in his recognition of the difficulties in his behavior that were causing his discharge and in his request for therapy and his favorite child care worker. Nevertheless, the very articulateness of our patient in calling attention to his particular needs may obscure the conclusions which we have reached regarding factors which we hold to be present in all work with these particular clinical groups.

Children who are constantly threatened by catastrophic discontinuity from within and without, and who therefore need our assurances the most, are those whose treatment is most likely to be disrupted. For they successfully assail in us that which they need most desperately—our sustained capacity for treatment continuity.

It is perhaps inherent in the phenomena which we report that one must close ruefully and with a lingering doubt as to whether we have in this presentation primarily raised technical questions or whether we have given primary expression to a mood still rooted in the experience which we have described.

PART II

COUNTERTRANSFERENCE IN SPECIFIC SITUATIONS

4

Racial and Cultural Issues Impacting on Countertransference

Donna M. Norris, M.D.
Jeanne Spurlock, M.D.

Although the concept of countertransference has been discussed by many scholars throughout the history of the development of psychodynamic theory, little attention was given to the significance of countertransference in psychotherapeutic work with children. Even less attention has been directed to the phenomenon of bicultural and biracial dyads. In this chapter we will discuss the impact of racial and cultural issues, with a particular focus on work with African-American children and adolescents. The concepts advanced by Giovacchini (1981a) and Ekstein et al. (1959) will be used as a frame of reference in exploring culture and race as underpinnings of countertransference reactions. Specifically, we will be guided by the concept that both homogeneous countertransferences (or reactions that are predictable given a particular transferential stimulus) and idiosyncratic countertransferences (those arising from unique features of the therapist's background and character make-up) can encompass the parent–child unit. We view some countertransferences as negative and impeding the therapeutic process, while others are seen as positive and possibly as serving to promote the treatment. In either case, it is essential for therapists to be alert to all of their countertransference responses and to manage these reactions such that the therapeutic process will not be thwarted.

The therapeutic situation may be likened to a journey in a strange land, with patient and therapist each having only part of the necessary map. The therapist's map provides an accurate route for the therapeutic process; the patient's part provides information about the culture of the territory. The two must work together to develop a complete map that provides direction to the end point of the journey.

When the patient is from a culture that is markedly different from the therapist's, certain prejudices and stereotypes are likely to evoke countertransference responses that have the potential to impact negatively on the treatment. Although the members of any cultural group share certain characteristics that serve to unite them, it is important to remember that all individuals within a group do not necessarily want the same things, share the same values, or desire the same treatment. Like individuals from other cultural groups, African-Americans represent a mosaic of differences. There is no single African-American culture; such factors as ancestral heritage, geographic residence, and socioeconomic conditions contribute to the shaping of each individual, and each person referred for psychotherapy deserves an individually tailored diagnostic assessment and treatment plan. Many of the issues that will be discussed in this chapter are applicable not only to African-Americans, but to other cultural and racial groups as well.

GLIMPSES FROM THE LITERATURE

Most of the psychiatric and psychoanalytic literature that deals with the impact of racial and cultural factors on transference and countertransference focuses on work with adults. However, some of these references are applicable to work with children and adolescents. For example, Thomas (1962) has noted that "pseudo-transference reactions" can be produced when therapists "exhibit a culturally determined, derogatory, stereotyped attitude toward the patient in terms of the latter's sex, race, religion, or socio-economic status" (p. 895). Bernard noted that "the respective subcultural groups to which patient and analyst belong can be regarded as constituting a special dynamic factor of the analytic situation and as such can be provocative of countertransference" (1953, p. 257). Bernard and others (Calnek 1970, Oberndorf 1954, Rosen and Frank 1962, Spiegel 1976,) have called attention to the fact that various issues related to prejudice are not always dealt with or worked through during the course of personal training analyses. Bernard concludes:

If an analyst has insufficiently analyzed his own unconscious material pertaining to his own group memberships and those of others, he and his patients may be insufficiently protected from the interference of a variety of positive and negative countertransference reactions stimulated by the ethnic, religious and racial elements that are present in the analytic situation, the patient's personality, and in the specific content of the patient's material. [1953, p. 259]

If the analyst is intensely race conscious, it is likely that his interpretations will be rooted in racial conflicts, and this lessens the opportunity to address and work through basic problems. Thomas (1962) provides a vivid illustration. He had received a referral of a black male patient whose previous experience in therapy had been unsuccessful. The referring therapist indicated that the root of the patient's problems lay in his lifetime of racial oppression, giving the impression that he could expect little, if any, alleviation of his psychoneurotic symptoms.

In a discussion of transference and countertransference in interracial analyses, Schacter and Butts (1968) note that the convergence of stereotypes and countertransference serves to retard the analytic process. Ticho (1971) describes the development of negative countertransferences that blocked her ability to empathize with a 17-year-old black female. Fischer (1971) notes that in a biracial treatment situation, he warded off repressed aggressive and sexual fantasies by denying his patient's blackness. In a description of three individual analyses with black female patients, Goldberg and colleagues (1974) write of "fantasies that the unconscious of these black patients would be different from that of whites." The analysts' stereotyped concepts were evidence of the expectations of some therapists that a patient's blackness is of no consequence in the therapeutic encounter. Some therapists, regardless of their racial identity, avoid addressing the fact that the patient is black (Calnek 1970).

Schowalter (1986) calls attention to the limited reports of studies of countertransference in work with children, especially in the arena of supervision. He provided an example from his experience. A white trainee speculated that a 7-year-old black male patient would not accept treatment if it were recommended. The resident's reluctance to make a commitment to offer treatment was out of proportion to the data he had reported to the supervisor. At the supervisor's initiation, an exploration of the resident's feelings about the various aspects of the case took place. It became clear that the resident's background of poverty and his shame about his roots had colored his clinical judgment.

Gartner (1985) discussed the range of countertransference reactions that are likely to develop in therapy with adolescents. A reactivation of therapists' adolescent struggles are commonplace, especially as related to aggressive and sexual impulses. A therapist's narcissistic investment in the patient's recovery was identified as another source of countertransference responses. The narcissistic injury triggered by a patient's acting-out behavior or devaluation of the therapist provokes countertransference reactions that can thwart the progress of therapy. Thus, when the therapist works with patients who are culturally different and who present with acting-out behavior, there is a potential compounding of the countertransference reaction. Similarly, it may be that "minor" acting-out behavior will be tolerated, whereas more aggressive and violent activity will be reason to exclude the patient from the treatment. The therapist may not exclude the patient overtly, but rather may gradually become more distant and punitive in reacting to the patient and may "allow" the patient to drift away, thereby terminating the treatment.

King (1976) has discussed the countertransference reactions stirred in treatment with violence-prone youth that are likely to provoke rejection. Christ (1964) provides an interesting account of countertransference reactions experienced in the treatment of an adolescent schizophrenic girl. Progress was delayed at times when the therapist was unaware of his countertransference reactions, but moved ahead when he recognized the basis of his use of particular defense mechanisms.

Barbarin (1984) discusses several countertransference themes that affect treatment in biracial encounters. Highlighted are the white therapist' unconscious racial attitudes, which may be expressed in avoidance, for example, or in passive acceptance of a patient's premature termination. Adams calls attention to the positive countertransference reactions experienced by white therapists who have "White Negro" tastes. Such a therapist tends to demonstrate a "preference for black patients, for whom he leans over backward, welcomes their abuse, and accedes to their demands that they be dealt with as 'exceptions'" (1970, p. 38). Obviously, such actions are of benefit to neither the patient nor the therapist.

Not infrequently, countertransference reactions are rooted in guilt. This pattern was often noted during the height of the civil rights movement of the 1960s, when "white guilt" was commonplace. Some black therapists were known to share in this "white guilt" when work with disadvantaged blacks stirred guilt about their own successes. Until these countertransference reactions were recognized and worked through, the therapists were inclined to identify with the patient's tendency to externalize their problems and to view their difficulties only in terms of racism.

Adolescents often become sensitized to their therapists' guilt and find ways to intensify the reaction. This, in turn, reinforces the mechanism of avoidance. A therapist's false perceptions of patients are often increased in bicultural therapy. In such encounters, therapists should ideally make use of "methods and behaviors that support clear and complete transmission" and be alert to identify and correct erroneous perceptions (Pinderhughes and Pinderhughes 1982, p. 264). Spiegel (1976) and Gorkin (1986) make distinctions between counter-transference errors and misunderstandings that arise out of a lack of knowledge about the culturally or racially different patient.

ENVIRONMENTAL FACTORS

Depending on where one has resided and attended college or postgraduate school, it is still possible in this country to meet one's first racially or culturally diverse patient in one's therapy office. White therapists who lack experience with African-Americans often fear, whether they recognize it or not, that such patients are potentially more impulsive or dangerous than others. Such fears may paralyze the therapist and prevent her from being appropriately active in the therapy. Furthermore, cultural naivete may increase the therapist's vulnerability to the biases of other clinicians. One of the authors supervised a white therapist's inpatient treatment of a child of the same racial group. A home visit was recognized as important to further the understanding of the family dynamics. When this plan was shared with other staff of the dominant group, the therapist was alerted that a visit to the home, which was located in a "black area," would place his life at risk. The validity of this warning was questioned in the supervisory hour; the child and family experienced neither harm nor risk in the neighborhood. In the exploration of this sequence, it became apparent that the staff's response seemed to betray their own countertransference responses relating to the black supervisor's ability to guide the psychotherapeutic work and, at the same time, to be aware of the therapist's educational needs. This example demonstrates the importance of the therapist's continual observation of factors outside of the therapy hour that may impact on the psychotherapy process. In large part, much of our education about racially and culturally diverse groups has come from the media. The portrayal of blacks as subservient or assaultive gives a stereotypic message that precedes the patient's arrival at the therapist's office.

Dr. Y's report of experiences in working with black male adolescents during her second year of psychiatry training are illustrative. The early phase of treatment of one patient, 14-year-old Marvin, coincided with a reported upsurge of violence in the community where both the treatment center and the patient's home were located. In response to Dr. Y's concerns about the patient's resistance (he was usually nonverbal until near the end of the session, usually arrived late, and denied any problems) and her question about the advisability of termination, the supervisor asked about the therapist's speculations as to why she was having so much trouble with this particular case. Her initial response was to focus on the patient's resistance, as she perceived it. The supervisor wondered whether there was anything about this patient that stirred particular concerns and responses. This question elicited no additional information. To the resident's credit, however, she gave further consideration to this question between supervisory sessions, and she finally recalled the following experiences:

When I was in the sixth grade, a black family moved into our neighborhood. There was a lot of unrest about this, and I remember discussions about avoiding contact with the black children, especially the boys, who were described as potentially violent. I saw them as big, and I must have incorporated my parents' and brother's admonitions, even though I remember liking the guy in the class ahead of me.

In further discussion with the supervisor, it became clear that the recent media reports about violence in the immediate neighborhood had activated the therapist's old concerns and had brought about a kind of paralysis in her work. She recounted that in previous work with adolescents who had assumed a passive or passive-aggressive stance, she had taken a more active role and had usually been able to achieve a therapeutic alliance. In the same supervisory session, Dr. Y and her supervisor recalled that the media's reports about the neighborhood were silent about any endeavors of a positive nature, and they drew a parallel between this observation and the discussions that had taken place in the therapist's childhood.

The media is a powerful determinant of our impressions of members of other cultures, capable of undermining even the greatest accomplishments. In an industrial state in the northeastern United States, the swearing-in of the first black woman judge was reported in the larger of two daily newspapers. In an adjacent column was a report of a black senior justice's questioned sobriety while driving. Therapists are not necessarily immune to the power of the press, lay or professional. Therefore, they must repeatedly examine their own hypotheses about culturally or racially different groups. Although segregation in housing and education has been outlawed in this country, the races remain largely separated from one another. For many white individuals, contact with blacks is limited to those who are performing menial services. This skewed exposure does not provide the opportunity for these individuals to become aware of or benefit from the broad diversity within the black population. Stereotypic attitudes can affect the establishment of the goals of the therapy, the scope of the work, and the consideration of alternative options. If the therapist accepts as valid the premise that black families cannot achieve "the American Dream"—extended formal education, economic security, and a stable family life—then the therapeutic process will be handicapped, and the growth of both patient and therapist will be thwarted. Patients are thus hindered in reaching their potential, and therapists are restricted in the utilization of their skills toward appropriate goals.

In working with African-American patients, therapists must be alert to the risk of assuming paternalistic attitudes in identifying and shaping the work and goals of the therapy. Goal-setting should be identified as a task shared by the patient, or the patient's parents, and therapist in line with the patient's cultural values. For example, a white clinician was working with an African-American boy whose treatment had been mandated by the juvenile court after the boy had become involved in a series of delinquent behaviors, primarily stealing. In presenting the case to her colleagues, the clinician noted a significant family history of emotional deprivation and poverty. She indicated that, given this history, the patient should be excused from any punishment by the courts. The long history of discrimination experienced by African-Americans, she explained, was reason enough to understand and excuse the patient's behavior. In this example, the clinician's countertransference interfered with her ability to focus on the problems and needs of this individual patient, and caused her to assume that advocacy was the most desirable goal. There was no acknowledgement that the attainment of her goal might be detrimental to this lad's future.

Within an inpatient therapeutic milieu, the therapist must also be aware of the influence of staff members' countertransferences in shaping the treatment process. The following composite of several clinical vignettes is illustrative.

A 12-year-old black male who appeared older than his age was admitted for his first psychiatric hospitalization following several suicide threats. He initially settled into the inpatient unit without difficulty. The staff noticed, however, that the patient was gradually becoming more irritable and loud in his interactions with others. In supervision, the psychiatric resident on call reported that the nursing staff viewed this patient's behavior as potentially dangerous and was urging that he be medicated with a neuroleptic. The resident believed, however, that this class of medication was not appropriate given the patient's symptoms and the medication's significant side effects and potency. The supervisor and the resident assessed the patient together and determined that there were no indications for a neuroleptic. There was no history of psychotic behavior before or after the admission, and the patient's irritability and loudness were attributed to his panic anxiety. In subsequent discussion with the nursing staff, it became apparent that one of the most vocal and assertive members of the team often tended to identify the agitated behavior of black male adolescents as potentially violent. When these patterns were discussed with the nurse, she was able to acknowledge their consistency. It became apparent to the unit staff that the phenomenon of countertransference would have to be addressed in all meetings focused on patient care.

INITIATING THE THERAPEUTIC PROCESS

It is acknowledged that individual psychotherapy with children cannot be undertaken without the permission of the parents or guardians, and that the parents or guardian must be treated with respect. Unfortunately, such respect is often absent, especially in public-sector work with families of nondominant cultures or races.

For example, it was noted during a case conference that staff members were referring to Hispanic parents by their given names, despite the treatment team's agreement that clinicians should not presume familiarity by using first names without explicit permission. This pattern was noted to be in contrast to the last-name form of address used with families of the dominant group. It became clear that there was an implied criticism of their parenting, but without documentation of any deficiencies. Children of culturally or racially diverse groups are cautiously protective of their families. Threats or denigrations of the "family," whatever the composition, will not be tolerated. Often, the response is withdrawal from treatment.

Children demand that their therapists be "real" people with ideas and answers. The therapist is expected to be responsive and to offer herself as an assistant in the patient's quest for a positive sense of self. Psychotherapy with African-American children may initially be less verbal than with children of the dominant group. This early period may be an evaluative process for both the patient and the therapist. Limited verbalization should not be stereotyped as evidence of inferior intelligence or an inability to benefit from therapy.

Although some African-American patients may be socioeconomically disadvantaged, they may not perceive themselves as impoverished. Therapists must be careful to avoid applying their own ideas regarding economic status as a measure of self-worth. For example, a family's decisions on what to purchase—a luxury car, expensive sneakers for their adolescent son—are often based upon their own individual values.

It is important, at the initiation of the therapeutic process, to acknowledge differences. In the United States, the factor of black skin has significant impact but may be ignored or go unrecognized in the therapy process. In speaking about blacks, West notes:

> For man, daytime is a good time, the safe time . . . when one can see what is going on and make his way in the world. The daydream is aspiration; but the nightmare is consummate error . . . and the man of the night is black. [1979, pp. 646–647]

When the therapist initiates a discussion of race-related issues, it helps the black patient to understand that blackness is important to discuss and that the clinician is not afraid of what it will bring. The therapist who has not resolved his own racist, stereotypic beliefs will not be able to work successfully with culturally or racially diverse patients. Similarly, the clinician who rationalizes, minimizes, or overlooks unacceptable behavior that is perpetrated either on or by the patient cannot do useful work. It is not helpful to the patient for the therapist to become so identified with the patient's struggles in a racist society that they both fail to work toward achieving the patient's potential.

Another important issue in therapeutic work with African-American children and adolescents is that of aggression. It is not uncommon for therapists to raise questions about the potential for aggressive behavior upon receiving a referral of an African-American patient—before the therapist and the patient ever meet. The therapist must carefully evaluate the evidence to support such a concern.

SOME EXAMPLES OF COUNTERTRANSFERENCES

Some therapists select patients from cultures different from their own because of a particular interest in the other culture. Intense curiosity about a patient's background often leads to an exploration of the patient's culture to satisfy the therapist's curiosity rather than to further the therapeutic task (Gorkin 1986). For example, in reporting a case to his supervisor, a psychiatric resident focused his discussion on his exploration of an adolescent's family's history of marriages across racial lines. Although the patient was biracial, there was nothing in the nature of the problem for which he was referred (specifically, predelinquent behavior following the murder of his black father, a police officer) that would have supported this focus. In response to his supervisor's queries, the resident spoke of his long-held interest in bicultural relationships, perhaps stemming from his own family background. This kind of countertransference reaction extends beyond traineeship. Devereaux (1953) wrote of a problem in curbing his curiosity about his patients' culture when working with native American patients. Gorkin (1986) addressed similar problems experienced by Jewish therapists in their treatment of Arab patients.

Significant countertransference reactions have been experienced by African-American therapists who have been purposely sought out by white parents seeking help for their children. One such therapist experienced fantasies that she was being viewed as a domestic who "understood the ways of children and could set them straight." Undoubtedly, she said, memories of her mother's tales of her work experiences evoked those countertransference reactions. Similarly, African-American families bring to the therapy their experiences of interaction with the dominant culture. Their transferences may be accompanied by heightened suspiciousness of the therapist's motives and potential influence over their children.

Ordway's account of a report of a white analyst reflects the potential adverse effects of countertransference in a biracial treatment situation: the patient, a black male adolescent, was described as sullen and verbally nonresponsive in the first few sessions. In the fifth hour he reported a dream in which a black car and a white car collided. Both were towed to a garage, but only one would be repaired. The lad couldn't remember which one—the black or white—was salvageable.

> Later in the hour Paul laughed as he said that he thought maybe the black car had driven away. At the analytic meeting itself the analyst recounted that, from the boy's subsequent interpretation of the dream, he under-stood that the patient had a feeling that a destructive clash between patient and doctor was inevitable and that the patient only hoped that he could survive his trip to the hospital (garage). He understood that the patient's fury at whites had led him in the dream to wishfully "bump off" his white therapist. But the psychoanalyst laughed heartily at the "unrealistic" thought that Paul had anything to fear from him. Only after the meeting . . . did he see that his hearty laugh was in large part sadistic joy over Paul's discomfort and his ability to "make a nigger patient squirm." [1973, pp. 136–137]

In another case, an African-American adolescent was asked why she had terminated treatment (with a white therapist). The patient immediately replied, "She [the therapist] didn't know nothin' about me or black people." She went on to say that the therapist had continually asked questions about "black life." Upon further exploration, it became clear that the patient perceived the therapist to be unable to help her because the therapist had no knowledge about where the patient had come from or where she might want to go. Unfortunately, the first therapist did not have the opportunity to reconstruct an alliance with the patient. We believe that the therapist's recognition of cultural differences in the first session may have prevented the abrupt termination. Lack of information about the background of a culturally different patient is evidenced by some faculty who are responsible for supervising the clinical work of trainees. This situation warrants long overdue attention and remediation. This lack of knowledge and concern may reflect unconscious negative racial attitudes. The following case examples might prove illustrative of such attitudes.

A white psychiatric resident was having difficulty setting limits with an African-American male adolescent. In supervision, the resident spontaneously spoke about negative childhood experiences with African-American and Hispanic peers in his neighborhood, and he acknowledged an awareness of his own barely suppressed rage about the physical assaults he had experienced in his youth. Clearly, there was a countertransference reaction that needed to be addressed. Unfortunately for all concerned, the supervisor, after acknowledging the countertransference phenomenon, recommended transfer of the patient. It may have been the supervisor's own countertransferences that prompted this recommendation.

A 16-year-old African-American girl was referred by the court for psychotherapy. The patient had been abandoned by her family and had been living on the streets for several years. The patient had been arrested for larceny immediately preceding the referral. Early in the sessions with a female therapist, the patient appeared to be developing a relationship; however, she soon disappeared from treatment. Several years later she "dropped by" the therapist's office "to say hello." In response to an inquiry about her abrupt termination, the patient acknowledged that she had been attracted to the therapist and feared that they might become involved in a sexual relationship. In a later consultation with this patient, the therapist recalled that she had known of the patient's lesbian relationships and had suspected that the patient might have some conflict about homosexual issues. She wondered whether the patient might have felt more comfortable if she, the therapist, had addressed this matter early in their relationship. Although the patient expressed uncertainty in responding to this query, it may be that the therapist's avoidance of the matter (particularly in view of the fact that she knew of the history of lesbian relationships) might have been interpreted as a potential rejection, to which the patient responded by flight.

Although this case is unrelated to racial differences, there is a parallel. That is, the therapist was aware of a cultural difference, experienced some discomfort about the difference, and then reacted in a way that served to further distance her from the patient.

As we have noted, a supervisor's countertransference often influences the therapist's responses in an individual treatment session and, subsequently, over the course of treatment. Calnek (1970) called attention to several issues that are of particular significance when the supervisor is white. Lack of knowledge about a patient's culture can make for major difficulties in the treatment. For example, the supervisor's misinformation or lack of knowledge about characteristic folkways of African-American communities can lead to misinterpretations of normal patterns of behavior as pathological. One would hope that there have been significant changes in training in recent years so that the patterns noted by Calnek more than two decades ago would no longer obtain. However, a recent report from a psychiatric resident, who happened to be the only African-American in his training program, speaks against such changes. In the course of a seminar, another resident spoke of the "genetic inferiority" of African-Americans. Only the black resident challenged this statement. The professor was silent then, and even later, when the black resident spoke to him privately; that is, he declined to discuss the fallacy of the statement. One can only conjecture that if this professor were ever in a position to supervise the treatment of a black patient, his negative countertransference reaction, based on his obviously biased beliefs, would surely have impeded the progress of the therapy.

Supervisors who announce to trainees that they know nothing about the culture of the patient who is being presented and therefore cannot be of help are guilty of negligence. As Morgan has exhorted, "It is the supervisor's responsibility to be sensitive to the issues of culture and race, both in the supervision as well as [in] the conduct of therapy" (1984, p. 63). To take this a step further, supervisors should be responsible for working with trainees in identifying ways and means to learn about the culture of the patient.

CONCLUSIONS

Although countertransference reactions triggered in white therapist–African-American patient dyads serve as the focus of this chapter, a number of these points are applicable to other cultural and racial groups. Most of the literature on this subject pertains to work with adults. Nevertheless, the observations and conclusions noted are clearly related to work with children and adolescents as well. The unconscious racial attitudes of therapists are the major roots of countertransference reactions that impede therapeutic progress. Unfortunately, these issues are often not dealt with in supervision of therapists in training. The authors strongly recommend that therapists and supervisors jointly take particular care to identify and emphasize the importance of racially and/or culturally based countertransference issues in the therapeutic work.

5

Depressed and Suicidal Children and Adolescents

Jules R. Bemporad, M.D., and Stewart Gabel, M.D.

Countertransference has come to include a large variety of feelings, fantasies, or behaviors that are elicited by a patient in a therapist during the therapeutic process. An entire spectrum of definitions of counter-transference has been proposed, from, at one extreme, the narrow meaning of the term, which limits countertransference to the therapist's unconscious reaction to the patient's transference, to, at the other extreme, a "totalistic" view (to use Kernberg's [1965] terminology), which includes any and all of the therapist's emotional reactions toward the patient.

As has been noted previously (see Chapter 1), the concept of countertransference in work with children and adolescents has been relatively neglected in the psychotherapeutic and psychoanalytic liter-ature. This is particularly true of the subject of therapy with depressed pediatric patients. Further advances in theory building and in clinical application demand additional attention and new perspectives. There-fore, our own contribution in this chapter will emphasize two major areas. First, we will focus on a model of countertransference that is based in part on the development of conflict within the therapist that may at times become particularly acute because of the therapist's own expectation of the role he must maintain. Second, in a effort to broaden the framework within which countertransference is sometimes described, we will emphasize the importance of the context in which the therapeutic work progresses, with particular emphasis on such issues as the developmental stage of the youngster being treated, the specific problem or disorder that is the focus of treatment, and the involvement or lack of involvement of parents in the treatment process.

The development of an affective reaction in a therapist (or in anyone) commonly occurs when an individual, through particular behavior, appearance, or characteristics, provides a stimulus that impacts on the therapist in a manner that confirms or challenges ongoing internal values or belief systems. The therapist's reactions, stimulated and altered by some aspect of the patient's presentation (intended or not), are reflected in somatic or affective change in the therapist. From the point of view of countertransference, this internal conflict becomes defended against and projected outward. The behavioral and emotional reactions to the patient, whether increased empathy and concern or anger and loathing, reflect the multiply determined internal-state changes of the therapist reflected onto the patient and the therapeutic relationship.

From analytic perspectives, countertransference reactions can be understood on the basis of anxiety that is produced because of conflict within the therapist. Defenses against this anxiety result in various therapist reactions that become operative in the therapy. From the perspective of cognitive dissonance, competing internal belief systems within the therapist result in confusion that is experienced as dissonant. The need to clarify and develop a more harmonious, less conflicted belief system may then ensue, thereby sometimes encouraging a distortion of actual events into a more compatible framework.

Regardless of which model is used in understanding these therapist reactions, they are typical of human interactive processes in general. They have particular relevance for therapist–patient interactions, as reflected in countertransference phenomena, because of their enormous impact on the treatment. Further, these typical human interactive processes, exemplified in therapist–patient interactions, often find particular relevance because of the unique role of the therapist and his expectations of that role, as understood within the concept of "professional role" or "professional identity." The therapist's own strongly internalized role expectations are crucial to an understanding of the development of countertransference.

Most therapists, for example, expect themselves to be helpful and positively disposed toward their patients. While overly positive reactions to the behavior or to particular characteristics of a child or adolescent may obscure or alter important aspects of the treatment, therapists often do not seem discomforted by these types of reactions. Negative, angry, frightened, or loathing reactions on the part of a therapist toward a patient may be more troublesome to the therapist's sense of himself as caring or helpful and may result in a variety of defensive responses. As we will note later, therapists who conceive of their role as requiring success in helping to relieve suffering or distress in others may have particularly strong negative reactions to patients who do not "get better." As understanding of countertransference reactions therefore must take into account both the notion of internal therapist conflict in a general sense, stimulated by the characteristics of a particular patient, and the notion of the therapist's own sense of professional identity and the threats to this role expectation engendered by particular patients.

The second major point of emphasis in this chapter is a consideration of the importance of the therapeutic context (including issues of development, the type of disorder being treated, and which family members are involved in the treatment) in an understanding of countertransference reactions. Contextual features of the therapeutic situation, such as those just noted, are instrumental in eliciting countertransferential reactions, even when disregarding unique or idiosyncratic therapist reactions. For example, suicidal and depressed children and adolescents, who often convey their own feelings of helplessness, despair, and worthlessness, elicit similar feelings in many therapists. Aggressive or antisocial children and adolescents, on the other hand, may convey their own feelings of anger, defiance of externally imposed structure, and indifference to the feelings of others (including therapists), thereby eliciting very different types of therapist reactions from those elicited by sad, depressed children and adolescents.

In this regard, the developmental stage of the patient is crucial. Adult patients are commonly seen as actors on their own behalf in social and therapeutic contexts. They are expected to arrange details of their own therapy, their own living arrangements, their own relationships, and their own lives. Inability to complete these and other tasks are looked on as problems worthy of study in the therapeutic context, since such inability constitutes a deviation from the expected social role—a role that is exemplified by the presumably well-functioning adult therapist. In contrast, therapy with children, especially young children, commonly evokes parental feelings in therapists that reflect their own conscious and unconscious views of themselves as parents and their expectations of the role of caregivers for children. As will be exemplified later by a case illustration, therapists who work with children may develop countertransferential reactions toward known or unknown parents when their child patients evoke strong parental feelings—feelings of anger, for example, that the child's own parents have not cared for her and have caused the child's unhappiness. These reactions seems especially prominent when working therapeutically with preschool and school-aged children. Adolescence is a transition phase during which individuals are expected by society to assume a more independent and potentially adult posture. Therefore, work with adolescents may lessen some of the therapist's expectable countertransferential parental, care-taking feelings, but may increase the possibility of countertransferential reactions based on more strongly expressed sexual, aggressive, or defiant behavior characteristics of this developmental period.

The following section reviews various characteristics of depression in children and adolescents. Typical countertransferential patterns involving young children are noted next. A case illustration of countertransference in a school-aged child follows. Subsequently, patterns of depression in adolescents are described, along with further clinical illustrations of countertransference in this age group.

DEPRESSION IN CHILDREN AND ADOLESCENTS

The subject of depression in youth is a controversial one. Classic papers (e.g., Bowlby 1960, Spitz 1946) have described signs and symptoms, such as sad appearance, weepiness, or apparent despair on separation of infants from their caretakers, that are similar to the characteristic features of clinical depression in adults. Yet questions have been raised about whether these reactions constitute a true depressive syndrome comparable to that seen in older children and adults (Poznanski 1979). Mendelson's review of the psychoanalytic literature concludes that "there seems to be a general but not absolutely unanimous agreement in psychoanalytic literature that depressive illness does not occur in children" (1974, p. 142). Mendelson emphasizes later, however, ". . . that in no other area of the psychoanalytic literature on depressives are the theoretical papers so far removed from the observations that any clinician can make in the course of his daily practice" (p. 165). Clearly, the notion of clinical depression in children has evolved considerably in recent years; nevertheless, as Bemporad and Lee (1988) point out, numerous controversies remain.

Recent mental health nomenclature and diagnosis has been dominated by attempts to establish a standardized classification for mental disorders, as embodied in DSM-III (American Psychiatric Association 1980) and DSM-III-R (American Psychiatric Association 1987). These manuals have taken the position that major depressive episodes in children and adolescents, including infants and preschool children, have similar "essential features" to major depressive episodes in adults, although some differences in associated features may occur. These differences depend on the child's developmental stage. DSM-III and DSM-III-R therefore challenge the concept of "depressive equivalents"— a still widely held belief that children and adolescents with somatic or externalizing problems, such as aggressive behavior, may have underlying depressive illnesses despite clinical presentations that include minimal symptoms of depression itself.

The DSM-III-R classification for a major depressive episode includes a minimum 2-week period of either depressed mood (or irritable mood in children and adolescents) or loss of interest or pleasure in most activities, along with such symptoms or signs as significant weight loss, sleep disturbance, psychomotor agitation or retardation, fatigue or loss of energy, feelings of worthlessness or guilt, poor concentration, recurrent thoughts of death, or suicidal ideation, plans, or behavior. Age-specific features in prepubertal children with a major depressive episode include somatic complaints, psychomotor agitation, and mood-congruent hallucinations. Anxiety disorder and phobias are commonly associated diagnoses. Adolescents suffering from a major depressive episode, by DSM-III-R criteria, are described as sometimes presenting with associated problems of antisocial behavior and substance abuse. They also may feel not approved of and misunderstood. Grouchiness, restlessness, uncooperativeness in family affairs, social withdrawal, and school difficulties are all common. Inattention to personal appearance and extreme sensitivity to rejection may also occur.

COUNTERTRANSFERENCE IN WORK WITH DEPRESSED CHILDREN

As we have noted earlier, an understanding of typical countertransference reactions in work with children and adolescents is facilitated by awareness of developmental considerations in the presentation of clinical disorders. A brief review of developmental aspects of depression in young children is therefore presented here.

Despite the infrequency of depression as a clinical syndrome in preschoolers, reactions of apparent sadness, withdrawal, apathy, and clinging to caretakers or others occur. These reactions are commonly found to result from difficulties in the caregiver–child relationship or from periods of separation from caregivers. Depressive disorders in older children and adolescents are more frequent, occurring in 1.8

percent of prepubertal children and 4.7 percent of adolescents 14 to 16 years of age (Weller and Weller 1990).

Bemporad and Lee (1988) describe characteristics of depression in middle and later childhood, emphasizing that longer periods of sadness are more commonly encountered as the child becomes of school age. Depressive affect in mid-childhood appears to be related more to punitive or depriving environments than to negative self-judgments, poor self-esteem, or concern about the future. Lack of a positive response from the parent, who is normally idealized at this age, is frequently found. Further, the apparent rejection or abandonment by the parent is often accompanied by the child's not receiving adequate substitute care from other figures. These children appear sad, lack interest in activities, and feel lonely and unloved.

The situation changes somewhat as children approach puberty, when they increasingly evaluate themselves and others. Whereas earlier periods of sadness were related by the child to environmental events and did not as readily include self-attributions, prepubertal children seem to feel a greater sense of personal blame or worthlessness in association with depression. They may feel that others do not want to be with them or that they have done something wrong. Their own actions and behavior (or "misbehavior," according to now more internalized standards) have produced their situation. Loss of important figures or inability to achieve according to parental standards are perceived as indicating personal defects. Low self-esteem, isolation, peer difficulties, and academic problems are common.

Countertransference reactions to depressed school-aged children commonly involve reactions to the child's affect, cognitions, and environmental situation, in both their realistic and their distorted manifestations. Parental feelings—a sense of wanting somehow to care for these children—are common. Depression and sadness in children and adults commonly elicit a sense of helplessness, futility, and pessimism in on-looking adults, and may also threaten the on-lookers' wishes for an emotionally rewarding life for themselves, and, in the case of child therapists, for children.

Mental health clinicians who work with children often want to correct or improve their own childhood experiences vicariously through their therapeutic work with young patients. Such attempts may involve, consciously or unconsciously, efforts to provide the child with a better adult (parenting) relationship than the child has had previously. To some degree this may suggest providing the child with some aspects of an "ideal" parental relationship—a relationship that contrasts with the child's present parenting and with the therapist's own previous parenting. The therapist commonly wishes to "correct" or "make right" the child's environment, arguing internally (and often accurately) that this would relieve the child's depression. The therapist may become increasingly frustrated and angry when the child's environment—or, more particularly, the child's parents—cannot or will not change in a manner that would be helpful to the child.

Much of the appeal that children have for adults, and that child patients have for therapists, may lie in the adults' recognition of, appreciation for, and amusement by developmental differences between children and adults. School-aged children who become depressed and blame themselves when their emotionally disturbed or abusive parents reject them may elicit strong care-taking wishes and feelings of anger on the part of therapists toward the parents, in part because children's developmental stage-specific cognitive reaction of self-blame appears so distorted in relation to the adult therapist's cognitive view of the situation, which emphasizes the inadequacy of the parents.

Similarly, adults are sometimes saddened when dealing with depressed or suicidal children because of their own long-term goals and wishes for these children. However, depressed children do not think of or plan for the future as adults do. Again, the therapist's countertransference reaction depends on his cognitive stage appraisal of the situation.

The child's developmental immaturity, helplessness, and vulnerability, along with his cognitive distortions (from an adult perspective) thus contribute to the therapist's sadness and desire to help the child by parenting him better. The depressed child's developmentally expected idealization of his often significantly impaired parent during this stage may also raise issues of frustration, anger, or even jealousy in the therapist, who is, through the therapeutic work, attempting to provide a better parenting model. Several of the countertransference reactions that are to be expected in work with depressed children are illustrated in the following case:

A. is a 9-year-old boy who was seen for psychiatric evaluation because of suicide threats he made to his teacher and primary therapist. The available early history is limited but indicates that A. was born to substance-abusing parents. Nevertheless, pregnancy, labor, and delivery were described as unremarkable. A.'s birthweight was normal, and his development in the first four to five years of life was said to be without significant difficulties.

The parents' relationship in the years after A.'s birth was stormy; there were periods of separation, and A. and his mother moved to live with A.'s maternal grandmother in another part of the country during his preschool years. The father had little contact with A. during this time, and A.'s mother's alcohol abuse seems to have been quiescent during this period. For reasons that are not clear, A. and his mother moved back to A.'s birthplace when he was 5 years old and ready for kindergarten. He rarely saw his father, and when he was about 6 years old he learned that his father had died by hanging himself. A. was informed of this event by his mother and reportedly showed little emotion. Periodically thereafter, however, he would talk of his father, wondering aloud why he had killed himself.

After A. entered first grade, he did fairly well for a while, but he was noted to have mild learning difficulties and periodic angry outbursts, with aggression directed toward himself or others. He reportedly brought a knife to school one day but would not say why he had done so. At times, he would hit himself or call himself stupid. On one occasion, he put thumbtacks into his mouth in what was thought to be a provocative, attention-seeking gesture; however, he denied intending to swallow the tacks. He was suspended from school several times because of aggression toward others; in one such incident he reportedly tried to hit a peer on the head with a chair.

When A. began to speak periodically of wanting to die, school personnel referred him for counseling, where his father's suicide some months before was discussed. A. was considered an anxious, dependent youngster with poor self-esteem. There was a pervasive sense of sadness about him; he was described as "somber," and teachers commented that he sought adult attention and related better to adults than to other children. A. was moody and affectively labile; the sad, somber periods fluctuated considerably with periods of impulsivity, anger, and irritability.

A.'s home situation during this period was characterized by marked instability. A.'s mother continued to drink, often heavily. There were several male figures involved with her, and thereby with A. His reactions to these men, who also seemed to be substance abusers, ranged from indifference to quiet anger, to overt hostility. On one occasion A. angrily challenged a man who he said had hit his mother, causing her to have severe bruises. Fortunately he himself was not attacked in response.

Child Protective Services (CPS) became involved with A. and with his mother on several occasions. The mother had been in and out of alcohol rehabilitation programs but had been unable to maintain sobriety for a sustained period. CPS found her neglectful of A.'s needs, although she had apparently not abused him. A. spent several months in foster care during times when his mother was not able to care for him, whether because she was drinking heavily or was undergoing inpatient treatment for alcoholism. A.'s adjustment in foster care was described as "fair," with continued intermittent explosive behavior and an ongoing sense of sadness and lack of enthusiasm or motivation for school work or in-depth peer relationships. A. talked openly of wanting to return to live with his mother, refusing to disclose anything negative about his life with her. He admitted that his mother had a "drinking" problem, but he denied that her problem had contributed to his own sadness or periodic self-abusive episodes, during which he would hit his head with his fists.

By age 9, A.'s behavior in school had deteriorated further. His lack of academic motivation and poor performance, aggressive outbursts, repeated self-destructive thoughts, physically self-abusive behaviors, and frequent minor "accidents" became more prominent. He was therefore referred to a day treatment program.

On initial psychiatric evaluation in that setting, A. was described as a thin, attractive, cooperative youngster. He maintained good eye contact, but his rather serious, somber demeanor was immediately evident. He complied willingly during the evaluation and spoke readily in response to most of the interviewer's questions. While he was obviously anxious when discussing his family background, he was able to share some details about his parents, sadly casting his eyes to the floor and fidgeting or drawing designs as he talked. He denied any thoughts about why the adults in his life acted as they did and would comment only briefly and superficially about his own reactions to important events in his life. He showed no signs of impulsivity or aggression during the evaluation, although he did admit to becoming angry and fighting with peers who "annoyed" him, especially by talking about his mother. It was clear that he was strongly attached to his mother and would accept no criticism of her.

Aside from chronic feelings of sadness and lack of motivation, A. admitted to no other symptoms of depression. His understanding of his difficulties with his peers was that they had simply gotten him "mad." He described himself as "bad" or "wrong" when he physically assaulted his peers, and he thought that his father had been "stupid" for killing himself. He claimed not to know why he himself periodically hit himself on the head, pounded his fist into the wall, or said that he wanted to die.

At the time of the interview, A. was in foster care because his mother's alcoholism had been particularly severe and CPS had removed him from the home. Several visits had been scheduled for A. and his mother with the Department of Social Services, but the mother's attendance at these meetings had been sporadic. A. always seemed especially sad and depressed after such disappointments. In talking with the interviewer, he acknowledged that he felt "very sad" after his mother had missed scheduled visits, but he would offer no criticism of her behavior, saying only that she had an "alcohol problem." He recognized that his suicidal ideation increased during these times, but denied feeling angry at himself or his mother. He felt that his desire to die or to hurt himself was related to his sadness, but not to anger. He also seemed to have little recognition that his stated suicidal thoughts or impulses might be a means of attempting to draw others toward him.

Countertransference

The psychiatrist's reactions during and subsequent to his interview with this youngster were a blend of sadness, hopelessness, and empathy for A., who seemed to have had more than his share of misery. The psychiatrist was quite aware of the long-standing nature of the boy's difficulties, lack of caretaking, and feelings of helplessness. A. seemed to have been placed into untenable and unfair positions by his parents, who had thoroughly neglected his needs, essentially abandoning him. The psychiatrist felt a strong attachment to the boy and a desire to care for him better than his parents had. He was particularly affected by the desperate measures A. had taken or threatened to take in an effort to relieve his feelings of depression or to punish himself as his mother seemed to have punished him by failing to arrive for their scheduled visits, the most recent series of disappointments for A.

Some of the psychiatrist's feelings of sadness and helplessness, and his desire to protect A. from further loss and rejection were, he realized, based on his own background and internalized sense of the rightful role of parents. A. himself, through his sad demeanor, his near-pleading enlistment of the examiner in games or conversation, his politeness, his ready compliance with requests, and his difficulty leaving the session, had provided the stimulus for these strong parental and nurturing reactions.

A.'s behavior had also evoked other feelings in the psychiatrist. Repeated contacts with social service agencies and with "unparented" children like A. had reinforced the psychiatrist's belief that such children are often helpless victims, caught between parents and agencies who are entrusted with their care but who are unable, because of psychological difficulties in the case of parents, and because of legal and financial constraints in the case of social service agencies, to care for them adequately or to provide consistent, nurturing environments for them.

In this case, the psychiatrist experienced frustration and anger in the face of his own helplessness to effectively improve A.'s long-term, seemingly obvious need for a consistent, nurturing parenting figure. He was angry and impatient with the social service department for not moving to terminate parental rights, thereby freeing A. from the "on-again, off-again" parenting his mother provided. The examiner felt that it was his responsibility as a psychiatrist to help A. as much as possible. The help that A. needed, it seemed to him and to other staff members, could be provided best by terminating A.'s mother's parental rights and freeing A. for adoption or at least placement in a consistent home environment.

From previous experiences with social service agencies, however, the psychiatrist knew that his perceived clinical judgment and expertise would not be sufficient to ensure an intervention that would be most psychologically beneficial to A. Legal entanglements and what the psychiatrist believed to be an exaggerated notion of "parental rights" would be placed against his training, experience, and clinical judgment about A.'s best interests. The recognition that A. was in chronic limbo between an inadequate home environment and foster care drew the psychiatrist closer to A. as he felt his helplessness more deeply, but it also made him feel more distant from A. as a self-protective mechanism, since he believed that neither his work nor that of the day treatment program staff could overcome the ongoing harm imposed by A.'s unstable environment. The psychiatrist therefore also felt some desire to withdraw from A. and not risk disappointment and failure, which had occurred in similar cases previously.

Reaction to the Parents

Among the strongest of the psychiatrist's reactions, however, were anger and resentment directed against A.'s mother and, to a lesser degree, against A.'s dead father. Little information about the mother was available at the time of the psychiatrist's interview with A.; she had failed to keep a number of appointments with the primary therapist, just as she had with A. and the social service agency. Based on information available, A.'s mother was of average intelligence and functioned reasonably well on public assistance between periods of acute alcoholism. Social service agency personnel believed that she was sincere when she stated that she wanted to stop drinking and that she wanted A. to get all the help he needed for his emotional difficulties. She herself could offer no reason for her periodic drinking episodes or for her self-destructive choice of male companions. Day treatment staff members described her as immature and dependent. On some issues, however, she was quite determined and resolute. She would not relinquish custody of A., and she would not allow him to leave her to live again with her own mother, as had been suggested repeatedly.

The psychiatrist wondered at his strongly felt and persistent anger at A.'s mother. He resented what he felt to be her destructive behavior that so negatively affected A.'s life, paralleling, it seemed, the destruction of her own life that was in progress. The psychiatrist was angry that A.'s mother had abandoned him and had failed to care for him, but he was also angry that she would clutch A. to her, refusing to relinquish custody, even temporarily, to enable him to obtain the consistent parenting and nurturance that he so obviously needed. A.'s father also received a share of the psychiatrist's internal invective for having abandoned his son, first when A. and his mother had moved away, and then a second time when he killed himself. The psychiatrist believed that A.'s lasting internalized image of his father would be of his suicide. This would remain forever a model against which A. would continue to measure his own choice to live or to die.

Conflict and Resolution

These strong, uneasily mixing impressions and feelings—of sadness, of desire to "parent" A. better than he had been parented, of desire to care for and nurture A., of frustration and anger at the slow-moving legal system and social services agencies, and of rage at A.'s unknown parents—continued to trouble the psychiatrist over the next few days as he considered an upcoming meeting with the child's primary therapist and the staff working with A. He had some concern that the strength of his countertransferential reactions to A., whom he had seen for one extended interview and several other times briefly, and to A.'s mother, whom he did not know at all, were potentially counterproductive. It seemed to him, as he further considered the situation and his reactions, that the strength of his warm, nurturing, parenting feelings for A. were in striking contrast to his rage toward A.'s mother. The psychiatrist came to suspect that his reactions to A.'s mother, which were themselves rejecting and, if she had complied, would have fulfilled his wishes to banish her from A.'s life, to "abandon" her as she had "abandoned" A., would not be helpful to A., to the staff working with the boy, or to A.'s mother.

On continued reflection, the psychiatrist came to suspect that his lack of contact with the mother during the evaluation and his lack of knowledge about her contributed to a form of splitting, whereby A. was given all of his positive feelings, as the psychologically victimized party, and A.'s mother was given all of his negative feelings, as the apparently victimizing agent. Clearly, A.'s mother, by remaining unknown, had contributed to this distortion. Nevertheless, the resultant split in which A. had received the psychiatrist's warmth, and his mother and, to some degree, the father and the social service agency had received his wrath, would not be helpful.

Recognizing this split in his own countertransference reactions, the psychiatrist decided that it would be in all parties' best interests, including his own, if he learned more about A.'s mother and father as "real people" who functioned with all the usual complexity of the parents and patients with whom he was accustomed to dealing. However, he could not actually realize this goal because A.'s father was dead and the mother was currently drinking and unavailable. The psychiatrist nonetheless met with staff members and with A.'s teacher and primary therapist for a case conference. He encouraged the staff, many of whom had engaged in the same type of splitting he had, to share whatever information and feelings they had about A.'s parents. It was found that, despite rather voluminous records of previous educational and therapeutic contacts, relatively little was known about A.'s parents.

The primary therapist offered that he knew nothing of A.'s father, but that he had spoken with A.'s mother on a number of occasions, both when she wasn't drinking and when she was drinking moderately. His assessment was that A.'s mother was quite dependent, but that she was also angry at her own mother and resentful of others' control in her life. Her numerous male companions and her drinking seemed to be attempts to deal with these feelings. A. was clearly important to her, and she depended on him to love her and be available to her, although she recognized that she was unavailable to him much of the time. About this she was troubled, and although she felt guilty, she was unable to change her own behavior or to allow A. to be parented by her own mother, who was willing to assume temporary guardianship.

A broader picture of A.'s mother gradually formed in the psychiatrist's mind. She seemed to share some of A.'s own qualities—dependency, anxiety, and immaturity, as well as an ability to relate warmly to others. She became more than merely a rejecting, selfish destroyer of A.'s potential. Partly through the primary therapist's report, A.'s mother began to emerge as a flawed parent, but a parent nonetheless. A. continued to seem a helpless victim, but the psychiatrist's increasing awareness of A.'s mother's problems and decreasing sense of anger and outrage allowed him to focus greater attention on what A., still a victim, might do to help himself, given his flawed parenting.

Working with the staff, the psychiatrist developed a treatment plan aimed at scheduling additional contacts with the department of social services to emphasize A.'s needs for more prompt decisions on custody and more emphasis on the mother's needs for treatment and consistency in attending sessions with A. Increased contacts with A.'s mother were encouraged, with the aim of establishing rapport and trust so that she would come to recognize that the treatment team was interested in her welfare as well as A.'s. Ultimately, it was reasoned, she would willingly relinquish custody of A. only if she also felt cared for herself, and only if she were enabled, with the staff's support, to recognize what her role as a caring, mature parent would require of her.

The psychiatrist agreed with the staff that therapeutic efforts would have to be directed toward enabling A.'s mother to gain self-esteem by making sound parenting decisions that were in A.'s best interests. To some degree, in this case, that meant showing added support, attention, and concern for the parent along with the child. The potential rejection and abandonment of A.'s real parent, which had accompanied an overinvolvement with A. and his needs for a "good" parent, had risked alienating his mother and prolonging his abandonment and rejection by her.

Finally, the treatment team would need to recognize A.'s love for, loyalty to, and need for his idealized mother, while also supportively allowing his expression of disappointment and anger toward her when these feelings could emerge without causing him to feel that he was rejecting her. Without blaming the mother, as was the initial tendency of the psychiatrist and some of the staff members, A. was encouraged to learn coping skills and more adaptive means to deal with times when his mother would not or could not satisfy his legitimate needs.

The therapeutic work was slow but ultimately fruitful. A.'s suicide threats, self-punishing behavior, impulsivity, and dysphoria remitted, and his mother agreed to his moving away to live with her own mother more than 1,000 miles away. There, it was reported, he was forming relationships and doing well in a regular school environment.

COUNTERTRANSFERENCE IN WORK WITH DEPRESSED ADOLESCENTS

Therapeutic work with adolescents places particular personal burdens on the therapist that usually do not encumber the treatment of children or adults. Adolescents may be as devoid of restraint as younger children, yet the consequences of their impulsivity are much more serious, leading to excessive concern in the therapist. The adolescent's tendency to externalize internal conflicts may cause the therapist to take action rather than deal with the underlying difficulty. Adolescents are notorious for expressing extremes in mood, rapidly shifting from maniclike ebullience to profound despair, thereby testing the therapist's ability to continue the task of exploration and clarification of psychic contents.

Positive aspects of adolescence may also arouse unwelcome feelings in the therapist. As noted by Galatzer-Levy (1990), the physical vigor, beauty, and limitless range of opportunities open to adolescents can elicit the envy of therapists. Their industry, sense of fairness, and open demand for recognition may also evoke the therapist's jealousy. There is little question that this stage of development can be a most unsettled—and unsettling—time not only for the adolescent, but also for those around him. Most therapists will readily recall their own adolescence as an unsettled and unsettling time in their lives, so working with adolescent patients can elicit a range of old feelings and desires, both pleasant and painful. Psychotherapy with adolescents revives the tribulations and gratifications of this developmental stage, and the degree to which these historical artifacts interfere with treatment depends largely on the degree to which the therapist has come to terms with his own adolescence.

One obvious danger is that the therapist will act out vicariously through the patient, subtly encouraging the adolescent into potentially dangerous activities in the name of psychological freedom. The opposite reaction is also not uncommon, wherein the therapist may be overly critical or contemptuous of the adolescent for behaving in a manner of which the therapist is secretly envious and that represents experiences the therapist wishes he had had as a youngster.

While these countertransference reactions occur frequently in the treatment of most adolescents, they are exceedingly rare in therapy with depressed youngsters. These patients are usually so inhibited or self-punitive that their plight can scarcely arouse envy or allow for vicarious excitement. Rather, depressed adolescents may cause the therapist to feel protective of and sorry for a youngster who is not able to take advantage of a potentially enjoyable time of life that is relatively free of responsibility. As therapy progresses, however, if there is little movement or change, these initial benevolent feelings may turn to anger, frustration, or boredom. These countertransference reactions usually result from the therapist's feeling defeated by the patient and his illness and sensing that therapy is at a stalemate.

Clinical depression in adolescents takes two major psychodynamic forms, and each may evoke different countertransference reactions in the therapist. Experienced clinicians such as Jacobson (1961) and Anthony (1970) have classified adolescent depressions as falling into two major types, similar to those noted in adults. A wide variety of labels have been used to classify these depressive types; however, Blatt's (1976) terms *anaclitic* and *introjective* seem most appropriate.

Anaclitic Depression

Briefly, anaclitic depression entails psychopathology resulting from the inability to separate psychologically from one's family of origin.

Individuals who suffer from anaclitic depression are not sufficiently individuated to function adequately without a parental figure, and they respond to demands for autonomy with despair, anxiety, and depression. When strong atavistic dependency needs emerge in times of stress, the adolescent, who is trying hard to see himself as an independent adult, feels ashamed of and humiliated by his own dependency. These youngsters continue to require an omnipotent, need-satisfying parental substitute and are exceedingly frightened by the changes that transpire in their social expectations and psychological functioning as a result of their maturation. They typically decompensate when they are forced to venture out on their own and realize their limitations, which had previously been hidden or compensated for by family and its attendant security.

One such individual presented for therapy a few months after starting his freshman year at a prestigious university. He had high hopes and expectations for his college career. Since arriving at the school, however, he had become increasingly anxious, withdrawn, and depressed. History revealed that he had been an outstanding student in high school, obtaining excellent grades and receiving numerous awards and honors. In contrast to his admirable academic achievement, however, his social and interpersonal skills were markedly underdeveloped. He had never established true friendships outside his family, and his few dates for special occasions had been arranged by his parents. He seemed not to have begun, much less mastered, the social tasks of the latency period as represented in our culture, during which the child begins to search outside the family orbit for companionship, closeness, and sources of gratification and self-esteem. Developmentally, this patient was an oedipal-stage child in an adolescent's body; he continued to need parental nurturance, approval, and direction. It was not surprising that he felt utterly lost and acutely lonely upon leaving home. His one major source of self-worth, his scholastic ability, was no longer a special asset, as his new peers were academically equal to him, and there was little importance afforded to academic ability as compared to dating and social skills. His lack of social and interpersonal abilities became increasingly evident with time; he was at a loss as to how to relate to others, and he experienced their neutrality or indifference as rejections and rebuffs. The final blow to his already shaky narcissism came when he achieved only average grades on his midterm exams; to him, this represented the loss of his one admirable or special quality.

This youngster's behavior in therapy reproduced his relationship to his parents: he expected the therapist to "fix things" so that he would feel better. He had little awareness of any obligation to help himself. He would come to therapy and complain for a while, relating the latest events that had made him miserable, and then would remain silent, expecting reassurance or directions.

He called his therapist frequently between sessions to complain of being unable to study or of being lonely, and he felt hurt if his calls were not returned immediately. After a few weeks he began arriving for sessions 2 to 3 hours early and sat in the waiting room, as if this location afforded him some security and relief from loneliness.

The patient's profound despair and his urgent demand for immediate relief prevented him from profiting from any sort of interpretations or historical reconstructions. Medication was tried, with some benefit from anxiolytics but no benefit from antidepressants. The therapist also assumed a more directive role, suggesting possible activities, such as joining clubs or working on the college newspaper or yearbook, that might ease the patient's loneliness and allow him to put his abilities to use in a social setting. However, this youngster found reasons for not following through on recommendations, eventually revealing a basic belief that it would be humiliating for someone of his intellectual ability to seek out or accept the menial tasks assigned to freshmen in the various campus organizations. Therapy stagnated, and little progress was made as the patient continued to resist change and the therapist felt increasingly helpless and frustrated.

This clinical situation is far from unique in the therapy of adolescents with anaclitic forms of depression. These patients' narcissistic mode of relating to others drains the therapist, who feels that he is constantly giving while receiving little in return. Anthony (1970) remarks that one such patient made him feel like the proverbial cupboard that offered constant nurturance as he occasionally hungered for some evidence of a more reciprocal relationship. Golombek (1983) also describes how therapists with demanding adolescent patients feel that they are merely filling stations or cows; that is, they are simply providers who do not merit the status of a whole person. When such demandingness is coupled with a lack of cooperation or of acceptance of mutual responsibility, the initial benevolence elicited by these youngsters can turn to anger and a sense of therapeutic futility. If the therapist acknowledges these feelings, he can honestly evaluate the appropriateness of or potential benefit from therapy for the patient. Peer supervision or consultation with another therapist can be helpful in finding hidden avenues by which to engage the patient or in objectively deciding the suitability of psychotherapy or the need for other treatments. However, if the therapist represses or does not acknowledge his countertransference feelings, he may find himself dreading the sessions with his depressed patient and may express his anger or contempt through critical interpretations or by subtly encouraging the patient to terminate therapy. A particularly difficult aspect of treating youngsters who are so overwhelmed with despair and hopelessness is that their dysphoria pervades the therapist with a sense of gloom and futility. This contagion of affect often results in the therapist's countering his own sense of melancholia by an exaggerated sense of good humor or by minimizing the depth of his patient's depression. This reaction may be especially selected by therapists who have a propensity to depression themselves and who find that their empathic resonance with the patient's dysphoria threatens to evoke their own depressive feelings. The obvious danger of this countertransference situation is that the patient will sense that his suffering is being trivialized or that the therapist does not appreciate the true severity of his illness.

The therapeutic task required for anaclitic depressions of adolescence is to relive as much as possible the period of latency at a later developmental period (Bemporad 1988). Problems usually arise, however, because it is difficult, if not impossible, for the patient to relive latency authentically while facing everyday demands of adolescent existence. Some depressed adolescents simply cannot fulfill age-appropriate tasks while simultaneously learning to cope with life outside their accustomed family structure. In such cases, individual therapy may be neither sufficient nor appropriate and may result in a therapeutic stalemate, wherein the patient desires only relief from dysphoria and protection from developmental demands while the therapist is still attempting to augment further development and encourage greater (if more painful) self-awareness. Such a situation is bound to evoke strong countertransference reactions, since the patient and therapist are at markedly cross-purposes. In the case just described, peer supervision helped the therapist realize that the patient was so overwhelmed by his daily college life that he could not participate in therapy. It was decided, with the patient and his parents' approval, that he would take a year off from school and attend combined group and individual therapy while living at home. Free of the pressures that were the immediate cause of his symptoms, this youngster was able to learn, in a gradual manner, to separate psychologically from his parents, to develop interpersonal skills, and to establish a more valid estimate of himself compared to others at his own developmental stage.

Introjective Depression

This form of depression occurs among adolescents who have been able to separate from their families and appear to function independently. However, they still carry within themselves irrational and unrealistic internalizations of parental values so that they are unable to deal with the opportunities for pleasure or freedom that are normally part of the adolescent experience. As their widening world presents them with the potential for new gratifications, new relationships, or new beliefs, they recoil from their own stimulated desires with shame, guilt, and a sense of betrayal of their loyalty to their families. These youngsters retain an idealized version of one or both parents whom they believe they must continue to please and placate. If they dare to break with familial expectations, they torture themselves with self-recriminations. On the other hand, if they hold to their often distorted sense of values, they perceive themselves as empty and lifeless and their existence as devoid of meaning or satisfaction.

Such adolescents are capable of the darkest despair and the deepest self-loathing—feelings that often lead to suicide as a means of removing themselves from what appears to be an irresolvable conflict. In contrast to adolescents with anaclitic depression, who present with agitation, panic, urgency, and a demand to be relieved of their suffering, youngsters with introjective depression more often present with psychomotor retardation, a sense of overall shame and guilt, and a feeling that no one can help them. Instead of clamoring for relief, they quickly convey their conviction that any relief is impossible and that they are doomed to an anhedonic, painful existence—which is mostly deserved. The following patient's case exemplifies introjective depression.

A college sophomore was referred for treatment, against her wishes, by her parents. She easily reconstructed the history of her illness and clearly stated her belief that she understood all there was to know about it, so that therapy would be a waste of time and money. This young woman described herself as having functioned quite well throughout most of her life. She had enjoyed her college days and had made the transition from home to university life without difficulty. At the start of her sophomore year, she started dating a fellow student and fell in love with him. As the relationship became more intimate, she acquiesced to his requests for intercourse, even though she had been taught by her family that she should remain a virgin until marriage. She continued to have sexual relations with her boyfriend, but she felt guilty about her behavior and did not allow herself to enjoy sex. She justified her behavior as being consonant with that of her fellow students.

While on a visit home for the Thanksgiving holiday, she told her parents about her boyfriend and let it be understood by her description that they were sexually active. At that moment in the conversation, her parents became hysterical, with her mother collapsing in tears and her father shouting, "How could you do this to us!" The patient recalled that at that moment her entire world collapsed around her. She ran from the room in tears, feeling that she had irrevocably injured those who had most loved and cared about her. Her parents regained their composure and after some time apologized to her for creating such a scene, stating that she was now an adult and could live as she chose. The matter was not discussed again, but the patient believed that a wall had fallen between herself and her parents. She felt sure that their considerate, understanding behavior was merely hiding their deep disappointment in her and served as further proof of her parents' love for her.

Upon returning to college, she vowed to conquer her "immoral" desires and never to disappoint her parents again. She gave up her boyfriend despite her strong feelings for him and devoted herself exclusively to making good grades so as to make her parents proud of her again and make up for the hurt she had inflicted on them. Even after she withdrew from socializing, she still felt guilty and ashamed about her former behavior, but, in addition, she found that she was losing interest in all of her activities. She started spending time alone in her room, trying to study but finding that school meant less and less to her. She became perpetually tired, had difficulty sleeping and eating, and soon doubted the purpose of existence. When she presented for therapy, she was severely depressed, with vegetative symptoms and marked suicidal preoccupation.

Adolescents with introjective depression elicit a different countertransference reaction from those with anaclitic depression. These youngsters are more psychologically mature, and their conflicts are similar to those of adults. Therefore, it is easier for the therapist to identify with them and to feel their depression more strongly. As Anthony (1970) comments, these adolescents are usually accomplished, responsible individuals, and therapists may genuinely admire them and like them, feeling all the more pressured to rescue them from their misery. The major potential countertransference pitfall is that these patients' despair will overwhelm the therapist, who finds in them a kindred spirit. They often present with very logical reasons for doubting the worth of living and have firmly entrenched belief systems that are not only difficult to alter but may even convince the therapist. In writing of such patients, Anthony (1970) cites a joke of Freud's about a meeting between a priest and a moribund insurance agent, at the end of which the dying man was not converted but the priest was insured.

Therapists who treat these depressed youngsters need to appreciate their depression while neither succumbing to it themselves nor defending against it with trivialization or jocularity. If they had similar feelings themselves as adolescents, or if they have not developed secure and satisfying moral systems of their own that can withstand the patient's existential questioning, then there is a danger of countertransference reactions that may be expressed by the excessive need to change the patient's values in order to reassure themselves.

The other therapeutic difficulty encountered with these patients is the likelihood of sudden and unexpected decompensation in the face of some environmental stressor. Youngsters with introjective depression give the appearance of adult, responsible functioning; in reality, however, they are still adolescents who lack a backlog of experience to moderate their reactions to everyday events. Their fledgling sense of self is still very dependent on the responses of the world around them, and a collapse of this sense of self may be expected on occasion. Therefore, months of painstaking therapeutic work may seem to evaporate if the patient fails an exam or is turned down for a date. In the event of such disappointments, there ensues a rapid and dramatic return of all the former self-recriminations and feelings of hopelessness and despair. Such "regressions" are common in the treatment of adolescents but may take the therapist by surprise when they occur in a patient who, despite his age, appeared so mature and self-reliant. Obviously, these disruptions are frustrating and disheartening to most therapists. However, these episodes may be seen as serving a crucial function in the adolescent's development. These reversals can be used to demonstrate that one can surmount difficulties with less dire consequences than were imagined and that human existence is seldom a continuum of achievement and satisfaction but rather is fraught with some failure and humiliation.

THE SUICIDAL ADOLESCENT

The overwhelming urgency of the adolescent's affects, his ability to project himself into the future coupled with his inability to moderate this predictive thinking, and his extensive reliance on external sources for a sense of worth contribute to the propensity to suicidal behavior as a means of immediate relief from what is seen as an unbearable situation. This propensity is understandably frightening to most therapists, and the prospect of a successful suicide by a patient who still had so much life ahead of him fills most therapists with a sense of dread, sadness, and personal failure. The possibility of an adolescent patient's suicide may be so difficult to contemplate that obvious clues are overlooked or minimized rather than considered seriously. In reality, the high frequency of self-destructive acts in this age group (Shaffer 1986) should alert the therapist to such a possibility in all severely disturbed youngsters. The suicidal adolescent represents a threat to the therapist's professional identity and to his sense of worth as a member of a helping profession. The range of reactions to such a profound threat can range from overprotection and grandiose rescue fantasies, in which the therapist believes that he is the one with sufficient ability to make the patient see that life is worth living, to the wish to be rid of such a disturbing patient and to blame the youngster for "controlling" treatment with powerful suicide threats. These reactions probably derive from the omnipotent fantasy that the therapist bears all the responsibility for the patient's behavior. When a patient in therapy presents the potential for destructive behavior that is beyond his control, other service agencies or individuals in the patient's life may be called upon for help. The therapist's fear for an adolescent patient's safety can be greatly relieved by informing other responsible individuals in the patient's life, such as family or school authorities, of this possibility or, ultimately, by arranging for hospitalization.

The suicidal adolescent, perhaps more than any other patient, lays bare the limitations of psychotherapy as a treatment modality. The best way to deal with the expected countertransference reactions aroused by such a confrontation with helplessness is to admit and accept these limitations and then act accordingly in the best interests of the patient.

CONCLUSION

This chapter has described some countertransference reactions that are commonly observed in psychotherapy with depressed children and adolescents. These reactions are determined partially by the patient's developmental level, partially by the nature of the disorder, and partially by the idiosyncratic personal characteristics of individual patients and therapists. The most prevalent countertransference reactions are those in response to the patient's profound dysphoria, which at times threatens to overwhelm the therapist and may lead to denial, minimalization, avoidance, and anger. The equally compelling desire to relieve such a young individual from his misery leads to protectiveness and, in the case of children, to displacement of negative feelings onto the parents, who are held responsible for the patient's condition. As therapy progresses, however, the patient's failure to respond rapidly may give rise to feelings of helplessness in the therapist and to threats to his own estimation of his professional ability. This sense of powerlessness and ineffectiveness, which reaches its maximum when the therapist is confronted by suicide threats, is difficult to admit in view of the injury involved to the therapist's narcissism. An honest acknowledgement of the limitations of psychotherapy for some patients and the search for alternate or supplementary treatments may be the best ways to deal with these countertransference reactions.

6

Treatment of Infants and Their Families

Barry M. Wright, Ph.D.

Therapists working in the model of intensive home-based infant–parent psychotherapy (Fraiberg 1980, Trout 1986, Weatherston and Tableman 1989, Wright 1986) rapidly discover that a good working understanding of countertransference is essential both for effective therapy and for their own psychological survival. The presence of an infant dramatically intensifies the preverbal and affectively primitive aspects of the therapist's countertransference experience. Even the experienced therapist is quickly drawn from emotional neutrality into the sea of painfully conflicted, emotionally volatile nonverbal communications that occur between parents and infants.

A practical yet theory-based approach to understanding and using the countertransference experience is a primary element in successful infant–parent psychotherapy. In developing such an approach, I will suggest a framework that can be of particular use in understanding the confusing and chaotic real-world relationships between parents and infants. This framework, heavily influenced by Racker's (1968) formulations of countertransference, focuses less on narrowly defining countertransference than on using the clinician's broad affective experience. It seems most pragmatic, yet theoretically sound, to start with the affective world as experienced by the therapist.

The first step in understanding and using the therapist's affective experience is one that may appear deceptively simple. We must begin by fully acknowledging the extraordinary intensity and range of emotions experienced in working with parents and infants. At times the experience is affirming, even joyful, as parents and infants are finally able to connect with pleasure and trust. At these moments the therapist is able to identify with the success of the parents and the pleasure of the infant. Obviously, however, these are not the affects that are difficult for the therapist to acknowledge. What *is* difficult, particularly when engaged in the lofty enterprise of helping infants and parents, is to acknowledge less-than-lofty feelings. At times we may feel disgust to the point of nausea, rage to the point of wanting to assault the parents more violently than they are assaulting their infant, depression and hopelessness to the point of falling asleep, or emptiness and disconnection to the point that the session becomes a silent movie.

The therapist must not only acknowledge but also sustain these strong and troublesome feelings. This is by no means a simple task. Yet if the therapist has sufficiently processed her own issues, then, in Heimann's words, it is possible to "sustain the feelings . . . as opposed to discharging them (as does the patient), in order to subordinate them to the analytic task" (1950, p. 82).

When the therapist can sustain these feelings, it is always possible to pursue two associative paths. One path leads back to the therapist's history and issues, while the other path leads to the parent's history and the issues in the infant–parent relationship. Sandler has commented on the inclination of the analyst to regard "some aspect of his own behavior as deriving entirely from within himself when it could more usefully be seen as a *compromise* between his own tendencies or propensities and the role-relationships which the patient is unconsciously seeking to establish" (1976, p. 47).

It is of theoretical as well as practical importance to avoid dichotomizing these two elements, which are always present and always intertwined. It is all too natural for the therapist, aware of those elements in the infant–parent dyad that may resonate with her own issues, to focus exclusively on her personal contribution to the countertransference experience. In so doing, she may miss a key element that the infant and parent are communicating. Instead, the therapist can stay more accurately attuned to the therapeutic moment if she presumes that *the countertransference is always a reflection of internal sensitivities and a communication from the patient.* Since these elements always intertwine, the therapist must continually attend to her own contribution to the countertransference experience. In so doing, however, she must not lose sight of the patient's contribution. This chapter focuses on understanding and decoding the patient's contribution: the induced countertransference.

THEORETICAL FRAMEWORK

Parents and infants communicate nonverbally with each other and with the therapist. Two parallel nonverbal channels transmit essential unconscious information to the therapist: the enacted parent–infant relationship and the countertransference induced in the therapist. Projective identification is the primary medium of communication in both channels. Through the first channel, the enacted parent–infant relationship, the therapist is able to learn about the parent's past. The parent's most archaic, preverbal internalized relationships come alive through the observed interaction between infant and parent. These are the phenomena that Fraiberg (1980) so evocatively described as "ghosts in the nursery." Analytically, the parent's projective identifications distort perceptions of the infant, the parent's self, and the affective linkage between them. This is a specific case of the formulation that an object relationship consists of an internal object affectively linked to a representation of the self (Kernberg 1976). The parent's old internalized relationship (for example, the archaic object relationship between self and mother) appears now between this parent and infant.

Typically, the parent projects one side of the old relationship onto the infant and then assumes the complementary role. Thus, the parent reenacts an old, unresolved internalized relationship in the current interpersonal relationship. The mother may see the baby as her old "bad" baby self and enact the role of her "bad" mother. Or the situation may be reversed: the mother may feel as if she is a helpless infant and perceive the infant as the frustrating or tyrannical parent.

Understanding the elements of projective identification can dramatically clarify the enacted parent—infant relationship. Phenomena that are otherwise astonishing and bewildering, such as a mother saying that her 3-week-old infant is "bad" and "out to get me," become transparent. The parent is projecting the role of the internalized bad parent onto the young infant and assuming the internalized role of the helpless and abused baby self.

Processes of projective identification are elegantly clear in theory, and sometimes in practice as well. At other times, kaleidoscopically shifting projections and real family chaos make it extraordinarily difficult to decode this channel of communication. Yet through this bewildering milieu, parents and infants are also communicating to us through induced countertransference.

Understanding induced countertransference as an element of projective identification conceptually parallels our understanding of distortions in the infant–parent relationship. This conceptualization also has the advantage of bridging the parent's intrapsychic structure and interpersonal processes directed toward the infant or the therapist. Very simply, the therapist may find the infant or herself, or both, experiencing one side of the parent's internal drama. In so doing, the therapist unconsciously identifies with the parent's self or with an internal object. Racker (1968) described these, respectively, as concordant and complementary identifications. This means that *in infant–parent psychotherapy, the countertransference experience typically involves identification with the position of the patient's infant self or of the archaic internalized parent.*

This framework for thinking about countertransference in infant–parent psychotherapy can be an extremely powerful tool for hypothesizing about three critical relationships: the parent's internalized relationships, the enacted infant–parent relationship, and the therapeutic relationship. In essence, the induced countertransference creates within the therapist an affective template through which to clarify all three relationships.

If the induced countertransference is a projection of one position of the patient's internalized parent–infant relationship, we can begin to hypothesize about the other, interlocking position. The therapist identifying with the internalized parent may find herself feeling terribly critical or punitive. We can guess with confidence that the patient, as an infant and young child, felt criticized and punished. If the therapist is identifying with the parent's archaic infant self, he may feel hungry, helpless, or abandoned. Again, it is not difficult to surmise that the parent's parent was emotionally depriving. The cluster of feelings induced within the therapist invariably suggests something about the relational complement, which is also internalized within the patient.

A therapist working over time with a distant and denying parent of a failure-to-thrive infant may come to feel hungry and abandoned. It could be important to hypothesize that the mother is defending against a ravenous infant self, particularly if she is presenting a rigid facade of indifference. The hypothesis that the mother is defending against her own internal hunger suggests avenues of therapeutic exploration. Of perhaps even greater importance, inferences about the patient's infant self can help the therapist stay empathically attuned in spite of the patient's discouraging defensiveness.

Hypotheses about the parent's internalized relationships also shed new light on the observed relationship between parent and infant. For example, the therapist may find herself wanting to avoid a particular family for no obvious reason. The patient may be ostensibly receptive, the house safe and organized, and the family relatively well functioning. The infant and toddler are receiving adequate care and are not the focus of particularly hostile projections. Nevertheless, the therapist may find herself hoping that the patient will not be home for a scheduled visit, or she may be delighted when the session finally ends. The affect induced within the therapist, the wish to avoid or abandon, suggests an affect that may be central to the parent's internalized relationships and the enacted relationship with the infant. Closer observation may reveal that beneath the relative adequacy of the parent's caregiving, both infant and therapist may be reacting to the parent's latent wish to abandon. Such a hypothesis can guide observation and suggest feelings that the parent needs help to verbalize so that they will not be acted out at the expense of the children.

The affect induced within the therapist may clarify what is being projected onto the infant, what the parent is defending against enacting with the infant, or what the infant may already be feeling. Since the induced countertransference can tell us about either side of the relationship, it can tell us about the infant as well as the parent. For example, the therapist may find herself feeling disconnected or nonexistent. This suggests a quality of the infant's—as well as the parent's—affective experience of self.

At a practical level, it is important to remember that the negative feelings, such as depression, anger, and frustration, that prompt a therapist to close a case may also be communications about the infant's experience. Thus the disturbing feelings that may provoke termination can also, when understood more fully, renew empathy with the infant and motivation with the family. In addition, the particular affects induced in the therapist point to the affective needs of the infant and parent.

The therapist can use each of the two parallel channels of nonverbal information, the enacted infant–parent relationship and the induced countertransference, to clarify the other. Because nonverbal communication can be so difficult to discern clearly, having two channels is enormously helpful. Distortions in the infant–parent relationship can help the therapist decode her countertransference reactions. For example, a highly eroticized baby game may clarify affects that have been unspoken in the transference–countertransference relationship. Or an understanding of the countertransference relationship may help the therapist pinpoint the unspoken problems in the infant–parent relationship. In this case, a therapist's awareness of feeling seduced suggests that she watch and listen very closely for eroticized interactions between parent and infant.

Induced countertransference illuminates not only the parent's internalized relationships and the enacted relationship between parent and infant but also the therapeutic relationship. The processes of projective identification that characterize the parent's relationship with the infant have a parallel life in the therapeutic relationship. In both relationships, the parent unconsciously recreates pathological internalized relationships. This recreation is defensive, as painful affects are projected and their origins are denied. Yet the recreations, particularly with the infant, are driven by hope. This hope, as in any repetition compulsion, reflects the drive for mastery. In infant work there is also the pervasive hope for affective attunement. The patient desperately hopes that her message will be received, decoded, and responded to, that someone will finally get it right. Without therapeutic intervention, this wish is often projected onto the infant. The parent will eventually punish or reject the infant for failing at this task, which is enormously complex even for the therapist.

A brief example can illustrate how induced countertransference allows inferences about all three critical relationships: the parent's internalized relationships, the current relationship between parent and infant, and the therapeutic relationship. While the range of possible examples is limitless, I have chosen an affect that is neither uncommon nor commonly discussed: repulsion. The patient who elicited these feelings of repulsion presented as a consciously dedicated parent who was also helpless, hopeless, and gratuitously unattractive. She appeared to be a "loser" who sought redemption through parenthood. As the therapist, I found it easy to like her initially, since she was genuinely motivated to get help for herself and her infant. Yet over time those feelings gradually changed as therapeutic efforts brought meager results. I began to feel impatient and critical of the patient's insatiable dependency needs. As a counterpoint to the patient's emotional morass, I found myself quietly entertaining sadistic thoughts. I began thinking of funny stories to tell my colleagues when I returned to the office, stories at my patient's expense. At least such an unpleasant reaction was sufficiently dystonic to signal the presence of induced countertransference.

This rudimentary countertransference experience of repulsion combined with distancing and sadism suggests implications for all three levels of relationship, beginning with the internalized relationships. It is not difficult to understand the induced effect as a complementary identification, an identification with the internalized parental object. This suggests that the internalized parental object was rejecting, yet demanding and perhaps sadistic. This hypothesis was of particular value, since this patient was more convincing than many in describing a secure, happy childhood. She spoke fondly of the family's maids and the abundance of presents she received on holidays. The patient could not approach the visceral rejection she felt as an infant, foreshadowed by the countertransference, until well into the second year of treatment.

The induced countertransference was also helpful in anticipating important issues in the relationship between mother and infant. The mother appeared all-suffering, keeping the infant at the center of her life and lavishing much more care on her infant than on herself. She described doing everything in her power to nurture her infant, even as she began to describe her infant as demanding and difficult to satisfy. These qualities are usually a welcome relief when working with a high-risk population. Consequently, the induced countertransferential elements of repulsion and sadism were of particular importance in signaling elements below the surface presentation.

If her projective identification became more primitive and intense under environmental or intrapsychic pressure, this mother might begin to see the baby as not only difficult but even "out to get" her. She would be at risk for reversing the projected relationship. She might give up the masochistic role, trying to meet *all* of her baby's needs, and assume the role of the internalized sadistic parent. At that moment she could then become rejecting or potentially abusive toward her infant. She would be enacting the affective role she had previously induced in her therapist.

As a general principle, the intensity and dissonance of the induced countertransference suggest the intensity of the split-off affect in the parent. The countertransference helps the therapist anticipate the complementary side of the projected relationship and the degree of danger to the infant when the projected role relationship switches.

The induced countertransference also guides the therapeutic relationship. It is obvious that the therapist must avoid being rejecting or sadistic in interpretations or actions. Yet this is not nearly as easy as it "should" be, given the way that characterologically disturbed patients, who desperately need confrontation, invite retaliation or abandonment. Simply censoring the negative countertransference is far from sufficient, since this would amount to a subtle but profound abandonment of the affective core of the parent and the infant–parent relationship. In this example, simply repressing the sadistic, rejecting countertransference might be benign but not particularly helpful. This mother desperately needed permission, guidance, and safety in exploring her own negative affects with respect to her parents, her infant, and her therapist. The induced countertransference underscored the absolute centrality of the patient's painful memories of rejection and her own rage and sadism. This was of particular importance, since these issues, latent in words and behavior, placed the infant at serious risk.

COUNTERTRANSFERENCE COMPLICATIONS IN HOME-BASED THERAPY

The infant–parent psychotherapist working in the home faces severe complications in the identification of induced countertransference. Four factors make it more difficult to identify induced transference: the presence of the infant, parental psychopathology, the home setting, and the complications of outreach. Each of these factors muddies yet intensifies the therapist's nonverbal perceptions. At the same time, these very factors make it all the more essential that the therapist identify and use the countertransference accurately. In the example of repulsion just described, the therapist could identify the induced countertransference relatively easily. The troublesome affect was dystonic for the therapist and relatively discrepant from the observed infant–parent relationship. In most situations it is much more difficult.

The first complicating factor, the presence of the infant, has a power that is difficult to describe in words. On all counts, the therapist's concern for the preverbal infant heightens the affectively primitive nature of the countertransference experience. Simultaneously, the therapist's "objective" countertransference reaction (Winnicott 1949) is intense when the infant is repeatedly the object of hostility, pain, and abandonment. The confluence of painfully observed interactions and concern for the preverbal infant pulls the therapist toward complementary or concordant identifications with the infant. The therapist identifies with the parent role or with the infant directly.

In the complementary identification, the therapist wishes to be the "all-good" parent and rescue the infant. Because this is a role-syntonic affective experience, the therapist can readily raise this identification to consciousness. Unfortunately, this identification in itself does little to help the parent or the infant. The therapist is not typically in the position to act out the role of rescuer and, when the empathic link with the parent is broken, nothing can be accomplished therapeutically.

In the concordant identification, the therapist merges with the affective state of the infant. This merger can easily lead to feeling emotional hunger, rage toward the parent, or detached hopelessness in the face of the "all-bad" parent. The therapist will defend more vigorously against awareness of these identifications because they are all painful *and* role dystonic. Yet the therapist who fails to acknowledge and process this affective experience will remain a captive of her preverbal identification with the infant. Obviously, working from an affectively primitive identification with the infant's anger, hunger, or hopelessness is an impossible therapeutic position. Instead, the therapist must become aware of the identification as a communication from the infant and, in all probability, the internalized infant hidden within the parent.

The second complicating factor is the level of parental psychopathology the infant–parent therapist encounters. Parents having psychodynamic problems relating to their infants are often characterologically disturbed, with deeply embedded preverbal conflicts and traumas. Even for parents with more psychological structure, conflicts with an infant spring from the earliest layers of their own development.

Parents communicate about their preverbal issues through interaction with their infants and the countertransference induced in the therapist. What they show through the infant and the induced countertransference is intense and often abhorrent, as primitive experiences of abandonment, rage, sadism, and despair are recreated viscerally. Through projective identification, the parents try to replicate and master their internalized relationships by provoking retaliatory abandonment or rejection from the therapist.

The third factor that complicates the identification of countertransference is the fact that the therapist operates on foreign territory—the patient's home. In office-based work, the therapist has some symbols of power and status as well as relative control over the environment. In home based infant–parent psychotherapy, the therapist's definition of herself and her mission is constantly challenged, diluted, or simply ignored. Unidentified neighbors drop by, people make drug deals, sad children stare through doorways, and the television drones on. The therapist's boundaries are pressed as she immerses herself in a chaotic, boundariless, and often nonverbal family.

In the home, extraordinary dramas affectively assault the therapist. Parents and infants do not report their pain; they enact it. Parents refuse to feed a hungry infant and then scream at him for crying. Parents display the angry wounds of fresh abuse on their infants' and their own bodies. The therapist's position and boundaries are weakened as her senses are flooded. From the affectively overwhelming home environment, she must tease apart the "objective," the personal, and the induced countertransference elements in her experience. While this can feel nearly impossible, it is imperative for her survival and effectiveness.

The very model of an outreach intervention creates a pervasive complexity. Fraiberg (1980) cautioned therapists from the inception of this model to "sit on their hands," to reflect rather than act, as parents struggle to relate with their infants. This caution came, in part, from the need to delineate infant–parent psychotherapy from traditional models of home visiting with infants and parents. To an even greater extent, the caution is a response to the fact that however strictly the therapist wishes to maintain the therapeutic frame, the therapist going into the home enters a milieu of actions. Going to the home, or perhaps the hospital, the jail, or the graveyard, are interventions that begin with the therapist's action. The therapist may take a sick infant or parent to a physician's office or to the emergency room. At other times the therapist may have to act quickly and decisively to maintain safety in the midst of chaos and family violence. There are times, for example, when the therapist must call the police or Children's Protective Services if the parent cannot.

It is an inescapable fact that actions are part of the basic currency of infant–parent psychotherapy. Actions are required as a response to the realities of infants living in extremely high-risk environments. At critical junctures, the therapist must respond in word and deed to necessity and danger. Actions are also an intrinsic element in responding to the preverbal world of infant and parent. This is not to argue that infant–parent psychotherapy is a therapy of actions instead of words. Rather, I am arguing that reality and therapeutic effectiveness demand that actions and words be congruent in communicating with both the preverbal and the verbal domains of the infant and parent. At critical junctures, it is not enough for the therapist to answer a phone call from a desperate parent by expressing concern verbally and offering to talk more the next time the patient can find transportation to get to an appointment. Words without the corresponding appropriate action, such as going to the home, hospital, or courthouse, cannot speak to the preverbal layer of distrust and abandonment in the parent.

Because actions are such an elemental theme in infant–parent psychotherapy, the therapist must be infinitely more aware of countertransference responses. The office-based therapist can presume that the urge to act is countertransferential and countertherapeutic. For the home-based infant–parent psychotherapist, there is not such a clear presumption. Instead, the therapist must determine whether she is acting out the induced countertransference (the pathological role that the patient is projecting onto her) or using her affective experience to guide actions therapeutically.

IDENTIFICATION OF INDUCED
COUNTERTRANSFERENCE

Even the most experienced therapist working with infants and parents in the home milieu needs operational rules for identifying induced countertransference. When affectively flooded by pathological transactions, the therapist needs practical, even oversimplified, guidelines to identify intense yet kaleidoscopic countertransference phenomena. I will suggest two guidelines or questions that seem of particular relevance in infant–parent psychotherapy.

The first question a therapist may ask herself is whether she is maintaining a "holding environment" for the infant and parent. The affective challenge in infant–parent psychotherapy is much like that which Winnicott (1958, 1960) described in good-enough mothering. Just as the mother must be able to withstand the instinctual assaults of the infant, the therapist must be able to sustain the assault of the transference–countertransference experience without retaliation or withdrawal. Further, the therapist must strive to provide such a holding environment for *both* infant and parent. It is all too easy to identify exclusively with one side of the relationship, often the infant, and retaliate against or emotionally abandon the other, the parent.

The therapist can easily tell when her wishes to retaliate threaten the holding environment, since blatantly negative affect so clearly violates the therapeutic ethos. Abandonment or passive aggression, however, can come in a variety of much more acceptable disguises. Consequently, these are perhaps the most common forms in which the therapist unwittingly acts out countertransference.

Particularly for the overextended therapist working in an outreach model, it is all too easy to taper off efforts to reach an avoidant family or to fail to make another phone call or drop-in visit. It is all too easy, influenced by reality and unconscious countertransference, to decide that a patient is "unmotivated" or "too low-functioning" to benefit from treatment. While these may be perfectly appropriate decisions that every therapist must make at times, the infant–parent therapist must be especially careful to weigh the contribution of the induced counter-transference. Since parents having difficulty with their infants so typically have historical issues around abandonment and loss, the therapist must decide whether she is enacting the role being projected onto her, the role of the abandoning parent.

Impulses to abandon or retaliate are pervasive countertransference experiences, especially in infant–parent psychotherpay with extremely dysfunctional families. When the therapist feels the wish to abandon the patient, the feeling need not be repressed. Repression leads to immo-bilization, depression, and burnout. Instead, the therapist can use the affect as a guide to the patient's issues around abandonment or rejection. The therapist can explore these affects with respect to internal objects, the infant, and the therapeutic relationship. If the therapist confronts the patient with these issues in as caring and consistent a fashion as possible, the therapist will not be acting out the evoked abandonment. Either a significant piece of the transference-countertransference relationship will open to processing, or the impasse will intensify. By observing the patient's responses, the therapist will be in a much better position to determine objectively whether therapeutic progress is possible.

The second question the therapist may ask herself is whether she is impeding the patient's self-awareness. This question speaks to a more subtle kind of countertransference, one that tends to be more chronic in contrast to acute, highly negative countertransference. The therapist can easily act out this countertransference within the nurturing ethos of infant–parent psychotherapy. When unconsciously acted out, this evoked countertransference can be unhelpful for the patient and terminally draining for the therapist.

I am referring to those cases in which the role of the good parent is projected onto the clinician, which can be a delightfully gratifying change from the norm with high-risk infant cases. Yet before long, the clinician becomes drawn into the impossible job of filling up the patient's emptiness and aloneness. This is especially easy to fall into, since home-based infant–parent psychotherapy is, of necessity, more "giving" or "nurturant" than traditional outpatient therapy. With borderline patients, the therapist can usually count on rapid shifts in projective identifications to jolt her into awareness. All too quickly, the therapist receives the projected role of the bad parent and is made painfully aware of her inability to fill up the patient.

With other, more dependent or avoidant personality disorders, it is easy for the well-intentioned clinician to try to satisfy dependency needs while unconsciously helping patients to avoid facing their issues. For example, a therapist may feel caught by a situation in which the parents have repeatedly run out of formula for the infant and have no transportation. If there is no alternative help, the therapist may be compelled to take the parents to get the formula. The therapist is acting into the countertransference, however, if she repeatedly fails to explore the dynamic meaning of this situation. In addition to reality-based problem solving, the therapist may need to confront the patient with the feelings that are being acted out with respect to the infant and the therapist.

The two questions I have suggested can be helpful guidelines in recognizing countertransference as it emerges. It is frequently the case, however, that the therapist's affective experience of the induced countertransference remains preverbal and unconscious. Avoidance, reaction formation, and other defensive operations can easily mute the therapist's emergent, preverbal, affective experience. At other times, the therapist may act into the countertransference before she can identify its presence. The therapist need not be overly self-critical about the difficulty of clearly identifying and articulating the induced countertransference. After all, these difficulties are inherent in the projective identification of preverbal issues, particularly in an infant's home.

The therapist must assume responsibility, however, for getting help with clarifying the countertransference experience. Consistent consultation with a supervisor or colleagues is an absolutely indispensable part of gaining awareness, decoding, and using countertransference. This may seem a truism, but it is one that is often lost in the therapist's hectic routine. Program directors all too rarely understand the need for true clinical supervision, much less the attention that must be paid to countertransference issues. While it should be the program director's responsibility to provide, directly or indirectly, for clinical supervision, this often fails to materialize. Ultimately, each therapist must assume responsibility for seeking out supervision and collegial consultation that deal openly with countertransference issues.

Finally, I want to emphasize the enormous advantage to therapists that comes from sustaining, understanding, and using the induced affective experience. When the therapist fails to do so, she stays unconsciously identified with the most horrific aspects of the patient's internalized relationships. This is painful and unsettling for the therapist and accumulates in depression and burnout. However, when the therapist sustains the identification until she can understand and use it, she is liberated from that position. Then she is vastly more energized, and knowledgeable, in her work on behalf of infants and parents.

7

The Severely Disturbed Adolescent

Peter L. Giovacchini, M.D.

Freud mentioned the word *countertransference* only four times in all of his written works (Guttman, Jones, and Parrish 1980). He viewed it in a negative light and admonished therapists to seek further analysis if they continued having emotional reactions to their patients (Freud 1910c). Since then much has changed, as has been well outlined in various books that, to a greater or lesser extent, review the burgeoning literature on countertransference. Attitudes about countertransference have become more sanguine because it has proven helpful to the psychotherapeutic treatment of certain patients, particularly very difficult and severely disturbed patients (see Giovacchini 1974, 1989).

Freud (1914b) limited the applicability of psychoanalytic treatment to the transference neuroses, which he considered to be hysteria and the obsessive-compulsive neuroses. Regarding the narcissistic neuroses, schizophrenia, and depressions, he believed that the psychoanalytic approach was contraindicated. He based his opinion on the belief that patients suffering from the narcissistic neuroses do not form transferences, and the resolution of the transference, as he postulated, is the essential feature that makes a successful psychoanalysis possible.

Clinical experience has taught us that transference does, indeed, occur in the so-called narcissistic neurosis, but the question remains as to whether it is analyzable. There are many questions that have to be reviewed if we wish to be clinicians operating in a psychoanalytic frame and also wish to treat patients who suffer from relatively severe emotional disorders.

To begin, we have to be as clear as we can as to what types of patients we are treating, or, more accurately stated, what types of patients are seeking our help. Some clinicians or institutions may at one time have had the illusion that they were selecting their patients. Within psychoanalytic institutes, committees of clinicians seek fairly healthy psychoneurotic patients who usually fulfill Freud's criteria of analyzability for their candidates to analyze as they are being supervised. Recently, however, we are hearing more and more about the difficulties that institutes have in finding psychoneurotic patients for their students. During my training in the early 1950s we were assigned patients, since many applied for control analyses, but as the treatment unfolded, practically all of them were rediagnosed as psychotic or as having a schizoid core or as borderlines.

I will not pursue this argument about the paucity of psychoneurotic patients and the overwhelming abundance of patients suffering from much more serious psychopathology further, since it is practically "old hat." I can simply refer the reader to Reichard (1956) who rexamined Freud's cases in "Studies on Hysteria" (Breuer and Freud 1893–1895) and made rather good arguments that these patients who represented the paradigm for his categorization of the psychoneuroses were, in fact, examples of patients suffering from borderline psychopathology.

Thus, if the patients Freud treated in developing the psychoanalytic perspective were not really examples of the psychoneuroses but rather belong to another group that included borderline patients, then psychoanalytic treatment can be a feasible approach to a more severely disturbed group of patients. Contrary to popular belief, psychoanalysis may have begun as a treatment for patients who, Freud wrote, were not amenable to analysis. This is an interesting paradox that is relevant to our changing ideas about the role of countertransference in the treatment process.

Basically, clinicians rarely see psychoneurotic patients whose psychopathology can be understood from a psychodynamic viewpoint—that is, in terms of intrapsychic conflict and clashing psychic forces. Instead, they usually encounter patients whose emotional problems are best explained as the outcome of structural defects. They suffer from defects in character structure, which also means that the course of emotional development has been traumatic and that various levels and types of psychic structure are defectively formed. These are similar to anatomical distortions rather than physiological upsets in emotional equilibrium, as might characterize the psychoneuroses. Character structure is imperfectly consolidated.

Within the last twenty years there has been an intensification of interest centering around adolescent development and the failures in development that frequently lead to psychopathology. Adolescence has been viewed as a transition period between childhood and adulthood, a time when the adult character begins to form. If, however, the course of childhood development has been punctuated by trauma, then the growth spurt that represents the adolescent phase will be stormy, and the psychic structures that are eventually consolidated will be imperfectly formed and inadequate to cope with the exigencies of the adult world. These structural defects may characterize the adolescent syndrome.

Character disorders are to be expected in the adolescent group, and the problems and technical factors involved in the treatment of patients suffering from structural defects might be expected to be encountered when dealing with adolescent patients. As mentioned, countertransference has become a technical tool for successful therapy, which requires the resolution of childhood trauma and the acquisition of functional psychic structures. It can also become a major therapeutic complication and obstacle. Therefore, it behooves us as therapists to examine some of our countertransference reactions to the adolescent patient.

Freud (1910c) would have disagreed, in that he viewed countertransference as a deficit in the analyst's character. If his early patients had, in fact, been examples of intrapsychic conflict accompanied by defenses against anxiety derived from oedipal wishes, then his admonitions about countertransference would be somewhat understandable. These patients would not need a strong supportive or holding environment (Winnicott 1960) because presumably their psychic apparatus would be sufficiently well integrated that their problems with the external world would be minimal. Survival is not at stake, as their main focus is on the inner world. Both patient and analyst become allies as they scrutinize the patient's transference reactions, which reflect irrational impulses of the childhood past. The transference neurosis supposedly unfolds in the context of a well-synthesized ego that is capable of developing a self-observing function (Sterba 1934). Other than occasionally identifying with the patient in order to gain empathic understanding, the analyst does not become engulfed in the treatment process as he remains an objective but compassionate observer who continues to analyze.

With patients suffering from structural defects, the situation is markedly different. They demand more than being understood, although being understood is very important. They are needy and feel helpless and vulnerable. In a sense, they require a developmental experience as well as the management that Winnicott (1960) described. This means that the patient expects the therapist to have a more palpable presence than merely that of observer. Other facets of the analyst's personality are forced into the treatment interaction, and inasmuch as the therapist wants to confine his activities to observation and interpretation with just a minimal involvement of his feelings, he may be facing an inner struggle, which we identify as countertransference. This countertransference manifests itself in many guises, depending on the specific nature of the patient's structural defects and his traumatic background.

DEFINITION OF COUNTERTRANSFERENCE

Before embarking on the discussion of specific countertransference reactions to particular types of psychopathology, I should be explicit as to what is meant by countertransference as it is used in this chapter. I view it in broad terms and consider all of the analyst's reactions to his patient to have a countertransference determinant. All of our thoughts, feelings, and impulses can be viewed in terms of a hierarchical continuum that contains elements' from deep, primitive primary-process operating levels to higher-order, well-synthesized, reality-attuned secondary-process orientations. The more primitive (primitive in the sense of corresponding to early developmental stages) levels of reactions constitute for patients the transference potential and for the analyst, the countertransference response. In some instances, the reality or higher psychic levels are dominant, and it may not be possible to work with or even acknowledge the transference or countertransference contribution. Thus it is a relative question; there are varying degrees of id and ego factors, at any particular moment, in the interaction between patient and therapist, and to the extent that the id gains ascendancy, both transference and countertransference become more manifestly acknowledged, or, at least, make their impact felt.

Returning to the countertransference per se, it can be divided into two categories, which I designate as *homogeneous* and *idiosyncratic*. These descriptors refer to expectable and nonexpectable reactions.

Racker (1968) also wrote of two types of countertransference, which he called *concordant* and *complementary* and which are distinguished by the analyst's reactions. In the complementary variety the patient projects destructive feelings and hated parts of the self into the analyst, but the analyst finds this uncomfortable and resists accepting the projections. By contrast, the concordant type of countertransference occurs when the analyst can feel a sympathetic resonance between himself and the patient. He identifies with him as he puts himself in the patient's place, a process that contains both projective and introjective elements, and that constitutes a projective identification instituted by the analyst. This could also be called an empathic reaction. Racker's distinction refers to the intermeshing of patient's and analyst's psyches, which can be understood on the basis of projective-introjective processes.

My categorization of countertransference reactions is somewhat more global in that it emphasizes general reactions that most analysts would have toward their patients. The homogeneous countertransference consists of responses that most therapists would have in particular situations. At the extreme, if a patient tangibly threatens our lives, as by pointing a gun at us, the fear we experience would make our own analytic objectivity inoperative. The patient who pounds away at our self-esteem will also cause us universal discomfort. Exploration of the homogeneous type of countertransference is clinically useful and will help us to make meaningful contact with our patients.

Idiosyncratic responses are determined by the unique elements of the therapist's personality, character structure, and infantile background. The patient's psychopathology can, so to speak, become complementary to the therapist's. This could have deleterious effects, because the therapist's blind spots about himself will obstruct his capacity to understand the patient. On the other hand, his emotional problems may enhance his intuitive appreciation of the patient's suffering, creating a concordant countertransference, as described by Racker.

We cannot make *a priori* remarks about the usefulness or harmfulness of countertransference as Freud (1910c) and Reich (1951) did. Both homogeneous and idiosyncratic responses can work for or against treatment, and both must be examined in the context of specific psychopathological constellations. I will focus mainly on homogeneous reactions to the manifestations of structural defects as they occur or are acted out in the treatment of the severely disturbed adolescent.

Furthermore, I believe that countertransference can best be understood in terms of two factors. The first involves the specific aspects of the therapist's character structure that are affected. What parts of the personality feel the impact of the patient's transference projections, such as the superego, ego ideal, or the self-representation?

The second factor refers to the interaction between patient and therapist. To be redundant, it focuses on the transference–

countertransference axis. The therapist's feelings and reactions are considered both from the perspective of the patient's transference projections and within the context of the repetition compulsion. As will be discussed further, patients tend to bring the infantile environment into the consultation room and try to force the therapist to take over the role of a significant and usually trauma-producing person of the past. The therapist, in turn, will have specific countertransference reactions to being coerced into such a position.

COUNTERTRANSFERENCE RESPONSES TO OVERWHELMING TRAUMA

The patient, a 19-year-old college student, described himself as being in a constant state of anxiety that at times escalated to terror. He was visibly agitated and finally had to leave school because his tension was overwhelming and he was no longer able to function. Although he continued receiving funds from home, primarily to pay for treatment, he took a series of menial jobs to support himself.

He did not believe that he could be helped and felt that the only way he could obtain relief from his pain and misery was by killing himself. Nevertheless, he decided to try treatment, although he doubted that any therapist would really want to treat him. He found a young psychiatrist who was willing to attempt therapy and who, in turn, sought supervision from me.

The patient complained about the intense pain he felt; it was so overwhelming that he could not describe its somatic qualities. It was simply horrendous. He also regressed to states that he later called "splitting" and "psychotic," in which he would fall and writhe on the floor, screaming and moaning like an animal. At the beginning of treatment the therapist was able to observe these states, which, to him, suggested the reactions to blows administered during torture or to being torn apart on the rack. At other times he seemed to be begging and praying for succor and help. He screamed so loudly that the therapist was concerned about his neighbors' objecting to the noise.

He also reported episodes in which he seemed to be experiencing what Erikson (1959) called the "identity diffusion" syndrome. He literally did not know who he was. Consequently, he did not go to work because he did not know he had a job. He described occasions when he was in a daze, without any feelings except numbness—which, paradoxically, he felt acutely. At these times he did not shave, bath, or change his clothes; he also did not eat. After several days he would spontaneously recover. These states, which were accompanied by some anxiety, were not overwhelming uncomfortable. Actually they were welcomed because they gave him some relief from the violently painful states that he produced during his sessions and that also occurred in the evenings three or four times a week.

The horrors of his background seemed unbelievable, but in view of the intensity of his current pain and misery and the bizarreness of his symptoms, they appeared to be more and more believable. He did not recall his parents ever showing any affection toward him or his younger brothers. He compared his upbringing to the experience of an experimental animal that was being coerced into developing conditioned reflexes. The stimuli, however, were always painful rather than rewarding. He was punished when he behaved contrary to his parents' wishes. Both his parents, but more often his father, would beat him mercilessly when he did something of which they disapproved. He believed that they beat him when he was 6 months old in order to toilet-train him, something that he claims to have achieved before he was 10 months old. He stated that he was beaten at least four to five times a week. Nevertheless, this was the only attention he ever received from them. When he was not being brutally punished, he was totally ignored.

He remembered his mother and father as never smiling, just looking at him sternly. His mother was unpredictable, and for no reasons that he could discern she would often become violently angry and attack him. This sometimes happened in the middle of the night when he was asleep. His alcoholic father, when in drunken stupors, would also beat him. Both his parents frequently walked around the apartment naked, and he claimed that he often witnessed them having intercourse.

During the first 6 months of therapy, he constantly questioned his therapist's ability to help him. He complained about the briefness of the sessions, even though they were at least an hour long and sometimes longer. He urgently demanded help but could not articulate what he meant by "help." He blamed himself for being too sick, but he also felt that his therapist was not doing anything that he found useful.

During each session, he vehemently complained that his condition was deteriorating; each day he was the worst he had ever been, and he blamed his therapist for his downhill course.

His dreams highlighted two themes. He dreamed of his therapist, only thinly disguised, beating and homosexually attacking him. He also dreamed of being totally ignored. For example, he was sitting in his therapist's backyard when a man walked past him without acknowledging his presence even though he looked straight at him. The patient complained that these dreams meant that treatment was not working. Both the therapist and I believed that they indicated that the transference was unfolding as it should, although perhaps it was developing too rapidly.

The patient continued to complain, accusing the therapist of being useless and insensitive to his needs. He could find absolutely nothing of value in the treatment relationship. The therapist kept in mind the patient's assaultive and rejecting infantile milieu and viewed the patient's protestations as an attempt to recreate the traumatic past in the consultation room as well as in his dreams. He gently interpreted that the patient saw the world as a dangerous place, and that it was not surprising that he would view the treatment in a similar fashion. It would take time until he could feel secure and develop trust. The patient paid no attention to what his therapist said and continued to complain and regress to the dissociated states I have described.

After several months of being ignored and attacked, the therapist, as benevolently as he could, told the patient that he could not allow himself to be helped, that he had a need to reject everything that the therapist interpreted and tried to give him. The patient felt that he was being criticized and viciously attacked. Once again, he fell to the floor and began to thrash around as he moaned and screamed. The therapist stated that if he had inadvertently been unkind, he was truly sorry. If anything, these remarks only caused the patient's pain to intensify. At the end of the session, he stormed out of the room, shouting that he would never come back. The therapist called the patient on the telephone to urge him to return, at least for one session so that they could review what had happened, but he adamantly refused.

The therapist felt confused and frustrated and wondered why he had ever accepted the patient for treatment in the first place. He also wondered whether the patient was, to some extent, correct when he accused him of being critical and attacking.

We discussed these issues in a supervisory session as we investigated countertransference. Regarding the first question, he admitted that perhaps he was indulging in some degree of grandiosity. He was trying to enhance his ego ideal and strengthen the cohesion of his professional self-representation by successfully treating a patient that most analysts would regard as hopeless. If he did not succeed, it would not be considered a tremendous failure, and he would not be blamed for anything except perhaps for being foolhardy enough to have accepted such a patient for treatment.

Nevertheless, the therapist was upset. More precisely, he felt a certain amount of sadness because he was aware of how acutely this adolescent was suffering, and he felt powerless as he was engulfed by the misery and anguish that inundated the therapeutic setting.

In addition to sadness, the therapist felt confused. Although he under-stood how the patient was recreating the traumatic infantile environment before his eyes, he was still bewildered. He knew he was being cast in the role of the assaultive or rejecting parents, but his attempts to make the patient aware of this had no effect whatsoever. Rather, the patient responded as if he were being criticized or attacked. On the other hand, if the therapist remained silent, then he became the rejecting parent who had no interest in helping him secure some relief from his disruptive inner agitation. This was indeed a frustrating situation, a bind, for the therapist, but his confusion was related to other issues beside this feeling of entrapment and frustration.

Cases like the one I have described are often found during adolescence, since the character has not yet consolidated. The sense of identity is in a formative state, and value systems are not firmly established. Some adults also have the same fluidity of character. I am referring to how the lack of stabilized psychic structures upsets the therapeutic interaction because there is a paucity of expectable reactions.

What might have been helpful to other patients was experienced as harmful to this patient. There was a topsy-turvy, "Alice in Wonderland" quality to the therapeutic interaction. The therapist was not counterattacking when he was being viciously attacked. He understood the patient's lack of trust and his need to view any experience as useless in view of the unpredictability of his traumatic past and the necessity of bringing pent-up rage into the therapeutic setting. As discussed, the understanding conveyed by the therapist to the patient had a devastatingly negative and destructive effect instead of helping construct a holding environment, as Winnicott (1962a) discussed. This caused the therapist to feel confusion—what might be called a countertransference confusion.

Within the treatment context, the usual values of the therapeutic process were shattered. What has ordinarily been considered good is now bad, and an empathic, understanding attitude is transformed into a traumatic experience. Under these circumstances, therapists may even become disoriented because their standard of values is precipitously rendered useless.

This patient reminds me of other severely disturbed adolescents whom I have tried, both successfully and unsuccessfully, to analyze. Some of them were closer to the schizophrenic end of the spectrum than they were to the better integrated nonpsychotic, yet vulnerable, ego state. Insofar as their environments have been both assaultive and rejecting, as was the case with the patient just described, they have developed practically no sense of security and safety. They perceive their current world as they have experienced the infantile milieu—that is, as violently impinging.

Their mothers have not provided them with the protective shield from destructive stimuli, the *Reizschutz* that Freud (1920b) described. Rather than providing a safe, protective holding environment for their children, these mothers, on the contrary, were themselves the source of destructiveness. They would create and intensify their children's vulnerability rather than enhance their sense of security. Therefore, what in therapy would have constituted the construction of a holding environment, was experienced as an attack. Nurturing experiences were equated with being destroyed. Life-giving interactions were perceived as deadly dangerous.

To have needs and to be dependent is devastatingly painful. For instance, Flarsheim (1975) writes about an anorectic adolescent who had been a "fussy" baby. Her parents hired a nurse who presumably knew how to handle such a situation. She meticulously responded to general infantile needs, but not to the need the child was having at a particular moment. If the baby was hungry, the nurse would change her diapers; if she was cold and wet, she would feed her. She also blocked any autoerotic gratification by putting on the baby a certain type of glove that prevented thumbsucking. The nurse succeeded in eliminating the fussiness by creating an apathetic, inert child. The parents were pleased in that they could continue to ignore their daughter with equanimity and without her protestations.

Flarsheim's patient lacked a sense of aliveness. She felt dead. At first, one's sense of being is determined by needs and how they are met. Successful nurture creates a state of satisfaction, of well-being, which leads to security and eventually comfort with a curiosity about the surrounding world. On the other hand, if the response to an inner need is experienced as an assaultive intrusion, the process of living becomes painful. To be alive is dangerous. This patient protected herself by apathetic withdrawal and a state of deadness. Living in the world meant being surrounded by murderous forces directed against her. She had to deaden both her perceptions and her inner feelings in order to survive. She existed on the basis of the fundamental oxymoron, which, to her, meant that to be alive is to be dead.

At the most elemental level, she had to deny that she had any needs so that, in a sense, she did not need anything from her current milieu. Then she could protect herself from painful, caretaking ministrations that were never directed to her needs or acknowledged her as a person with a sense of aliveness. This was especially evident in her anorexia. If she did not need to eat, then she was totally in control and would be independent. She rejected food, since she had no needs for external sustenance. This was practically a delusional autonomy.

The need for protective defenses against threatening and dangerous impingements from the external world is especially prominent during adolescence. As stated, this is a period of life when the self-representation and adaptive mechanisms are not yet well constructed. Consequently, adolescents tend to have difficulty fitting into their current milieu, which, at times, is felt as traumatic.

Trauma, as with many emotional constellations, has to be viewed on a relative basis. The two significant variables are a person's vulnerability and the destructiveness of the stimulus. If the ego is extremely vulnerable, a relatively nonthreatening stimulus will be traumatic, as was true of the supervisee's patient. The converse is also true; the more secure and less vulnerable ego requires a greater destructive stimulus in order to feel traumatically threatened. There are variations in reactions to situations and relationships, dependent on susceptibility. Certainly these have been dramatically noted in combat, where some soldiers would become incapacitated with panic whereas others might adjust to such danger with relative ease.

The position of the adolescent in the external world is comparable to that of the soldier in combat. Prior to adolescence, the child has learned to adapt first to the world of infancy and, later, to the world of childhood. Children develop a variety of adaptive techniques within the context of a dependent orientation. After puberty, this adaptive balance is suddenly disrupted. It is no longer acceptable, in terms of sustaining self-esteem, to be dependent. Of course, the adolescent remains dependent in most respects, but there are expectations that go beyond this basic childhood orientation as it is defined by our culture.

Adolescence is a transition period between childhood and adulthood; youngsters find this sojourn in limbo somewhat disconcerting. Their childhood techniques of adaptation are no longer appropriate, and they have not yet learned how to relate at an adult level. Thus they feel vulnerable to the implicit and explicit demands made of them because they have not yet acquired the coping techniques required to respond to the exigencies of an emotionally mature environment.

As stated, the external world is experienced as traumatic if we conceptualize trauma in terms of the two variables I have described, the ego's vulnerability and the impact of the stimulus. Adolescents are similar to the patients described but, of course, to a considerably lesser degree, in that for some period of time, they feel unprotected. They do not totally lack a protective shield, but their skins are relatively thin. Therefore, if their childhood was also traumatic, they become even more vulnerable during adolescence. Lacking an adequate stimulus barrier, they are more susceptible to emotional collapse as their already precarious psychic structures face an even more dangerous and demanding external world than that of childhood and infancy.

Many such patients have constructed some type of stimulus barrier that is part of a false-self orientation to the external world. During adolescence, they are struggling to establish an identity, and whatever false-self orientations they have constructed only intensify their conflict and strengthen the barrier against acquiring a true identity. Although they may perceive the world of impending adulthood as similarly traumatic to their infantile milieu, the psychopathological adaptations they have acquired do not function well in this new adolescent setting.

The patient my supervisee presented had practically no defenses, which, among other things, meant that he lacked a protective shield. Rather than having a thin skin, he had no skin, and in one of his painfully regressed states, he screamed that his whole body was an open, festering, raw wound, oozing with pus and unbearably, painfully sensitive to the slightest stimulus. Adolescence, to him, represented additional trauma, "the straw that broke the camel's back," trauma he had felt surrounded by ever since he could remember, and with which he had no effective way of dealing.

For my supervisee, a young, relatively inexperienced therapist, there was a special negative resonance between himself and the patient that contributed to the disruptive countertransference. This patient would be a difficult patient for even the most experienced therapist, but there were specific problems because of the therapist's relative professional youthfulness. I do not believe that this represents an idiosyncratic countertransference; rather, it is homogeneous in the sense that it is a more likely reaction for therapists who have fairly recently begun treating patients psychotherapeutically or psychoanalytically.

I am referring to a parallel process taking place in the therapist's orientation in reaction to the failure of consolidation of the patient's own adolescent process. The therapist was facing a type of professional adolescence in that the world of clinical practice was relatively new to him. Unlike his patient, he had acquired many adaptive techniques during his training to cope with the exigencies of therapeutic work. But they were relatively untried and had not yet become fully incorporated and integrated into the ego's executive system. In addition, this patient presented problems for which the therapist could find no suitable method or technique; none of us could.

Consequently he felt anxious, although he was not always aware of it. Later he realized that he felt inadequate to deal with the bind in which the patient had placed him. In relating to this borderline and sometimes psychotic patient, he felt as if he were a borderline therapist. The therapeutic tools that he had at his disposal were now ineffective, in the same fashion that the adaptive techniques of childhood are no longer operational when facing the more complex and demanding adult world. Again, like the adolescent, the therapist was having problems moving from the dependency of his training to the responsible autonomy required to function as a mature, competent clinician. Comparable to the adolescent phase, he had one foot in the training setting and the other in the clinical arena. This limbolike state was further stressed by his being in supervision rather than operating in a totally independent fashion.

These are not phenomena that occur only with therapists who are still consolidating their professional character. To a large measure, these countertransference disturbances are created by the particular psychopathology I have discussed. These patients are capable of provoking most therapists to regress to states of adolescence, insecurity, and turmoil. They can make borderline therapists of many clinicians who accept the challenge to treat them, since they trap us in the paradox of viewing us as either assaultive or rejecting. We find ourselves between the Scylla of assaultive understanding and the Charybdis of silent abandonment.

COUNTERTRANSFERENCE AND THE PSYCHOANALYTIC PARADOX

Admittedly, the clinical phenomena just discussed represent extremes. We might hope that these forms of psychopathology will rarely be encountered, but patients as severely disturbed and traumatized as the one just described are coming increasingly to our attention. Psychoanalysts may not often see this type of patient because they usually do not seek insight-promoting treatment, and if they do, analysts tend not to accept them for therapy. However, the countertransference problems that they provoke illustrate certain general principles about the transference-countertransference axis that have relevance for many different forms of psychopathology, some of which are more commonly encountered in a standard psychotherapeutic or psychoanalytic practice. I wish to focus particularly on therapeutic interactions that interfere with the analyst's modus operandi.

The patient I have described interfered with the therapist's modus operandi in that he created a situation that rendered the therapist helpless and at a loss as to what to do. Now I will discuss patients who are disturbed but not nearly as vulnerable. With these patients, the appropriate course of action soon becomes clear, but the therapist or analyst is reluctant to follow that course because it is counter to his professional ego ideal. The therapist may, however, unwittingly be drawn out of the professional role. He may feel threatened because his therapist identity is encroached upon.

The interactions I am about to describe are examples of what I have called the psychoanalytic paradox (Giovacchini 1979, 1986). I define the psychoanalytic paradox as a situation in which the treatment setting, at some level, resembles the infantile environment; or as a situation in which, because of particular qualities of the analytic frame, the patient is not able to experience certain primitive feelings that have to be resolved in the transference regression.

In some instances, the patient tries to get the therapist to change his therapeutic stance in order to alter the setting so that it no longer resembles the world of childhood and instead approximates a milieu that he wished he had to make up for the deficits that he had to endure.

Invariably there will be countertransference responses to the patient's expectations, at best, or demands, at worst. The strength and disruptiveness of such reactions depend on whether analysts are aware of what is going on between themselves and their patients. If the therapist is not aware of how he is being manipulated, he is more likely to feel uncomfortable and, in some ways, react adversely to the patient. In short, there will be some disturbance of the therapeutic interaction.

The following case histories are two examples of the psychoanalytic paradox that are benign in that they caused no intense, untoward reactions, nor did they irreversibly upset the treatment process. They are, however, good illustrations of the psychoanalytic paradox. Because most of the treatment interaction was occurring at conscious levels, these situations did not create special problems.

A 19-year-old patient complained that she needed to relive a fundamental state of loneliness, a sadness and isolation that had been particularly intense and poignant during her childhood. Consequently she did not feel as if she were a person; rather, she saw herself as a "babbling weakling" without substance. Throughout the years she had developed a series of attitudes and had adopted a posture that stood her in good stead in that she was able to maintain an active social life, but she felt that it was all a sham. She knew that she was viewed as shallow and flighty, but she was sufficiently charming and attractive so that she was fairly popular. Nevertheless, she knew this was all a cover-up and a response to how she was expected to behave. Most of the time she was "down on herself," feeling self-conscious and drawn into her wealthy parents' "meaningless" social world.

She was not satisfied with coasting along, and for a while she indulged herself in an adolescent rebellion. She let drugs and sex dominate her life, but finally she realized that this frenetic activity provided neither self-satisfaction nor freedom from anxiety. In therapy, she wanted to cut through the superficiality of her life and get down to her basic lonely core. She could not do this, however, because of my constant presence. I interfered with the sense of isolation that she was trying to magically summon up.

She did not blame me for "interfering with her analysis," and I had no conflictful feelings that might have added to the tension she felt. Still, at a surface level, the analytic setting, because it is constructed around a transference–countertransference axis, a dyadic relationship, does not permit the patient to feel alone.

I realized that the patient had not developed what Winnicott (1958) called the "capacity to be alone in the presence of another person." She had not yet acquired the ability to be able to maintain the internalization of an external object without the actual presence of the object, what Fraiberg (1969) called evocative memory. Conversely, this patient was not able to lose, or even temporarily decathect, an internal object representation in the presence of the external object.

This clearly was an ego defect that had to be repaired by the work of analysis, which occurred as we were able to construct a supportive matrix that created a sense of trust. She was eventually reassured that while she was in therapy I would continue to be there for her even between our sessions. She became able to carry a memory of me (and more particularly, of me as I represented the analytic interaction) with her in her daily life, and, finally, she was able to feel the sadness and loneliness of childhood in my presence. It was interesting that during these moments she did not perceive me as a distinct person. Rather, she felt herself as being enveloped in a warm, soft comforter and, at the same time, she felt utterly desolated. She believed that she could allow herself to feel such painful feelings because she was protected by the warmth of the comforter. As a person, I had receded into an invisible background. The psychoanalytic paradox had been resolved, and she had succeeded in symbolically manipulating the treatment setting so that she could, if not entirely comfortably then at least safely, regress to early traumatic infantile levels.

There were no significant countertransference difficulties because I had some understanding of the patient's characterological problems. When she first complained about my intrusive presence, I felt a twinge of disruption in that she was making an implicit demand that I modify my therapeutic modus operandi. Nevertheless, I was not too impelled to respond to her on the basis of the content of her material. Obviously, I could not withdraw so that she could be alone. I did not feel any more compunction to respond to her than I would in the face of a delusional request. Still, the twinge I felt was comparable to the signal anxiety about which S. Freud (1926) wrote. My usual analytic techniques were no longer adaptive in view of the patient's background and ego defects. Thus I was able to recognize that analysis and, more specifically, my physical presence, were not intrinsically in opposition to the course of therapeutic progress.

Another patient, a 20-year-old student, teasingly accused me of being too rational and soothing. He stressed that he had to get in touch with the irrational and anxious parts of himself, and that my interpretations interfered with his being able to bring them to the surface. Or if he did, my comments would immediately place them within the realm of logic, and they would therefore lose their raw and wildly irrational native qualities.

Regarding my activities, he stated that no matter how irrational his thoughts and feelings were, I would cause them to make sense through my interpretations and reconstructions. He felt that the same thing happened with his anxiety. I could always locate its infantile source and then would no longer feel afraid. He felt some relief, but he was also reprimanding me.

Because of the mild manner of his reproaches, I was neither particularly concerned nor moved to do something about them. As he continued, however, I began to question my technical perspectives. I examined some of my concepts about the effectiveness of interpretations. They seemed to work against the best interests of this particular patient. Again, this was a situation that threatened my modus operandi. What I had been taught was the essence of psychoanalytic techniques—that is, the fostering of insight through interpretation—now seemed to be the wrong thing to do. Should I stop interpreting? I was experiencing countertransference confusion. With the previous patient it was the dyadic nature of the analytic relationship that was being threatened, whereas with this patient it was a technical device—interpretation—that was being challenged.

My confusion, a countertransference reaction, was again the outcome of inroads being made into both my professional self-representation and my ego ideal. I believe that there is a significant distinction here that emphasizes both a global response and a more focalized reaction that stems from related but distinct psychic structures. Regarding my professional self-representation, these two patients caused me to have doubts about the total treatment process, including the formal aspects of analysis as well as the techniques involved. The formal aspects refer to the setting and include the frequency of appointments, the use of the couch, and the analyst's nonjudgmental and nonintrusive presence, which helps make him available as a receptacle for the patient's projections. Both patients upset my equanimity when they stressed that at least one of these factors, my constant presence, was detrimental rather than helpful in providing a target for transference feelings and a reliable holding environment.

The second patient further upset my security about my analytic identity when he found my interpretations to be obstructive rather than liberating. To repeat, he was undermining an important aspect of my modus operandi. I refer to these reactions stemming from encroachments on my professional self-representation as global, because they could crumble the entire psychoanalytic edifice. Within the psychoanalytic context I might have been functioning well, but the fundamentals, the validity of analyses, were being challenged.

I wondered whether my interpretations were correct. I scrutinized their content, depth, and timing, and I questioned whether I was stressing the transference sufficiently, or whether I should have concentrated more on genetic factors.

I was taking what the patient had said literally. Regardless of the accuracy of my interpretations, it could be argued that it might have been better if I had said nothing. Obviously the patient was dealing with primitive, primary-process–oriented material. I was responding in another language, that of secondary-process logic. The differential between his level of discourse and mine was sufficiently great that the patient could not operate in his frame of reference and mine at the same time. If he joined me at my level, he had to leave his infantile feelings behind. He could not jump up to my level without abandoning his. Furthermore, translating his highly emotional experiences into the conceptual framework of language totally destroyed his feelings.

By gaining cohesiveness and structure, the interpretations lost their impact. I was interfering with whatever constructive potential a regression might have in helping the patient regain painful, split-off parts of the self and reintegrate them into the main psychic current, as Freud (1938b) stated. I finally realized that the patient was, in fact, correct, and that my need to interpret to him was based on my failure to recognize his need to recapitulate early ego states. I was interpreting at levels that were, for the moment, beyond his level of comprehension. As the patient later exclaimed, I was interpreting upward.

Unlike the first patient, he simply needed me to be there when he was feeling painful anxiety states. My presence supplied him with the security that enabled him to face dangerous feelings and introjects. I learned that I could make an occasional remark that emphasized that I was still present and that I understood how he felt. For example, I might remark that it made me sad to see him suffering as he did, but that we both knew that he had to get in touch with his basic anxiety so that he could eventually feel in control. I had become careful not to go beyond his feelings or my reactions to them. My responses were limited to observations about his current mental state. At most I would elaborate what he presented to me or ask him for further details and connections.

At times his misery reached such proportions that he felt it was unbearable. Then he felt hopeless about ever being able to work it through. His hopelessness was based upon his feeling that he could never regain split-off lost parts of himself because they were too painful to incorporate—that is, to once again make part of his psyche. I firmly believed that he would eventually be able to modulate the pain. When the dissociated parts of the self became integrated with the main currents of the psyche, they would gain structure and organization and lose their painful qualities. I did not say this to him, because I feared that once again I would be "interpreting upward" and prematurely end his regressive experience. Nevertheless, my attitude must have been evident, since he believed that even though he sometimes felt hopeless, I represented constant hope. This was verbalized, and I acknowledged my hopeful attitude.

I initially had some difficulty in maintaining what turned out to be a resonating interaction rather than making interpretations designed to foster higher levels of ego integration. Finally, I recognized that my "sophisticated" interpretations were not empathic because I was not dealing with the patient's current emotional state.

I thought that investigating the sources of his anxiety and seeking to clarify traumatic constellations would eventually lead to higher levels of ego integration. What I did not realize was that I was bypassing infantile ego states by converting the patient's primary-process material into secondary-process ideas. If the patient had responded to my insights, he would have moved up to a higher ego level, but in so doing, he would have lost contact with earlier ego states. There would be a psychic discontinuity; that is, there would be no connecting bridges between primary-process and secondary-process orientations.

I learned that interpretations dealing with split-off material cannot be effective. From one viewpoint my interpretations were not transference interpretations, even though the patient's feelings were directed toward me. His feelings were not, however, integrated with the self, and not a part of a smooth, hierarchically arranged continuum. I was talking about phenomena that were split off and external to the psyche.

I understood that the patient's regression was designed to bring dissociated parts of the self back into the psychic stream. He was trying to establish continuity, and only after having achieved a degree of such continuity could transference interpretations be effective. Much later in treatment, the same interpretations I had made in the past were effective, and the patient gained considerable control over feelings that had been previously painful and split off from his psyche.

The two case histories just described refer to clinical situations in which a routine but actually robotlike adherence to the psychoanalytic method worked against therapeutic progress. The method failed because of the patients' specific ego defects. The first patient was unable to form stabilized inner representations and decathect them. The second patient was not able to contain traumatic introjects and painful parts of the self, and he therefore had to dissociate them from the main psychic current so that they were not perceived as being part of himself.

There are other treatment relationships that can lead to counter-transference impasses based on the construction of a psychoanalytic paradox. The following is a discussion of a treatment relationship in which the therapeutic setting, in some ways, resembled the infantile environment. As mentioned at the beginning of this section, this resemblance is the essence of the psychoanalytic paradox.

The patient, a schizoid young man, behaved like a stereotypic adolescent. I found the first interview to be particularly tedious, since he never elaborated in answering any of my questions. His replies were pithy, sometimes terse, and usually monosyllabic. Often his response would be a grunt or a shrug of his shoulders. Contrary to the way I had felt in the past toward a similar patient, I did not feel that I was being intrusive or particularly probing. I believed, however, that to some extent I was being manipulated and that the patient was gaining some sadistic pleasure from my discomfort.

During the second session, I asked him to lie on the couch and with some trepidation explained the rudiments of free association. He acknowledged what I said, but I had the impression that he really did not hear me. This and many later sessions were punctuated with long periods of silence.

Ordinarily I am not bothered by silence. It may represent the patient's need to withdraw, and I can usually respect that need. Or it may be a nonverbal, but often deep, form of communication. Silence can have varied meanings, and many analysts who treat patients suffering from severe emotional disorders have learned to adapt comfortably to it. With this patient, however, I was afraid that if the silence continued, the treatment would end before it started.

I had put together various bits of information that I had sporadically gathered from various sessions. I derived a picture of parents who looked after his material needs but who had very little emotional involvement with him. They gave him expensive sports cars and praised his good academic record, but the patient did not believe that they were truly interested in him as a person. He stressed, in his laconic fashion, that they never spontaneously talked to him or ever inquired or showed any concern about what might interest him. He depicted his household as cast in gray shadows and characterized by silence.

I now felt that his silence had a tendentious quality. I believed that he was exacting revenge by treating me as he had been treated. It was at his parents' urging that he had come to analysis. Furthermore, I believed that he was protecting himself from the silence he expected from me. Rather than being passively vulnerable to silent rejection, he would take the active role and make me the victim.

He was also recreating the low-decibel environment of his childhood, in which there was little if any spontaneous talk. Analysts usually conduct themselves in a low-keyed fashion, and analytic treatment is often a low-decibel procedure. However, I began to feel uncomfortable and confused because my relatively silent nonjudgmental stance, rather than setting the pace for the therapeutic relationship, seemed to lead to stagnation.

When the patient spoke, which was rarely, he emphasized how pointless it was for him to come to see me. He explained that he simply did not have the courage to defy his parents by terminating his visits. His life continued in the same dull fashion; nothing had changed. I, in turn, felt similarly discouraged and found his constant complaining about the uselessness of the treatment tedious.

I considered this relationship to be another example of the psychoanalytic paradox. Phenomenologically, the infantile environment and the analytic setting had some similarities. Consequently, it would be difficult to analyze the transference because the patient would be unable to distinguish his projections from the actual treatment setting. I felt as if I were in a bind, because to maintain my objective and relatively quiet analytic perspective meant that, at one level, I was behaving as if I were one or the other of his parents. Furthermore, his complaints about the uselessness of the treatment began to aggravate me, partly because I was beginning to acknowledge that he was correct; that is, conventional analysis could not give him what he needed.

Fortunately, he helped me work out this dilemma. Perhaps to denigrate me further, he brought me a problem in logic. I had not heard of this particular problem, but I recognized that it was similar to one that I solved many years ago, so it did not take me long to give him the answer. After solving his problem I promptly gave him one in return. He noted it but could not solve it at the moment. However, he brought it home with him, and during the next session he proudly presented me with the solution.

As I recall these sessions, I am struck as to how involved we both were in this problem-solving activity. The previously funereal atmosphere of the consultation room suddenly changed and was replaced by intense and lively exchanges of puzzles and conundrums. I found myself eagerly responding to his questions as well as asking for information that had not been available to me. I realized that the treatment setting was no longer confused with the infantile environment when he asked rhetorically why his parents could not have shared his interests with him as I was doing.

The treatment was now being conducted in a higher-decibel context. I must stress, however, that there was nothing contrived about my reactions. I had considerable feeling about what we were doing; with my background in mathematics I have had a life-long interest in puzzles of this sort. We had succeeded in finding an area of mutual interest. If I were simply play-acting, I am certain that he would have been able to pick up the falseness of my position, and this would have been therapeutically disastrous.

Some clinicians might object that what we were doing was not analysis.

This depends on how analysis is defined. Certainly, he was not free-associating, and I was not making any insight-promoting interpretations. On the other hand, I was creating a setting that he could differentiate from the pathological elements of past object relationships. This makes it possible to analyze the repetition compulsion as, later in treatment, the past is recapitulated and the transference neurosis develops.

My patient finally tired of discussing riddles, and I encouraged him to apply his problem-solving abilities to unraveling the mysteries of his psyche. He was intrigued by this poetic way of expressing the analytic task and started free-associating. What transpired from this point on certainly fits the analytic mode.

Actually, it does not make any difference, as far as I am concerned, how we label the treatment interaction. I had to create a background that was markedly different from what he had experienced as a child so that he could develop sufficient interest and trust to enable him to believe that he was in treatment because he wanted to be. He had to develop a certain amount of enthusiasm to explore how his mind worked, rather than feeling that he was submitting to parental demands.

Winnicott (1945) would have considered our early interaction as an attempt to construct a holding environment. In a similar fashion, I view it as a foundation or background that is required to initiate and facilitate the analytic process. I believe that every analytic relationship has a background, which can be conceptualized as a holding environment, and a foreground, which refers to the analytic work itself. For adolescents and patients suffering from characterological problems, the background may be even more important than the foreground. The analyst's countertransference discomfort may unconsciously motivate him to find a method by which he can engage the patient, although in my experience the patient supplied the means to make contact. I believe that my countertransference disruption caused me to be receptive.

CONCLUSIONS

Adolescents in particular provoke disruptive countertransference reactions because the intensity of their neediness and defiance may completely dominate the therapeutic setting and disrupt the orderly course of treatment. To a large measure, the therapist participates in the chaos that the patient has precipitated. Some patients have specific impacts on their therapists that are experienced as countertransference reactions. Countertransference may destroy the treatment relationship, or it may lead to therapeutically beneficial insights.

I have defined countertransference as a ubiquitous reaction of therapists that may or may not be consciously manifest. The homogenous variety refers to the therapist's average expectable reactions to whatever the patient presents, especially threatening situations. I also distinguish an idiosyncratic type, which is largely determined by specific and unique features of the therapist's background and personality.

It is useful to scrutinize the therapist–patient interaction microscopically. This means that it is important to understand how the patient's material and behavior impinge on and threaten specific elements of the therapist's psychic structure. I discuss situations that involve the therapist's ego ideal and professional self-representation and the ego's executive system. These encroachments are often designed to interfere with the therapist's modus operandi.

Specific forms of psychopathology provoke particular types of countertransference reactions. I discuss especially difficult therapeutic situations dealing with patients who have suffered overwhelming trauma in childhood. These relationships frequently deteriorate in unresolvable impasses, primarily because any type of help that the therapist offers is experienced as an assault.

I also discuss the psychoanalytic paradox, a situation in which the treatment setting, at some level, resembles the infantile milieu. This similarity creates specific countertransference reactions that may cause therapeutic impasses. The patient and therapist often can work out such stalemates by creating a mode of communication that eventually constructs a background holding environment, and analytic treatment then becomes possible.

This chapter stresses that the treatment process is not unilateral. Two persons are involved, and the way in which the patient's feelings interact with those of the therapist must be understood. Especially with severely disturbed patients and adolescents, the transference–countertransference axis is the important hub that determines the course of therapeutic progress. The recognition of the reciprocal interplay of transference-countertransference feelings can be rewarding to both patient and therapist.

8

Psychodynamic Psychotherapy of Eating Disorders

Nancy Burke, Ph.D., and Bertram J. Cohler, Ph.D.[1]

Anorexia nervosa, which occurs most frequently in young women between the ages of 12 and 30 (Kaufman and Heiman 1964), is a modal psychosomatic syndrome characterized by a psychologically determined refusal of food, a relentless pursuit of thinness, and, often, a frenetic level of activity. Psychodynamic studies of this disorder have highlighted the complex factors underlying the syndrome, stressing the sadomasochistic and compulsive structure of the illness (Coles 1988), its depressive aspects (Bruch 1973, 1978, Katz 1987), and its frequent association with borderline and narcissistic personality disorders (Gartner et al. 1989, Lyon and Silber 1989). Yet the readily observable diagnostic characteristics associated with the illness make it possible to identify a discrete patient population and to assume a course and outcome within a reasonably narrow range, including the possibility of self-starvation to suicide (Bachrach et al. 1965, Blinder et al. 1970, Bruch 1974, Cohler 1976, Eissler 1943, Feiner 1982, Groen and

---

[1]This chapter is dedicated to the memory of the late Alfred Flarsheim, M.D., whose courage in discussing the analyst's experience of the analysand and the analytic process fostered innovative approaches to the study and treatment of the more troubled patient.

Feldman–Toledano 1966, Hallston 1965, Lang 1965, Leitenberg et al. 1968).

Indeed, the potential fatality associated with the illness has a decisive effect upon the course of psychotherapy, but other factors also play a role in rendering problematic the treatment of the anorectic patient (Cohler 1976). Significantly, these women show primitive psychological defenses when confronted with personal conflict, stress, or adversity (Steiger et al. 1989), do not appear to be willing to reflect on their own experiences or to participate in a process of self-inquiry, and are particularly suspicious regarding psychological intervention (Bemporad and Lee 1988). Such women find it difficult to maintain therapeutic alliances (Zetzel 1956), often undermining efforts at fostering increased self-understanding regarding the meaning and origin of their present distress (Deering 1987). Perhaps most difficult to manage, however, are the complex feelings engendered in the psychotherapist attempting to work with these anorectic patients.[2] This chapter considers countertransference responses to the psychologically "primitive" or archaic worlds of these anorectic women patients.

COUNTERTRANSFERENCE, ANOREXIA, AND THERAPEUTIC PESSIMISM

Many anorectic women report striking similarities in family background: these women show problems in presentation of self and response to treatment, which, paradoxically, foster strikingly similar responses reciprocally to this psychopathology among those attempting to intervene to reduce their suffering. Considering the psychologically primitive nature of the anorectic's experiences, their frequent expressions of rage, their destructive wishes regarding both self and others, and their feelings of depletion and depression, the therapist faces particular problems in working with these patients. The psychological discomfort posed for the therapist, essentially a reflection of the anorectic patient's archaic and chaotic experience of self and others, poses unique challenges for attempts to maintain the working or

---

[2]This chapter assumes psychoanalytically oriented psychotherapy as the mode of psychological intervention. Whereas psychoanalysis may be a useful intervention in the treatment of anorexia, most of these patients are seen in psychoanalytically oriented psychotherapy. The term *therapist* is used generically to refer to those working with the more troubled anoretic patient, recognizing that the issues raised here apply equally to psychoanalysis and to psychoanalytically oriented psychotherapy.

therapeutic alliance and to respond empathically to the patient (Fliess 1942, 1953, Kohut 1959, 1971, 1977). As a consequence, in an effort to avoid confrontation with the sense of despair engendered through work with these patients, the analytically oriented therapist may recommend behavioral manipulations, hospitalization, or psychopharmacological treatment, even though these approaches do not yield results superior to those obtained with the best intensive psychotherapy (Bruch 1974).

Many of those involved with the treatment or study of anoretic patients have noted that "the literature on the psychoanalytic treatment of anorexia nervosa is generally pessimistic" (Fischer 1989, p. 42, see also Birksted-Breen 1989, Bruch 1982, Sours 1974). A major reason for this pessimism may be the failure to recognize counteridentification responses in therapeutic work with anorectics. The therapist's experience of the patient's sense of hopelessness, engendered through empathic appreciation of the patient's profound experience of distress may, in turn, lead the therapist to conclude prematurely that anorectic patients are not suitable for psychodynamic intervention; countertransference concerns, rather than technical aspects of "analyzability" or professional ethics, may be the principal factors leading to this decision to abandon the psychoanalytic situation (Stone 1961) in favor of alternative behavioral approaches (Feiner 1982, Fine 1984, Smirnoff 1988). While recognizing the significance of biological factors in the origin of the illness and the benefits of such pharmacological approaches as antidepressant therapy, it is all too often assumed that psychodynamic approaches add little beyond pharmacological or behavioral treatment in fostering the anorectic patient's recovery.

Consistent with pessimism regarding the psychodynamic treatment of anorexia is the paucity of reports providing in-depth understanding regarding the nature of the psychoanalytic process with these patients. With the exception of Johnson's (1990) edited volume, there has been little sustained focus upon the course and treatment of anorexia from a psychodynamic perspective. Further, even though a small number of helpful and sensitively written accounts of psychodynamically oriented therapies with anorectics have been published in recent years (Berenson et al. 1989, Birksted-Breen 1989, Coles 1988, Fischer 1989), there have been even fewer reports regarding the therapist's own experience of the psychotherapeutic process reciprocal to that of the anorectic patient (Wooley 1990, Zerbe 1986); however, psychoanalytic treatment can be useful precisely as a result of the therapist's ability to reflect on his own experience of the analysand as understood within their collaborative work.

Personality Development, Countertransference, and Psychoanalytic Theory

Across the past several decades, the view of the therapist as a "blank screen" (Freud 1914a) has been replaced by a view that portrays the therapist as a partner in a collaborative relationship demanding his own continuing self-inquiry (Gardner 1983, Horney 1942). This relational emphasis (Mitchell 1988, Modell 1990) reflects a shift within psychoanalysis from an analysis of the nuclear or oedipal neurosis, portrayed by the topographic and structural models of therapeutic change (Freud 1900, 1915a, 1923,) toward a developmental model in which the analysand reenacts experiences with others from earliest childhood within the relationship with the analyst (Balint 1935, Bowlby 1960, Erikson 1950/1963, M. Klein 1928, Middlemore 1941, Spitz 1946, Winnicott 1949). This developmentally oriented model highlights the significance of the mother–child relationship and the emergence of intersubjectivity as significant for the course of personality development and later change within psychoanalysis (Friedman 1978). The developmental approach has also been important in understanding the therapist's experience and response to the analysand's struggle to resolve deficits stemming from experienced failure to attain a coherent and vigorous sense of self within the parent–child relationship of early childhood (Kohut 1971, 1977, Racker 1968, Winnicott 1953).

Contemporary psychoanalytic theory, as presented in the work of Kernberg (1975, 1976), Giovacchini (1979, 1986), Gedo (1979, 1981), and Kohut (1971, 1977), has enlarged upon this notion of developmental deficit. While current formulations vary in terms of their accounts of the sources of deficit in personality development, as well as in terms of implications for the therapeutic process, these apparently dissimilar perspectives emphasize disturbance in the young child's experience of self and others as central both for the origin of distress and course of treatment (Modell 1990, Zetzel 1965, Zetzel and Meissner 1973). These developmentally focused discussions provide evidence that symptoms as diverse as perversions, feelings of rage, fantasies of destruction of self or others, profound sense of depletion, and loss of vitality all reflect deficits in development prior to the onset of the nuclear conflict, rather than regressions from the conflict associated with the nuclear neurosis.

This elaboration of the developmental perspective as a means for understanding variations in personal psychopathology has dramatically altered the conception of the psychoanalytic process from an emphasis upon "mutative interpretations" designed to alter the analysand's super ego to an emphasis upon the "diatrophic bond" (Friedman 1978, Gitelson 1962), reflecting the child's tie to the mother of childhood. In addition to interpreting enactments referring to disguised expression of wishes associated with the nuclear conflict, traditionally understood as the "transference neurosis," developmentally oriented analysts interpret those enactments as referring to the effort to maintain a fragile psychological adjustment through the use of others as a source of psychological oxygen or as an aspect of missing psychological structure.

The increasing significance of this developmentally oriented therapeutic approach has highlighted both transference and countertransference as particularly important in the successful treatment of those patients showing particular deficits stemming from the experience of caregivers during the first years of life. Hoffman (1990) observes that even when the therapist acts in ways consistent with customary therapeutic activity, "those routines themselves provide little or no sanctuary from the more or less turbulent currents of interpersonal responsiveness and self expression that run through every analytic encounter." He continues:

> In the first place, the very fact that one has elected to be in this peculiar role of the therapist is probably saturated with personal meaning. And then, within that role, the conventionally expected acts such as listening and interpreting are invariably self-expressive in terms of their timing, manner, and—in the case of interpretation—their content. So even when therapists find themselves and their patients in the relatively calm waters of critical reflection on what has transpired between them, they are also in the midst of new, personally expressive actions which are eluding critical scrutiny at that moment. [Hoffman 1990, p. 6]

While, at least to some extent, this use of others as a means of enhanced comfort and solace is essential in the human condition (Kohut 1977), among more troubled persons this search for aspects of oneself experienced as missing leads to a desperate search for tension reduction or a "holding environment" (Modell 1990, Winnicott 1960). These more troubled persons are particularly sensitive to even momentary breaks in empathy, which may lead to enhanced feelings of fragmentation and disintegration. Reciprocally, the therapist may feel particularly burdened by this expression of despair and demand for reparenting, leading to additional breaks in empathy; increasing emphasis upon countertransference presents new challenges as well as new resources for the psychotherapist.

Self-Inquiry, Countertransference, and Counteridentification

Psychotherapeutic intervention supposes both the therapist's knowledge of personality development and psychopathology and the therapist's self-knowledge, fostered first through a personal analysis, and then through a lifelong process of self-inquiry (Gardner 1983, Horney 1942). Both Ticho (1967) and Calder (1980) have noted the significance of this continuing self-study for maintaining the analytic attitude. Gardner notes that such self-study must be differentiated from the lay concept of the "examined life"—that it is, rather, an "experiencing, attention-paying, sense-making" activity (1983, p. 18). There has been little study of the analysand's continuing self-analysis after formal termination (Calder 1980). This capacity for continuing self-inquiry, founded on the empathic response emerging from the intersubjectivity that evolves from the jointly constructed analytic relationship (Atwood and Stolorow 1984, Stern 1985, Winnicott 1953), together with the variety of the analysand's own enactments of wish and intent emerging across the course of life, differentiates psychoanalysis and psychoanalytic therapy from all other therapeutic approaches.

Contemporary psychoanalysis has its roots in Freud's own self-inquiry, resulting from his recognition of ambivalent feelings in the aftermath of his father's death in 1896 (Anzieu 1986, Gedo 1976, Sadow et al. 1968). As a result of Freud's self-analysis, he first came to appreciate the "nuclear complex" accompanying the shift from early to middle childhood (Gedo 1976, Kohut 1976, Sadow et al. 1968). Freud's (1937) recommendation in "Analysis Terminable and Interminable"— that analysis should be continued throughout the therapist's career— reflects continuing commitment to self-inquiry as the basis for therapeutic change within the psychoanalytic process.

Continuing self-inquiry reflecting enhanced self-understanding resulting from the therapist's own personal analysis, remains the essential therapeutic "tool" both for maintaining an empathic stance toward the analysand and for recognizing and making sense of unresolved psychological issues in the therapist's own personality reciprocally evoked by those of the analysand. It is important that we consider the role of resistance to recognizing feelings elicited in the therapist as a consequence of working with these more troubled patients, just as, more generally, we must consider the concept of psychoanalysis as an "impossible profession" (Malcolm 1983) to reflect unrealized counteridentifications that become additional resistances in maintaining the psychoanalytic situation (Fine 1985).

Countertransference in Early Psychoanalytic Technique

Surprisingly, although Freud was clear in emphasizing the importance of self-inquiry for the practice of psychoanalysis and as an important source of analytic insight, he nevertheless viewed the therapist's feelings as a potential obstacle rather than as a resource for the treatment. His observation of the problems in understanding the origins of the patient's wishes in the triadic situation of early childhood suggested that the analysand's transference neurosis was capable of reciprocally stimulating unresolved conflicts within the therapist (Freud 1910c). This insight regarding the significance of unresolved conflicts in the therapist's own life as a source of disruption of the treatment provided the basis of Freud's discussion of countertransference.

Freud offered unwitting illustrations of the difficulties that arise when countertransference intrudes into the psychoanalytic situation. Perhaps nowhere are its detrimental effects more dramatically illustrated to the modern reader than in Freud's (1905b) report on the case of Dora (Decker 1991, Marcus 1984). Studies of problems of technique in this case (for a complete review of the literature on this case, see Decker 1991) have suggested that Freud responded to Dora as though she were the governess of his own childhood. Freud's own unresolved conflict regarding his governess and her possible seduction of him during early childhood made it difficult for him to recognize the nature of the transference (Decker 1991, Glenn 1986). Consistent with Freud's discussion of the psychopathology of everyday life, the choice of this pseudonym was based on the name of the governess of his sister's children.

Freud characterized the psychoanalytic process as a form of unconscious-to-unconscious communication between analysand and therapist, demonstrating the importance of both the interpretation of otherwise unconscious wishes enacted within the transference and the significance of the therapist's "evenly suspended attention" (Freud 1912b, pp. 115–116) as a means of understanding the analysand's free associations. However, much of this discussion appears to have been one-sided, focusing on the analysand's transference enactments, while less explicitly acknowledging the therapist's own unconscious process reflected in the countertransference.

As suggestive as Freud's description of the unconscious-to-unconscious communication between analysand and therapist might have been in another context, within the context of his drive to establish the method by which the patient's free associations could be met by the therapist's "evenly suspended attention" (Freud 1912b, pp. 115–116), attempts to recognize the usefulness of countertransference

responses could only be seen as intrusions into the process of developing specifically psychoanalytic techniques. Grounded in Freud's
(1915a,c, 1915–1917, 1923) conflict psychology, the concept of countertransference was limited to those sentiments evoked in the therapist
as a function of unacknowledged and unresolved wishes focused on the
nuclear conflict of early childhood. This critical view of countertransference was congruent with and supported the scientific perspective of
his time, which emphasized the investigator's objectivity regarding the
data of the natural world (Galatzer-Levy and Cohler 1990).

Countertransference, Counteridentification, and Counterresonance

Ironically, Freud's assumption that the intrusion of the therapist's own
personality into the therapeutic relationship was detrimental to the
therapist's neutral stance, and therefore to the well-being of the patient
(Freud 1910a, 1912b), discouraged exploration of the nature of countertransference as it occurred in individual cases. Following Freud's
(1910a, 1912b) effort to describe countertransference vicissitudes as
tantamount to admission of therapeutic "failure," and despite his
willingness to portray at least certain selected therapeutic failures in the
interest of furthering psychoanalytic inquiry (1910a, 1912b), therapists
of more modest professional reputation were understandably reluctant
to provide accounts of failed cases. In retrospect, it is clear that Freud's
claim that the intrusion of the therapist's personality into the psychoanalytic setting was detrimental to the therapist's neutral stance and
therefore to the patient's well-being (Freud 1910a, 1912b) effectively
limited willingness to explore the vicissitudes of countertransference as
an inevitable aspect of the psychoanalytic process.

Discussion of countertransference in the years since Freud's initial
comments has challenged both his assumption of psychoanalytic
neutrality and his claim that it is possible to eliminate countertransference as an inevitable element of the psychoanalytic situation (Racker
1968). Particularly over the past three decades, there has been increasing
interest in the study of the therapist's personality as a factor determining
both process and outcome in psychoanalysis (Flarsheim 1975). From
initial accounts by English analysts (Heimann 1950, Little 1951,
Winnicott 1949) to Abend's (1989) most recent review of the countertransference literature, recognizing the analytic relationship as one
between two persons requires a consideration of sentiment and wish
among both participants in this relationship (Gill 1982). Current
perspectives on countertransference highlight its presence as a ubiquitous element of the therapeutic relationship. Psychoanalysis is unique in

fostering the therapist's own self-awareness and continuing self-inquiry as an essential component contributing to the realization of a positive therapeutic outcome.

This reformulation and extension of the concept of countertransference presents issues requiring more extended discussion: (1) the role of sentiments and intents experienced by the therapist related to personal psychopathology other than those determined by the reactivation of the therapist's own nuclear conflicts first experienced at the time of the transition from early to middle childhood (Freud 1900, 1910a), and (2) extension of the concept of countertransference to include not only the therapist's own psychopathology reciprocally evoked by the patient's psychopathology, but also any and all sentiments reciprocally elicited for the therapist by the analytic relationship, including those related to empathy or counteridentification. At least in part, study of these issues has been furthered by the effort to provide more inclusive accounts of the therapist's experience as encompassed by the term *countertransference*.

The concept of countertransference may refer either to the experience of the patient that serves predominantly to inform the therapist regarding his own wishes and sentiments, or to those sentiments evoked within the therapist that contain information particularly relevant to understanding the patient, and that are experienced reciprocally and empathically in connection with the patient's own personality and psychopathology (Casement 1986, Grayer and Sax 1986). In addition, the concept of countertransference is sometimes used to refer to responses reflecting the specific phase of the treatment in which therapist and client find themselves (Vaslamatzis et al. 1986). Other theorists have suggested that the concept of countertransference portrays the therapist's position within the treatment situation, the unique content of the patient's own life history, or the analyst's personal emotional response to those of the patient (Missenard 1989). These personal emotional responses include both concordant and complementary identifications, through which the therapist is cast in the role of the patient or of a significant object in the patient's life (Racker 1968).

Tansey and Burke (1989) have further refined Racker's views, noting that we must distinguish not only between the therapist's concordant projective identifications (i.e., empathy) and his complementary projective identifications (i.e., tendency to play one historical or object-relational role while the patient plays the other), but also between those enactments in which the therapist embodies the role of the patient and those in which the therapist takes on the role of significant other to the analysand. Following Fliess (1942, 1953), it is important to distinguish countertransference from counterresonance with the patient's experiences (Boyer 1989, Casement 1986, Grayer and Sax 1986). It is important to differentiate the analyst's empathic, reciprocal experience of the patient's feelings of emptiness and terror from the analyst's own unresolved wishes and sentiments evoked counter to the analysand's enactments of wish and sentiment. The analyst's own unresolved wishes and sentiments may interfere in the process of a deepening and enlivening therapeutic relationship, and may make it additionally difficult for the analysand to achieve greater self-understanding. The analyst's own capacity for continuing self-reflection is important in facilitating the analysand's capacity for self-understanding.

Emergence of unrecognized wishes within the therapist, whether parallel, counter, or reciprocal to those of the analysand, may compromise the effectiveness of psychoanalytically oriented treatment. The task of self-inquiry regarding the therapist's own understanding of the analysand's distress is further compromised by the assumption, based on a misreading of Freud's (1912b, 1914a) papers on technique, that the ideal therapeutic stance is akin to that adopted by the surgeon. Psychotherapy is a relationship between two persons, and it is the very humanity of this relationship that is so essential for the therapeutic change. Success in assisting the analysand to make implicit wishes and sentiments explicit, to develop additional perspectives on the presently remembered life history (Cohler 1991), and to realized enhanced solace and capacity for personal integrity depends in large part upon the therapist's own prior capacity for self-inquiry.

Empathic resonance, facilitated by continuing self-inquiry, which fosters increased understanding of the analysand and appropriate therapeutic intervention, must be differentiated from enactment of sentiments and intentions that are not in awareness and not accessible to the therapist's own self-inquiry. Countertransference is facilitated by continuing self-inquiry and must be differentiated from the therapist's effort, counter to the evocation of the analysand's own enactments, to provide protection from reenactment of aspects of the therapist's own unresolved nuclear neurosis or psychologically primitive wishes and sentiments. Precisely because they are not accessible to self-inquiry, issues in the therapist's own life may interfere in the therapeutic process, mitigating against effective therapeutic change.

Countertransference, Counterresonance, and the More Troubled Patient

Countertransference is a ubiquitous aspect of psychotherapy, but perhaps nowhere is it as significant as in the treatment of the more troubled patient. More difficult patients elicit more powerful and more psychologically primitive countertransference, which require particularly courageous and continuing self-scrutiny on the part of the therapist working with these patients; failure to recognize and assist the patient to recognize wishes and sentiments evoked anew within the therapeutic relationship presents serious problems for the vitality of psychoanalytic intervention with the more troubled patient. Continued awareness of frustration and rage, reciprocally experienced in response to the intensity of the analysand's demands, taxes the capacity for self-inquiry of even the most personally integrated therapist. Perhaps it is for this reason that there is agreement in the literature that these patients are particularly likely to elicit intense countertransference feelings, which may be expressed as therapeutic pessimism or even as premature termination of psychotherapeutic work (Renik 1986, Thoma et al. 1986). Countertransference responses appear to be more prominent (Denis 1990), more difficult to manage (de Urtubey 1989), and more integral to the therapeutic encounter (Shectman 1989) among patients for whom psychologically primitive or archaic personality characteristics are predominant.

Reflection on psychoanalytically focused intervention with more troubled patients suggests that their "powerful projective tugs may cause the clinician to flee or rely on previously renounced characterological defenses" (Greene et al. 1986). Unresolved developmental deficits may be elicited as a consequence of the intensity and the psychologically primitive quality of the analysand's sentiments and intents. These deficits may interfere with the therapist's access to continuing self-inquiry, critical in maintaining capacity for an empathic response to the patient.

THE PSYCHODYNAMICS OF ANOREXIA NERVOSA AND THE THERAPIST'S COUNTERRESONANCE

Although the significance of anorexia, together with eating disorders more generally, has been highlighted over the past two decades, concern with etiology and treatment may be traced back to the nineteenth century. Freud provided the first psychoanalytic account of anorexia, describing the concurrence of melancholia and loss of appetite in an early paper addressed to Fliess (Freud 1895). Following Freud, other early efforts, gaining almost unanimous acceptance in the time after the Second World War, stressed the origin of this illness in the analysand's failure to resolve issues associated with the nuclear neurosis. According to this perspective, the anorectic patient was believed to be struggling both with and against fantasies of oral impregnation, and to be defending against incestuous oral wishes through the refusal to accept food (Berlin et al. 1951).

Contemporary Psychoanalytic Views on Anorexia

Viewed from contemporary perspectives provided by ego-psychological, self-psychological, and object-relational approaches within psychoanalysis, and in the light of pioneering work of Bruch (1973, 1978), the study of anorexia has shifted away from reliance upon this classical view of the anorectic's dilemma as motivated by a defense against primitive expressions of oedipal wishes toward increased concern with the illness as a reflection of a deficit in psychological development. However, at least some clinical theorists who have questioned the universal applicability of the classical "oedipal" model stressing unresolved elements of the nuclear neurosis nevertheless have retained the model for use in particular cases, suggesting that the "classical" formulation may apply for a subgroup of anorectic patients, usually those who show evidence of less intense and long-standing psychopathology (Sours 1974).

Three themes emerge from review of the current psychodynamic literature regarding the etiology of the more severe forms of anorexia nervosa: (1) conflict regarding the patient's capacity for individuation and for resolution of the mother–infant symbiosis (Armstrong and Roth 1989, Beattie 1988, Boris 1984, Bruch 1974, Fischer 1989, Friedlander and Siegel 1990, Goodsitt 1984; Lerner 1986; Mahler 1968, 1972), (2) feelings of loss of control of the patient's capacity to determine her own life, reflecting, at least in part, an impoverishment of mature defenses (Steiger et al. 1989, Wagner et al. 1987), and (3) difficulties in consolidating a gender identity (Orbach 1978, Wooley 1990).

Virtually all published reports regarding the importance of family relationships in the development of anorexia nervosa stress the significance of the mother's personality, life experiences, and relationship with her child from birth through adolescence as the most critical factor determining the development of the syndrome (Bruch 1973, 1978, Cohler 1976, Palazzolli 1963). However, more recent accounts have highlighted the manner in which a combination of the father's absence and a sense of entitlement facilitates the mother–daughter enmeshment as well (Gordon et al. 1989). These accounts have highlighted the counterintuitive fact that "detached, depressed or unexpressive fathers intensify rather than compensate for maternal involvement" (Wooley

1990, p. 259). By failing to provide a "third term" through which psychological differentiation can be achieved (Lacan 1977), the father effectively abandons and isolates the mother–daughter dyad.

Recent studies of anorectic patients have observed that the anorectic presents herself as an extraordinarily competent, self-controlled, and independent young woman. However, this sense of independence masks long-standing confusion regarding the capacity for maintaining a vital and "true" sense of self (G. Klein 1976, Kohut 1971, 1977, 1984, Winnicott 1963). Prior to adolescence, the prospective anorectic may have been viewed by her parents as a model child, extraordinarily compliant with parental needs and wishes from very early childhood. Clinical accounts of babies with anorecticlike symptoms have pointed to the potential long-standing nature of this compliant or false self in which eating has been regulated by parental concerns rather than by the baby's own perceptions of hunger (Chatoor 1989).

The anorectic's parents have generally become alarmed by her predicament by the time that they seek psychological intervention. Nevertheless, they may continue to view her as an ideal child, perhaps failing to acknowledge her present difficulties. The patient may respond by presenting the family in a brittle and idealized manner (Uphoff 1990), as though the family as a whole constituted an impenetrable and yet strangely deserted fortress. Just as the child's needs appear to be dictated by her parents, her illness is apt to be viewed by them as an indication that they, too, are ill; they may view their daughter's illness as if it were their own, protecting themselves against recognition of their daughter's distress with increased intensity.

Relinquishing her awareness of her self in favor of attending to that of her mother, the anorectic patient finds herself in an impossible position. As Sprince (1984) and Birksted–Breen (1989) have observed, the anorectic patient is caught between "the terror of psychic annihilation" and "the terror of aloneness." For the anorectic patient, denial of her own needs is tantamount to destroying herself, denying her own life force, while denial of her mother's needs is equated with destruction of the person upon which she depends for life itself. The anorectic finds herself in the predicament of sharing "one body for two" with her mother (McDougall 1987), responsible for a situation without which neither partner is able to survive. As a consequence of the psychologically primitive or archaic origins of the most severe forms of the syndrome, anorectic patients may be unable to distinguish between food and the mother herself as provider of this food (Birksted–Breen 1989). As a result, either taking in food or accepting the mother's comforting presence constitutes a threat both to the anorectic's own survival and to that of her mother. At the same time, the denial of food and nurturance threatens the patient with both physical and emotional death through starvation.

Although the anorectic patient may rely upon archaic defenses in the effort to master her fears of being engulfed and abandoned, an overly simplistic description of her defensive strategy does not fully portray emerging transferencelike reactions within the treatment situation. On the one hand, evidence of the anorectic's unmediated rage abounds, reflected in the brutality with which she inflicts suffering upon her own body. On the other hand, the patient may rely upon psychologically primitive mechanisms of splitting, disavowal, and denial in an effort to preserve sentiments of personal integrity. The anorectic patient reflects a personal psychology most consistent with Klein's (1946) concept of a paranoid–schizoid position. There are a few gray areas in her world; good is meticulously isolated from bad, as shown by the tenacity with which she clings to her idealizations. The patient's thought and language are remarkably concrete, as is apparent from the way in which she talks about food; she shows a marked proclivity for the symbolic equations (Segal 1957) through which fantasy comes to be responded to as though it were reality itself. In this way, as has been observed (Gartner et al. 1989, Piran et al. 1988), the anorectic's rage responses may resemble those of the borderline patient, despite the fact that her rage is only indirectly expressed through starving both herself and the therapist by withholding within the transference.

Descriptions offered by M. Klein (1946), Winnicott (1949), and other object–relational theorists regarding the nature and defensive strategies characteristic of persons psychologically functioning within the paranoid/schizoid position are important in understanding the anorectic patient. This approach to understanding the origins and course of the anorectic's suffering can be complemented by drawing upon descriptions provided by Ogden (1989). Consistent with earlier observations by Tustin (1984), Ogden describes an autistic–contiguous mode of functioning that is extra-linguistic and sensory dominated, and "in which the most inchoate sense of self is built upon the rhythm of sensation (Tustin 1984), particularly the sensations at the skin's surface" (Ogden 1989, p. 31). Tustin (1984) has suggested that persons functioning within this mode experience the world either in terms of a sense of being held in which "the 'otherness' of the holder is of almost no significance" (Ogden 1989, p. 36), or in terms of "hard, angular impressions upon the skin . . . associated with the most diffuse sense of danger" (p. 37). These persons often experience either a pure sense of being soothed, or else a sense of "nameless dread" (Bion 1955), as they feel their skin giving way and leaking into the world.

Ogden reviews a number of self-stimulating behaviors that reflect difficulty in moving beyond this autistic-contiguous mode. He suggests that these behaviors constitute an effort to affirm a "second skin formation" (Bick 1968) as a protection against formless dread; these self-stimulating behaviors, he notes, often seem to crystalize into regular activities whose "tyrannical power . . . derives from the fact that an individual relying on an autistic mode of defense is absolutely dependent on the ability of the perfect recreation of the sensory experience to protect him against unbearable terror" (Ogden 1989, p. 42–43).

Descriptions provided by object-relational clinical theorists regarding the paranoid-schizoid and autistic-contiguous modes may provide a useful means for understanding the anorectic's experience of self and others as reflected within the transference. The anorectic patient struggles to maintain sensory integrity juxtaposed with the struggle to maintain the split between good and bad, which serves to protect the anorectic's necessary and yet terrifying feelings of merger with her mother. In some severe cases, there may be a vicious cycle in which the anorectic's need to be perfectly soothed drives her to take comfort in her mother, only to discover her mother's intrusiveness. This discovery leads the prospective patient to feel an intolerable threat to her own existence which, in turn, leads her to split off rageful and loving feelings, and to a continuing, ever more desperate search for the opportunity to be soothed.

According to this portrayal of the psychodynamics of anorexia nervosa, cyclical alternations of modes of functioning render the anorectic both passive and rageful, desperately seeking comfort, yet also impossible to comfort. The anorectic simultaneously insists upon preserving a constant distance, as though molding the therapist to her shape, while permitting the therapist to be a repository for her feelings of terror and rage, only tentatively acknowledged as real and helpful. Even when functioning psychologically from within a predominantly paranoid-schizoid mode, although the anorectic may have begun to split off her infantile rage from her capacity for actual merger, experience of this split within the analytic situation may not foster enhanced personal integration. Indeed, viewed from within the paranoid-schizoid position, love is experienced as dangerous in the same manner as hate and as equally likely to result in being devoured.

The annihilating threats of intimacy and aloneness are exacerbated during the "second individuation phase" of adolescence (Blos 1979), when psychologically more archaic separation issues may be reactivated. During adolescence, the anorectic daughter seeks psychological distance from her mother that differs both in kind and in degree from the expected adolescent drive to separation; self-starvation may be used simultaneously to provide that distance and to maintain the premenstrual, oddly "ungendered" physique of her girlhood. The anorectic patient is confronted during adolescence with the prospect of moving away from her mother's regulatory and soothing power, leading to the adoption of an exacting control system, impelled by unmodulated rage, as her split-off infantile brutality is directed against the self.

This self-directed destructive activity reinforces the defenses arising in response to failures to maintain the integrity of the patient's primitive sensory core. Considering its importance in the mother–daughter relationship, as well as the demands of a broader social world in which thinness is marketed as a form of perfection, food becomes an important medium through which this control may be exercised. Effects of the anorectic patient's dieting are almost immediately apparent, providing the patient's only reassurance of control over a fate of either devouring or being devoured; as a consequence, the anorectic patient experiences control and soothing as coming from within, rather than from without, in the person of a controlling mother.

Within the clinical situation, in addition to attending to the patient, work with the anorectic patient requires that the therapist maintain a dual focus on both mother and daughter transference-like enactments. This issue is of particular importance for women therapists, who are particularly likely to become the container of primitive enactments of the dangerous and alluring mother (Wooley 1990). Clinical reports suggest that the mother of the typical anorectic patient may be emotionally impoverished, experiencing her own mother's care giving as inadequate (Gordon et al. 1989, Sheppy et al. 1988). The mother of the anorectic patient continues to be dependent upon her own mother, who she experiences as a controlling woman, providing much criticism but little support, and experienced again within the transference as overcontrolling.

The anorectic's mother may have felt unprepared for parenthood, resenting having to care for another when she still wants to be cared for herself. Unable to understand her own wishes and sentiments, she may be similarly uncertain of the meaning of the baby's cry, or of the relationship between signs of the baby's distress and the baby's needs. Feeling unsatisfied herself, she cannot understand that her infant's needs may be different from her own, looking to her daughter to fulfill these needs. Unable to foster individuation, the mother of the anorectic patient may remain tied to her daughter in special ways that are not true for other children in the family.

During her daughter's adolescence, at least in part as a response to reactivation of her own fears of separation during her own adolescence, these ties to her daughter may be threatened. Fears of what might happen lead the mother to intensify her own enmeshment with her daughter at just the moment at which social and other developmental expectations pressure the daughter to move away. This intensification generally coincides with the onset of the anorectic's self-starvation. Considering the distinctive challenges facing mothers and daughters in their effort to resolve ties formed in earliest childhood (Benjamin 1988, Chodorow 1978, 1989), it is important to note that because the child is a girl, self–object differentiation is vastly more difficult for the mother of an anorectic than it might have been had the child been a boy. These dynamics of anorexia can be illustrated in the description of a young woman seen for psychotherapy in a college counseling center.

Sharon had reluctantly sought treatment when her parents became frightened by reports of the patient's condition provided by the family physician. At the age of 19, Sharon weighed only 90 pounds and had numerous symptoms. She ate only one meal a day, generally a salad, and exercised for more than two hours each day. She was consumed by fear when she felt her pants to be too tight; she both assumed that she had gained weight and feared the contact of the pants against her skin. Later in treatment she began to portray her fear of eating as a monster; she reported fearing that, when her jeans were too tight, she thought she might grow so large that she would explode into bits. At the beginning of the treatment, she regarded her therapist with condescending indifference and indicated that she was pursuing treatment only at her mother's insistence.

The patient and her mother had a complex relationship characterized by daily phone calls from college involving such trivial matters as the patient's outfit for the day (the patient noted in a caustic manner that her mother was markedly obese) and frequent weekend trips home because, she said, her mother needed her; these trips required a four-hour bus ride and made it difficult for Sharon either to complete assignments or to make friends at college. After each such weekend home, Sharon returned to college indirectly voicing anger and disdain toward her mother for interfering in her life and for attempting to bribe her into eating by cooking her favorite foods.

Early sessions were characterized by prolonged periods of silence alternating with intricate and detailed descriptions of her study habits and eating. She arrived five minutes early for her sessions but sat stiff during the hour, warily evaluating the possibility of an attack by the therapist, and wary of revealing anything about herself. Talking terrified the patient and was equated with the terror that she felt when she was "full" or when her pants were too tight and touched her skin. Long periods of silence led the therapist to experience the patient as absent from the room; at the same time, the patient warily scrutinized the therapist, continuously alert to the possibility of attack.

While portraying her daily round, the patient actually provided few details of her life, other than her frenetic exercise and her lack of contact with others beyond her exercise partners. Her look implied that there was little else to say.

A turning point in the treatment resulted from a change in the patient's attitude toward her roommate, whom she began to regard in a cold, callous, aloof manner following failure on a math test. The roommate retaliated by calling the patient's parents and informing them of her continuing weight loss and physical symptoms and refusal to eat food sent to her. The family physician confirmed the seriousness of the patient's condition and, alarmed by continuing deterioration in the patient's physical condition, requested a family meeting. The patient sat stone-faced throughout the meeting, saying little while her mother sobbed as she related the difference between the patient's present distress and her earlier accomplishments. The father looked on dispassionately, halfheartedly reassuring the mother that things would soon be all right. The parents were demoralized by the problems of their "once-perfect daughter" and agreed to seek help for themselves.

Countertransference in the Treatment of Anorexia

Discussions of psychoanalytic psychotherapy suggest that more re-gressed and troubled patients evoke more powerful countertransference responses that are more difficult for the therapist to recognize and understand. It is not surprising that accounts of long-term psychother-apy or psychoanalysis with severely anorectic individuals particularly emphasize difficulties inherent in the therapeutic relationship. This difficulty is often apparent from outset, either as a result of the immediate intensity and powerful enactments from the patient's past characterizing the therapeutic relationship (Fischer 1989), or as a result of the intensity of the lack of intensity itself, which may characterize this relationship from the first phase of treatment. Clinicians often describe their first difficulty working with an anorectic patient as a difficulty in formulating a working alliance. The therapist's discomfort in failing to cement an emotional tie may be experienced as quite active and aggressive (Bemporad et al. 1988, Debray 1987).

While anorectic patients generally do not appear for either psy-chotherapy or medical treatment until the family becomes alarmed and recognizes an obvious physical illness, patients may deny that they have any problem at all (Deering 1987), leaving the therapist with simulta-neous sensations of urgency and helplessness. The intense feelings of anger and inadequacy engendered in this situation may arise before the therapist has had time to establish rapport or a therapeutic alliance (Greenson 1960, 1965, Zetzel and Meissner 1973).

Those working therapeutically with anorectic patients often report that the disjointed intensity characterizing even initial interactions often continue unabated for at least the first several years of the treatment (Birksted-Breen 1989, Fischer 1989). The first therapeutic encounter, in which the patient meets any show of urgency or concern on the therapist's part with a denial of her need for help or nurturance (Bemporad 1988, Deering 1987), is continually replayed throughout the first years of treatment. Negotiation of this process of alternating expressions of need and denial of need constitutes the first phase of the treatment: Fischer (1989) has well paraphrased the "push-pull" drama enacted during the first phase of the treatment: "I feel so helpless, inadequate and alone," she felt her patient to be saying. "You must help me to function—but if you do I will feel hurt and enraged—your help will make me feel more helpless and overwhelmed—you must help me" (p. 45). With these words, the anorectic patient expresses anew the experience of the early mother–child tie unfolding once again with full force in the transference.

In this current staging of the drama, the therapist is assigned multiple roles. In order to appreciate the manner in which these roles are allotted, it is essential that the gender of the therapist be taken into account as a part of treatment, along with the social context of gender relations in which the treatment unfolds. In one of the very few contributions to the discussion of countertransference in psychoanalytic intervention in anorexia nervosa, Wooley (1990) observes that the issue of gender is particularly germane when considering countertransference responses arising in the treatment of anorectic patients. Always an issue in the therapeutic intervention, the problem of gender-related counter-transference is particularly difficult to understand within the context of psychoanalytic treatment of anorexia, characteristically a psychoso-matic illness particularly resonant with psychological issues confront-ing late adolescent and young adult women.

The woman therapist may be cast as the mother upon whom the anorectic silently depends and with whom the patient is enraged; even the therapist's most tentative expression of interest and concern threat-ens to destroy the symbiosis, which the patient experiences as a reenactment of the mother's voracious intrusiveness. Within the coun-terresonance of the therapeutic process, the therapist feels constantly helpless and inadequate, experiencing uncontrollable resentment of the power over her life that is held by another. Wooley (1990) suggests that even a male therapist will eventually find himself in a similar situation, although perhaps somewhat later in the treatment. The intensity of this process is somewhat modulated by the anorectic's idealization of his perceived, characteristically male, competence, self-sufficiency, and restraint.

Countertransference pressures may also be extraordinary. Considering the divergent and often contradictory roles in which the therapist may be cast, feelings of therapeutic competence become elusive. Aware of the patient's desire that the therapist magically know everything there is to know about her, and yet afraid of the control implied by this knowledge, efforts at intervention are experienced by the anorectic patient as a violent and irresponsible intrusion, while every admission of ignorance on the therapist's part is subject to the patient's rage at the therapist's imperfections. Nothing seems to make sense within this foreign world, where eating is equivalent to dying and starvation to living (Cohler 1976). Even the therapist's concern is experienced as hurtful, a fact that can be profoundly alienating, even among therapists who harbor little expectation of becoming a magical rescuer. The therapist may feel, as did Birksted-Breen in her sensitive and insightful portrait of work with an anoretic young woman, that "[her] identity as therapist, or even [her] very existence," was threatened (Birksted-Breen 1989, p. 34).

Psychotherapeutic competence may be easily undermined at the very moment at which there is a feeling of being engulfed within the mother transference. The therapist may be more precisely understood as the recipient of intense malevolence, alternating with the anorectic patient's desperate use of the therapist in an effort to buttress a self experienced as disintegrating. Relying upon an empathic stance, and reciprocally experiencing the analysand's fears of disintegration, the therapist must stand otherwise intolerable and painful affects and become the container of otherwise intolerable sentiments that the patient experiences as threatening psychological survival. To the extent that unresolved deficits, outside of the therapist's awareness, interfere in the capacity for maintaining an empathic stance, the therapist responds with terror elicited counter to the patient's sense of terror. This terror may lead the therapist to attempt to flee from the situation, transfer the patient to another therapist, or emotionally withdraw from genuine engagement in the therapeutic process.

Viewed from the perspective of relational psychology, the anorectic patient functions alternatively within a psychological modality in which splitting is a dominant defense and the therapist is treated as a malevolent object to be envied and expelled; further, it is a mode in which the therapist's presence is seemingly recognized only diffusely, even in the patient's moments of most acute distress. Ogden has noted that therapists working with these more troubled patients may experience "feelings of being tyrannized by an automaton, feelings of inadequacy for having no compassion with the patient, unable to make any connection, together with both intense feelings of protectiveness for the patient" and enhanced experience of physical distance from the patient (1989, p. 44).

The experience of being both intensely loved and intensely hated by a psychologically fragile patient may alternate with a sense of being simply nonexistent, or of being gently taken for granted, like a chair or a blanket. The therapist may experience the patient as alternatively disengaged and aggressive. At times it may be difficult to differentiate between these two responses, as the patient presents an often indistinguishable combination of rejection and pure lack of recognition. Intense aggression may alternate with feelings of emptiness in the therapist, as s/he attempts to deal with the anorectic's feelings of isolation and rage (Flarsheim 1975). If anorexia has been described as "an attempt to annihilate the very nature of human existence" (Birksted-Breen 1989), then the therapist's feelings of impending annihilation may appear "double," occurring through both isolation and destruction, which together intensify the impact of the patient's distress upon the therapist.

It is precisely at the moment when the therapist may be most aware of feelings of anger and helplessness evoked by the patient, that the process of recovery may be under way. The therapist's capacity to "accept [the anorectic's] anger and rejection without retaliation or withdrawal" (Wooley 1990, p. 260), and to understand and mobilize counterresonance reciprocal to the patient's experience of rage and isolation in the service of therapeutic response (Carpy, 1989), is perhaps the most important element contributing to therapeutic change (Berenson et al. 1989, Lerner 1986).

Only when the anorectic is able to experience the therapist's ability to absorb her hostility, and to remain concerned and empathic even when confronted by the patient's feelings of terror, is she able, slowly and at first often only implicitly, to recognize the presence of another person in the room. Only then might the patient begin to suspect the existence of alternatives in addition to those of annihilation through merger or abandonment. The anorectic patient is able to consider the possibility that she possesses an independent self only when she feels sure of the therapist's capacity to allow her the development of a protective skin, to show the ability to survive the ravages of her brutal and devouring love, and to serve as an accepting container for her split-off projections.

The difficulties that the therapist experienced in the treatment of Sharon (discussed earlier in this chapter) may help to illustrate the dynamics of the therapist's own response to the patient's difficulties, the use of this self-inquiry in fostering the therapeutic process. Already at the first meeting with this clearly troubled young woman, the therapist was aware of feeling intimidated by Sharon's perfect clothes and grooming, and by the striking contrast of these elements with her gaunt appearance. While experiencing the patient's smoldering anger, the therapist was able to be empathic with the patient's fear of seeking treatment. The therapist's feeling of helplessness increased reciprocal to the patient's report of her serious medical problems in an offhand and disinterested manner.

The therapist's initial response to this diffident presentation was to feel hopeless about the patient, then a sense of isolation and fear set in as the patient demonstrated a lack of awareness of the life-threatening nature of her problems. The therapist's resentment of the patient increased as Sharon denounced psychotherapy and the therapist's ability to help her. The therapist recalled particular fantasies at this point in the interview, one in which the physician would report that the patient's condition was so serious as to require hospitalization, so that the patient would have to discontinue psychotherapy, and one in which she saved the patient against all odds. At the end of the first hour, the therapist was aware of conflicting feelings of expectation regarding therapeutic progress, including both fear and hope that the patient would not return for a second appointment.

During subsequent meetings, the therapist experienced an increased sense of engagement that the patient could not yet acknowledge. As Sharon sat stiffly in her chair, her index finger would slowly inscribe a small circle on its arm, and the tactile quality of her relationship between Sharon and the chair seemed somehow to expand to include the therapist as well, cementing their contact even at those times when the therapist felt most aggressively attacked by her. Further, while at times this effort at creating unity was felt as soothing, at other times it left the therapist with an uncomfortable and anxious sense of having lost direction and as unprepared for the patient's next attack, with her circling finger tracing patterns on the arm of the chair. The therapeutic atmosphere was marked by complete diffidence toward the therapist, in which periods of icy silence alternated with mockery and derision regarding the therapist's effort to understand the patient's distress. The therapist's efforts at clarification of the patient's distress were greeted with disdain and as irrelevant to her problems.

Even the most minimal gestures were welcomed by the therapist as evidence of ability to communicate the pain and rage that the patient was experiencing. During these periods of silence, any evidence of the patient's experiences became magnified; the silence enhanced the therapist's experience of even the slightest indication of the patient's thoughts and feelings as particularly significant.

The therapist's anxiety regarding the patient's problems increased following the family meeting and revelation of marked deterioration in the patient's condition. These concerns led to impatience with the patient's provocations and difficulty in maintaining a therapeutic alliance. The therapist's recognition of her wish to disavow fear, guilt, and responsibility for the patient's increasing distress provided important information in recognizing that these feelings represented resonance with the patient's own disavowal of her distress, concurrent with the effort to have the therapist serve as the container for painful feelings and unacceptable wishes. The place of the mother transference as a representation of the patient's own feelings of disavowal became clear over time as Sharon increasingly demanded that her mother, and not herself, be held responsible for therapeutic failures. The therapist's initial realization of her own disavowal through continuing self-inquiry fostered reciprocal understanding of the significance of disavowal by the patient through enactment of the experience of the therapist as her mother.

Therapists report that the process of working through the painful dilemma of the anorectic tends to occur in two roughly distinguishable stages. Initial phases of the treatment focus on formal aspects of the therapeutic relationship itself, rather than the origins, course, and content of the patient's distress (Fischer 1989). Early in treatment, anorectic patients are highly self-critical and disparaging regarding their own lives as a continuation of their parents' experienced lack of responsiveness to them (Sohlberg et al. 1989, Wassel-Kuriloff and Rappaport 1970). These patients identify with their parents' aggressiveness and recognize that the parents "regard actions, not words, as the ultimate conveyers of reality" (Myers 1987). Just as in Sharon's case, these factors undoubtedly contribute to the anorectic patient's need to reenact, rather than to recollect, past relationships. At the same time, the patient's self-starvation provides a particularly graphic reminder of her struggle to contain her unmodulated impulse life.

The effect upon the therapist of this action-oriented process—albeit often *inaction*-oriented—may be to seek protection for both participants through increased therapeutic distance, which reduces the sense of exposure and vulnerability on all sides (Herdieckerhoff 1986). The anorectic patient's refusal to talk is less a symbolic expression of this vulnerability than an enactment in itself (Burke 1991); any attempt to treat the anorectic through an analysis of her symbolic life is particularly difficult (American Psychoanalytic Association Panel, 1988). Much of the work of the first years of treatment proceeds almost nonverbally, allowing the therapist little recourse to the mediating force of symbolization available in other psychotherapeutic situations as a means of moderating the patient's regression. Symbolization occurs only upon the successful navigation of the development of a sense of bodily integrity and separateness, its substantive appearance in the therapy acting as a signal that inroads into the underlying process have been made.

Entrance into the second phase of treatment is marked by the evidence of the emergence of the capacity for symbolic function, heralded by an increasing willingness to speak to the therapist, an increasing tendency to use the word *I* when referring to herself, and the appearance of themes of envy and rivalry. In contrast with the first years of treatment, generally characterized by problems in engaging and maintaining the patient's collaboration, the last years of therapy may be characterized by the effort to understand in words and to express those wishes and sentiments connected with the therapist as an extension of other significant past experiences (Fischer 1989).

While the countertransference challenges facing the therapist during this second phase of the treatment are in many ways less intense than they had been during the early years, they nevertheless remain formidable. Therapists may feel exasperated, having weathered storms of rage and self-destructive actions during the early phase of treatment only to discover an envious, attacking, greedy, psychologically fragile patient (Sohn 1985). Even the satisfaction that the therapist experiences with a shift to collaborative focus on understanding the patient's life experiences must be carefully monitored in the light of the temptation to participate in a fantasy in which the "good" therapist replaces the "bad" mother (Wooley 1990, p. 262), especially when the therapist alludes to apparent progress in their collaborative work that the patient is not yet ready to accept.

If each of the two phases of the treatment is marked by characteristic countertransference dilemmas, there is a third dilemma that is reflected in the therapist's effort to make a transition between these two phases. As the patient develops new capacities, the therapist's role must shift from remaining in the background to becoming active in interpreting the anorectic patient's wishes and fears. As Wooley has observed: "Constrained in the early phases of the treatment to relinquish as much control as can safely be done and to absorb hostility, the female therapist reaches a point at which confrontation and the assertion of her feelings are vital to the successful completion of the therapy" (1990, p. 260), while the male therapist's "crucial juncture comes when the patient . . . demands a glimpse into his feelings" (1990, p. 263).

Other therapists concur with Wooley's assessment. Fischer (1989) observes that, "In the second half of the analysis there was a distinct change. . . . There had been a rather dramatic shift from a preoccupation with struggles involving a critical developmental lag to a focus on the intrapsychic conflicts surrounding phallic Oedipal wishes and fantasies" (p. 51). Birksted-Breen (1989, p. 34) describing the shift in countertransference that occurred, observed: "I no longer felt that I had a fragile baby on my hands whose survival depended on my perfect handling and tuning into. Simultaneously I noticed that I became less patient with her silences and less able (or willing) to tune in and read the nonverbal communications during these silences. I now expected more of her" (1989, p. 34).

While the appearance of such a shift may be gratifying, reflecting evidence of therapeutic progress, negotiating this relatively abrupt transition is a delicate matter, inevitably entailing risk on both sides. The therapist may feel overwhelmed by the intensity of the patient's demand for a person with whom to merge, to use as a "selfobject" (Kohut 1971, 1977) or to fight with, thus expressing the patient's rage. At any point in this process the patient may either regress or act up, either beginning once again to diet or escalating her rage at the therapist (Bromberg 1983). Continuing self-inquiry on the part of the therapist fosters recognition both of the patient's fear of changes taking place in her self-concept and the experience of being with others and also that action directed against the therapist and the analytic situation is an inevitable accompaniment of change. The danger is that countertransference will go unrecognized, enhancing the patient's tendency to action and encouraging the patient to maintain a psychologically fragile sense of self.

The therapist begins to adopt new strategies for participating in the treatment at least partly in response to indications from the patient that it would be important to do so. However, the timing of this decision rests at least partly with the therapist, leading to yet further vulnerability to an exaggerated sense of responsibility at just that moment when the patient is beginning to take increased responsibility for her own life. As Mitchell has commented: "Transitions in the process of the therapy, like transitions in the parent–child interaction over time, are "best understood not only as . . . transformation[s] of motivational states in the child [or analysand], but . . . [as] transition[s] of modes of interaction in a relationship" (1991, p. 10). Rather than viewing this transition as dictated solely by the patient's readiness, it may be more useful to view it as negotiated by patient and therapist together, prompted by their mutual sense of frustration and readiness for change.

CONCLUSIONS

The therapist working with an anorectic client experiences a range of sentiments and wishes in response to the patient's distress, including rage, hopelessness, and despair. These feelings are uncomfortable to bear, and they compound the reality of the anorectic's often life-threatening illness. At least part of the effectiveness of psychoanalytic psychotherapy rests on the therapist's capacity to experience reciprocally the patient's subjectivity, leading to counterresonance that is accessible to the therapist's own reflective consideration. The process of counterresonance must be differentiated from countertransference in general, which refers to the therapist's reenactment of deficits and conflicts not experienced in the context of those of the patient, and maintained out of awareness through compromise formations or disavowal.

The literature on countertransference distinguishes between the therapist's responses arising out of his life history and those arising out of a developing sense of the patient in the course of their continuing work together. Empathic resonance with the patient's distress (Fliess 1953, Kohut 1959) fosters enhanced understanding of the patient's subjectivity and provides important clues regarding more effective therapeutic intervention. However, enactments out of awareness, complementary to the patient's distress, interfere with the capacity for counterresonance and lead to the patient's experience of a serious break in empathy, in which the patient feels very much alone and not understood. To the extent that the therapist is able to recognize countertransference and to empathically experience the patient's response to this enactment, helping the patient to resolve these feelings of disappointment and distress, it is still possible to realize a positive therapeutic outcome (Kohut 1977, 1984).

The concept of countertransference normalizes characteristically strong responses evoked as a consequence of work with anorectic patients, providing an increased psychological distance from the patient's painful struggles when working with patients whose psychopathology affords the therapist little personal space. On the other hand, it is important to emphasize the therapist's responsibility for recognizing those responses that might interfere with the deepening of the therapeutic relationship, and encouraging those sentiments that might foster his or her collaborative work with a patient.

The nature of the therapist's experience in working with an anorectic patient provides a modal treatment situation for appreciating the integral role played by the therapist's role within the treatment setting (Fliess 1942, Kohut 1959, 1971). Those working with anorectic patients often experience strong feelings of rage, hopelessness, and incompetence. The therapist beginning work with an anorectic may be regarded by the patient as not existing or as incompetent and subject to annihilation. Birksted–Breen (1989) has portrayed anorexia as "an attempt to annihilate the very nature of human existence." However, this annihilation is really double, occurring through both isolation and destruction, which together intensify the power of the experience. Ironically, it may be at the precise moment when the therapist is most prone to feelings of anger and hopelessness that the process of real recovery may begin. The therapist's capacity "to accept the (anorectic's) anger and rejection without retaliation or withdrawal from the patient" (Wooley 1990, p. 260) and to tolerate the countertransference responses evoked by this rage and withdrawal (Carpy 1989) are essential elements of the restorative power of this mode of psychotherapy (Berenson et al. 1989, Lerner 1986).

Only when the anorectic can witness the therapist's ability to absorb her hostility and yet remain concerned and empathic is she able to acknowledge the presence of another person in the room other than through annihilation through merger or abandonment. Just as in the model of infant personality development portrayed within relational psychology, only when the anorectic patient can be assured of the therapist's capacity to allow her the security of a protective skin is she able to acknowledge existence of self and to begin to relate to others.

The therapist's sentiments of hopelessness and rage, resonating with those of the patient, are accompanied by the capacity for enhanced self-awareness, fostered by continuing self-inquiry, and by the ability to make that which is implicit in human relations now explicit within the therapeutic relationship. Self-inquiry fosters continuing recognition of those sentiments evoked by the patient's illness, which, if not recognized, could compromise the therapist's continuing ability to maintain an emphatic position within the therapeutic situation. Continuing self-inquiry, reflecting the therapist's own continuing self-analysis, fosters empathy or counterresonance, which makes it possible to bear the often painful and explosive sentiments and wishes from which the analysand seeks flight and from which, in a complementary manner, the therapist might otherwise take flight. Recognized as relevant to the patient's own experience of self and others, this recognition fosters counterresonance, which provides the foundation for helping the patient to bear and to resolve her sense of despair and turmoil through enhanced self-understanding.

9

Psychotherapy with Abused Children and Adolescents

Jamshid A. Marvasti, M.D.

COUNTERTRANSFERENCE DEFINED

Countertransference has been defined in several ways, and these definitions exist along a continuum from global to rather narrow. The broadest definition refers solely to those feelings in the therapist that are evoked by the patient; in its narrowest usage, it is defined as those unconscious feelings or reactions that are induced in the therapist by the patient's transference. Other clinicians may label countertransference as the therapist's transference to the patient. This definition suggests that the therapist's unresolved conflicts with significant people in his past are displaced onto the patient and the therapeutic situation.

In this chapter the author uses the concept of countertransference to refer to the sum of all intense feelings in the therapist toward the abused young victim and her[1] family, and toward the offender, the offender's therapist, and the offender's lawyer. The definition is close to Heimann's (1950), Alvarez's (1983), and Racker's (1968) definitions of

---

[1]For the sake of simplicity, a female pronoun is used for the victim and a male pronoun is used for the offender. This should not imply that there are never female offenders or male victims.

countertransference, which differ from the classical position that restricts countertransference to the pathological aspects of the therapist's response. The clinical material in this chapter is derived from clinical experience at the Sexual Trauma Center in Manchester, Connecticut, where the author has been involved in the treatment of victims of child abuse, in supervisory work and in the psychotherapy of therapists who were victims/survivors of child abuse. Some of these clinical findings are derived from the author's work with abused children while he himself was under personal psychoanalysis.

A review of the clinical literature reveals a dearth of articles on the issue of countertransference in work with children, especially in the treatment of sexually abused children and incestuous families. Some authors have speculated that clinicians are not comfortable in talking about themselves in general, which may account for the scarcity of articles that address countertransference. Another reason to believe that little has been written about countertransference in cases of sexual abuse is that the therapist not only must talk about his own feelings, but must acknowledge his own reaction to the incest taboo. Frequently a therapist will react with disgust at the disclosure of an incestuous relationship. On the other hand, he will, on occasion, be sexually stimulated and even have fantasies about the patient. Some therapists have been brave enough to write about their experience of such sexual stimulation and fantasies.

REVIEW OF THE LITERATURE

Briere (1989) defines countertransference in working with sexually abused victims as "biased therapist behaviors that are based on earlier life experiences or learning." Ganzarain and Buchele (1988), in treating sexually abused victims, define countertransference as "the whole of the therapist's unconscious and conscious attitudes and behaviors toward the patient." This broader definition goes beyond the therapist's repetition of childhood conflicts and incorporates the therapist's specific responses to the patient's personality. Other therapists who have worked with child abuse victims have acknowledged countertransference reactions, and generally define these phenomena in broader terms than what is usually encountered in psychoanalysis. Friedrich (1990), in psychotherapy with sexually abused victims, considers countertransference to be the therapist's reactions that are based in part on who the therapist is and what he or she brings to the therapy process: "Given our early 'training' to be therapists in our own families, we can expect that some of what we bring to therapy are overdeveloped skills at listening, facilitating, controlling and supporting" (p. 269). Generally, clinicians who work with sexually and physically abused children may encounter intense feelings and emotions both from and toward the patient. Therapists need to acknowledge that some of these intense feelings may have to do more with their own personal issues than with the victim's circumstances and the therapeutic situation. The therapist's intense feelings and personal issues may interfere with therapy and may be identified in supervision or through personal psychotherapy.

A variety of countertransference situations may be observed in the treatment of abused children. For example, the subject of incest can be roughly divided into two categories: (1) countertransference in the therapist who does not identify any incestuous activity in his or her past, and (2) countertransference in a therapist who is a survivor of incest and child abuse. In the latter group, the countertransference may vary on the basis of the individual's perception of past incestuous involvement. The following scenario occurs frequently among therapists who were themselves survivors of incest:

The therapist, ex-victim, finds herself treating a patient for a situation that she experienced in her own childhood. It seems that her past is almost recreated in the therapy room, except that it is the patient who is the victim and not the therapist. This clinical scenario is therefore quite reminiscent of her own childhood victimization, although with certain modifications. The following modifications usually occur: The outcome is different from that in the therapist's childhood past because now the father is being confronted, and the mother is being criticized for her passivity. Further, the child is believed, protected, and encouraged to talk; the secret is out, the child is being empowered, and the fear of disclosure has subsided. At this point, the therapist may mistakenly suggest a solution she would have wished for in her own family situation. In this respect, countertransference can influence the therapist's treatment goals for her patient; these goals may well be a reflection of the therapist's wishes for herself and a solution to her own victimization experience.

The Need to Be with an Abused Child

Working with abused children may reveal the overdeterminants of the therapist's motivation and may indicate the professional's personal need, (conscious or unconscious) to be with abused children or abusive families. Friend (1972) skillfully hypothesized about the personal life of a psychoanalyst who works with children. He mentioned a few characteristic needs of such a therapist:

1. The need for an opportunity to defend against the incompletely analyzed infantile–parental problems of the therapist.
2. The omnipotent need to maintain a nurturing feminine identification.
3. The need to maintain a powerful, authoritative masculine identification with the adolescent as a figure for projective identification.
4. The possibility of unconscious seductive/erotic determinants and a desire for leadership. [p. 325]

Friend (1972), in the course of his work supervising child analysts, frequently encountered analysts who had experienced the loss of a parent during their adolescence. Such losses may reinforce an unconscious narcissistic aim to undo similar reactions experienced by adolescent patients.

VARIETIES OF COUNTERTRANSFERENCE

In child abuse intervention, professionals may demonstrate three kinds of countertransference reactions:

1. Countertransference reactions in *selecting* the treatment modality.
2. Countertransference reactions in *reporting* the suspected child abuse incidence or reoffense.
3. Countertransference reactions in *psychotherapy* with the victim and her family.

Countertransference Reactions in Selecting the Modality of Therapy

The clinician's ideology and life history influence not only the clinical findings, but also the therapeutic approach toward abusive and incestuous families. Countertransference also influences the selection of the therapeutic modality. For example, a therapist who is excessively confident in her belief that family therapy is the best and only type of treatment for these abusive families may be reenacting her childhood role of peacemaker in her therapeutic efforts at "keeping the family together." Another clinician, who insists on initiating play therapy with child victims, remembers that during her childhood she was assigned by her mother to pacify her younger siblings with toys and games whenever they cried.

Countertransference Reactions in Reporting Child Abuse Cases

Failure to report suspected cases of child abuse or neglect by mandated reporters is a national problem (Zelman 1990). This failure may be a strong indication of countertransference involvement, although the reporters' characterological makeup may also play a role. Various professionals may fail to report, but clergy members may have a particularly difficult time with this responsibility.

A priest was counseling an anxious and depressed father who "confessed" to the priest that he touched his daughter sexually. The priest advised him to stop it and to fight with the "evil thoughts" in his mind; the father promised he wouldn't do it again. After a few months he confessed to the priest that he had not been able to fight the "evil thoughts," that his faith was getting weaker, and that at times he was acting upon his temptation toward his daughter. The priest then suggested to the father that he might need more intensive counseling and referred him to a pastoral counseling clinic. He was seen there by another priest, who in turn referred him to a psychiatrist for treatment of pedophilia. Neither priest reported the case to state authorities, although the state law considers clergymembers to be mandated reporters of child abuse. However, the second priest told the father that the psychiatrist would probably report it.

Primary-care physicians may also fail to report child abuse, as evidenced in the following example:

A pediatrician had taken care of a family for more than twenty years when the youngest daughter, who by then was an adolescent, informed him of incest with her father. The pediatrician was also aware of the warm and caring relationship between the father and his family, and he felt that reporting the incest to the state would have a very destructive impact on this "respectable" family. Furthermore, he believed that the father had stopped his sexual advances toward the girl. The pediatrician rationalized that the Hippocratic oath (*Primum non nocere:* Do no harm) was more important than state law. [Marvasti 1985]

Although in both examples there may be conscious rationalizations for not reporting, there are indications that countertransference is the main issue. The clergyman felt that he "could not spy" on others and had been trained in his childhood to keep family secrets hidden. He himself had masturbated in his early teen years and felt extremely guilty about it. He had tried to repress his sexual feelings and went to confession many times, but he did not talk about his "sin." He was afraid that the priest to whom he confessed would inform his parents about his sexual activity.

The pediatrician was paralyzed by his excessive need to please his patients, a need that had been a learned survival skill in his past. His childhood was generally unremarkable except that he had established his self-esteem and self-image on the basis of not hurting others, pleasing everyone, and then "feeling good" about himself. As his father had told him before he died, "Be a peacemaker, not a troublemaker."

In the following example, a psychiatrist mandated to report suspected abuse failed to do so because of his own unresolved oedipal issues.

A very attractive single mother had a boyfriend who was babysitting for her two daughters. The girls eventually reported some inappropriate sexual touching by the man. The mother brought her children to a therapist for evaluation and treatment, and the therapist, who was fascinated by the mother's beauty and charm, failed to report the incident to state authorities. His rationale was based upon the following:

1. The children were not at risk anymore.
2. The mother was protective of her daughters and was a reliable woman.
3. The offender was seeking help from an alcohol counselor.
4. The children would not testify against the offender because of their close relationship with him.
5. It would not be beneficial for the mother and her girls to see their friend arrested and jailed.

These conscious rationalizations by the therapist did not represent the principal countertransference issues but were superficial elements that covered the underlying unconscious dynamics: The therapist was attracted to the mother, wished to have her as an intimate partner, and concomitantly wished to get rid of her boyfriend. He defended against these unacceptable wishes by the mechanism of reaction formation and undoing, eventually preventing separation of the mother and her boyfriend. This therapist gained insight into his countertransference reaction during his own psychoanalysis and was able to modify some of his clinical interactions.

Pollak and Levy (1989) have suggested a framework based on four categories of countertransference responses in mandated reporters who fail to report.

1. *Countertransference fear:* Fear of verbal and/or physical assault by the client. Although this fear may be stimulated largely by a

realistic situation, the clinician's psychodynamic issues should not be ignored as a contributory factor.

2. *Countertransference guilt and shame:* Such feelings may be present when the mandated reporter views the act of reporting as a betrayal of trust, a punitive action, or an indication of treatment failure.

3. *Countertransference anger:* A mandated reporter may experience anger and resentment and displace it onto the family. The reporting may be viewed as a personal assault on the professional's sense of perfection, especially when personality variables such as grandiosity, excessive need for control, and difficulties with authority are present (Pollak and Levy 1989).

4. *Countertransference sympathy:* Families presenting emotional deprivation, victimization, and economic need coupled with a genuine desire to change may evoke sympathy and support (Krell and Okin 1984). A professional may overidentify with such families, based upon his own personal issues (such as guilt over having had a more advantageous background, or similarities with his own childhood experience or current situation). These professionals tend to make excuses for families that evoke such reactions and simultaneously fail to recognize a family's need for limit-setting (Pollak and Levy 1989).

Therapists as Ex-Victims and Survivors

For the following reasons, the most effective therapist for an incest offender may be a trained therapist who is also a survivor of incest:

1. The therapist may easily understand the victim's ambivalent feelings toward her parent because she herself experienced the same feelings toward her own incestuous father.

2. The therapist may be able to separate the offender from the offense, acknowledge his human part, and not experience global hatred toward him.

3. The therapist may also be aware of the positive response of the victim toward the offender's sexual stimulation and thus be able to explore all aspects of the victim's feeling about it.

However, there may also be disadvantages:

1. The therapist may personalize the treatment, imposing and projecting her own situation onto her patient.

2. The therapist may overidentify with the victim.
3. The therapist may have preconceived ideas about the cause-and-effect relationship.
4. The therapist may identify with the aggressor in her own childhood abuse, which may lead her to overidentify with the patient's abuser.
5. Posttraumatic stress disorder may develop in the therapist; the patient's description of her victimization may trigger a flashback in the therapist.

Mrazek (1981) notes that a puritanical, repressive upbringing or personal experience with sexual assault may make psychotherapy with sexually abused children more difficult, or even impossible, unless the experiences are understood and worked through. However, in my experience, the therapist, as an ex-victim or survivor, may demonstrate superiority over the nonsurvivor therapist, if he has arrived at a certain degree of resolution of his own trauma. As Briere (1989) stated, the experience of having "been there" can be an asset in working with survivors. Taking the hand of the patient and carrying her through the "dark side" of her life may be very gratifying if the therapist has partially accomplished this task himself.

The Issue of the Therapist's Self-Disclosure

Should the therapist who is herself a survivor of incest disclose details of her own incest history to her patient who is an incest victim? One of the disadvantages of the therapist's self-disclosure is a potential lack of confidentiality on the part of the patient with regard to the therapist's personal life: the patient has no obligation to keep her therapist's personal disclosures confidential, while the reverse is guaranteed by both law and ethics.

Some counselors argue that lack of self-disclosure by the therapist is dishonest. Those therapists who disclose their past victimization to their sexually abused patients report the development of a rapid and intense therapeutic alliance and mutual trust. It may be an important factor for a therapist, as an incest survivor, to disclose her victimization to her patients. If disclosure does not occur, then the therapist may think she is repeating the "secrecy of incest," particularly if the patient suspects her therapist's past victimization and asks about it.

If the therapist opts for self-disclosure of her own past victimization, she should be aware that the patient may believe that her therapist has attained the "correct" or "healthy" view of both the offender and the nonoffending parent. This may deny not only the individual response of a traumatized patient in coping with a similar trauma, but also the variety of her reactions to it.

In recent years, a stumbling block for some survivor/therapists has centered on their court testimony regarding their sexually abused patients. Defense attorneys have demanded that these therapists reveal certain aspects of their personal lives, and more specifically whether or not they themselves were victims of incest and rape.

THE TREATMENT OF SEXUALLY ABUSED CHILDREN AND INCESTUOUS FAMILIES

In incestuous families, separation of the offender from the victim and her siblings at the time of disclosure is indicated. The child should be protected not only from incest but also from "revictimization" by family members who may scapegoat her for "blowing the whistle." In some cases, children may interpret sexual contact not as negative but rather as an expression of parental nurture and love. Children may hesitate to disclose sexual abuse for a variety of reasons, including the cultural stigma associated with sex, self-blame, fear of the offender and of possible retaliation, and fear of not being believed. Even after children have revealed abuse, they may decide to recant (Sukosky and Marvasti 1991).

Therapeutic Principles and Goals

General therapeutic principles and goals in the treatment of such children and their families include the following:

1. The establishment of a therapeutic relationship that allows the child to express and ventilate negative feelings and repressed emotions
2. Provision of corrective emotional experiences
3. Development of awareness and knowledge of her emotional traumas
4. Reworking of the trauma and resolution of the developmental crisis
5. Increase in self-esteem, self-confidence, autonomy, and impulse control
6. Improvement in coping skills, object relationships, and reality testing

7. Breaking the cycle of victimization in the next generation; breaking the intergenerational cycle of victimization may be understood as the most important therapeutic test

Treatment modalities in father/daughter incest include:

1. Crisis intervention
2. Group psychotherapy with victims
3. Group psychotherapy with mothers of victims
4. Play therapy with child victims; individual psychotherapy with adolescent victims
5. Family therapy
6. Therapy for the sex offender

COUNTERTRANSFERENCE IN CRISIS INTERVENTION

Crisis intervention is applicable immediately after the disclosure of incest. When the incest is perpetrated by the father, the mother's reaction is usually denial, shock, and disbelief, while the victim experiences guilt feelings, self-blame, and fear. Fathers rarely admit to their offense, and the equilibrium of the family is shaken when the "conspiracy of silence" is broken. Family members demonstrate reactions that are usually geared toward rebalancing the family's equilibrium. The usual countertransference of professionals is characterized by anger toward the mother. Male professionals, especially, may get caught in "blaming the mother syndrome" (Marvasti 1991).

In some cases an adult female may be the sex offender of a male teenager. There may be a very different reaction from the male therapist toward the female sex offender (Marvasti 1986). Such reactions may include sexual stimulation of the therapist and undermining of any possible negative effect on the male victim.

At this stage of treatment, the victim should be believed, understood, and praised for appropriate action in disclosing the secret. She should be encouraged to acknowledge and deal with her self-blame, guilt feelings, and ambivalence toward her father. The mother–daughter relationship should be evaluated, and attempts should be made to reestablish the mother–daughter bond.

Countertransference issues in this stage of therapy are multiple and divergent. The female therapist, who has a need to believe that incest between a father and daughter must be painful to the daughter, may not allow the patient to discuss her positive physical responses to sexual contact with her father. The patient gets the message from the therapist that everything related to incest should be negative, or that the therapist wants to hear only the negative aspect of the experience. This countertransference reaction is a barrier to effective therapy, because the positive side of the child's ambivalent feelings toward her father are not explored. The therapist's unacceptable sexual feelings toward her own father are being rigorously defended against when the therapist is capable of viewing incest only as painful and negative.

The therapist's reluctance and discomfort in exploring sexuality and incest may prevent him from asking the incest victim "sexual questions" in the first session. This difficulty may be rationalized as "waiting for the patient to become more comfortable." The impact on the patient may be negative; this is such a bad, shameful, and frightening subject that even the therapist has difficulty talking about it.

Therapists who work with these patients should be comfortable with their own sexuality and aware of their own sexual "hang-ups." The therapist who intensely defends against his erotic excitement toward the patient is intolerant of any seductive behavior from her, as is evidenced in the following vignette:

Mary, a teenager who was rejected and abandoned by her father for the entire period of her childhood, was sexually abused by her mother's male friend. She was involved in therapy with a young male therapist and exhibited some mildly flirtatious behavior toward him. The therapist, frightened by this behavior, prematurely interpreted the patient's behavior and directed her to stop it; the message received by the patient was that flirting is wrong, unacceptable behavior. This interpretation may have helped the therapist, because his sexual conflicts were greater than his patient's, but it did not permit the patient to explore, test, or become comfortable with her own attractiveness. The therapist also ignored the patient's deprivation in the father–daughter relationship, which was being recreated in the therapeutic situation. The therapist later explained to his supervisor that he could not allow "promiscuous girls" to get his attention through seductiveness, since he believed that girls should also become aware of their nonsexual value.

Gottlieb and Dean (1981), in group therapy with sexually abused girls, suggested a dramatically different approach to dealing with the seductive behavior of female patients toward male therapists. "When one of the girls put her breasts against the male therapist's back, no interpretation was made because such a comment might have been viewed as a rejection of her need for close physical contact. By modeling the ability to be physically close through touching which was not sexualized, the girls could feel cared about without being exploited" (p. 217).

The Therapist's Emotional Response to Incestuous Families

Clinicians working with physically abusive families need to maintain a balance between compassion and control (Rosenfeld and Newburger 1977). However, many therapists find this dual role difficult, if not impossible, to maintain. For some clinicians, compassion, which is vital in treating sex offenders and victims, does not come easily. Anger, overidentification, or helplessness can all get in the way (Mrazek 1981). Ganzarain and Buchele (1988) explained that clinicians working with sexually abused victims experience tense and contradictory feelings such as horrified disbelief, excited curiosity, sexual fantasies, related guilt, a need to blame, and rescue fantasies. These countertransference feelings influence the treatment approaches used with such patients.

The sexually abused patient in therapy may assume contradictory roles learned during childhood. These roles influence countertransference through projective identification inducing, role suction (Redl 1963), and/or role reversals (Ganzarain and Buchele 1988). Patients assuming contradictory roles in therapy may shift from one role to its opposite. For example, roles may switch from abandoned child to favorite child; perverted to normal; prostitute to nun; sexual expert to shameful ignorant; victim to offender; seducer to seduced; and child to caretaker/parent.

Ganzarain and Buchele (1988) explain how these fluctuating roles between two opposite poles confuse the therapist. When a patient assumes one role, the therapist is under pressure by the patient to assume the complementary opposite, effecting a *role suction* through projective identification. A female adolescent, who grew up in an incestuous family with a seductive father, may recreate her childhood milieu in therapy with her male therapist. She splits off and projects a sexual parental introject onto the therapist. The therapist may begin to feel that he is being "seduced" into responding with a counterprojective reaction.

Ganzarain and Buchele (1988) explored the therapist's feelings during group therapy with sexually abused individuals. Voyeuristic curiosity can be stimulated by the patient's stories, and conflicted responses can fluctuate between lust and repulsion. Whenever the male therapist responds to seductive messages conveyed by female patients, the anger at the offender is reenacted in the female therapist's feelings (Ganzarain and Buchele 1988).

Other therapists who have worked with sexually abused children, such as Krieger and colleagues (1980), report that their seductive behavior was sexually arousing. They felt irritated, annoyed, and disturbed by their reactions, fearing that their discomfort would result in covert expressions of anger and distancing. The patient may split off and project the unwanted parts of the self onto the therapist, who in turn comes to experience these parts as his own affects and attitudes. This point does not prove that all of the erotic feelings that the therapist develops toward the patient are induced by the patient. For example, the patient's feelings of love and hatred toward the therapist are generally considered to be displaced (transference) feelings. The patient may develop strong sexual feelings toward her therapist, but such feelings do not indicate that her therapist has acted in a seductive manner toward her.

Mrazek explains that sexually abused children and their families can evoke particular types of responses in clinicians. She describes three such responses, which take the following forms:

1. *The therapist's collusion with the family system:*
   The therapist may be pushed by the incestuous family to collude in their laying of blame for the sexual abuse. The family may completely blame a "seductive" adolescent or "alcoholic" father while overly protecting or rescuing other family members, and the therapist may join the family in this scapegoating and splitting.

2. *The therapist's response to the sexual milieu*:
   Some incestuous families live in a highly erotic milieu, and both their verbal and nonverbal behavior is manifestly seductive or sexually provocative. Although the therapist may at first find such sexual practices disquieting, he may soon begin to feel that he is being too moralistic and rigid in his world views, especially in dealing with such a family.

3. *The therapist's unrealistic expectations:*
   The therapist may have unrealistic, excessively optimistic expectations in regard to the improvement of family members. He may spend a year in rehabilitating the parents while the child remains in foster care with much uncertainty about her future home. The therapist's own self-image and personal investment do not allow him to "give up" on a particular family, although other professionals may have given up any expectation of substantial improvement in the parents. [Mrazek 1981, p. 163]

COUNTERTRANSFERENCE IN GROUP THERAPY WITH SEXUALLY ABUSED CHILDREN AND ADOLESCENTS

Group therapy with victims of incest frequently serves as a vehicle for the development of transference and countertransference, especially if male and female co-therapists are present. The rationale for having co-therapists of different genders includes facilitating the resolution of transference issues, attending to and resolving the sexualization of relationships, and working through the lack of trust toward both sexes. Male and female co-therapists represent surrogate parents who provide appropriate limits and, as Ganzarain and Buchele (1988) have noted, provide the group with "a good mothering environment" in which it is safe to be oneself.

Male and female co-therapists give the group a chance to rework the issues of competition for the attention of same sex–opposite sex adults. The therapists focus on anger toward both the offender and the nonoffending parent, and on ambivalence, guilt, self-blame, amnesia, problems in expressing feelings, assertiveness and passivity, abandonment, and feelings of confusion.

In the group context, the patients may try to reenact their families' dynamics. The male therapist may become idealized by the female patients and the female co-therapist may become the target of subtle jealousy and competition. Sibling rivalry also may occur when patients want the total attention of the therapist. Secrets between two patients may develop as a re-creation of the secret of incest (Marvasti 1992).

In therapy with a group of adolescent girls, one of the patients developed a crush on the male co-therapist. She wrote a poem to this therapist and asked to have individual sessions with him. In a letter she expressed negative feelings toward the female co-therapist and asked the male co-therapist to keep her feelings secret, as she didn't want the female therapist "to get hurt by my crazy feeling toward her." The patient's effort to induce a desire in the male therapist to keep the secret represented her need to be reexposed to secrecy. The male therapist, by analyzing his countertransference, discovered that the patient had induced a sibling rivalry in him toward the female co-therapist; he eventually remembered how in his childhood he wished to be better than his sister. He was tempted to keep the secret and not to inform his co-therapist of the patient's negative feelings, since he felt that the female therapist was already disappointed at being unable to develop a "therapeutic alliance" with her patients. He eventually shared his feelings and the patient's letter with the female co-therapist. Both therapists brought up the issue of secrecy in the next group session, and the patient was confronted by other patients with her violation of the group agreement regarding secrecy. The co-therapists reaffirmed the group policy—namely, that all erotic feelings by patients toward the therapists should be disclosed and discussed in the group, and that negative feelings toward the therapists should be disclosed as well.

Co-therapist's Task

Gottlieb and Dean (1981) relate that, in group therapy with sexually abused victims, they felt that an open dialogue between co-therapists and communication about countertransference was necessary. Their patients saw the male co-therapist as a sexual threat to the female therapist and displayed curiosity about the co-therapy relationships. Both therapists acknowledged to each other that they would need to explore the presence of sexual fantasies about one another. When girls expressed anger toward the male co-therapist and the female therapist became the idealized object, the male co-therapist experienced a reaction toward his colleague because she was the positively valenced object. The girls' attempts to provoke the therapists to act out their anger toward each other then became evident (Gottlieb and Dean 1981, p. 215).

In a group that I led for sexually abused girls, I had been a target of hostility for several group sessions. These girls tried to victimize me as they themselves had once been emotionally victimized. Female patients may distrust the male therapist, may criticize, belittle, and reject him, and may make him believe that he is the barrier to therapeutic progress in the group, as is demonstrated in the following example.

Group therapy for adolescent girls who were victims of paternal incest was conducted by a male therapist. In the beginning, the patients were very reluctant to talk about personal and sexual issues, letting the "secrets" remain secrets. The male therapist eventually began to feel that he was a barrier in therapy, and he experienced guilt about this. He tried to focus on issues other than incest and attempted to discuss nonthreatening subjects for the purpose of developing a rapport with the patients. After several sessions, the therapist became aware of the lack of progress in the group and, in analyzing it with his own psychoanalyst, he found that his countertransference and behavior in the group was largely evoked and directed by the group's transference. He discovered how the patients had placed him in the position of the incestuous father who was able to survive at home with the help of secrecy. These girls recreated the secret of incest in a group session and evoked countertransference in the male therapist by contributing to the conspiracy of silence. He, like their fathers, avoided talking about the real issues and maintained his contact with the girls on the basis of exploring non sexual subjects, such as school performance and sibling and peer-group relationships. The therapist, in analyzing his countertransference, was able to learn about his patients and their need to recreate a scenario where they were the passive players. The therapist also speculated that these girls, by evoking this sense of secrecy within him, may have demonstrated their fear of disclosure and the concomitant efforts that they themselves engaged in that may have contributed to the secrets they kept with their fathers. He later explored this issue in the group, and his speculation was confirmed by a few patients.

In group therapy with female adolescents who are victims of sexual assault by a male offender, a variety of transference and countertransference configurations may develop. Patients may express negative feelings toward the male co-therapist and idealize the female therapist, or, on the contrary, may become seductive toward the male therapist and resent the female co-therapist. Gottlieb and Dean (1981) reported that their adolescent girls in group therapy viewed the female therapist as passive and ineffectual or as a potential victim of male therapist aggression. Conversely, they also observed that girls idealized the female co-therapist as a strong, maternal protector from the aggressive male, and that the female co-therapist would then become an object for identification.

The seductiveness that female adolescents display toward male therapists may represent a value system that was taught to them at home by their incestuous parents. These girls may feel they have no value to others except when they are sexual. Since paternal attention was given to them only when their behavior served the sexual needs of their parents, their self-esteem became dependent on whatever sexual affections they could evoke in men. During therapy, these overly sexualized girls may evoke sexual feelings and excitement in the male therapist by seductive or provocative behavior. They may be able to relate to men only by being sexual and submissive. If the male therapist feels sexually attracted to one or more of these girls in group therapy, he may consciously or unconsciously give special attention to the one to whom he is more attracted, or he may defend against his unwanted sexual feelings by ignoring her or interpreting her seductiveness prematurely. By analyzing his erotic countertransference feelings, the therapist may become aware that these girls grew up in homes where no boundaries existed, particularly insofar as father–daughter boundaries were violated, ultimately transforming the father–daughter relationship into an erotic one. The same phenomenon may be recreated in therapy sessions as the therapist–patient relationship is subject to pressure for transformation into a sensual and sexual one. The therapist must resist this change, interpret and confront the erotic dynamics of his patients, and bring up the issues of sexual seductiveness and attraction as subjects for open discussion. If the therapist succumbs to his erotic countertransference feelings, then these girls will lose their last chance to experience a caring and nonsexual relationship with an adult male and may never discover their value as nonsexual beings.

COUNTERTRANSFERENCE IN THE TREATMENT OF FATHERS IN FATHER–DAUGHTER INCEST: NEUTRALITY VERSUS REALITY

It is difficult not to develop powerful feelings toward an incest offender or victim. Breaking the incest taboo evokes a range of subjective reactions that must be acknowledged and analyzed. In effect, neutrality is almost impossible, although the inexperienced therapist may feel guilty when he does not feel "neutral" during therapy with the abusive parents. The therapist's awareness of his subjective reactions is the important element, however, regardless of how negative or positive these reactions may be. Not only may a "neutral" feeling toward the abusive parent be an unattainable ideal, but the great effort put forward to remain neutral can have negative consequences: the abusive parent cannot believe that the therapist is neutral and may therefore consider this neutrality to be a deception or a pretense.

If countertransference includes all feelings or subjective reactions of the therapist toward the patient, then it is first necessary to explore feelings that the therapist may develop even prior to seeing the patient. These may be based upon only the information given at the time of the initial telephone contact. This information may include the reasons for referral, the type of sexual offense or victimization, and news media reports (about the offender's arrest) that include data on the patient's and offender's race, age, name, ethnicity, and socioeconomic class.

I have developed a method that prevents the emergence of obstructive negative feelings in work with child rapists. Almost all the rapists with whom I have worked have a childhood history of physical or emotional abuse or of rape and sexual maltreatment. Picturing the offender as a child who is being beaten, or who is being chased in order to be raped, or who has been abandoned and emotionally traumatized enables me to reduce my negative feelings.

Jack was a big, burly man with a thick moustache and a booming voice. He had been labeled a child rapist and an incest offender. The therapist immediately developed negative feelings toward him when he was described by the therapist's female office manager as "scary." In order to reduce these negative feelings, the therapist attempted to view the patient through a developmental perspective. He told Jack that he knew he was there because of allegations of rape and incest, and asked him to provide some information about his past, especially his childhood.

When the patient spoke about his childhood, the therapist began to visualize instead of this "rapist" a 6-year-old child who had been abused, raped, and emotionally battered throughout his childhood. The therapist felt as though he wanted to get up and hug and comfort this "6-year-old child." His negative feelings toward the rapist were transformed into feelings of caring because he no longer saw a burly sex offender but a child victim instead.

In the treatment of juveniles or adults guilty of sex offenses against females, cultural attitudes and beliefs should be addressed in a manner that is both cognitive and confrontive. Especially significant are those attitudes such as "boys will be boys" and that women are helpless and passive and enjoy being "grabbed, forced, overcome, and possessed" during sexual activity. Cognitive distortion is present in almost all incest offenders and rapists, to the point that a rapist may consider the victim's physical struggle against rape to be bodily movements associated with sexual orgasm.

The therapist who is overly defensive about his incestuous feelings toward his daughter would be "shocked" and "astonished" by a case of intercourse between father and daughter. Such a strong reaction was evident in an interview when a father confessed to a therapist that he had had sexual contact with his daughter. The therapist's questions revealed his own astonishment and incredulity: "Are you sure?" "Is it possible?" "Are you just trying to shock me?" "Could it be a drug-induced delusion?"

Countertransference in the therapist, induced by the patient's transference, is illustrated in the following example:

An incest offender constantly blamed his mother for the problems in his life: "She rejected me, put me down, hurt me, and told me I was nothing . . ." The therapist developed a strong mothering attitude toward him, and the focus of therapy shifted from the sexual offense to mothering issues. The therapist identified with the patient's "poor me" attitude, and because it was the patient's need to have a good mother, the therapist was induced to become one. This revealed the therapist's negative and resentful feelings toward his own mother. An overidentification with the patient developed, and the therapist's countertransference became evident. He began to see the patient as himself (a rejected, poor, innocent child) and then displaced his feelings for his mother onto the patient's mother. Finally, he acted upon his need to be a good mother for a "poor child," thereby proving that he was a better mother than either his own mother or his patient's.

CHILD PHYSICAL ABUSE

Physical abuse is defined as the infliction of injury such as bruises, burns, or any other form of physical harm that lasts for at least 48 hours. Many professionals consider excessive corporal punishment as well as close confinement of a child (such as locking and binding the child) to constitute physical abuse. A rare kind of physical abuse identified as "Munchausen by proxy" is a syndrome in which parents subject the child to unnecessary medical procedures, medication, and surgery for which there is no medical basis. Each year it is estimated that 2,000 to 5,000 children die as a result of some form of abuse or neglect. Abusive parents may belong to any socioeconomic group, race or religion, or educational level.

Countertransference in Treatment of Child Battering

For years, since the case of Mary Ellen[2] became public in 1875, the customary response to child abuse was to remove the child from the abusive environment and to punish the batterer. Treatment for abusive parents did not exist until recently, when such parents began to be diagnosed as "sick" people in need of therapy rather than as "bad" or "criminal" people in need of punishment.

Treatment is based on complete and intensive evaluation of the parents, victim, and siblings. If one or both of the parents are suffering from any psychotic, neurotic, or substance-abuse disorder, the first goal is the treatment of these psychiatric disorders. However, removing the child from an environment that puts him at risk should always be the first step. Child abuse is a medical emergency, and in any suspected case the immediate protection of the child should have priority.

Child abuse is also a manifestation of dysfunctional parenting. Individual and group psychotherapy with the victims and treatment of the abusive and nonabusive parents are essential. The involvement of parents in self-help groups (such as Parents Anonymous) and the arrangement of help from organizations such as Time Out for Parents

---

[2]Mary Ellen was the first case of child abuse and was brought to court in 1875 by attorneys from the Society for the Prevention of Cruelty to Animals, because at the time there were no agencies protecting the interest of children.

and visiting nurse associations is beneficial. Abusive parents are in need of counseling, support, role modeling, and stress-reduction education. They need psychotherapy to focus on their sense of rejection, isolation, loneliness, and poor self-image, and they need to ventilate and explore old injuries such as their own parental deprivation and unmet dependency needs.

For the victim, in addition to milieu therapy, long-term psychotherapy is needed, and this may later be combined with possible family sessions after the parents have achieved a certain amount of progress in their own individual therapy. The following case examples indicate the variety of countertransference phenomena encountered in the treatment of the battered child and the battering family.

A young victim of a father's physical abuse did not improve in long-term therapy despite the therapist's efforts to do whatever he could to help his patient. The therapist eventually felt helpless and developed a sense of failure. With the help of his own therapist, he found that the feelings of helplessness and failure were what the patient evoked in him. Both the patient and her mother had felt helpless for a long time and had given up any hope of changing the battering behavior of the father. The patient recreated this scenario in therapy and put the therapist under pressure to play the roles of both herself and her mother. At the same time the patient, by not changing her behavior, exhibited her father's brittleness and inflexibility. By identifying the patient's transference and her need to locate the therapist in the same place that she and her mother had been, the therapist was able to break through this therapeutic stalemate.

In the eyes of the parents of an abused child, the therapist may be viewed as "authority," especially if there is court-mandated treatment for both victim and parents. They may consider the clinician an extension of the justice system and place him in the same category as that of a probation officer. Some abusive families respond only to power and authority, even when the power is abusive. When a therapist is in the position of controlling a family's destiny, various countertransference reactions may occur. The therapist who guards against his excessive authoritarian or grandiose wishes may use reaction formation and resort to a humble, down-to-earth attitude; on the other hand, the therapist who has a need to be important and powerful may experience a euphoric state when the patient's transference evokes feelings of omnipotence, benevolence, and power.

The following case exemplifies the countertransference of a therapist with unresolved childhood feelings of rebelliousness toward his parents:

A therapist who had an unresolved conflict with his own parents, and hence with authority, indirectly encouraged his child patient to "assert" himself to his teacher. Eventually the child became aggressive and spat at the teacher. The therapist's initial reaction to the episode was long, hearty laughter, a reaction that signaled a certain amount of gratification. The child in this case had been encouraged to act out his therapist's conflicted wishes toward authority.

A patient may also try to direct the therapist's behavior toward himself, as a reenactment of what he is being exposed to at home.

Jimmy came to the therapy room while his mother and his younger brother remained in the waiting room. For some time the therapist had felt that the patient's brother was an extremely cute and attractive little boy, and he had a desire to hug him. However, the therapist felt uncomfortable about not having the same feelings toward his patient. By analyzing his countertransference feeling, the therapist understood his simultaneous resentment toward the patient and attraction to the patient's brother to have been induced by the patient. The therapist eventually found these feelings in himself to be an extension of identical feelings of the patient's parents. The parents favored the younger brother, and the patient tried to evoke identical feelings and behavior in the therapist by talking about how he had hit his little brother, and how nasty he was to the boy. In analyzing his countertransference, the therapist was able to uncover the patient's unconscious motivation, and was then able to intervene in a therapeutic way. He tried to avoid satisfying the "sick part" of the child, but rather confronted the child's wish to create resentment in adults toward him (Marvasti 1989, p. 38).

Countertransference toward the young child's parents may be as common as the parent's transference toward their child's therapist. Except in court-mandated therapy, the parents are in charge of their children's treatment. Children are "hostages" of their parents, so to speak; if the therapist dissatisfies the parents or alienates them, the child may not attend the next session. The following example demonstrates how the mother of a patient, through transference, evoked a counter-transferential fear in the therapist.

June, the mother of an abused patient, wore a necklace with the engraving "Irish Bitch." She had been raised by an alcoholic, unstable father who had repeatedly terrorized her. In conversation with her child's therapist, June evoked a feeling of terror and intimidation in him as she played out the role of the "Irish bitch." She recreated what her father had done to her by interro-gating her child's therapist and attacking his competence and clinical judgment. The therapist's fear and intimidation were most likely similar to the feelings that June had experienced in her childhood toward her tyrannical father. She was able to evoke these feelings in the therapist because he had once experienced identical feelings in childhood toward his own selfish brother.

During therapy sessions with abused children, the therapist may unconsciously recreate his own childhood conflicts alongside those of his patient. The interaction of these two "recreations" is the basis of either improvement or regression and deterioration in treatment.

A therapist who has been the scapegoat of his siblings in childhood may become very passive in the therapeutic playroom and allow the child patient to act out her aggression on him. Once again he becomes the victim of another child's tyranny and humiliation. By using displacement, the child may also act out, vis-à-vis the therapist, the anger she feels toward the violent males in her family. In order to determine what is truly in the best interest of the child, the therapist needs to recognize this countertransference. He must eventually renounce his needs—to recreate his past events—in favor of the child's need—to ventilate her anger appropriately toward the original object.

Therapy with survivors of child abuse presents a special set of challenges to the therapist. McCann and Pearlman (1990) have skillfully explained that, just as trauma strongly affects victims, working with victims/survivors will alter therapists' ways of understanding the world and their beliefs about themselves and others. The varieties of transference that abused children may develop may give rise to countertransference in the therapist.

A child of a single mother expressed wishes to have the male therapist as her father or as a man "who could come and live with" her family. She initiated the conversation by telling the therapist that she wished to invite him to her birthday party. She said that her mother made the "best meatballs," and if the party ended late he could even stay overnight in the guest room. She went on to say that her mother would make a delicious breakfast for him. The child's desire to have the therapist as her father induced erotic feelings and fantasies in the therapist toward the patient's mother. The therapist continued to fantasize a romance with the patient's mother until he was able to recognize how his own childhood oedipal fantasy was playing a role in his feelings toward his patient's mother.

Countertransference has been viewed by some as a reflection of the therapist's own unresolved past issues. McCann and Pearlman (1990), however, use the phrase *vicarious traumatization* to describe a phenomenon that many trauma therapists experience, and in specific ways that are related to their own personalities, regardless of whether or not they have unresolved past issues. "Just as posttraumatic stress disorder is a normal reaction to an abnormal event, vicarious traumatization is an inevitable result of working with survivors" (McCann and Pearlman 1990, p. 3). The therapist's identity and frame of reference are often affected in work with survivors, and traumatic experiences in the victim shape the assumptions and beliefs about self and others in both therapist and victim in six "central need areas": safety, trust, esteem, independence, power, and intimacy. McCann and Pearlman (1990) explain how our individual life histories determine which of these six need areas are most important for each of us. For example, the therapist whose safety needs are a central issue may experience an increased sense of personal vulnerability, hypervigilance, and fear, while another therapist whose trust needs are paramount may become painfully aware of the many cruel and sadistic ways in which people can betray the trust of others.

CONCLUSIONS

Countertransference as defined in this chapter includes the totality of the therapist's feelings toward the patient and significant others who are involved with him. These feelings may be due to the therapist's past unresolved issues, or they may be induced in him by the patient or the patient's transference. This totalistic view of countertransference also includes the therapist's reactions to the patient's projective identifications.

Countertransference may be a barrier in psychotherapy, but it may also be used as a tool for discovering the patient's transference and unconscious wishes.

Abused children and abusive parents evoke intense feelings in many clinicians, from denial, distance, and avoidance, to overprotectiveness and overinvolvement. Abusive parents may evoke intense negative feelings in therapists; similarly, incestuous families may stimulate sexual urges in therapists, with attendant feelings of guilt as the counterpart of the "forbidden pleasure."

The therapist who is an ex-victim may be more effective than a nonsurvivor therapist if she has arrived at a certain degree of resolution of her own traumas. As Briere (1989) has stated, the experience of having "been there" can be an asset in working with survivors. There are also possible disadvantages for the therapist with a past history of child abuse, one of which is the risk of overidentification with the patient and the loss of objectivity.

Many therapists may become frustrated or, as Touhy (1987) has observed, develop "narcissistic depletion" when dealing with abusive families. This occurs because the therapist constantly provides inputs to the family but receives little in return. The result may be a drained, used up, and burned out therapist. However, my own experience with therapists who are ex-victims is different: since these therapists could not substantially change their own parents' personality disorders, they seem to know better than to try to change the pathology of the patient's parents. When improvement is not seen, acceptance of the immutable truths may occur in its place, with recognition that "all the king's horses and all the king's men could not put Humpty Dumpty together again."

10

Children Who have Experienced Parent Loss and Parental Divorce

Benjamin Garber, M.D.

T he patient's transference reactions to the therapist and the therapist's countertransference reactions to the patient are seen as the drive that constitutes the essence of the therapeutic process. Whatever other interactions may occur, whatever the therapeutic strategies may be, it is the transference-countertransference interplay that gives the therapy its dynamic direction and its energetic component. The variety and range of transference and countertransference reactions set each therapy apart from all others. The style and substance of these interactions will be determined in large part by the psychopathology and personality of the patient as well as by personality and, hopefully to a lesser extent, the psychopathology of the therapist. Such individual variables can be addressed and examined only on a case-by-case basis. However, in certain psychopathologic configurations or as the result of particular traumas, there occur transference and countertransference interactions that seem to be ubiquitous in their presence and repetitiveness. Aside from other variables, a particular form of psychopathology manifests itself in a particular transference gestalt and also elicits a specific countertransference response. Freud (1905b), in his early cases, especially that of Dora, set the precedent for these types of interactions, and since then therapists have expanded and contributed to the fund of knowledge and understanding of the various transference–counter-transference configurations.

Clinicians have learned that the seductiveness of the hysterical personality will typically elicit a mixture of sexual excitement and anger from a male therapist, while the sterile speculations and intellectualizations of the high-level obsessional will invariably draw the therapist into discussions about somebody's hostility. The mood swings of the narcissistic patient will stimulate feelings of excitement, boredom, hopelessness, and ultimately confusion in the therapist. A similarly repetitive clinical interplay occurs between the child who has lost a parent by death or by divorce and the therapist who treats him.

THEORETICAL CONSIDERATIONS

Before proceeding with an elaboration of the more common transference–countertransference interactions in parent loss and divorce, it may be useful to introduce some general comments about countertransference in the work with children. Much has been written about therapeutic work with children (A. Freud 1965, Glenn 1978, Smirnoff 1971), and their transference reactions to the therapist have been described and elaborated. However, the subject of the therapist's countertransference responses to the child have been dealt with only sporadically (Berlin 1987, Bornstein 1948, Gartner 1985, Kabcenell 1974, Kohrman et al. 1971, Marcus 1980, Marshall 1979, Schowalter 1986).

One of the main reasons that countertransference issues are rarely covered in the literature is a concern that our unreasonable emotional responses to children would make us look bad. Since we are seen, and sometimes see ourselves, as "model parents" vis-à-vis our child patients, the public admission of these reactions might indeed tarnish such an image.

Countertransference reactions may be more intense than they are in the work with adults, and that may be another reason for their avoidance. But that in itself is a compelling reason to examine and study their nature and specificity.

In recent years the concept of countertransference, and even the term, has largely dropped out of the awareness and the vocabulary of child psychiatrists. The current emphasis on descriptive and biological psychiatry as well as the difficulty and discomfort that is part and parcel of any method of self-examination have been largely instrumental in banishing countertransference from awareness (Schowalter 1986).

At various times, all possible behavior and reactions to the patient on the part of the analyst have been called countertransference. Kohrman and colleagues (1971) prefer to use the term *counterreaction* to cover all forms of counterbehavior of the therapist. This group distinguishes universal countertransference as a total response of the child analyst to the patient, the parents, and the therapeutic situation. Then there is the more specific and spontaneously occurring unconscious reaction of the analyst to the patient's transference, which originates in the unresolved conflicts that complement those of the patient. This is countertransference proper.

The most encompassing and clinically useful definition of countertransference is one offered by Marcus (1980): "Countertransference is a complex phenomenon which has its origin in unconscious and preconscious processes of the analyst, has specificity to the patient, to the transference or to other components of the patient's material, and defensively interrupts or disrupts the analyzing function" (p. 286).

While these concepts and definitions have been derived from the psychoanalysis of children, they are applicable to the psychotherapy of children. The clinical configurations may not be as stable nor as intense; nevertheless, they do occur in nonanalytic psychotherapy as well.

In spite of the usefulness of the concept, transference and countertransference issues as they occur in work with children have rarely been written about in the child psychiatric literature (Berlin 1987). Perhaps a closer clinical examination of the transference-countertransference configurations in various forms of psychopathology will help to bring back this neglected area to clinical consciousness.

COUNTERTRANSFERENCE REACTIONS IN REGARD TO DEATH AND DIVORCE

Children whose parents have died and children whose parents have been divorced are viewed by society and by therapists as unique victims of circumstance. In one instance by fate and in the other by seemingly unconcerned parents, the child has been dealt a cruel blow over which he has no control. Consequently, such children are looked at as victims who are in need of care, attention, and support. Such youngsters elicit our deep sympathy and concern, so that we tend to overprotect and make special allowances for them.

The basic concerns for the child who has experienced the loss of a parent by death or divorce may have similar origins, but in the initial evaluation our reactions begin to diverge, and in part this divergence is rooted in intense countertransference reactions.

DIAGNOSTIC ISSUES

When a child who has lost a parent is brought for an evaluation, the most common overt reason for referral is a need by the surviving parent to determine whether the child is intact and whether the parent is dealing reasonably well with the crisis. The surviving parent wants affirmation that he or she is doing an adequate job of parenting under adverse circumstances. Such parents approach the diagnostic process from a position of underlying emotional stability, except that fate has been unkind to them. Since the approach is from a position of intactness, there is a wish for short-term advice but there is scant motivation for long-term intervention. The perception is that life was perfect prior to the loss, and that the lost parent was exceptional and psychopathology was nonexistent; and that since the loss there may be some transient problems but these are appropriate responses to a real-life situation.

Mrs. B, a 32-year-old widow, requested an evaluation for her 10-year-old son. The father had died seven months earlier in an auto accident, and Mrs. B was concerned about how her son was dealing with the loss. An attempt to elicit a history of specific problems was fruitless, as the boy was functioning well. His schoolwork had improved since his father's death. Both the diagnostician and Mrs. B were puzzled about what had precipitated an evaluation at this time, since there was no evidence of psychopathology. After two sessions of nonspecific complaints and concerns, Mrs. B said in desperation that she merely wanted feedback about whether her son was doing well and whether or not she was being a good parent. She then talked about the difficulties of being a single parent and her wish to start dating. She thought that they were handling the loss well, but she had just wanted the opinion of an expert.

In the past it was fashionable to suggest that almost every child who experienced the loss of a parent needed treatment (Furman 1974). Recently this position has shifted, so that we respect the surviving parent's and the bereaved child's adaptive capabilities (Altschul 1988). In part this clinical decision is based on such histories as the foregoing one, and in part it is based on the recognition that during the initial phase of bereavement the family's priorities do not include therapy. Perhaps at a later point a reevaluation would be useful and then the issue of treatment may be reconsidered.

In divorce the initial presentation is different. The referral is usually the result of a child's conflict with his environment. There has generally been a lengthy predivorce history of conflict and strife that has finally come to a head. Each parent recounts in detail the numerous flaws and deficits of the partner. There is a marked emphasis on psychopathology and conflict, so that the parents approach the diagnostic process from a position of defectiveness. The expectation is that the therapist will correct the flawed product of a flawed marriage; the position in these cases is pathology-oriented, and expectations are unrealistic. Since the conflicts usually continue after the divorce, there is the expectation of a long-term, drawn-out therapeutic process.

As a result of such initial self-presentations we tend to see the bereaved parent as stable, and, consequently, we see the child who experienced a parent loss as more intact than the child of divorce. In divorce there is the immediate assumption of psychopathology, which may or may not be valid. There is also an immediate assumption of parental lack of cooperation, which may be equally invalid. From the beginning the initial contacts may thus suffer from countertransference intrusions. There may be an initial idealization of the grieving child and parent, in much the same way the grieving family idealizes the parent who died. In divorce, however, there may be a depreciation of the child, just as the child depreciates the strife-torn parents. In both instances there is an identification by the therapist with the position of the child.

TREATMENT PROCESS

In work with a child whose parent has died, the therapeutic task is relatively straightforward: to assist the child in carrying out a mourning process that is in keeping with his or her developmental capabilities (Garber 1981). The treatment goals are presented to the surviving parent with a sense of certainty and directness. The child or the surviving parent may choose not to accept these therapeutic goals; nevertheless, the therapist has a clear notion of what needs to be done and some idea of how to do it. There is also, in addition to a consistent theoretical framework, a vast amount of clinical data to buttress our theoretical position on how to work with the child who has experienced the death of a parent. Moreover, every culture and religion has a prescribed set of rituals to help people deal with death. These rituals are in part derived from how other generations have dealt with similar crises.

Consequently, in approaching a child who has lost a parent, a therapist does so from a solid position of knowledge, certainty, and expertise. While much in the work with children is vague and uncertain, there is a consensus that mourning is essential if development is to proceed. Although there are various models of mourning, with diverging frames of reference, there is general agreement that mourning is essential for emotional well-being, adaptation, and stability.

In divorce, on the other hand, the therapeutic goals become more vague and uncertain. Although there is agreement that it is important for the child to come to terms with the divorce, the best and most informed way of doing so is not clear. In divorce, just as in loss by death, the child is expected to mourn something; however, that mysterious something is not explicit. While the child may not necessarily mourn the absent parent, he needs to mourn the predivorce intact family constellation, and he has to relinquish the image and fantasy of the intact family.

The child of divorce is also expected to deal with a range of affects in response to the loss. There is sadness, shame, and guilt—and most importantly, there is anger. In addition, the child has to confront profound loyalty issues and to resolve his disappointments with both parents. While in theory there may be a consensus about therapeutic goals, in practice the therapeutic task becomes vague and murky. Instead of dealing with internally constituted issues of which we are cognizant and with which we are comfortable, we are put in the unfamiliar position of mediators. Instead of being able to deal with internally constituted psychological configurations, we must mediate between the child and each parent as well as between the parents, and we must also mediate between the family and the external milieu.

Since the pervasiveness of divorce is a recent phenomenon, culture and tradition have not provided us with the necessary wisdom and rituals to approach such a complex issue. Consequently, as therapists, mediators, and advice-givers, we float in a sea of uncertainty. Clinical theory and research have not yet given us the best approach and the optimum solution to the multiple conflicts that beset the child of divorce. We do not know what to advise, what to say, or how to say it because we are uncertain of the consequences. This uncertainty leads to confusion and anxiety in the therapeutic stance.

Robbie was an engaging and articulate 12-year-old whose parents had divorced six months earlier. Both parents called with complaints that Robbie had been avoiding his customary weekend visits with his father. The parents were puzzled by this behavior, as the divorce had been relatively amicable and the parents were able to cooperate on the child's behalf.

When we discussed his avoidance of his father, Robbie was as puzzled by this as his parents were, since he loved his father and wanted to be with him. When he began to arrive late and miss sessions, I expressed some annoyance at his lack of cooperation. Perhaps something similar was keeping him both from his father and from me. After a lengthy discussion of the issue, he told me that he was confused by the sessions because there were no rules or expectations. Robbie was an orderly, organized youngster who withdrew when there were no visible guidelines in the interaction. Similarly, there were no rules about what he should be doing with his father. He knew that their time together was valuable, but they were always at loose ends about what to do. Either they sat around and watched television or they chased around from activity to activity. The unevenness of the interactions confused Robbie and made him anxious. He wished that the judge who had presided over the divorce would give him "a bunch of rules" as to what a kid should do when he visits his divorced father.

The treatment of a child whose parent has died begins with a sense of certainty that is missing in the treatment of the child of divorce. Our uncertainty causes us to approach the treatment of the divorced family with anxiety and trepidation. There is a sense that we will be called upon to do things that we do not feel capable of doing.

In our compassion for the bereaved child there is an overwhelming eagerness to recommend treatment as a way to compensate for the loss. The question of whether the child has the cognitive or emotional tools to use psychotherapy becomes irrelevant. To enhance therapeutic enthusiasm, the therapist makes a great effort to view the child as likable. His positive traits are overemphasized, while his unappealing traits are ignored. There is a concerted effort to see these children positively at all costs and to overestimate their suitability for treatment. They may be seen as perceptive, insightful, and cognitively mature, when in reality they are incapable of sustaining a mourning process. In the eagerness to treat such a child, the clinician may not make a careful assessment of the ego capacities that are necessary for mourning. Because of our inflated expectations and idealization of these children, we expect them to attach and to mourn on command. We may use an adultomorphic model of mourning that has limited relevance for the child.

When such expectations do not bear fruit and the child does not respond to our interpretations or demonstrate the expected affects of mourning, there is disappointment, which may result in hopelessness and anger. We may tend to label the child as stubborn and assume that he is capable of mourning but just will not do it. The treatment may then reach a stalemate. While we are engaged in an unproductive struggle with the child, the surviving parent may have come to terms with the loss and may be proceeding with his life. Because of this disparity, the parent may remove the child from treatment in order to avoid being reminded of and confronted with the loss.

Eight-year-old Josh had been in treatment for eighteen months without making significant progress. His father had died when Josh was 5 years old, and his mother, who was in therapy, felt that the boy needed treatment to deal with the loss. Josh was a likable but somewhat morose youngster who engaged very superficially. Any effort to have him talk about his loss was futile. He had no idea what I wanted or why it was necessary for him to talk about his father, since his mother was getting married again and he liked his future stepfather.

Just as I was becoming thoroughly frustrated with this youngster, his mother requested a meeting. She came with her fiancé and told me how upset she became with Josh before and after each session. He would refuse to go and would become angry and sullen after the sessions. She had finished her own therapy and suggested that Josh and I also bring our work to a close. Her fiancé had similar feelings and told me that there was no sense "mucking around" in the past. I felt hurt when Josh told me in our last session how relieved he was not to have to see me any more.

In divorce the therapeutic expectations may be more realistic in the beginning of treatment. Nevertheless, we expect the child to express his anger and resentment toward both parents for turning his world upside down. While some children may indeed conform to our expectations, others may not, because of a sense of loyalty to both parents. Children of divorce are reluctant to reveal their thoughts because they have evolved a cynical view of adults. They may come from environments in which disappointments were many and promises were not kept. Thus it is not surprising that children of divorce are often slow to trust their therapists. In such instances, pressure from parents and impatience on the part of the therapist will obstruct the unfolding transferences.

Since children are exceptionally dependent on the environment and reactive to events in their surroundings, it is important for the therapist to be aware of significant shifts in the child's milieu. In analysis, because the transference unfolds in a more detailed manner, significant events in the child's life may be reconstructured in the treatment. In psychotherapy, on the other hand, it is useful that the therapist be apprised of upcoming changes. The communication between parents and therapist must be maintained in an ongoing manner.

When a child's parent dies, the circumstances surrounding the death are known and thus the environment may respond accordingly. Teachers, fellow students, relatives, friends, and the community will know about the loss and may respond accordingly to the child and the surviving parent. Significant changes that follow in the child's life, such as a move, a change in schools, or a parental remarriage, will also be known and will be recognized as legitimate adaptations to the trauma. The therapist is usually informed of such changes in the child's life.

In divorce, the opposite occurs. An ongoing lack of information and a veil of secrecy surround the major players in the drama. The school is often not informed of the dissolution of the marriage because of embarrassment and shame. Teachers and fellow students will find out indirectly when it is discovered or revealed that the child spends weekends with one parent. The reasons for the divorce become the subject of speculation. Suspicions of sexual acting-out by one or both parents are ever-present. When one of the parents decides to date, to change jobs, to move, or to remarry, it is often kept a secret. In most instances the therapist is the last one to be informed of such changes since his importance to the child's well-being is often trivialized and diminished. Consequently, therapy with the child of divorce is likely to be laced with surprises that keep the process, and the therapist, off balance. This withholding of information brings a precariousness and an instability to the treatment. The child's sudden removal from treatment in response to such changes is not uncommon.

Nina, a very anxious 9-year-old girl, had been seeing me twice a week for two years. She was referred for school problems in response to an imminent parental divorce. She was an outgoing, verbal youngster who spent much time talking about her friends and her material possessions. Her parents' divorce became final about a year into the treatment, and custody was awarded to the father.

In our sessions, Nina flitted along the surface and seemed totally uninvolved. She seldom discussed the divorce or the frequent battles between her parents. Despite her surface stance and her sporadic complaints about the sessions, however, her academic performance and social functioning improved markedly. Both parents seemed supportive of the treatment and noted that she was less anxious.

During the last session, prior to Nina's departure for summer camp for four weeks, she seemed uncharacteristically sad and thoughtful. She became tearful as she talked about missing her friends and her dog. She conceded that she might even miss her "boring Dr. Garber." I was puzzled by the intensity of her reaction. We said good-bye and set the date for her next appointment. Two days after her return from camp her father called and announced that she would not be coming back. He gave finances as the reason for termination.

Since the therapist knows little about what is going on with each parent, it is not surprising that therapists will fantasize about the parents' sexual and aggressive acting out. The countertransference response may be evidenced by an ongoing questioning and cross-examination of the child, who may know very little. The therapist may then assume that the child is lying, sneaky, evasive, and withholding, "just like the parents."

Loyalty commitments are internalized patterns originating from something owed to a parent or to an internalized image of a parental representation. Every divorce situation is permeated with loyalty conflicts for the child. Every decision within the disintegrating family involves loyalty issues and conflicts. These loyalty conflicts within the child of divorce are a major contributory element to the child's psychopathology, for they tend to destroy the child's relationships to both parents (Garber 1984).

The therapist may also experience loyalty conflicts if his allegiance shifts from one parent to the other. This may be a function of an identification with the parent and an attempt to overprotect and cater to the child's needs and demands by making suggestions to the parents. As the treatment progresses there may be an increasing identification with the child's position as the therapist finds himself feeling closer to one parent than to the other, with a resulting sense of guilt.

Parents who are divorced or separated usually find it impossible to present a united front. While the child may use this split to turn one parent against the other, in the long run it is the indecision about loyalties that may lead to a passive-aggressive stance and a paralysis in functioning.

The therapist may initially experience more empathy and compassion for the parent of the same sex; however, this may shift as the treatment progresses. Consequently, the therapist may choose to emphasize the child's positive attachments to the other. Such to-and-fro shifts may be discomforting and unsettling, so that the therapist may ultimately move to a position of greater detachment and distance for the preservation of even-handedness. Such shifts by the therapist may confuse the child in his loyalty struggles, for he expects the therapist to remain constant.

In situations of parental loss, the conflict centers around maintaining loyalty to the dead parent. How quickly should the child begin to seek a replacement, and how soon after the death should the surviving parent date and remarry? Such questions evoke significant loyalty issues.

The child in the oedipal and early latency stages will exhibit longings for a replacement at the parent's funeral. We may be horrified by such demands, and we may dismiss them as babblings of an immature mind. With the older child, however, there may be a tendency to lecture and moralize about the wish to forget the lost parent prematurely. Lecturing and hints of disapproval of parent and child are not uncommon and may be presented therapeutically as the wish to avoid mourning the dead parent. This is evoked in part because of an identification with the dead parent. There is anxiety that the child may forget us just as quickly as he is trying to forget the lost parent. Consequently we may insist on memorialization of the dead parent, but not in a way that is spontaneous or ego-syntonic.

When a child's parent has died, there is very little that the therapist can realistically do to make the child's life easier. The therapist is unable to replace the dead parent, so the child's hopefulness and expectations are bound to be frustrated—especially if the therapist and the lost parent are of the same sex. The younger child will not wish to dwell upon his grief; he longs for an immediate replacement, and anything less is not useful. Consequently, a recurring external issue and internal conflict is that the child whose parent has died will harbor the fantasy that the therapist will replace the lost parent. This type of restitutive fantasy is often supported by the surviving parent. When the child begins to realize that his wish will not be fulfilled, profound disappointment may ensue, along with anger and a feeling of betrayal. Once the child senses that the therapist will frustrate his longings, a major component of the initial motivation for treatment falls away.

The therapist may unwittingly contribute to the child's expectation of a replacement. Passing comments by the surviving parent about the child's expectations of a replacement are sometimes ignored because of the therapist's embarrassment. The child may ask recurring questions about the therapist's "real life" outside of the office; the therapist, not wanting to frustrate the already traumatized child, will answer such questions readily, without pursuing their underlying motives. In either instance, the therapist's countertransference response will cater to the child's need and expectation of a replacement. It is indeed possible that the underlying motive for such countertransference responses is the therapist's competitiveness with the dead parent and the notion that he or she could be a much better parent than the deceased.

Seth was an extremely friendly and verbal youngster who talked effortlessly about his dead father. This 10-year-old boy settled into the treatment easily. As he talked about his friends, schoolwork, and activities, he would occasionally ask questions about where I lived, whether I had children and where they went to school. He also wondered about my athletic interests. Because he seemed so involved in treatment, the answering of such questions seemed insignificant. In our last session before my summer vacation, Seth asked where I was going and how I would spend my time. When I attempted to explore his curiosity, Seth became furious. He could not see the harm in my answering "one little question."

After the vacation Seth began to arrive late for sessions and talked less and less. In my irritation I confronted him with the change in his manner from cooperation to avoidance. Seth announced that he wanted to discontinue treatment.

In a subsequent meeting with Seth's mother, she told me that her son had complained about how I had changed. He told her bitterly that I used to be such a "nice, friendly doctor" and that lately I had become "mean." He wondered why I had changed and speculated that maybe it was his fault, although he did not think that he had done anything "bad."

In cases of divorce, the therapist has the leverage to influence the child's outside life. He may be called upon at various times in the divorce process for his input regarding custodial arrangements, and he may have an impact on visitation by supporting one parent's position as a more active and involved caretaker. The therapist may also become involved with lawyers and teachers in a manner that could affect the child's daily interaction with his environment.

While such involvements may indeed have some impact on the child's daily life, they may have a detrimental long-term effect on the treatment. As therapists we are trained to address and deal with the internal world of our patients. Interventions that make use of dreams and fantasies are focused internally, for that is a familiar and comfortable milieu. Such is the essence of therapeutic work to assist a child whose parent has died and who is thus struggling with a reassessment of the internal image of the lost object. In working with children of divorce, however, we are frequently forced out of that position and called upon to deal with the external realities of the child's world. We are asked to deal with issues that frustrate us and make us uncomfortable and angry, since they require a deviation from the traditional therapeutic role. When the parents are not readily available as a focus of discharge, then the anger may be displaced to the child. Since anger usually leads to guilt, resulting aloofness and emotional distancing are frequent companions in the therapy of the child of divorce.

One of the common countertransference problems in the treatment of parent-loss cases is the making of special allowances, which leads to a moving away from and a distortion of the treatment contract. The verbal agreement about the mutual responsibilities of patient and therapist constitutes the essence of the practical framework around which therapy is constructed. The basic interaction in any therapeutic process is spelled out in the beginning of treatment and is then periodically reexamined and renegotiated as the treatment progresses.

In cases of parental loss, there is a greater tendency to overlook the elements of the original contract. Such issues as missed appointments or failure to adhere to the agreed-upon frequency of sessions are just a few of the practical day-to-day aspects that are often overlooked. Such oversights can be rationalized as realistic results of the hardships encountered by a child who has experienced an overwhelming trauma. The therapist may ignore these oversights in an attempt to strengthen the relationship or to compensate for the child's deprivation. Lesser variants of the foregoing may include the giving of food or presents to fill a void, albeit symbolically. Such interactions are part and parcel of any therapeutic encounter, except that in cases of parental loss they are accentuated by the therapist's easily rationalized collusion with the acting out.

Eventually the therapist has a difficult time following the continuity of the process, since the only process available is one of missed appointments, cancellations, lateness, and avoidance. The surviving parent, aware of this pattern, feels guilty and is likely to demand a progress report. When the therapist has nothing to report except his sense of frustration, there is a chance that the treatment will phase out, with a mutual sense of disappointment and relief.

Therapy in cases of divorce is also characterized by frequent departure from the treatment contract, but under different circumstances. After the initial honeymoon period it is not uncommon for the child to miss appointments because the warring parents did not communicate. It is even more likely that the bill will not be paid, because each parent feels that it is the other's responsibility, or because each parent is evading the truth about his or her own hidden financial resources. Due to parental conflict, the treatment is unevenly supported and the contract becomes distorted beyond recognition. The therapist may then begin a chase after the parents, with limited success, since each parent will blame the other. If the parents cannot be recommitted to the treatment, then the therapist's anger at the parents may be displaced to the child. In response to this anger, the therapist may withdraw or make special allowances for the youngster. At such a juncture it is not uncommon for the treatment to phase out, to everyone's relief. Children of divorce are very difficult to engage in ongoing treatment. While inconsistent parental support has a detrimental effect on the process, it is just as likely that the therapist's anger at the child as a countertransference response exerts a powerful disorganizing effect on the process.

TERMINATION ISSUES

Every treatment process is loaded with explicit and implicit expectations. While we feign neutrality, we have underlying expectations for our patients, and this is especially true for children. There is a plan and an accompanying fantasy that follow along predetermined lines. Within this fantasy there is a notion of developmental progression that may involve specific steps and milestones that we anticipate with a sense of eagerness and expectation.

The child who has lost a parent is expected to mourn, and that in and of itself is a reasonable expectation. However, the child should not be expected to mourn as an adult would. We subscribe to a psychodynamic model of the mourning process that, as developed by Bowlby (1960), Pollock (1961), and others, follows predetermined stages, and we expect the child to conform to this schema. Such expectations are unrealistic for children and are probably unrealistic for most adults. This unreasonable expectation has something to do with idealization of the child and with a wish that the child have a better life and be happier than we are. Such inflated expectations may confuse and frustrate the bereaved child and contribute to a feeling of badness and guilt. We may spend much time engaged in a therapeutic push and pull with such a youngster, demanding that he think, talk, and feel about the dead parent. While there are children who are capable of such work, there are many others who are not (Furman 1974, Garber 1981, Miller 1971). Most children fall somewhere in between, such that they can address isolated components of the mourning process but are unable to sustain it. However, as therapists we find ourselves dealing with children who are unable or unwilling to deal with the pain of the loss. There may evolve a tenacious struggle in which the therapist becomes frustrated and angry at the resistant child, while the child complains bitterly about being in treatment. Not uncommonly, the treatment reaches a stalemate and the child leaves in anger.

In reassessing therapeutic strategies with children who have experienced parent loss, we may consider the possibility that if the child is unable or perhaps unwilling to deal with the loss at this stage in his development, he may be able to do so at a later time. An attempt to mourn at a later time and another place is feasible. However, a return to therapy may not occur if the child leaves in anger, so that future exploration of the conflict is less likely.

Jennifer was an intelligent, attractive, reticent 15-year-old who seemed to be functioning adequately in school and with her peers. On two occasions her mother had caught her drinking, and there had been sporadic outbursts with teachers, but overall she seemed to be functioning acceptably. Jennifer's father died when she was 9 years old after a long battle with cancer. Jennifer began to act out after her father's death by failing in school, staying out late, and fighting with her mother and younger brother. She had been close to her father, and they shared athletic and artistic interests. Jennifer felt very guilty about his death because she had refused to visit him in the hospital in the last few weeks of his life. Her mother, who was in treatment, had tried to get her seen by three different therapists. In each instance Jennifer had refused to attend or to talk.

Jennifer's mother had been surprised when her daughter requested treatment six years after the loss. We began working together, and after a successful three-year insight-oriented psychotherapy, we terminated.

During the termination phase we explored why she had decided to seek treatment when she did. The precipitating incident was a walk by the cemetery, which had made her very anxious. She had had dreams about her father for weeks after this incident. She had refused to cooperate with earlier treatment attempts because they felt to her like a punishment for not visiting her father in the hospital. She experienced her mother's anger and saw the therapists as her mother's agents, who were going to punish her for being bad. She did not feel that she was bad, as she loved and missed her father very much. Six years later, when, she reported, her father's ghost came back to haunt her, she finally decided that she was ready to deal with the loss.

In work with children of divorce there is a different set of expectations. The main one is that parents who have been unable to agree and cooperate on most matters should suddenly work together for the good of the child. While there are situations in which this is possible, as shown by the work of Cohen, Cohler, and Weissman (1984), it is generally an unrealistic expectation. Since disruption and disruptiveness are inherent characteristics of divorce, they are likely also to become elements of the treatment. Expressing anger at the parents and child and lecturing about what is good for the child are neither useful nor workable approaches. Parental guilt may carry the treatment for a few weeks or a few months, but as a long-term motivation for therapy, it is not effective.

Just as it is unrealistic to expect the parents to be totally supportive of the treatment, it is equally unrealistic to expect them to settle their lifetime differences for the good of the child. It would be beneficial for the child if the divorce were a clean break and if each parent could get on with his life. Unfortunately this is often not possible, and each time divorcing parents come together, all of the old angers and recriminations are likely to reappear as if the divorce happened yesterday. It is essential for the therapist to be aware of these possibilities, for such an awareness may diminish countertransference.

The therapist who is overidentified with the parental roles is likely to experience particular difficulties with the termination process. Like the parents, he will experience conflicts about how long one holds on to a child and when it is the optimum time to let go. Concern and anxiety about the child and an uneasiness about the child's ability to make it on his own will influence the therapist's thinking about the optimum time for termination.

According to Anthony (1982), countertransference reactions are more likely to arise in work with children than in work with adults. Some of the most troublesome countertransference reactions may occur during the termination phase with children.

When therapy has been successful, the therapist's narcissistic investment may lead him to prolong the treatment unnecessarily. If the therapist's own children are growing up and in the process of leaving home, then his patients, especially those who are successful in doing so, may serve as substitutes. It may well be that the therapist's most intense countertransference response emerges around prolonging the termination or refusing to allow its introduction into the therapeutic work.

The most frequent countertransference reactions, and those most likely to be noticed and recognized, are those involving anger, hate, or fear because they are the most likely to cause anxiety in the therapist. The therapist's sadness about the potential loss of the patient may be more subtle and more difficult to discern. Therapists invariably feel sad about terminations, and this feeling is a sign of their countertransferences. In parent-loss situations, this feeling may be compounded, since it is also a response to the patient's sadness, which intensifies as the patient reexperiences the original trauma. The therapist may then deal with his sadness in one of two ways. He may attempt to extend and prolong the treatment, ostensibly as an attempt to protect the child from experiencing another loss; or it may be that the cloud of sadness becomes so palpably thick that a termination may occur abruptly, to the relief of both parties.

In those instances in which the child has not conformed to our expectations of a normal and appropriate mourning process, it may be tempting to make dire predictions about his future. Such pronouncements are an indicator of anger at the parent and child in response to the termination, for while we have ideas about what constitutes "good treatment," our ability to predict the future is reasonably poor. Termination is successful in a case of parent loss when the patient and the therapist can say good-bye to each other while secure in the knowledge the patient can come back some day if he chooses to do so.

Termination in cases of divorce may be easier than termination in parental loss. Just as the treatment process in divorce is usually buffeted by external circumstances, so is the termination. There may be a forced termination due to a parental move, remarriage, rearrangement of finances, or just a sudden decision that they have had enough. Often there is little hint of an impending change, so both patient and therapist may be surprised. If the child knew about the upcoming change he might have repressed it from both the therapist and himself. While termination in cases of parental loss is permeated with sadness, termination in cases of divorce is characterized by feelings of helplessness and rage. Consequently, in the end, as in the beginning, there may be a palpable identification with the child's feelings. The anger is based on the impression that the treatment, whether successful or not, was not allowed to run its natural course. It is not uncommon for patient and therapist to engage in a kind of sullen mutual withdrawal. In the course of the treatment the parents may seek frequent contact with the therapist to ask advice and to complain about the other parent. Toward the end of treatment, however, the parents are likely to avoid the therapist because of guilt, anger, and disappointment that he did not fix the flawed product of this flawed marriage. At this point the parents may feel optimistic that a new life in a different place or with a different partner will compensate for the deficits of the past.

Parents may also avoid the therapist because they are reluctant to face his disapproval and potential dire predictions for their child. Despite the therapist's withdrawal and anger, he may also feel relieved at not having to deal with this situation. Nevertheless, like the divorcing parents who seek a new therapist, we proceed to the next case with the same sense of hopefulness and unrealistic expectations.

CONCLUSIONS

Although countertransference always comes from the therapist, a countertransference response is triggered by the psychopathology of the patient or some other element of the situation. Therefore, countertransference is usually the result of a fit between the needs of the therapist and the needs of the patient.

Bornstein (1948) comments that therapists often make great efforts to describe their child patients as cute, lovable, and appealing, and are reluctant to see them as "naughty" or unintelligent. This is a manifest attempt to cover negative feelings about a child. It is also an attempt to maintain the fiction that every child is workable, and that it is only the parents who make the work impossible. With the passage of time and an accumulation of clinical experience, there has emerged the recognition that children do elicit countertransference responses, and that these responses are part and parcel of every therapeutic encounter. Although these responses may be qualitatively and quantitatively different from those that arise in treatment with adults, they do occur, nevertheless.

Countertransference reactions may be evoked by the demanding, stubborn, or hostile child as well as by the passive, submissive one whose fear of object loss and need for love remain concealed. Both the domineering angry child and the withdrawn needy child may evoke countertransference reactions in the therapist. Countertransference thoughts and feelings may occur around issues of restraint, retaliation for emotional and physical pain, seduction, sexuality, competitive feelings, hate, fear, anger, rage, and helplessness.

Those who praise countertransference often indiscriminately confuse it with empathy. Empathic feelings, as differentiated from countertransference, are less intense and relatively short-lived. While countertransference reactions may allow us to orient our thinking about what is going on, they are nevertheless an interference with the smooth progression of the therapeutic process.

In the subjective world of individual insight-oriented psychotherapy, it is extremely difficult to make comparisons and draw conclusions from the examination of differing therapeutic approaches with two problems as diverse as the impact on a child of his parents' divorce and the effect of a parent's death. However, there are clues in the clinical experience of others that may allow us to arrive at some tentative impressions.

Rutter (1971) found that the loss of a parent by separation or divorce was more traumatic than loss by death, and that the traumatic feelings lasted longer. It has been noted that rates of delinquency are nearly double for boys whose parents had divorced or separated as compared with boys who had experienced no parental loss, but only slightly elevated when the boys had lost a parent by death. In a study of adolescent girls (Hethrington 1972), self-esteem was higher in girls who had lost a parent by death than in those who had lost a parent by separation or divorce.

Many factors would seem to explain such differences, the main one being the pretrauma familial constellation and its stability. We assume that the family was intact prior to a parent's death, and that the predivorce family has already experienced much strife and turmoil. The fact that the loss of a parent is an event while divorce is a lengthy, traumatic process is also a significant factor that impacts on the outcome. There are also significant differences in how families and the community at large respond to the child who has experienced the death of a parent versus one who has experienced divorce. When a parent dies, the family is supportive and helpful, at least in the short run. The school, church, and other community resources may be marshaled to assist the grieving child. In divorce, on the other hand, such supports are very limited, as families divide into warring camps while the community ignores or avoids the child.

By extension, then, we may assume that the therapist's reaction to the child in cases of death and cases of divorce may also be significant for the outcome. Our countertransference reactions may have a truly significant impact on how children adapt to each trauma.

11

Treatment of Borderline Children and Adolescents

Judith Mishne, D.S.W.

THE BORDERLINE SYNDROME

The label *borderline* has come into increasing use in the last thirty-five years. In fact, there appears to be an actual increase in the prevalence and severity of pathologies due to family disorganization and break-down, substance abuse, and resultant alienation. The borderline diagnosis was first applied to bewildering adult patients who presented "in-between" pathology—that is, pathology between neurosis and psychosis. Sigmund Freud (1914b) first noted the role of narcissistic defenses of projection and denial in the more severe forms of mental illness. In 1925, Wilhelm Reich placed the impulsive character, the neurotic character, and the psychopath between neurosis and psychosis and observed the ambivalence, hostile pregenital impulses, ego and superego deficits, immature defenses, and primitive narcissistic features of the impulsive personality.

Stern (1938, 1945, 1948) was one of the earliest to elaborate on the dynamics and treatment dilemmas with patients he labeled as border-line. He emphasized the underlying characteristic of narcissism and such personality features as psychic bleeding, which he defined as (1) internal reactiveness and distress over any and every life occurrence;

(2) extreme hypersensitivity and sense of insult and injury at the mildest provocation; (3) rigidity; (4) lack of self-assurance and self-esteem; (5) self-pity and chronic depression manifested by masochistic tendencies; (6) pseudo-equanimity, despite inner chaos; and (7) a distorted sense of reality because of excessive projection and denial.

Deutsch (1942) presented her conception of what she called "as-if" patients, because of their tendency to imitate those around them. Their superficial interpersonal relationships and their tendency toward clinging, due to faulty early mothering, results in impaired identifications, internalizations, and distorted ego and superego formation. Knight (1954) made significant observations regarding ego malfunctions and disturbed object relationships. Earlier (1953) he had noted that the ego labors badly and is a feeble and unreliable ally. By the 1950s, these bewildering adult patients were viewed as profoundly more disturbed than neurotic patients but not as impaired as schizophrenics.

At this time, child therapists were noting the same perplexing characteristics in child and adolescent patients. Mahler was one of the first to describe these atypical children in the early 1950s, and she observed a kind of benign psychosis that made them appear more neurotic than psychotic. Weil (1953) stressed, in her accounts, the seeming lack of emancipation of such children from their mothers. Ekstein and Wallerstein (1954) observed the striking similarity of borderline adults and atypical children, given their tendency to succumb repeatedly to intense anxieties and panic reactions, due to repeated ego regressions and temporary transit psychotic episodes, when under stress. These clinicians concluded that reality testing was maintained, although the sense of reality was distorted by magical thinking, grandiosity, basic ego deficits, and an inadequate defense system. Ekstein (1966) described the children studied at the Menninger Foundation as demonstrating markedly shifting levels of ego organization. Rosenfeld and Sprince (1963), in their research efforts with Anna Freud and colleagues at Hampstead, London, observed in their child patients a lack of phase dominance; thus a child or adolescent would simultaneously evidence marked oral and phallic features, seemingly due to inadequate repression and neutralization. Chethik and Fast (1970) and Chethik and Spindler (1971), working with children at the University of Michigan Medical School, wrote a series of articles that focused on the infantile period of development in which the child failed to make the transition out of narcissism.

Later research by Mahler (1963, 1968, 1972) and her colleagues (1975) emphasized the pathology as being due to ongoing symbiosis of child and parent and the child's failures both in achieving separation/individuation, and in attaining object constancy. Kernberg's work on the borderline syndrome (1966, 1967, 1970, 1974a, 1975, 1978) closely parallels Mahler's work. He emphasized specific characteristics of the weak ego and superego structure—more specifically, failure of normal repression; persistence of primitive mechanisms of defense, with reliance on projection, regression, denial, and splitting, and with resultant breakthroughs of aggressivity; fluid ego boundaries; poor reality perception; poor frustration tolerance; deficient differentiation between inner and outer stimuli; poor impulse control; and object splitting (i.e., the all-good or all-bad mother and the all-good or all-bad self). An immature primitive superego results in the child's having inconsistent standards, values, controls, and guilt. Ego-syntonic antisocial trends indicate a poor prognosis (Kernberg 1975).

Kernberg (1966) followed Mahler in his reliance on ego psychology and object-relations theory, noting the development of normal and distorted internalized object relationships and the pathologic chronic characterological organization of the borderline. Kernberg (1978) emphasized the basic ego defect and developmental arrest, rather than specific complaints and symptoms such as anxiety, antisocial behaviors, and narcissism. Pine (1974) underscored the need to map the borders of the borderline child and distinguish between high-, middle-, and low-level functioning. Similarly, Kernberg delineated between what he assessed as higher and lower levels of organizations, reflective of the degree of intactness of ego and superego, and the quality of object relations. Many adolescents who are appropriately diagnosed as borderline have early histories that reflect what appear to be solid and appropriate development and achievements, with the borderline features not appearing until some stage of adolescence. Momentous steps, such as departure for school in childhood and, later in adolescence, departure from home for college, and then the conclusion of college, are precipitants for disorganization and fragmentation because such milestones entail separation and the expectation of more independent, autonomous functioning. With others, just the entrance into chronologic adolescence stimulates profound disorganization and acting-out behaviors. We now have a better understanding that the earlier "good and solid" adjustment was, in fact, fragile, and that what balance was maintained was, in fact, superficial and precarious. Under the pressures of growth spurts, hormonal changes, expected greater emancipation from parents, peer pressures, and increased academic and other expectations, the initial separation-individuation crisis that was not mastered in toddlerhood erupts later, with drastic consequences. The borderline syndrome in these cases existed earlier, in dormant form; but when the young patient was faced with the second and final process of separation/individuation, a necessary part of adolescent development, a collapse occurred. Such a collapse happens because the developmental steps and accomplishments of adolescence prove to be overwhelming for the teenager, who is crippled with specific ego weaknesses; these weaknesses are (1) predominance of primitive defensive operation of the ego, (2) lack of impulse control, (3) lack of anxiety tolerance, and (4) lack of sublimatory channels (Kernberg, 1975, p. 129). Masterson's (1972) conceptualizations correspond to the ego-psychology and object-relations perspective of Mahler and Kernberg, and his emphasis is on what he labels as the "abandonment depression," which results in frequent acting-out behaviors to ward off depression and guilt that the child and adolescent feel because of their wish to individuate.

Additional to the aforenoted *psychoanalytic perspective* is the *biological constitutional approach*, which posits inborn physiological factors as predisposing a child to become borderline. Stone (1981, pp. 6–7) points to three groups of children who may develop borderline disorder: (1) those with a high degree of genetic vulnerability, (2) those with a less severe degree of vulnerability, affected by parenting and the psychosocial environment, and (3) those with the worst forms of parenting and psychosocial environment, who are thereby swamped even if they were normally endowed. The diagnosis in this approach is based upon a combination of clinical symptoms, familial/genetic history, treatment response, and the presence of biological markers. Hereditary links are stressed in this approach, and pharmacotherapy is the recommended treatment.

Grinker (1975), Gunderson et al. (1978), and Spitzer et al. (1979) represent the *eclectic/descriptive* approach and view the borderline as a specific personality disorder. These researchers differ among themselves, citing different criteria for diagnosis. Overall, they emphasize symptoms, behavioral observations, psychodynamics, and psychological test data. The etiology is unspecified, and the population is considered heterogeneous. Treatment is unspecified. Like other theorists, these clinicians pose a spectrum of psychopathology, according to different criteria. Rinsley (1981) points to the patient's position on the spectrum according to his self and object differentiation, whereas Mahler, Pine, and Bergman (1975) emphasize other variables—namely, symbiosis and separation/individuation, specific ego weaknesses, the self system, and the particular point of developmental fixation.

The *family persepective* presents a conceptualization on which there is general agreement regarding families of borderline patients. Zinner and Shapiro (1972) emphasize parental pressure on children to serve as collusive participants in sustaining mutual projections. Mandelbaum (1977) highlights volatile marital relationships, disagreements about parental discipline, parents' enmeshment with their families of origin, poor family boundaries, and, usually, a family history of overall failure to achieve separation and individuation, with resultant severe difficulty in interpersonal relationships.

We have been increasingly struck by the overwhelming volume of confusing, complex, and diverse literature on the borderline patient. Chatham notes that "there was, and still is, disagreement about whether the borderline is primarily a hereditary, constitutional disorder involving disregulation of the central nervous system (an affective spectrum disorder) or a deficit in the sense of self and regulation of impulses due to problematic early nurturing" (1989, p. XI). In the literature on the borderline child, some of the same diversity of opinion exists. Shapiro's (1983) objection to the concept of borderline disorder in childhood rests on the fact that, to him, the data is currently inadequate to designate a discrete diagnostic entity. He advises seeking a better label, unless we believe that the disorder represents a continuum with and to adult borderline personality disorder. With similar reservation, Vela, Gottlieb, and Gottlieb (1983) question the clinical usefulness of a concept that has not in their view been systematically examined. These authors are satisfied with the *DSM-III* classification for adults, but they believe that minus this similar classification for children, the borders of the borderline become increasingly blurred. Echoing Shapiro's reservations, they believe the term should be abandoned until a closer relationship is drawn between childhood and adult borderline states. Ego psychologists and developmentalists (Mahler, Pine, and so on), who believe that there is a continuity between childhood and adult borderline patients, hold a differing view. They see the disorder as rooted in childhood and as due to biogenetic and psychodynamic factors, with resultant failures both in separation-individuation and in the attainment of self and object constancy. Sometimes the disorder is concealed or disguised until adolescence or young adulthood, life stages that require greater autonomy and separation.

Despite such different foci and divergent views, theorists from the various perspectives would agree on features and characteristics commonly found, to varying degrees, in borderline patients. These include identity diffusion, primitive defense operation, existence of the capacity to test reality, impulsivity, unstable intense interpersonal relationships, and affective instability. In addition to the above criteria, the *DSM-III* adult borderline syndrome includes inappropriate, intense, out-of-control expressions of anger and rage; separation anxieties; intolerance of being alone; and chronic feelings of boredom and emptiness. Chethik (1976), in his discussion of borderline children, reminds us that in evaluating a child or adolescent it is the whole gestalt that determines diagnosis, rather than single symptoms or characteristics.

THERAPEUTIC CONTACT WITH PARENTS: THE CLINICIAN'S RESPONSE

Amid the noted differences and points of argument is one other major point of accord. Most experts would agree that individual psychotherapy is the treatment of choice for borderline patients, because they are still caught in the primary dyad, and they therefore require dyadic treatment to allow the original difficulties to emerge and be resolved. Here the agreement ends, as clinicians posit the advantages and disadvantages of adjunctive, additional interventions, including pharmacotherapy, family therapy, and group therapy. There are divergent views about contact with the parents of child and especially adolescent patients treated on an outpatient or inpatient basis or in some sort of day treatment program.

Some analysts and therapists contend that the parent should be seen as infrequently as possible because therapist–parent contact contaminates the treatment, obstructs the true development of a therapeutic alliance, and interferes with an analyzable transference. Concerns voiced are that the child may feel that the treatment is for his parents and not for him or may fear betrayal of confidentiality, and that information from parents may mislead the therapist, especially because parents commonly distort facts and see things from their own perspective and not the child's. If the therapist uses and relies on this distorted information, he may err seriously in work with the child or adolescent. I disagree with the propositions of those opposed to meetings between therapist and parents: "Reassuring explanations are necessary to maintain the parents' cooperation in continuing the analysis [therapy]" (Glenn, et al. 1978, pp. 406–407). "During the consultation and opening phase, educative work may be necessary" (p. 411). "There are times when analysis [treatment] will not prove effective and the child will not improve unless the environment changes" (p. 412).

Borderline children and adolescents are not commonly viewed as appropriate candidates for classical, uncovering psychoanalysis. Rather, intensive psychotherapy or supportive psychotherapy is considered the treatment of choice, during which time contact with parents seems crucial, given the common phenomena of family regression and parents' feeling devoured by their child's dependency needs or hatefully abandoned as the young patient attempts separation. Parental contributions and the borderline child's and adolescent's alienation, aggressivity, and inadequately structured self-image all contribute to family turmoil, all far beyond the turbulence, commonly observed in families of normal adolescents (Giovacchini 1973). Often, both parent and child suffer from deficits in self-esteem, self-reliance, and object constancy and are therefore too fragile for family therapy, because they cannot share the therapy hour or the therapist's attention. This generally requires concurrent work with child and parents. Such work can include parent guidance, parent education, marital therapy, and/or individual treatment for the parents as well as the child.

Parents often present the phenomenon of repetition compulsion and relive their own earlier problems, including lack of separation-individuation, as their child attempts to individuate. Esman (1985) routinely recommends parent–therapist contact in the treatment of adolescents, and this perspective appears all the more crucial with borderline children and adolescents due to the lack of genuine separation and individuation. Clinicians commonly strive for an informational alliance (Glenn et al. 1978) and a therapeutic alliance with parents to parallel the therapeutic alliance that is established with the young patient.

Many parents of young borderline patients cannot surrender their child to someone with whom they are not in contact. They often fear the loss of their child and will compete with the therapist or unconsciously sabotage the therapy unless they have a trusting and sustained alliance or symbiotic merger with the therapist as well. Because of the fluid boundaries in such families, they frequently do not effectively use separate therapists for each family member but instead tend to split and to make little or no progress. Treatment principles and parameters for more intact neurotic patients are misplaced in work with borderline patients and families, where self–other boundaries are blurred, and where there is an absence of self and object constancy. Often the therapist must gain entry into the symbiotic family mass in order gradually to effect boundaries and individuality. When this is attempted too rapidly, via insistence on separate therapists, treatment commonly flounders or is prematurely disrupted and terminated.

In considering countertransference responses in work with borderline children and adolescents, it is crucial to expand the focus all but universally to include the therapist's emotional reaction to the parents. Many of the clinician's reactions can be classified as identification with the child. Parents can be inappropriately blamed, or they may be "overlooked" in an effort not to condemn them; alternatively, they can be objects of competition for therapists, who act out rescue fantasies and attempt to be better parents than the biological parents. It has also been suggested by Ticho (in Feigelson 1974b) that antagonism toward parents can occur as a result of displacement of hostility from the young primary patient.

Glenn and colleagues (1978) suggest that clinicians react to parents as real people. A clinician's response to parents' actual manner and personality traits may include transference and countertransference responses, but "they are not exclusively [such]" (p. 400). Parents can evoke empathy, or, in the face of a hostile barrage, the therapist can become defensive or counterattacking. If the parents appear to be provoking the child's resistance, the therapist's response can be one of irritation and impatience, or of anger or disappointment at the parents' deficiencies. Parental feelings of failure and inadequacy often evoke similar feelings in the therapist, who may then feel a sense of therapeutic nihilism, helplessness, and confusion, or a sense of guilt toward the parents for not achieving rapid resolution of the child's problems.

TRANSFERENCE PHENOMENA

Borderline children and adolescents commonly exhibit modifications of classic transference. One such transferential phenomenon is habitual modes of relating in which children reveal various aspects of their character in treatment just as they do elsewhere (e.g., at home, in school, etc.). Another such phenomenon includes transference of current relationships, wherein the child's mode of relating is but an extension of, or a defensive displacement from, the relationships of primary objects (Sandler et al. 1980). The other subtypes of transference occur in more intact children and are not relevant in clinical work with borderline youth.

In sum, transference as manifest by children and adolescents must not be understood to represent displacement from old objects, in that young patients residing with their parents most commonly present current thoughts and behaviors about the parents in therapy sessions. There is spillover, often both ways, in that the child may act out at home as a result of the treatment, while simultaneously presenting the therapist with affects and defenses that originate in the parent–child relationship. The transference neurosis observed in more intact children involves three people: a subject (the patient), a past object (the parent), and a present object (the therapist). These distinctions are rarely seen in a sustained fashion with child patients, even with those who have achieved object constancy. With the more damaged child, we see self-object transferences and split-object transferences, wherein the therapist, like the mother, is all good or all bad.

The basic cause of these transference developments in borderline patients is the patient's failure to integrate the libidinally determined and the aggressively determined self and object representations (Kernberg 1975, 1976). Within the transference exhibited by borderline patients is often intense distrust and fear of the therapist, who is experienced as attacking the patient. The patient can at times have awareness of his hostility, but he generally feels that it is an appropriate response to the therapist's aggression. Thus the borderline patient, especially the adolescent, feels justified in being angry and aggressive. The patient attempts to control the therapist, much as efforts are made to deny dependency and to control the parents. The patient's aggressive behavior inevitably tends to provoke counteraggressive feelings and attitudes from the therapist. It is as if the patient were pushing the aggressive part of himself onto the therapist, and the countertransference reaction then represents the emergence of this part of the patient from within the therapist (Money-Kyrle 1956, Racker 1957). This self-defeating projection is not pure aggression, but rather a self-representation or an object representation linked with that drive derivative (Kernberg 1982a, p. 474). Commonly, in the borderline's unstable transference, the patient may project a primitive and frightening mother image onto the therapist while experiencing him- or herself as the attacked, panic-stricken, anxious child. Moments later the patient can behave and experience him- or herself as the stern, sadistic mother, and see the therapist as the guilty, defensive child. This transference phenomenon is described by Racker (1957) as "complementary identification."

The vicissitudes of the treatment process are apparent, because the transference–countertransference relationship may be pushed into a replication of the original parent–child interaction, and a vicious cycle may develop, which thereby produces a confusion of what is inside and outside in the patient's experience of the interactions with the therapist. This pattern produces a breakdown of ego boundaries and a loss of reality testing in the transference. The recommended therapeutic stances and treatment interventions to manage the transference phenomena are numerous, contradictory, and dependent on the clinician's theoretical perspective.

Despite general agreement with Kernberg's (1975) comprehensive presentation of borderline personality organization and the vicissitudes of the transference and countertransference phenomena, clinicians increasingly disagree with his major recommendations for dealing with borderline patients' transference manifestations. Similar reservations have been raised about Masterson's approach, which closely parallels Kernberg's. Both these clinicians make interpretations in the here and now, and they present with a stance of technical neutrality. I have grave reservations about what Chatham (1989) describes as Kernberg's persistent and strongly worded interpretations and Masterson's firmly stated and persistent confrontations. I have actually never encountered a borderline patient—and certainly no adolescent or child—who could tolerate persistent, strongly worded interpretations and confrontive interventions. The aftermath of rage at such approaches appears endless.

The following clinicians offer approaches that seem to be more in keeping with borderline patient's ego deficits and distorted object relations. They also reflect modification of technique necessary in work with children and adolescents. Young patients do not fully internalize the analyzing function of their therapists, nor do they acquire or retain a full genetic understanding of their internal conflicts. Neubauer (1980) reminds us that the lack of introspection is "based on a general ego attitude characteristic of childhood and adhered to by the child as an effective deterrent against mental pain" (p. 36). Anna Freud (1978) notes that while adolescents are often introspective, they are not interested in their past because their current difficulties and apprehensions about the future so absorb them. Spotnitz (1969, 1976) observes that patients suffering from preoedipal disorders usually require considerable time for the resolution of resistance. Havens' (1976) reliance on the work of Sullivan emphasizes the patient's distress and resistance to interpretations. Epstein (1979a) suggests containment, reflection, investigation of the projections, and keeping a low profile while working (gently) with transference projections in the here and now. Giovacchini (1985) cautions against classic analytic neutrality, which, for some patients, rekindles their early rejections and abandonments.

As expected, self psychologists, such as Kohut, take strong exception to any stance that favors strongly worded interpretations and confrontation. Kohut (1971) emphasizes the narcissistic injury and assault that frequently follow interpretation and cause patients to feel robbed of the competence and omnipotence that they might well need in their defensive repertoire. Stolorow and Lachman (1980) emphasize the holding qualities of the therapist. Gedo and Goldberg (1973), particularly in work with adolescents, caution against confrontations and recommend empathy, tolerance of self-object transferences, and patients' idealizations and deidealizations.

The most significant clinical contribution of self psychology has been the delineation, description, and elaboration of self-object transferences. Kohut described "new transference configurations: mirror transferences (which includes merger, alter ego or twinship, *and* mirror transferences in the narrower sense); and idealizing transferences. The former relate to the therapeutic remobilization of the grandiose self and the latter to that of the idealized parental image" (Goldberg 1978, p. 6). Self-object transferences often reveal what appears to be a paucity of reference, interest, and engagement with the therapist. Indeed these transference manifestations are very different from object-libidinal transferences. In patients who exhibit disorders of the self, we are dealing with the threat of temporary fragmentation of the self, and there commonly exists a lack of psychic differentiation between self and object.

Preoedipal conflicts, which originate at an earlier developmental period, prior to psychic structure formation, require a concept of transference that considers the period of structure building, the development of self and object representations, the phases of internalization of archaic objects and of object relations and functions, and their transformation into psychic regulatory systems. The transference manifestations concern archaic representations of part-objects, self-objects, or primitive object relations (Palaci 1980). In sum, the foregoing varied perspectives are noted as essential in considering the parameters of transference in work with young borderline patients.

COUNTERTRANSFERENCE PHENOMENA

Varying perspectives can be applied in attempting a precise definition of countertransference. The restricted sense of the term refers only to those instances in which the child analyst or child therapist "uses his child patient as a transference object" (Maenchen 1970, p. 194). However, there is real value in regarding countertransference in a broader sense to include the "child analyst's [child therapist] reactions to the parents and to some elements characteristic of the child [treatment] situation" (Kramer and Byerley 1978, p. 230). I subscribe to this broader view and believe that the child and the parents or parent surrogates cause countertransference and counterreaction responses. Additional conscious and unconscious variables that affect responses to young patients include the therapist's own personality and personal history, parenthood experience, training and theoretical base, and trainee or candidate status, as well as the stage and phase of the treatment process and the treatment setting or milieu. The patient's symptoms, impulsivity, acting out, and the like inevitably cause counterreactions and countertransference responses. In addition, it is now well recognized that the therapist's conflict about authority, fear of parents' jealousy, and competition with the child's parents can severely compromise child therapy.

I agree with Marcus's definition of countertransference. He defines it as a reaction to the specific patient, to the patient's transference response, or to other components of the patient's material. It can "activate a developmental residue [and] create or revive unconscious conflict, anxiety or defensiveness" (Marcus 1980, p. 286). If unrecognized and unchecked, it is a negative contaminant, but if examined and understood, it can be a positive therapeutic tool to aid in the interpretation of a patient's unconscious. It is the idiosyncratic, unique response of a given therapist based on his specific character, personality, and life history. In sum, I believe that countertransference proper is an unconscious or preconscious phenomenon of which the therapist must become aware, and must properly modulate. In contrast, I consider reality-oriented, secondary-process factors to constitute counterreactions, or "reactive countertransference" (Giovacchini 1985, Wolf 1988).

There is general consensus that child and adolescent therapy is particularly taxing. Young patients are rarely, if ever, voluntary patients; they are captives, brought by their parents or referred by schools, pediatricians, child welfare agencies, and courts. Treatment of a child or adolescent can rarely proceed without ongoing contact with the parents. In addition, collaborative contacts between the therapist and camps, child care workers, child welfare workers, and teachers are often necessary. Given these added dimensions, the potential for intense counterreactions and countertransference responses is heightened and is vastly greater than in treatment of the self-contained, self-referred adult patient. Children offer unclear communications, as well as behaviors, drawings, and play enactments, and these media can be enlightening or perplexing or both, stimulating frustration or empathic attunement.

Adolescents are viewed as a most taxing patient population, since they have a "propensity for creating problems within the treatment setting because of their reticence about becoming engaged, or their inclination to express themselves through action rather than words and feelings" (Giovacchini 1985, p. 447). In addition, adolescents commonly blame the environment, the parents, school, and so on, and often refuse to communicate. They often appear narcissistically self-preoccupied. All of this can threaten the clinician's sense of competence and professional identity (Giovacchini 1974).

All of the aforenoted complexities in clinical work with children and adolescents are compounded and exacerbated in treatment efforts with borderline youth. This group presents the clinician with all of the special challenges of the young patient, but with the added ingredients of turmoil, identity crisis, oscillating and uneven ego functioning, depressive states, heightened narcissism, failure of normal repression, persistence of primitive mechanisms of defense (i.e., projection, regression, denial, and splitting), deficient differentiation between inner and outer stimuli, poor frustration tolerance, poor impulse control, severely impaired parent–child relationships, and frequent destructive acting-out behaviors.

Proctor (1959) noted that countertransference problems are greatest in work with impulsive, acting-out patients and highly narcissistic patients. Such patients tax therapists, who attempt to defend themselves with counterresistance. It is further suggested that countertransference and counterreactions tempt clinicians to counterattack or mobilize infantile aspects of their superego against the patient's id. This mobilization of the therapist's superego can result in rejection, punishment, or hostile demands for conformity by the patient. Proctor uses the term *countertransference* to mean the reverse of transference: therapists displace their infantile object relation patterns onto patients. Often, interpretations of the therapist's countertransference "can be a highly effective tool, but [it] requires some finesse. Such interpretations must be correctly timed, and should be aimed at the most superficial level that is effective (Proctor 1959, p. 305). Ekstein (1966), in work with borderline latency-age children, recommends the same precautions—that is, of not attacking the child's defense and of interpreting "within the metaphor" so as to avoid disrupting the child's fantasy, play themes, or denial. This entails following the child's material empathically, until the child relates in a part-object fashion. Required is the containment and management of counterreactions and countertransference responses of anger, impatience, and frustration. The therapeutic goal is to help the patient trust the therapist via fusing the good and bad object—that is, to achieve a greater degree of object constancy in the treatment relationship as a result of the therapist's constancy and calm.

Other therapeutic challenges occur when the therapist is bombarded by primary process material, primitive expression (often of rage), fluctuating ego states, and resistances and inconsistencies demonstrated by parents (Pearson 1968). Borderline adolescents exhibiting paranoia, radicalism, narcissistic overevaluation of the self, regression, and alienation can often confront the therapist with rageful tirades about society, institutions, and the like. Such tirades conceal the rage and disappointment they feel toward their parents and family, even as they reflect real social and political convictions, values, and concerns. Meissner (1985) describes the need to wait and listen, and the need to avoid questions and confrontation. Often the application of firm limits and boundaries is necessary, such as in the example of the hospitalized patient. Counterreactions and countertransference responses require that the therapist contain the endless temptation and invitation to respond defensively in regard to personal, political, and professional values. Objective inquiry must be sustained. "The therapist must be as able and willing to recognize the pathological and destructive aspects of the social environment as he is able and willing to recognize and acknowledge the pathological aspects of the patient's psychic functioning" (Meissner 1985, p. 507). It is critical to perceive not only personal pathology but also social processes and societal realities that concern the borderline older adolescent with a social conscience.

The acting-out or severely symptomatic young borderline patient may elicit the same attitudes from the therapist that he elicits in others in his life. The therapist's "overwhelmed" response can reach or come close to reaching the traumatic proportions that may be simultaneously occurring in the patient's outside life. Some patients can and do arouse in the clinician the same degree of helplessness and despair that they arouse in their parents (Wallace and Wallace 1985). Therapists may react to the degree of primitive regression, the shifts and changes of tone, and the emotional attitudes that such patients exhibit toward the professional relationship with potentially dangerous responses. Such responses may include (1) the reappearance of anxiety connected with early impulses, especially those of an aggressive nature, which are now directed toward the patient; (2) a possible loss of ego boundaries in interaction with specific patients; (3) the strong temptation to try to control the teenager based on an identification with an object of the therapist's own past; (4) masochistic submission to the adolescent's aggression; (5) disproportionate doubts about one's professional capabilities; and (6) nihilistic attitudes about the necessary work with persons and systems on behalf of the adolescent patient (Kernberg 1975).

The capacity to experience ongoing concern and empathy for the patient, and attunement to the latent issues, can generally help in overcoming and neutralizing the aggressive countertransference responses. Empathy is key to understanding the techniques and approaches of self psychologists. Kohut (1959) defined empathy as "vicarious introspection"—namely, an attempt to live the inner life of another while simultaneously retaining the stance of the objective observer. Empathic failure on the part of the clinician can arouse an all-engulfing rage in the patient, with corresponding negative countertransference responses of hurt, anger, and a wish to withdraw from the patient. The clinician must attempt to surmount such a therapeutic impasse via self-scrutiny and additional empathic focus, and to recognize along with the patient the understandable early origins of such rage and the reasons that it is being reverberated in the present. "The therapist seeks to understand the cause of the interruption, not by a confrontation but by allying him/herself with the individual's fear of humiliation, injury, or exposure once more, to a repetition of past trauma echoed by something in the present" (Elson 1986, p. 56). Goldberg (1978) notes other potential problematic countertransference responses, including the fear of merger on the therapist's part during the merger transference; the resistance to being overstimulated by the therapist's own overly grandiose, exhibitionist drives during an idealizing transference; the discomfort with being a self-object; and fear of retaliation during a phase of de-idealization.

THE CASE OF A BORDERLINE COLLEGE STUDENT IN CHAOS

Joan, age 20, was referred by her parents. Her mother is a teacher, and her father, a lawyer. Joan was in a state of crisis upon her return home following a year-long Hispanic study program in South America. She seemingly fragmented at the conclusion of the academic year and was therefore unable to do the traveling she had planned. She and her parents described in exquisitely painful detail her incapacity to make any choices or decisions about travel destinations. This resulted in reservations being made and canceled and remade repeatedly amidst frantic calls home that could often number well over a dozen per day.

Once home, Joan enrolled in a summer school course, and the same indecision prevailed as she ran back and forth from class to class, uncertain about which course to settle on. The same obsessive ruminations and indecision prevailed regarding her residence at home or at the university dormitory facilities. Every decision, big or small, took on the aspect of crisis and momentous proportions. She was paralyzed when confronted by decisions regarding the purchase of a piece of clothing, social plans for an evening, or her daily schedule. Her frenzied state, nonstop talking, and literal hysteria over any and every choice were described as unprecedented and new, although Joan and her parents noted that indecision in milder forms had plagued her since puberty, especially when it came to making a choice of clothing to purchase. Later decisions on social and school-related activities, and still later decisions concerning which college to attend and what course of study to pursue, all reflected the same anxiety and indecision. Her parents acknowledged with hindsight that Joan had always simply appeared to be "flaky," disorganized, compliant, and "too good," and that they'd fallen into the habit of giving her a great deal of direction and advice, all of which she was now holding against them. Joan described feeling dismissed and overlooked because her parents, until recently, were preoccupied with the behavioral, academic, and dyslexia problems of her older twin brothers. Joan said, "Literally and figuratively, my brothers took up all the space and attention at home."

An attractive older adolescent who is blond, diminutive, and usually casually dressed, Joan was hesitant and spoke with the voice of a young child. She veered between presenting as a tiny, compliant child and an imperious, stubborn, assaultive teenager. She could badger with complaints, attacks, and projections of blame, or insistent demands for direction and instantaneous advice and solutions. Some sessions revealed a thoughtful, self-aware, introspective college student, while others reflected a regressed, unreasonable child who would not accept a reality limit. For example, she would become enraged when informed that a session was over, and that unresolved issues would have to be contained for the next appointment. Joan would come close to refusing to leave the office; she would return and ring the bell, presenting herself at the door with more demands and questions and complaints. At other times, upon hearing the bell (which signaled the arrival of the next patient), she would leave, slamming the door in rage. She would call when she was supposed to be in the office to request a change of hour, and when this was not granted, she would slam down the phone. She would then arrive half an hour later and be amazed when she couldn't have a full session.

Just as she was unable to decide which course and professor to study with, she could not decide which therapist to work with. I had referred her for a psychopharmacologic evaluation, and Joan decided that the other clinician, a man, was better and that she preferred him. When given the chance to change, however, she would not do it, and against the prohibitions of her parents and both clinicians, she continued to meet with both therapists. This was finally resolved when her parents, with my support, were helped to state firmly that they would not pay two therapists concurrently, and that she could not continue to schedule with both. As she ran back and forth between her parents, so, too, did she run back and forth between the therapists.

Joan would generally want to use sessions for ranting, complaining, projecting blame, and demanding advice, or complaining about what she surmised had been advice. At times she would acknowledge that as she scanned the environment for clues about what direction to take and what choice to make, she would be prone to misapprehensions about information that she felt was being provided to her. She also recognized her inner emptiness and the subsequent efforts to fill herself up with "creative, fun, interesting activities." She further began to acknowledge that such activities frightened her, so uncertain was she of her competence to handle them. She conveyed either basic distrust or misplaced, childlike, instantaneous and total trust. Her terror at facing her senior year, and the adult autonomy and responsibilities that were soon to follow, was something that she could recognize in isolated moments. More commonly, however, Joan's concentration, synthesizing ego functions and frustration tolerance were nonexistent, and she succumbed to primitive defenses of denial, projection, splitting, or primitive dissociation. On occasion Joan's frenzied indecision caused her parents anguish, explosiveness, and fragmentation. Over a particularly stressed weekend, her mother acknowledged a total loss of her ordinary "patience beyond endurance"; when harranged and badgered by her daughter, she succumbed to yelling and beating her fists on the wall while Joan smirked sadistically and made provocative comments. Clearly Joan externalized her sense of helplessness and frustration.

In the prematurely activated transference, which was apparent almost at once, I, like Joan's mother, felt drained, momentarily helpless, and frustrated—this in spite of my awareness of the impact of Joan's externalization of her own inner struggles. I often felt powerless to intercede in what was becoming the vicious cycle described by Kernberg (1982a), whereby Joan was "projecting aggression onto me, and under the influence of the projective aggressive drive derivatives, was reintrojecting a severely distorted image of the therapist, the perpetuation of the early pathological internalized object relationship" (p. 474). Although I was theoretically clear about the rapidly alternating projection of self-representations and object representations, I felt at times impotent to provide any relief or soothing (Goldberg 1972, Stolorow and Lachman 1980), so profound was Joan's regression, distorted thinking, and intolerance for the chaos she had been living with for months. "For several weeks I've come to see you three times a week, and you're not helping me," she would say. My attempt to soothe and reassure her, and to explain that more time was needed to help her feel less chaotic, fell on deaf ears. A similar fate befell my efforts to move her from her insistent focus on the manifest content and choice of the moment and from the complaints and projections that she would repeat over and over, despite her recognition of this obsessive tendency.

In the psychological testing sessions, Joan revealed herself to be a frantic, borderline older adolescent girl who wanted answers and who would badger the examiner, as she did her therapist, with questions, and delays in leaving sessions. Joan's depressed intelligence quotient score of 98 strongly indicated that her emotional disorder was interfering with cognition and intellectual functioning. Her thinking was viewed as fuzzy and concrete, with little evidence of a capacity for abstraction. Given the degree of distraction and interference in concentration, she would tend to "lose the forest for the trees." Preoccupation with details made her lose the overall picture and rendered her unable to remember issues and variables inherent in a situation that she was attempting to resolve. Her intolerance of ambiguity and her desire for closure and instant solutions created both inconsistent planning and impulsive decisions that she would then undo, and do, and again undo. This vulnerable thinking clearly led to Joan's poor and inconclusive judgment and her frantic efforts to seek outside guidance from anyone and everyone. She was incapable of planful, purposeful assessment of choices and alternatives. Her inability to tolerate or to defend against unbearable anxiety caused her to escalate, flood, panic, and think in an ever more confused fashion.

Joan seems as adamant as she is uncertain about her "choice" to return to college, and there to seek some temporary therapeutic intervention. Both the psychological consultant and the therapist have recommended that planning for long-term intensive therapy be the first priority, and that academic planning be secondary.

Discussion of Diagnostic Impressions as Elucidation of Countertransference Considerations

During this abbreviated course of therapy (in effect, an extended diagnostic assessment), I have had more than a few moments of doubt over my capacity to help Joan, due both to the degree of her regression, panic, and ambivalence about working with me, and to her parents' inability to hold firm and to set needed limits. Their historic capitulation and excessive advice-giving has not enabled Joan to develop an age-appropriate frustration tolerance or a capacity to endure ambivalence and ambiguity. She is therefore unable to tolerate the time and struggle necessary to think through issues or to problem-solve with autonomy and independence. Inconsistency and overgratification contribute to her ego weakness and lack of anxiety tolerance (Kernberg 1975).

I felt bombarded and assaulted by the primitive defenses of projection that Joan exhibited. I felt frustrated when our rapport and alliance, apparent at times, was so quickly erased. Although intellectually I grasped the basis of Joan's erratic mode of relating, it was nevertheless difficult to endure, especially because her parents could not hold firm to support and sustain Joan's commitment to work with me. Although they saw her defensive doing and undoing and dashing back and forth between professors and therapists, they wavered with her, wanting her to make age-appropriate choices for herself despite the ample evidence that she needed reality limits and parental constraints. These would have enabled her to sustain and expand on her fleeting flashes of insight so that she could stay and work. Starting and stopping things was not new, and neither was incessant change, as Joan, with hindsight, often despairingly recounted her recognition of her "predictable unpredictability."

The parents failed to follow through on the recommendations for some ongoing parental guidance, despite their portrayal of themselves as emotionally exhausted and frightened by Joan's wild swings and panic-induced expenditures. When the financial costs of Joan's actions were assessed, they were found to be excessive and unrealistic. These expenditures included her intercontinental long-distance calls and funds laid out for tuition, therapists, dormitory space, and so on. While her parents recognized her symptoms of indecision and of impulsive commitments she could not sustain, they failed to accept the fact that despite her chronological age, reality required stronger parental action and limit-setting. Instead the parents would take a stand, fail to hold to it, and—like their daughter—would vacillate and waver, and split any coalition they managed to achieve.

Prognosis and Treatment Recommendation

Until they can hold firm with unanimity, it is expected that Joan will continue to flounder and to be in the endless pain she describes. Her distress is expressed via sleeplessness and by the bombardments of unmodulated contradictory directives she gives herself, which appear to be echoes of her parents' anxious contradictory, impulsive advice and direction. Joan's mother appears to be the firmer, more consistent parental voice, but she is undone by the father's explosive ultimatums, which he counters by offering overly indulgent, permissive courses of action to Joan.

When her defenses are down and she is not projecting and denying, Joan confesses to feeling crazy, recognizing that she is not out of contact with reality but rather burdened by a distorted sense of reality. Increasingly, Joan and her parents are becoming aware of her isolation and her superficial friendships, and an associated immaturity in her gender development. Both Joan and her parents have begun to perceive her pattern of distancing from peers and family, all of whom become exhausted by her indecisiveness to make and keep even the most inconsequential decisions or social plans. Parental efforts to overindulge Joan with the most gratifying alternatives served neither to placate nor to please her. She would push her parents into making decisions, for which she would then assault them, accusing them of advising her, or commanding her, unwisely. She cannot recognize, of course, that it is she herself who is incapable of accurately presenting them (or herself) with an overview because her obsessive–compulsive attention to detail precludes realistic choices and planning.

Despite Joan's complaints and her assaults on my professional competence, her frequent harangues and bombardments, I saw her behavior as replicating her exchanges with her parents. Because I was in empathic contact with her basic sense of emptiness, low self-esteem, fearfulness, and anxiety, I have not felt sustained counteraggression, nor have we worked together long enough for me to feel "hate in the countertransference" (Winnicott 1949). I have felt myself struggling to refrain from making a hostile demand for conformity (Proctor 1959), and at the same time I have firmly refused to accept unrealistic blame (Meeks 1971). I have tried to show Joan that neither anger nor doubt will deter me from the goal of trying to be of help (Basch 1980).

I have wondered whether Joan might settle into treatment more easily with a male than a female therapist, since she portrays herself as "Daddy's little girl," and as more in conflict with her mother than her father. I've pondered whether this is a therapist's rationalization, or whether Joan is the rare adolescent whom I simply cannot engage and sustain in therapy. I do believe that her core conflicts regarding the lack of genuine separation/individuation from her mother requires that she ultimately work these conflicts through, and ideally with a female therapist, given her gender-identity immaturities. Joan needs the borderline adolescent's transitional parent (Ekstein 1983) to permit age-appropriate growth and autonomy, and the hope is that one will be chosen in the near future. Joan is aware that her difficulty in making choices keeps her bound to her parents with the wish that they make all choices for her. Her fear is that she might reject me simply because her mother selected me, and that she might then be sorry, as she has been repeatedly, about changing courses for the "better professor." Always looking for someone and something better (a "better" social plan, a "better" roommate, a "better" travel destination), she often ends up empty-handed, with no plans and no one. In brief moments of insight, Joan recognizes her endless searching as emanating out of her own sense of emptiness, loneliness, and low self-esteem.

In sum, I believe that the emotional responses evoked in me by my struggles with Joan are conscious, reality-oriented, homogeneous reactions and responses. I believe that such reactions and responses commonly occur when therapists attempt to engage such an over-whelmed and fragile borderline adolescent, a patient who is at the mercy of her disrupted thinking and of a primitive defense system. In fact, the collaborating psychologist mirrored my reactions and re-sponses. The atypical aspect of this case is the adolescent's and the parents' shifting posture in regard to therapeutic commitment and to the decision of which therapist will conduct the treatment. The parents are unable to hold themselves or their daughter to staying in therapy without endlessly shopping for yet another clinician. On the one hand the parents believe that Joan is old enough to make this decision for herself, but on the other hand, they recognize that she has demonstrated total inability to make a firm choice on the most inconsequential of matters. Clothes are frequently held in "layaway" because Joan cannot finally decide. At moments, I, too, have felt depersonalized, on reserve, or in layaway, uncertain about whether Joan would keep appointments because of her chronic indecision and ambivalence. This habitual way of relating and behaving is both recognized by the patient and her parents and also disavowed, via rationalizations, denials, and projections. The presenting symptoms of indecision, doing and undoing, obsessive ruminating, and doubting undermine the needed commitment for actual engagement in treatment.

THE CASE OF A 10-YEAR-OLD BOY MANIFESTING EXTREME ANXIETY REACTION OF CHILDHOOD

Chris, age 10, was referred by his mother in a series of frenzied phone calls during which she verbalized mounting terror at her son's most recent suicidal ideation. Chris's mother described her son as a very gifted child who had lately been saying, "I'm depressed and don't see the point of living." Such statements, understandably, greatly alarmed the mother. In addition, Chris was described as not wanting to see his father, and he had been refusing to attend school on Mondays after weekend visitations with his father and stepmother. Mother and son were getting into major struggles about the visitations and about school attendance.

Struggles also occurred over homework preparation. Chris frequently panicked and claimed he couldn't understand or complete the assignments; soon the panic would escalate and Chris refused to go to school because he had not completed his work and feared reprimands from the teacher. Chris had been an outstanding student, accustomed to all-A report cards, and was attending a program for gifted and talented pupils. Chris's mother said that although she and Chris are very close, of late he'd had temper eruptions when minor limits were set, during which he became explosive and volatile, screaming, swearing, and even gesturing to hit his mother (over such issues as her directing him to do his homework, her refusal to purchase a $175 skateboard, her expectation that he complete his minimal chores, and so on).

Chris's father and stepmother denied that Chris had problems of any sort, and they blamed the mother for sabotaging the visitation schedule. Chris's mother refuted this accusation and noted her extensive efforts to maintain Chris's contact with his father. The parents have had a lengthy course of disharmony and conflict over Chris. Chris substantiated his mother's account that he was often resistant to the visitation plan: "I don't have a real or open or good relationship with them. Whenever I go there, I must be on my best behavior, and they organize family conferences over each and every thing I do that isn't perfect. I'm afraid of my Dad. He can get real mad, furious in fact, though most of the time he's real quiet and I don't know what he's thinking. But then he can explode. I'm scared of my Dad. He really hit and hurt me when I was small. He often insults me and calls me 'stupid.' I'm nervous because I'm afraid of him. I'm less nervous with his wife, my other mother, than with Dad. My Mom gives in to them, so stuff won't be taken out on me. I'm sick of being in the middle. I know I also take stuff out on Mom, my real Mom, because I'm afraid of Dad, and not at all afraid of my Mom, even when we argue. I love my Dad, but most of the time I don't like him because I'm afraid of him."

In contrast to the accounts given by Chris and his mother, Chris's father and his wife stated that Chris exhibited no signs to them that anything was wrong. They described Chris as very bright. In fact, he was attending a school of which they did not approve, and they believed that placement in a private school would be more appropriate. Chris's father and stepmother described Chris's superior academic achievement, his love of reading, and his cooperative attitude in their home, which they attributed to parenting differences and to their greater demands. "One lives down to the expectations" was the view of father and stepmother, who stated that Chris's mother was too lenient, permissive, and nurturant and wanted them to be involved with Chris only on her terms. Chris's father and his wife recognized that Chris might at times feel caught in the middle, and they initially agreed to the therapeutic suggestion that such differences are common in divorce situations and might well necessitate a series of meetings between the parents on the child's behalf. They initially indicated a willingness to participate in such meetings, if recommended. Since that time, however, except for a note suggesting a phone conversation, they have not responded to the recommendation for parent guidance or mediation sessions with Chris's mother.

History

Chris's mother reported that Chris's resistance about visitations with his father was not new. When Chris was 2½ his father is reported to have bruised him by spanking him ("tanning his bottom"). His mother regarded this as abusive, and as reflective of his father's long-standing temper, which was exacerbated by an excessive use of alcohol. Father–son contact diminished following that incident. Chris's father volunteered that this outburst did indeed occur but he implied that he no longer drinks excessively, although Chris's accounts raise questions about the father's current alcohol consumption.

When Chris's father entered into a relationship with his present wife, she pushed for more regulated, consistent father–son contact, and so contact resumed when Chris was 4½. It ended a year later, when Chris was 5½ or 6, when Chris refused to see his father without the presence of his natural mother. The mother said that she believes her ex-husband and his wife do care about Chris, but that their conflicts and poor communication have taken their toll on him so that Chris believes he can't succeed in anything. He is overwhelmed with the pressures of trying to please everyone—parents, teachers, and grandparents. School has become an obsessive and frantic arena for performance, and the strain of maintaining his long-standing all-A report cards causes Chris to fragment and become hysterical over each and every homework assignment and test in school. Chris's comments have indicated that he is aware that his father and stepmother criticize everything, especially his mother, his maternal grandparents, his friends, and his school.

In sum, Chris's contact with his father has been characterized by a long-standing pattern of separations and inconsistency. Over the last four years, however, contacts have become more routine and now include a month in the summer. However, whenever Chris protests and refuses, his mother is accused of "putting him up to it." This is not my impression, however, in that Chris is a highly intelligent child who often describes himself as weary of feeling forced to comply or to be silent out of fear.

Treatment

Chris's treatment began on a crisis-intervention basis, given the urgency of his needs, regression, and panic states. The immediate goal was to calm Chris and his mother in order to diminish the panic and to stave off the regression inherent in his tantrums, school refusal, and academic difficulties so that he might regain a progressive line of development. At the outset, all parental figures conveyed a willingness to cooperate on behalf of the child, although the father and his wife indicated shock at the crisis, having seen "nothing wrong." They tended to minimize the degree of Chris's fears, performance anxiety, and apprehensiveness about time spent with them.

Then, abruptly, Chris's father and stepmother reversed their original agreement to participate in ongoing contact on Chris's behalf, stating that an overdramatized situation had been created by Chris and his mother. Quickly and suddenly they became abusive and rude to me, seeing me as allied with Chris's mother, and as opposed to their view that therapy was not necessary. The stepmother impulsively dismissed all notions of civil discourse and proceeded to rail at me as she had done for years at Chris's natural mother. Their sarcasm and demeaning deprecation of me was presented with stated entitlement: "We have every right to be rude and sarcastic, and we intend to be just that, since you weren't our choice as therapist. In fact, we never have any choices in relation to Chris. We're expected to just pay whatever bills his mother dreams up. We are furious that you see Chris as a kid in need of substantial help." Chris's father said that his insurance would cover twenty sessions, and he expected me to do whatever was needed within that time since he would not pay any further therapy costs.

Finances have been a long-standing battleground in this family, and the mother reports chronically late child support payments and inordinate delays in the father's payments of healthcare bills. Chris's father, an accountant, has a good income that is supplemented by the earnings of his wife, a nurse. Chris's mother, who works as an historian and museum curator, earns little money.

In addition to his rejection of Chris's need for open-ended treatment, Chris's father has reversed his earlier stated willingness to consider parent-guidance and mediation contacts with Chris's mother. With my help, the mother located several mediation clinicians, but the father, after agreeing to such a contact, abruptly dismissed the plan and said that he was willing to meet with his ex-wife on an informal basis only. They had several such meetings, but Chris's mother refused to acquiesce to the father's demands. This was a change from her historical stance, wherein she would submit to pressures from her ex-husband out of fear and a wish for "peace at any price." She also was concerned that if thwarted, her ex-husband would take out his frustrations on Chris, a pattern she states had occurred throughout the child's life.

During this last year, treatment has proceeded effectively with mother and son, both of whom have been helped to accommodate to and deal with the father's opposition more calmly. The mother has retained legal services to obtain what she believes is long-overdue child support. Chris's life and therapy are compromised both by father's habitually late partial support payments and by his lack of contact with his son. As before, Chris has declined to see his father at all. "I refuse to see my father, and I'm old enough to make my own decisions," he has said. "I won't be pressed to see him just to keep the child support money coming. I won't see him until he sees a counselor or a therapist. I'm tired of his temper and anger, and I'm tired of being in the middle. He'll think you and Mom put me up to this, but I've refused to see him before. My decision is nothing new. My reasons are just more grown-up. I love him, I guess, but I don't like or trust him, and I won't see him until I can be with him, unafraid."

In fourteen months of therapy, Chris has been seen weekly (due to financial constraints) and biweekly for short intervals when his panic recurred. Chris rarely plays in therapy sessions, but rather talks steadily and thoughtfully. On occasion, with playful humor, he has used the blackboard to demonstrate school-related topics and assignments or successful soccer plays from his league games. Overall, he uses his outstanding intellectual and verbal capacities to discuss feelings, thoughts, questions, ideas, and events in his life. He speaks of enjoying sessions, and he comes in eagerly. He tells me that his close friends knew about his therapy and his estrangement from his father. He has several friends who are also in therapy, and Chris believes that he has a better time of it than they do because he trusts me and feels close, respected, and understood. On occasion, when he feels overwhelmed by school assignments or by his perceptions of others' expectations, Chris has fragmented—exploding, crying, harranging, and badgering me, as he does at home in his conflicts with his mother. I believe that what has proved helpful is an absence of confrontation and interpretation, and instead the provision of empathy and acceptance of Chris's experiences, in which I am treated as an extension of or a substitute for missing pieces of psychic structure, rather than as a separate, independent person (Bleiberg 1987).

In addition to working with Chris, I have had weekly therapy contacts with his mother. The focus is a combination of reality-oriented parent guidance and psychotherapy, as we examine her chronic, life-long helplessness. This sense of helplessness began in her family of origin, and continued into her short-lived marriage; it is apparent, post-divorce, in transactions with her ex-husband and his new wife, with her child, and with supervisors at work. Chris's mother has made enormous gains in the management of her own anxiety, depression, and anger. She has consequently been able to move from an overwhelmed, passive position to one of greater energy and effectiveness, with resultant improved self-esteem. The parallel improvements are striking and demonstrate the undifferentiated dyad that still exists between mother and son. More separation and individuation is slowly occurring, but without paralyzing abandonment anxieties.

In sessions with both child and mother, I have avoided confrontive interventions and have instead attempted empathically to reflect the recognition of both mother's and son's responses to failure, humiliation, or injury. Soothing and reassurances have been fruitful, since both mother and son lack specific abilities to self-regulate due to their shared borderline chaos of the nuclear self. There appears to be greater calm, via the connection with the therapist, who serves as a partnering self-object (Elson 1986).

Assessment of Countertransference in the Treatment Process

Chris's father's and stepmother's abrupt reversal and unexpected bout of hostility evoked many countertransference reactions. I initially anxiously reviewed my notes, wondering whether I had done anything to set in motion their barrage of hostility. I had tried to draw on my knowledge of their histories to summon up some objective, empathic view of them. Although I was aware of Chris's father's abuse at the hands of his own volatile, authoritarian father, I nevertheless found it impossible to respond empathically to his assault on his son's therapy or to his blandness in the face of an absence of contact with Chris. I had attempted to soothe and reassure the father and stepmother about Chris's overall strengths and positive prognosis, while also attempting to clarify his need for longer-term treatment. I also tried to support their resistance to a treatment plan set forth by someone not of their choosing, and thus I urged them to seek the needed parent guidance and mediation elsewhere, where they could participate in the selection of the clinician in tandem with Chris's mother. To date, my efforts to restate the need for more cooperative parenting have fallen on deaf ears, and they have remained silent, absent, unreachable, and begrudging, with extremely late and only partial coverage of Chris's therapy costs. I am aware that this tendency to dismiss Chris's therapy, and the therapist, is not new; a similar event had occurred years before, when Chris's mother had sought help, and a similar phenomenon occurs now in regard to Chris's need for orthodontia. Chris's father and stepmother have stalled, claiming that they want to find the orthodontist and obtain a second opinion as to whether such dental care is even necessary. Regardless of my intellectual knowledge of these realities, I experienced countertransference reactions of uneasiness and anxiety in response to the conflict with Chris's father, and the resultant estrangement between father and son.

My concerns created more countertransference responses—anger at Chris's father and stepmother, for example, and a struggle not to overprotect Chris or his mother. Mother has assumed the unpaid balance of the therapy costs at great hardship to herself, as she has excessive financial burdens; these were exacerbated when she changed jobs and found herself in an extremely stressful work situation, caused by such pressures as tight deadlines and an overwhelming and unreasonable supervisor. My concerns for all of the pressures on her and her son, I feared, would compromise our work if I remained caught up in the real, manifest issues. I found myself struggling to limit her obsessive, detailed accounts of outrageous outbursts from her ex-husband, child, and supervisor in order to have time to explore the early etiology of this helplessness. Similarly, I found myself temporarily hard put to make role-appropriate demands on the mother in regard to Chris's needs for greater order, limits, regular meals, and a reasonably kept home. In response to the increased financial pressures, to Chris's mounting anxiety at his change of schools, and to stressors on the job, Chris's mother regressed. She became overly permissive with Chris, letting him stay up until all hours as he engaged her in the homework battle. She also let him miss school while she rushed off to her office. In the evenings she worked on office tasks at home, neglecting to cook and clean, and to appropriately limit and parent. Chris was very open in his complaints about the disorder at home and the inner chaos it engendered in him; he was clearly suffering from the lack of external structure in his living milieu. He had difficulty concentrating, and for months he could not complete his homework amid the disorder in the home. Chris's anxiety mounted in response to his mother's inattentiveness, as she ordered in dinners and tried to handle her own office work at home. She was becoming more and more emotionally distant and unavailable. In addition to our focused work during her appointments, Chris's mother needed some phone calls between sessions for help in better managing her environment. She needed advice and advocacy help to support a more self-protective stance, not only with Chris but also with her ex-husband and his wife, her lawyers, her supervisors at her job, and her own well-to-do parents (who heretofore had resisted providing needed financial help).

Direct therapeutic work with Chris and his mother required flexibility and shifts in the traditional therapeutic stance. In my effort to be unwavering in reliability, accessibility, and predictability, I could not be the blank, nondirective screen, withholding advice, direction, or my own value system. Chris's regular school attendance and an ordered living situation were my obvious bias in the face of his mother's increasingly disordered lifestyle (e.g., their extraordinarily messy apartment, her inability to discipline or to set limits for Chris, and his temporary status as a "latchkey" child).

I have no question that my age and gender stimulated maternal countertransference as I struggled to hold mother and son firmly to their age-appropriate tasks. It was critical not to adultomorphize Chris and to refrain from pushing this already precocious child into a more adultlike empathic response to his mother's pressures. He must not be pushed to be his mother's peer or surrogate husband. It was equally critical not to be overprotective and underdemanding of the mother (given my recognition of her excessive burdens) due to my maternal, positive countertransference and counterreactions to this young woman. Without self-awareness and vigilance, I feared I could easily overidentify with Chris's mother given my own past history, in which I had once experienced some similar stressful life circumstances. Idiosyncratic countertransference reactions arise from unique features in the therapist's background and character makeup (Giovacchini

1981b). Given my own highly organized management of personal and professional demands, I was aware that I must not force this young woman into some passive compliance, or attempt to push her too fast or beyond her capacities, so that she might better order and regulate her work, parenting, and homemaking responsibilities. Similarly, I did not wish to push Chris and cause an empathic breach or rupture with the mother and/or the son (Polombo 1985).

Efforts to effect a more reasoned level of communication with the father and stepmother had created "narcissistic depletion or exhaustion" (Touhy 1987). I was also aware of my negative responses to accounts of their handling of Chris, who often expressed his relief at the conclusion of weekend visits in his father's home. Chris often told of exchanges such as the one during which his father admonished, "Chris, stop this crying at once! You're too old to cry like a baby, and if you must, then go to your room. We'll not have tear-stains on our new couch." Chris's father had threatened to come to school, to force Chris into his car, and to enforce his visitation rights if the child persisted in avoiding contact. Chris's panic at this short-lived threat caused me some momentary counterreactions of helplessness, impotence, and lack of control (Mintz 1981), and I was acutely aware of what Racker has termed concordant identification and direct and indirect countertransference (1968). Direct countertransference occurred in response to my patients—Chris and his mother—whereas indirect countertransference occurred in response to those outside the therapy situation whose good opinion could not be secured—specifically, Chris's father and stepmother. My countertransference toward Chris and his mother proved to be a valuable tool for better understanding the dilemma of their self-experience of helplessness.

CONCLUSIONS

This chapter attempts to acquaint the reader with newer conceptions regarding transference and parallel concepts of countertransference. As noted earlier, Sandler and colleagues (1980) state that transference as manifested by children can be divided into four subtypes: (1) habitual modes of relating, (2) transference of current relationships, (3) transference that is predominantly that of past relationships, and (4) transference neurosis.

The borderline child or adolescent commonly exhibits only the first two subtypes of transference, while the latter two are manifested by more intact young patients. Anna Freud (1971) notes that borderline young patients lack the capacity to form genuine transference, and that even more intact children present only a short-lived, circumscribed transference neurosis. A lack of transference proper alters countertransference; in other words, when it is patently clear that one is being faced with a child's habitual way of relating, one counterreacts, and this is not necessarily due to one's unique personal history.

The parameters of the parent–child model of treatment and self psychology are offered as eminently suited to work with severely disturbed borderline children and adolescents and their parents. It is also posited that these perspectives stimulate different kinds of countertransference responses. With a different conception of transference manifestations by borderline young patients (using the therapist as a self-object), clinicians' responses are better distinguished as countertransference proper, counterreactions, or aspects of the real and human intersubjective experience.

Self psychology perceives countertransference as essential in order to understand the help that an individual seeks as a means of transmuting missing functions into self-functions. The self-object functions that the therapist performs have been described by Gedo and Goldberg (1973) as "pacification, unification, optimal frustration, interpretation, all . . . hopefully resulting in self-awareness. Ideally the therapist's calm unfolding understanding and empathy provide the conditions for an empathic merger." It is with the therapist as a new self-object in the here and now that the process of healing and filling in of earlier deficits takes place (Elson 1986, p. 56). Through myriad bits of interplay, the missing functions of stress-monitoring, self-soothing, and mastery are realized (transmitted) in self-functions of a cohesive, expanding self.

In addition to models of therapy and theoretical perspectives is the therapist's "distinct personal style, as an important facet in the construction of the holding environment. The therapists' nonjudgmental attitudes, serenity in the face of disruption and anxiety, stability and constancy are all responsible for preserving organization and structure in what might otherwise become an unmanageable regression" (Giovacchini 1989, pp. 136–137). The aforementioned nonjudgmental attitude is particularly pertinent with regard to significant variables that commonly induce varied emotional reactions to patients. Studies have shown that such significant variables may include the patient's gender (Broverman et al. 1970, Chesler 1972, Fisher 1976), socioeconomic class (West 1979), race (Blake 1973), or motivation; the therapist's expectations regarding prognosis, specific problems or symptomatology, fee amount (Shapiro 1971), and sexual preference (Geiser 1980); and the treatment setting. Therapists bring their own personal style, tolerance level, value base, beliefs, and attitudes to the treatment relationship, and they must be aware of their own biases, values, and stereotypes. Both case presentations demonstrate operationalization of these variables.

The self psychologist Ernest Wolf distinguishes between "countertransference proper" and "reactive countertransference." He underscores the therapist's residual archaic self-object needs and their correspondence to the patient's demands for self-object experiences. These self-object needs can become mobilized in treatment situations in both positive and negative ways. Depending on the therapist's need for some recognition by the patient and the usual need to have a patient who is at least potentially "admirable," the treatment either proceeds or flounders. "In all cases some responsive self-object experience is always needed" (Wolf 1988, p. 39). The "fit" between clinician and patient cannot be overestimated in understanding, examining, and regulating countertransference, counterreactions, and the therapist's role in the "real" relationship and the transference relationship.

Too often, scant mention is made of the need for a basic core of humanness around which to build a respectful, empathic relationship in clinical work with children, adolescents, and their parents. We too often fall prey to the clinical fallacies of *blaming the victim*, the *environment*, or *cultural differences* as justification for treatment failure without fully examining our own actions, reactions, and feelings. We must have a deep understanding of ourselves to be able to enter into another's inner world. Examination of one's own emotional responses is one of the greatest challenges in becoming a clinician.

In a seminal paper, Kris (1956) describes the vicissitudes of insight. He notes three integrative functions of the ego that are essential to a therapist, both for the treatment process and for the achievement of insight in both patient and therapist: (1) self-observation, in which the ego is split into observing and experiencing parts; (2) control of the discharge affect, which is related to therapists' tolerance of need tension in themselves and in patients; and (3) control over regression, which permits therapists to empathize with patients' regressions, manifested by their transferences, without loss of their own identities or reality-testing functions.

Particularly in work with children and adolescents, therapists must come to terms with their own childhood and their own infantile needs so that they are not seduced or endangered when confronted with their patients' affects, fears, symptoms, and defenses. As clinicians, we may or may not have encountered, struggled with, or lived through the pain and stressors that our adult patients experience. But as children we were all engaged in the same struggles for autonomy, separation and individuation, and identification. Clinical work with children and adolescents strikes continuous responsive chords in all therapists in a unique, stressful, and universal manner, and these chords must be faithfully recognized, monitored, and controlled.

12

The Child with a Life-threatening Illness

Barbara M. Sourkes, Ph.D.

Look long and hard at the things that please you,
even longer and harder at what causes you pain.

Colette

In the course of fifteen years of psychotherapeutic work with children and adolescents confronting life-threatening illness, I have often been asked, "How do you do it? It must be so *depressing*." In fact, depressing is one of the few things it *isn't*, for if it were, I could not continue. The words that do come to mind for me include rich, fulfilling, sad, poignant, and always profoundly moving. Frustration is often present as well. Everyone involved, including the therapist, comes face to face with the relentlessness of illness, if not with the inevitability of death itself.

Colette's words capture the essence of the therapist's task in working with these children. To avert one's eyes is to lose the patient, from a psychic point of view. For while the child living the experience may need *not* to focus on the fulcrum of life and death, the therapist must be capable of the intensity of this gaze, and able to sustain this intensity. At a profound intrapsychic level, the therapist's own strength must come from the ever-present knowledge of that fine line that separates living from dying. In a sense, this "knowledge" is the therapist's burden to bear, for if the child senses that the therapist is holding that reality for both of them, then he or she is free to venture out. This knowledge of life and death, whether implicit or explicit, becomes the containment of the psychotherapy.

The therapist must possess a high threshold for witnessing and tolerating pain—the pain of threatened separation and loss. To witness is not a passive process (Sourkes 1990). In working with a child facing the possibility of death, the therapist must be able to enter the threat with the child, accompanying him or her through the steps while knowing that this may be a journey that they cannot complete together. There is a paradox intrinsic in the process: the therapist accompanies the child down a road toward what may be ultimate separation. In traditional psychotherapy with children, psychological separation is part of the normal developmental process of growing up. In the case of the child facing the threat of death, the child is negotiating an experience utterly unknown to the therapist. Again a paradox appears: closeness between the child and therapist is what eventually allows the child to feel safe in letting go.

A life-threatening illness is a disease whose diagnosis portends the possibility of death as a final outcome. Death, when it occurs, is often preceded by a prolonged period of living with the illness. Many illnesses that were once uniformly fatal have become, through medical advances, life-threatening in nature. While in many instances recovery and even cure may be achieved, the child and family will nonetheless experience the reverberations of anticipatory grief. Thus, whether or not the threat of death is transformed into actuality, the psychological reactions throughout the illness trajectory reflect this profound uncertainty.

A child or adolescent diagnosed with a life-threatening illness throws an assumed sequence out of order. In the normal course of events, there is the expectation of a period of role reversal when children will care for their dying parents. When parents instead find themselves watching their child face death, a sense of tragic absurdity prevails. Not only is time shortened, but its order is shattered.

The spectre of a life-threatening illness represents to the family a premature separation. Even before the child has become a differentiated individual through a natural developmental sequence, that child is wrenched away. There is little preparation for separation by death when a psychological separation has not yet been effected. The adolescent, who is just beginning to negotiate an independent existence, is often the hardest to face when that "moving forward" is disrupted or irreversibly halted. A child has not even had the time to begin to form life goals. A seriously ill 5-year-old patient commented pensively to his therapist: "It takes a lot of days to be grown up, doesn't it . . ." (Sourkes 1977, 1982).

In most cases, the child enters psychotherapy because of the stress engendered by the illness, rather than more general intrapsychic or interpersonal concerns. From a psychological point of view, this is a normal population in which the majority of children and families are well adjusted. Psychopathology is the exception, not the rule. A 6-year-old child explained his understanding of psychotherapy in these words: "I felt much better because I knew that I had somebody to talk to all the time. Every boy needs a psychologist! To see his feelings!" (Sourkes 1982).

REVIEW OF THE LITERATURE

Countertransference in psychotherapy with the life-threatened child remains, to an overwhelming extent, uncharted territory in the clinical literature. In fact, on an even more basic level, there is very little literature on *psychotherapy* with these children. Most writing in the field of childhood cancer identifies the clinical issues faced by the child and the family, and delineates coping strategies for particular milestones and stressors (Brunnquell and Hall 1982, Chesler and Barbarin 1987, Kellerman 1980, Schowalter 1977, Spinetta and Deasy-Spinetta 1981, Van Dongen-Melman and Sanders-Woudstra 1986). However, the focus is not on psychotherapy as a context for adaptation and change. Thus, while these readings are essential for a cognitive grasp of the clinical issues, they do not address the vicissitudes of the therapeutic process. One exception in the pediatric literature is an article by Geist (1979). He states: "Unlike the physician, who can allow himself an emotional distance from these evocative encounters—a space which preserves, for example, his ability to operate—the psychotherapist must remain empathically in touch with the patient despite an ominously looming shadow of disease" (p. 19). In order to avoid impeding the "creative intimacy" of the clinical work, the therapist must maintain awareness of such countertransferential reactions as guilt, helplessness, and depression.

In the broader category of literature on "death and dying" and bereavement, mention of countertransference reactions is also quite limited. The focus tends to be on "burnout"—the culmination of caregiver stress resulting in psychosomatic symptoms, exhaustion, and disturbed involvement with or withdrawal from the patient (Rando 1984, Raphael 1983). However, the implications of this response for therapists in relation to psychotherapy patients are not pursued in depth.

A discussion of the caregiver's personal concerns in working with dying patients and the bereaved focuses on the need to grieve (Rando 1984). This need can be underestimated, since the caregiver may perceive it as somehow "inappropriate" to mourn a patient. By denying this aspect, however, the caregiver becomes vulnerable to the sequelae of unresolved grief, and to being overwhelmed by multiple loss. Work with dying patients can be a threat to the caregiver's sense of power, mastery, and control. In an attempt to counter the sense of impotence, the caregiver may become a "rescuer"—an unrealistic role in which the patient loses emotional support and the caregiver is eventually left with a sense of frustration and failure.

Awareness of one's own past losses and consciousness of potential or feared loss is critical for the caregiver (Raphael 1983, Worden 1982). In a related vein, Weisman states: "As a prerequisite for asking patients to confront mortality, I have advised professionals first to confront their own" (1977, p.119). He further admonishes therapists not to underestimate their own vulnerability in this realm. Raphael explains that the empathy so critical in this work "touches off in each one of us the most personal of terrors. We all have to learn to live with loss, but the person who works in this sphere must confront it every day" (1983, p. 401). This heightened empathy can put the therapist at risk for overidentification with the patient. Raphael believes that in order "to bear the enormity of much of the pain and loss and death he helps others encompass" (p. 405), the therapist must have ongoing support and consultation available from peers. Shneidman states:

> In my belief, the transference and countertransference aspects of death work are unique, different in subtle ways from any other human exchange. . . . For one thing, the situation itself, because of its obvious poignant quality and its time-limited feature, permits a depth of invest-ment which in any other circumstances might border on the unseemly, yet in this setting is not only appropriate, but perhaps even optimal. We can love a dying person, and permit a dying person to love us, in a meaningful way that is not possible in any other psychotherapeutic encounter.[1973, p.9]

This chapter will focus on selected facets of the countertransference in work with children and adolescents with life-threatening illnesses. The examples are taken from children with cancer but may be applicable to those with other illnesses. The chapter extends the existing literature in two important ways. First, it delineates the psychotherapeutic themes that set the stage for countertransference reactions to develop. Second, it focuses on children who are living through a life-threatening situation, but who are not necessarily dying. The word *child* will be used inclusively, unless the issue is specific to the adolescent age group. Countertransference will be understood in a broad sense, as the therapist's reactions to the child in psychotherapy, or, in Shneidman's words, as "the flow of feeling from the therapist to the patient" (1978, p. 213). This is a fitting definition for the therapist's responses to these physically ill, but psychologically intact, children.

COUNTERTRANSFERENCE THEMES

The Experience of Loss and Grief

Therapist: Are you in any pain? Does anything hurt?

Child: My heart.

Therapist: Your heart?

Child: My heart is broken.

These words were spoken by a 12-year-old girl two days before her death. The power of the words derives from their simplicity and directness, unfettered by any qualification. Distilled to the essence was her profound grief at her impending death.

The therapist must be able to absorb such words in the moment of their speaking and integrate them as a whole, without any defensive posturing. The overriding task is to be able to contain and channel the onrush of one's own grief *in order to allow the child full access to his or her own.* This is especially important because children often try to protect their parents by not disclosing the extent of their awareness. Or the parents, consumed by their own grief, may be unable to tolerate hearing such words. Thus, the therapist may be the first person, if not the only one, to whom the child can express such feeling. The therapist who, because of his or her own difficulty, blocks the child's disclosure commits an injustice that may be irreversible under life-and-death circumstances.

The therapist's own loss history has significant impact on his or her present work with these children. It is particularly important that the therapist be aware of personal reactions to loss during childhood, since these memories will often provide pathways toward the patient. Unresolved losses loom large in such encounters. The child has an acute sense of vision, through which the therapist's difficulties often become transparent. There is little place to hide. Thus, introspection must be the therapist's constant companion, with the attendant willingness to acknowledge vulnerability (Sourkes 1982).

Younger children often express the fear of their own death as a worry that something may happen to the parent, or to the therapist. This poignant projection is evident in the following example:

A 6-year-old child disclosed his fear in these words: "What if my mother dies? Then there will be no one to take care of me." When the therapist talked about how his mother attends to her health so that she *can* care for him, he responded, "Yes, she is trying very hard to stay alive. She eats all the time and she kisses me a lot." When the therapist asked the child what else frightened him, he answered, "I am scared that when I come back to the hospital, you will not be here."

In a conversation two weeks later, the child expressed his fear even more explicitly:

Child: Did you ever have bad dreams?

Therapist: Yes, sometimes I have had bad dreams. Usually when I have bad dreams, it means that I am worried about something.

Child: What are your bad dreams, usually?

Therapist: I think that they are a bit like yours. You know, monsters and things like that.

Child: And snakes . . .

Therapist: What else do you have bad dreams about?

Child: A snake biting . . .

Therapist: When you have those bad dreams, what do you think you are worrying about?

Child: You dying. Everyone dying in the world and leaving me alone. [Sourkes 1982]

On the one hand, by the projection or displacement of the issue of dying, the therapist has more time to respond—a luxury not afforded by the child who states directly, "I am afraid that *I* am going to die." On the other hand, the projection itself, the use of the pronoun *you* (as in "you dying"), can be quite threatening for the therapist to hear. The unexpected upsurge of anxiety that the therapist may experience is the very state in which the child actually lives. Thus, in some ways it is a test for the therapist: Can the therapist tolerate—in projection only—that which is the fact of the child's existence? It is the security of the therapeutic relationship that permits the child such candor. In turn, the agenda is set for exploring the child's sense of overwhelming loss.

It can be troubling for a therapist to hear and respond to statements about the future from children with guarded or poor prognoses. Such statements may appear to be inconsistent with reality. Yet the child with a life-threatening illness lives within the duality of adult (clock and calendar) time and child (magical) time. While the context for psychotherapy is finite time, a shift into child time does not necessarily imply denial or blocking (Mann 1973, Sourkes 1982). The child who makes plans for the future—however short- or long-range, however realistic or not—is living in the present with a view to continuity. This is, in fact, a definition of hope. When hearing of plans that probably will not come to fruition, the therapist must bear the sadness alone. It is not the therapist's place to dictate the boundaries of time to the child.

Through certain statements involving the future, the child may also be letting the therapist know that he or she is well aware of life's precariousness. Or the child may be testing the therapist's tolerance for the uncertainty that is at the core of his or her existence. When the child refuses to explore further the implications of a comment, the therapist must realize that the child has made a profound acknowledgment and accept it in its integrity.

A 10-year-old girl told the therapist, "If I have a Sweet Sixteen party, I want you to sit at the head table." The therapist was left with the "if" resounding in her ears.

A 13-year-old girl with widespread disease recounted to the therapist, "I know how to read palms, and I read my own. I'll be famous. I'll be married once. I see a break in my life when I'm about 17. I wonder what that is. . . ." The therapist privately envisioned a fault line, as before an earthquake. However, the girl could not elaborate further.

A 14-year-old girl complained constantly of being "bored" with being a teenager. "I'm just tired of it. I want to be grown up, travel, marry, and have kids." When questioned by the therapist, she was able to say that she wanted to hurry up time to ensure that she would make it to adulthood.

In working with these children, the therapist must engage in ongoing, honest appraisals of his or her capacity for repeated cycles of attachment and loss. An awareness of and respect for one's limitations is an integral part of such an assessment. It is only within the context of one's own psychic reality that the ability to take emotional risks, to experience and witness deep feelings, has meaning. Emotional risk-taking, without recognition of these limits, leads to an intensity that burns itself out (Sourkes 1982).

Guilt at One's Own Health

"My friends don't know how lucky they are. In fact, *you* don't know how lucky you are either. Or maybe you do know, since you see the kids here in the clinic. . . ." A 17-year-old boy hurled these words at the therapist in response to her greeting him and asking how he was feeling. His outburst, somewhat tempered by the end, is that of an adolescent angered and frustrated by serious illness. It is quite common for children to express a sense of injustice at being struck by illness, and to refer to the luck of siblings and friends who have "escaped." Implicit in these statements is the inclusion of the therapist, who is also perceived as belonging to the healthy world. Explicit accusations directed toward the therapist, usually verbalized by adolescents, occur much less frequently.

The backdrop for the therapist working with life-threatened children is a heightened appreciation for one's own health and that of one's family. Such awareness is a constant that does not interfere with the work. *Guilt* at being healthy, in contrast, peaks unexpectedly and can intrude on the therapeutic process. The therapist may, in response to the guilt, make inappropriate attempts to "make it all better" for the child. Examples of such maneuvers would include flooding the child with reassurances that cannot be fulfilled, or buying the child a gift. Or the therapist may respond defensively to a child's suggestion that, not being sick, the therapist cannot really understand. Withdrawal on the part of the therapist may occur, instead of a focus on the child's anger and isolation. Another possibility is that the therapist may simply feel overwhelmed by the tragedy of the circumstances, and wonder what he or she could possibly have to offer the child. In all of these instances, a loss of perspective occurs.

With young children who have been ill for most of their lives, the therapist may be confronted with a different reality. Unlike the child who can distinguish between "before" and "after" the diagnosis, these children may simply know of no other life for themselves but one including illness.

Child:	Did you have a lot of needles when you were 6 years old?
Therapist:	No, I didn't. . . .
Child:	Why not?
Therapist:	Because I didn't have leukemia when I was 6 years old.
Child:	Well, maybe you'll get it when you're grown up.

This type of interchange can trigger a chain of guilt and anxiety in the therapist. Yet it must be seen as a child's own matter-of-fact portrait of reality.

Tolerance for Witnessing Physical Pain

Therapist:	If you could choose one word to describe the time since your diagnosis, what would it be?
Child:	PAIN.

I can tolerate seeing pain and disfigurement, but not when those bruised bodies and bald heads belong to children (Sourkes 1982).

These latter words reflect the reaction of many medical professionals to the spectre of seriously ill children. For the psychotherapist who does not usually see physical aspects of illness in any form, the confrontation can be even more shocking. The ravages of disease in life-threatened children are a visible presence to be reckoned with, not a psychic abstraction. The therapist who works with these children must be prepared to witness first-hand the assault of life-threatening illness in all its harsh reality. Thus, he or she must be able "to stand" physical aspects as a child undergoing an invasive procedure, or reactions of nausea and vomiting, or startling disfigurement, or extreme pain. Then the therapist must be able to tolerate the profound helplessness that can be evoked by watching a child endure such hardship.

Exposure to suffering is a given in the daily routine of the therapist who consults at a medical center. To an important extent, the therapist's credibility with the seriously ill child is based on his or her ability to tolerate these physical aspects. A child gains a sense of safety in undergoing painful procedures if he or she knows that the therapist can at least bear to witness them. If the therapist cannot, then the child may feel "stronger" than the therapist and thus lose a crucial sense of protection. The therapist who sees the child in an office removed from the treatment center does not escape entirely. In this case, the therapist must be able to extract and respond to the child's detailed recounting of the physical distress without flinching.

The therapist can "construct" such tolerance from several sources. A cognitive understanding of the illness and its treatment and side effects is an essential foundation. If the therapist understands the potential life-saving value of a particular treatment, it is much more possible to tolerate the stress that the child must undergo. In such cases, the suffering of the immediate present is at least in part counterbalanced by the hope for the future. (In contrast, it is exactly the absence of such hope that makes a child's terminal agony so excruciating for everyone to witness.) Participation as a member of an interdisciplinary team provides the therapist with an arena for questions and reactions. Most important, as the child's sense of control grows through the process of psychotherapy, the therapist's helplessness is in turn assuaged by the evidence of his or her own contribution.

Responsibility for Continuity

Uncertainty and unpredictability are the hallmarks of life-threatening illness. In the child's vulnerable life situation, the therapeutic role is highly specific: the therapist is an anchoring presence. While continuity is important in any psychotherapy, it is an absolute requisite in working with the life-threatened child. Within the context of the therapeutic relationship, the person of the therapist comes to embody the essence of that continuity. Availability, implying the therapist's consistent and abiding presence, is the foundation. Whether or not a child actually questions the therapist explicitly, as in the following examples, the concern about continuity is paramount.

An adolescent who had recently been diagnosed asked the therapist, "Will you be here the whole two years I come for treatment?"

A 6-year-old child, in the course of a play therapy session, asked, "Will I come to see you for the rest of my life?"

It is the continuity that affords the child the safety to discuss the ultimate discontinuity of death. The recognition of the therapist's continuity (past, present, and future) is implicit in the following dialogue with a 6-year-old child on his return to the hospital after a month at home:

Therapist: Do you remember what we talked about last time?

Child: (*Without hesitation*) About dying. . . . (*A few minutes later*) If I don't feel like talking about dying today, there will be other days.

These examples illustrate the need for continuity "through" time, as in a linear dimension. Less evident, but of equal importance, is the therapist's constancy "across" time. That is, at any given moment, the child must feel certain of the therapist's presence. In general, this aspect becomes internalized as the relationship develops. Especially for younger children, however, the use of symbolic transitional objects can be important. In other instances, children may wish to give something of their own to the therapist. Adolescents often ask for the therapist's home telephone number, and then rarely use it. However, they express appreciation for the security it affords.

In the last session before the therapist's vacation, a dying 6-year-old child asked, "Could I have a teddy bear sticker?" He then hurried to specify, "I want the same one that you have on your beeper." The beeper (pager) was, of course, the most concrete symbol of contact with the therapist.

A 12-year-old girl brought in her school photo, insisting that the therapist carry it with her "all the time" and "always." Upon questioning, the child stated, "That way, I know you're thinking about me even when I'm not here." Her explanation was laden with significance: first, as her wanting to maintain the link in the present, when she and the therapist were apart; and second, in her desire for continuity after her death.

From the outset, the therapist must recognize the enormity of his or her responsibility to maintain the commitment of continuity. It requires a willingness for an ongoing availability and accessibility more pronounced than in traditional child psychotherapy. Lest this be misunderstood, the words "continuity," "availability," and "access" refer more to the therapist's conceptual framework in taking on the life-threatened child than to the actual day-to-day work. That is, the therapist may not see or be in touch with the child any more than usual, most of the time. However, the *potential* for heightened contact must be accepted by the therapist as an *a priori* condition.

In practical terms, the therapist must be prepared for the possibility of "off-hours" calls that demand return. Prior to vacations, careful planning for contact—symbolic or actual—is often necessary. In a teaching institution where trainees rotate for short periods, the impact of assigning "temporary" therapists to these children must be carefully assessed. When such an assignment is made, the supervising therapist should meet the child in preparation for taking on the case after the trainee leaves. Then, at the time of transfer, the child has already met the supervising therapist and knows his or her connection to the trainee. Both of these factors preserve a certain continuity.

The need for continuity is a subtle yet powerful underpinning of psychotherapy with the child with a life-threatening illness. Without an appreciation for its importance, the therapist may feel irritation, impatience, and resentment. This negative countertransference can emerge in response to what may feel like unjustified demands. While there are certainly children who do test and even abuse the therapist's boundaries, these are the exception. Most children, once secure in the commitment of continuity from the therapist, require little further "proof" outside the structure of the psychotherapy session itself.

Disclosure of Emotion

Psychotherapy with the child with a life-threatening illness demands the therapist's use of self to an extraordinary degree. On an intrapsychic level, the therapist draws from his or her own experience with separation and loss in order to witness and facilitate the child's process. However, the use of self also operates on an interactive level *with* the child—the therapist's disclosure of his or her own emotion within the psychotherapy. Over and above the mirroring of the child's material, the therapist must be prepared to share feelings more directly than in traditional psychotherapy. This assertiveness is congruent with the stress under which the child is living, unequaled by any other. As emotions—fear, anger, and sadness in particular—emerge as markers of the child's experience, the therapist may join the child in expressing and exploring them, thus taking an emotional stand. This does not give the therapist license to blur boundaries or to recount his or her own life content. Rather, the therapist's disclosure of emotion should be intimately linked to the child's experience at hand.

Fear and anger about the illness—both its physical and its emotional hardships—are the most straightforward emotions for the therapist to enter with the child. The therapist can acknowledge that he or she would also be frightened if faced with similar circumstances, or, more immediately, that the therapist feels fright with and for the child in the present. Through the therapist's disclosure, the child feels less alone, and any connotation of cowardice is minimized. In a related way, and perhaps even more powerfully, the therapist can acknowledge feeling anger at what the child must endure. This legitimization of anger is crucial, especially for adolescents.

The sharing of sadness, with an emphasis on mutuality within the therapeutic relationship, can strengthen the child's sense of safety immeasurably.

A 6-year-old child was being discharged home for a month's break between treatments. The child told the therapist that he was "a little bit scared" of going home and leaving the therapist alone. What then emerged was that he was scared that he was going to miss the therapist.

Therapist:	I am going to miss you too. I wonder what it will be like to miss each other. . . .
Child:	(*Shaking his head*)
Therapist:	You are shaking your head. . . . I don't know what that means.
Child:	(*Whispering*) That means "no."
Therapist:	That means "no"? That means . . .
Child:	That means it wouldn't be too good to miss each other.

The fear of replacement is a poignant aspect of the sadness shared between the child and the therapist. When this issue arises, the therapist's participation is essential in offering assurances of the child's uniqueness.

Over a year-long period of psychotherapy, a 10-year-old girl had become exceedingly attached to a stuffed polar bear in the therapist's office. She used the polar bear to voice her own emotions. One day, to the girl's chagrin, she came in to find that a stuffed dog had been added to the therapist's collection of toys. She spent the session having the polar bear beat up the dog, with the attack gradually abating over the hour. As she was preparing to leave the office, she said:

Child:	The dog's okay, I guess, but I still like the polar bear better. I wonder why the polar bear doesn't like the dog at all.
Therapist:	Maybe he's jealous that we might like the dog too much. But that polar bear should know that he is special . . .
Child:	And NOBODY can take his place.

In traditional psychotherapy, the deflection of emotion back to the child is a basic tenet. Thus, disclosure of feeling becomes a countertransference issue when the therapist feels uncomfortable, intruded upon, or seduced by the child's search for a response. The therapist may react defensively, thereby blocking the flow of the ongoing process. It is the therapist's recognition of the child's confrontation with an overwhelming reality that enables more flexibility in disclosure. Such emotional assertiveness on the part of the therapist is crucial when the child's situation is most precarious. As children go into long-term remission, and the threat to life recedes, the need for therapist disclosure tends to diminish accordingly.

Sexuality

A myth persists that in the battle for survival, sexuality is of little psychological importance. In fact, concerns about sexuality are quite pronounced in children with life-threatening illnesses. At one level, sexuality in all its facets represents a life force, exactly the struggle in which these children are engaged. Furthermore, the body is the focus of illness, and sexuality is an integral part of that same body. Sexual identity and functioning, and fertility—and the potential or actual losses thereof—are major issues. While adolescents are far more likely than younger children to address them, the effect on all age groups should not be overlooked.

Denial of sexual issues by the therapist serves only to close off a crucial avenue of disclosure. Acknowledgment of sexual activity, and in turn the impact of the illness upon it, is necessary if the adolescent is to communicate with candor.

An 18-year-old boy who had had a leg amputated expressed fears about his sexual functioning, and about how his girlfriend would react. On a clinic visit shortly after his surgery, he greeted the therapist: "You'll be glad to know I still work!" Before the therapist had time to respond, the boy added, laughing: "I was glad, too!"

There are concerns more subtle than those about actual sexual performance. For example, most children undergoing chemotherapy will temporarily lose bodily hair, a common side effect of many drugs. There is much overt focus on the visible loss of hair on the head, from both a cosmetic and symbolic point of view. In contrast, adolescents rarely mention the impact of the loss of pubic hair. Yet as a perceived threat to a newly emerging sexual identity, this may actually be a more devastating loss. Another topic that the therapist must be open to initiating is that of masturbation. For children whose bodies are undergoing assaultive medical regimens, the "permission" for private touching for comfort and pleasure can be a meaningful intervention.

At another level is the pain the therapist may feel at understanding implications that the child is not yet capable of grasping, or chooses not to look at in the present. Future sexual dysfunction or infertility, either as a direct result of the tumor location or as a side effect of treatment, are sobering prospects. The therapist bears the knowledge that one cost of long-term survival will be the negotiation of these losses.

A 3-year-old boy with a bladder tumor required radical surgery and extensive radiation therapy. Although the treatment would cause sexual dysfunction and sterility, the prognosis for cure was excellent. Of course, the parents consented immediately to the protocol. However, they questioned the therapist extensively on how their son would react when he reached adolescence.

A 13-year-old girl who had had surgery for a vaginal tumor confided to the therapist, "I started my periods when I was 9. I never felt that getting my period was right for me. So I'm really glad that I don't have them anymore." She exhibited no anxiety in this disclosure and would not elaborate further.

A 12-year-old girl insisted on reading the informed consent for her bone marrow transplant in the presence of her physician, her therapist, and her mother. When she asked what "sterility" meant, her physician replied, "It means you can't have babies." She retorted quickly, "Then I'll adopt!" Her spirited response, for which the therapist felt admiration, was highly adaptive at the time. Yet the therapist was fully aware that should the child survive, that loss would reemerge.

A 17-year-old girl who had been treated for uterine cancer cried, "The biggest scar is not having babies." Her grief was palpable and profound.

Medical personnel are often unprepared to broach sexual issues with the child. All the more pressure, therefore, falls on the therapist to take on the subject. As is evidenced in the examples offered here, these children have to progress not only through the normal developmental milestones of sexuality, but also through the inextricable overlay of the immediate and long-term effects of their illness or treatment. The therapist's discomfort in handling sexual concerns—or denial of their importance—can handicap the therapeutic process.

Relationship with the Parents

When asked who would visit him in the hospital, a 6-year-old child listed many individuals, but did not include his mother. When the therapist commented on the omission, the child retorted indignantly: "My mother doesn't visit. She *stays* with me!"

An adolescent girl stated matter-of-factly, "My parents and I are in this together."

In work with children with life-threatening illnesses, the therapist will encounter the parents more frequently and more closely than in traditional psychotherapy. Such contact occurs especially in the care of young children. The therapist often identifies with parents who are facing the potential lost of their child. This reaction may intensify when the therapist is also a parent, especially if his or her healthy children are of the same age as the patient. For the therapist who does not yet have children, the spectre of a seriously ill child may loom threateningly. As long as the therapist's identification is integrated into a balanced sense of empathy for the parents, such reactions do not interfere with the psychotherapy (Sourkes 1982).

However, an aspect of the countertransference that may be aroused particularly in working with these children is the "rescue fantasy" of the therapist. In wanting to protect or save the vulnerable child, the therapist encounters the danger of overinvolvement, a loss of boundaries and role. By moving in to achieve a great deal of closeness with the child, the therapist can in fact supplant the parents by becoming a surrogate. The pitfalls of this "parent surrogate" approach are evident.

The parents will feel estranged just at the time when they are desperately trying to "keep" their child. Parents' pervasive guilt about the illness (whether conscious or unconscious) will only be exacerbated if they feel that the therapist is "better" than they are at achieving closeness with the child. It is critical that the therapist not become a divisive wedge between parents and child, or be viewed with a sense of threat as the bearer of secrets that cannot be shared. The therapist must be aware of feelings of competition with the parents: such rivalry often serves as a danger signal of inappropriate involvement.

The child may be quite threatened by an inordinate amount of closeness to the therapist, while at the same time welcoming and needing this relationship. The sense of threat arises from the child's guilt at being close to a "new" adult other than the parents. The child may feel trapped in "having to choose" between parent and parent surrogate, with a simultaneous fear of alienating either. The therapist must be exceedingly careful not to contribute to such an undesirable dilemma (Sourkes 1977, 1982).

The therapist's anger toward parents must be managed delicately in any clinical setting, but especially in the intensity of life-threatening circumstances. This anger arises when the therapist feels hostility directed toward him- or herself, or when the parents' behavior is somehow hurtful to the child.

A mother had reluctantly granted permission for her child to be seen in psychotherapy. One of the presenting problems was the child's verbal abuse of the mother. At the second appointment, the mother greeted the therapist sarcastically: "He *wanted* to see you. What's your magic?" It was crucial that the therapist understand the source of the anger—the sense of vulnerability and threat—and not react with any sort of retaliation.

An 18-year-old boy was dying in the hospital. His parents had a long history of marital problems. Normally quite taciturn, he responded explosively to the therapist's question regarding how he felt about the parental conflict: "*That's* what's killing me—not the disease. I don't want to live if they aren't together. Some nights I cry all night. My father came in one night and I couldn't hold it in anymore. I told him what I was so upset about, and he just said: 'It'll be all right.' What's the good of that?" The therapist had to contend with her own inner fury at the parents for causing their son such anguish.

Negative countertransference reactions toward parents are almost always absorbed by the child as well. In such cases, the child will side with the parents and withdraw from the therapeutic relationship. Whereas other countertransference reactions impact selectively, the effect of conflict between the therapist and parents is dangerous in its breadth. Thus, the management of problematic interactions with the parents is crucial in preserving the therapeutic alliance with the child.

"THANK YOU FOR GIVING ME ALIVENESS"

These are the words of a 6-year-old child to his therapist. While life itself cannot be guaranteed, psychotherapy can "give aliveness" for however long that life may last. Such is the essence of the therapeutic relationship as captured in these words. For the therapist, the sense of fulfillment is profound.

The power of psychotherapy under life-threatening circumstances cannot be underestimated. The therapist must respect the responsibility that he or she bears in the process. With the power must come the ability to admit powerlessness, to acknowledge one's own limits.

Otherwise, caught up in the drama of children facing their own mortality, the therapist runs the danger of a narcissistic overinvestment.

Children with life-threatening illnesses tend to be idealized by their own families and by the public at large. One constantly hears the word "special" attributed to these children, spoken in almost reverential tones. In fact, they *are* "special" on one dimension: they develop a precocious wisdom of life and its fragility. However, as in any random group, they are not all necessarily likable. For the therapist entering the field, to "dislike" a child who is facing the threat of death can engender enormous guilt. A measure of adaptation to the work is the ability to admit comfortably that one finds a child irritating or difficult. It is important to note the children quoted in this chapter *are* gifted: they express what others feel. The articulateness itself, however, is not typical of all children in life-threatening circumstances.

Psychotherapy with children with life-threatening illnesses is rich in its rewards for the therapist. To know that one has contributed to a child's life is the therapist's gift. In the words of Saint-Exupery's Little Prince, "One runs the risk of weeping a little, if one lets himself be tamed." The depth of the therapist's tenderness and commitment sustains the child in his or her confrontation with separation and loss.

The author gratefully acknowledges the consultation of Margaret C. Kiely, Ph.D., of the Department of Psychology at the University of Montreal.

13

Substance-abusing Adolescents

Maryann Amodeo, Ph.D.,
Ann Drouilhet, M.A.

THE COMPLEX TEXTURE OF COUNTERTRANSFERENCE WITH SUBSTANCE-ABUSING ADOLESCENTS

Numerous authors have described the potential perils of clinical work with adolescents (Bernstein and Glenn 1978, Bonier 1982, Gartner 1985, Giovacchini 1975, Halperin et al. 1981). A common clinical experience for the therapist involves encountering a difficult, opposi-tional, recalcitrant patient who is usually in the consultation room against his or her will. Add to this picture the adolescent who has an active relationship with alcohol and other drugs, which he likely views as his right and as a badge of honor within his social group, and the phenomenon of countertransference becomes a more complex and even more salient issue. In working with substance-abusing adolescents, the therapist must create and sustain what is often a fragile therapeutic alliance, made vulnerable by four major sources of countertransferential responses.

1. *The effects of drugs on the adolescent's functioning.* This is the tendency for drug use to distort ego-functioning and relational skills.

2. *The therapeutic context in which treatment occurs.* This is the social system surrounding the patient, including the family, the school, courts or child protective agencies, the therapeutic setting in which the patient is seen, and the voluntary or mandatory nature of the referral.

3. *The attitudinal and emotional "filters" or prisms of the therapist.* Those are the early personal, professional, and societal experiences related to drug–dependent individuals and mind–altering drugs that shape the therapist's view and reactions to patients in the present.

4. *The adolescent's personality and the nature of the transference.* These are the unique qualities of the patient that contribute to the patient's reaction to the therapist, and the relationship that develops between them.

Broadly, the definition of countertransference to be used here is that described by Kernberg (1976) as "totalistic," comprising the total emotional reaction of the therapist to the patient. This definition subsumes the classical characterization of countertransference as the therapist's unconscious response to the patient's transference. This broader conception includes the reactions of the therapist that are induced primarily by external or patient behavior as well as those responses that primarily comprise the internal promptings of the therapist. This totalistic view allows for positive as well as negative countertransferential effects (Gartner 1985, p. 188).

Specifically, with adolescents who are alcohol and drug involved, countertransference is seen as including not only the therapist's response to the patient's transference, which is the classical view of the concept, but also the other dynamics in the foregoing list: the effects of drugs on the adolescent's functioning, the therapeutic context in which treatment takes place, and the "filters" of the therapist.

This chapter discusses these four sources of countertransference in detail and provides case examples that illustrate common clinical dilemmas. In addition, a theoretical model is proposed that describes the interaction between the sources of the therapist's countertransference and the stages of the patient's recovery. The model proposes that the countertransference phenomenon changes as the adolescent progresses along a continuum of treatment and recovery. This continuum begins with the assessment and diagnosis of the active substance abuse; extends through early abstinence, which is focused on building structures and supports for non-drug-use behaviors and addressing family behaviors that undermine abstinence; and concludes with ongoing recovery, focused on the working through and resolution of dynamic individual and family issues. The clinician experiences a series of shifts in therapeutic posture and emotional response that corresponds to movement along this continuum. Such shifts are affected by the nature and severity of the substance abuse and the character structure of the adolescent.

SUBSTANCES OF ABUSE

It is important to note that the majority of writers who address countertransference and substance abuse do not distinguish among addictions to different kinds of drugs. Alcoholism, for example, is included as part of the same pathology as other drug abuse or addiction (Yorke 1970). However, as early as 1983, Imhof and colleagues said that "today we have a far more diverse population . . . who might categorically be classified as 'drug abusers': recreational marijuana users, prescription drug misusers, individuals who use hallucinogens and similar mind-altering substances, and alcohol abusers" (p. 495). They concluded that historical writings must be applied very carefully to drug issues in 1983, taking into account a far more diverse and clinically demanding patient population. Now, in the 1990s, this point must be underscored. Drugs of use and abuse have increased in number, adolescent use patterns have become more diverse, and the effects of various drugs have become more complex due to drug use combinations and various routes of administration (Doweiko 1990).

The term *substance abuse* as used in this chapter refers to a range of mind-altering drugs, including alcohol; other sedative-hypnotics, including the benzodiazepines; other hallucinogens including marijuana and hashish, phencyclidine (PCP), and MDMA (known as "ecstasy," a mild hallucinogen prescribed originally for use in psychotherapy); stimulants, including cocaine, crack cocaine, amphetamines, and methamphetamine, which has recently taken the form of "ice"; inhalants, including gasoline, kerosene, glue, and cleaning fluid; and opiates, including heroin, meperidine, and oxycodone. Therapists working with adolescent substance abusers will generally find that alcohol is the most widely abused drug and is often used in combination with other drugs.

Use versus Abuse

How does one distinguish among chemical dependency, dangerous use and abuse, and normal oppositional behavior on the part of adolescents seeking to achieve a healthy separation from parents and establish an individual identity? Bratter, in writing about adolescents, states, "The ritual of using drugs, for example, permits them to relate to others without being close and enables them to share a part of their life. Adolescents view chemicals as the primary magical elixir which produces an immediate, but ephemeral, feeling of unity and oneness, a feeling of kinship" (1973, p. 586). However, Bratter also points out that a "distinction must be made between essentially productive adolescent curiosity and experimentation, and self-destructive drug abuse and dependency" (p. 585). "When drug experimentation and exploration becomes a preoccupation or an adaptive mechanism to compensate for a personal, social, or intellectual deficiency, then it becomes abuse" (Bratter 1973, p. 586).

Bean (1982), focusing on adolescent drinking, recommends distinguishing between normal adolescent experimentation and problem drinking by examining whether developmental arrest is occurring. She points out that the most pernicious result of frequent heavy use of any drug to cover feelings and to cope with stress is the blocking of social and psychological maturation and growth: the age at which heavy drinking begins may be the highest level of emotional development that the adolescent ever reaches, although some maturation may occur despite drinking. Sharoff (1969), in Bratter (1973, p. 586), states that "an individual may be considered to abuse a drug whenever his use of it results in behavior which is harmful to himself or his environment." In this chapter, the term *abuse* will refer to a pattern of use that repeatedly results in negative consequences.

Although some adolescent literature describes experimentation with alcohol and other drugs as a natural and "healthy" part of growing up, it is not the intention of this chapter to reinforce the notion that use or abuse of substances is an essential part of growing up for adolescents. Rather, even the occasional use of many of the drugs listed earlier is considered risky and dangerous, and heavy use may well interfere with achievement of many of the normal developmental tasks required for successful separation, individuation, and eventual adult adjustment.

LITERATURE REVIEW

Chemical use by children and adolescents is not a new phenomenon. According to Wheeler and Malmquist (1987, in Doweiko 1990) in the time of Charles Dickens, more than a century ago, alcoholism was rampant among the youth of England (Wheeler and Malmquist 1987). A small percentage of adolescents have always used alcohol or other drugs for recreational purposes, but in the last two generations, large numbers of adolescents have begun using drugs. However, because little well-controlled research exists, our information about use and addiction among children and adolescents, including patterns of use, etiology, and effects on emotional and physical development, is very limited (Newcomb and Bentler 1989, in Doweiko 1990).

It is therefore not surprising that little has been written on countertransferential reactions in work with substance-abusing adolescents. Most patients highlighted in the literature are a subgroup of chemically dependent adults who are in the middle to late stages of addiction, who are often seen in acute medical or psychiatric settings or in long-term residential drug treatment programs, and who are part of the drug subculture. This subgroup of addicts has been hardened by life on the street and interaction with the criminal justice system. They come to treatment with negative attitudes about authority figures and about the therapeutic process, and therapists' responses to them tend to be intense and dramatic. But even this literature on countertransferential reactions with adults who are alcohol and drug dependent is sparse.

While there are clear differences between these adult groups and the adolescents who will provide the primary focus for this chapter, literature on adult alcoholics and drug addicts, and on substance-abusing adolescents who are described as alienated and unmotivated, is briefly reviewed here to provide insight into the range of therapist responses to this issue. We will then discuss adolescents who have not yet been referred for intensive substance abuse treatment, but rather are commonly seen by mental health, social service, and youth service agencies, or are on the caseloads of the juvenile courts. Such adolescents are likely to have a polydrug abuse pattern, have experienced problems with drinking or drug abuse or both for six months to three years, be in the early to middle stage of dependence with few signs of physical addiction, and be in school and living with family.

Imhof and colleagues (1983), in an article on countertransference and the treatment of drug abuse and addiction, point out that over a period of 50 years, a vast amount of literature has explored drug abuse and addiction from a variety of vantage points, but scant attention has been paid to the countertransferential and attitudinal experience of the clinician. They quote Ausubel (1958), who describes physicians, even in the best institutions, as having openly cynical, unrealistic, and hostile attitudes toward addicts, behaving with indifference to patients' genuine complaints, and assuming in advance that patients are lying. He speculates that these negative attitudes probably pave the way for addict relapse.

Moore (1961, in Imhof 1983) notes that the constant seeking of indulgence by the alcoholic patient stimulates anger. The therapist may express this directly, through rejection of the patient, or, because the therapist needs to defend himself against awareness of his anger, through reaction formation in the form of an overly indulgent and permissive attitude. This reduces the patient's chances for recovery because it impairs his reality testing and promotes denial of the severity of the problem. Rosenfeld (1964) points out that the drug-involved patient is a particularly difficult one to manage because the clinician is confronted with the combination of a mental state and the intoxication and confusion caused by drugs. Other authors (Craig 1988, Levine and Stephens 1971), writing about addicts at an advanced stage, see them as able to engender powerful countertransferential reactions even in a brief interview. Imhof and colleagues (1983) describe several common countertransference reactions, among them the therapist who acts in the role of a good parent rescuing a bad, impulsive child; the physician who is manipulated into prescribing medications with high abuse potential as a defense against a barrage of patient complaints; the therapist who aligns himself with the patient by identifying with antiauthority stories or by vicariously romanticizing the addict lifestyle; and the therapist who experiences "burnout" as a self-protective distancing mechanism, which manifests itself as indifference, tiredness, and separation from the therapeutic interaction.

Bratter (1973, 1976, 1985), whose writings focus on adolescents who have a long history of substance abuse and dependence and who are often candidates for residential treatment, characterizes these patients as angry, defiant, and antagonistic. They have adopted antisocial lifestyles that conflict with the values of the therapist, and their current drug involvement could culminate in death, incarceration, or personality decompensation. Therapists find themselves responding to frequent crises so that long-term goal formulation is undermined. Despite the high level of emotional and practical involvement required from the therapist, establishing a therapeutic alliance is still extremely difficult with this group.

SOURCES OF COUNTERTRANSFERENTIAL RESPONSES

The Effects of Drugs on Adolescent Functioning and Relational Skills

The regular or heavy use of mind-altering drugs changes cognitive and emotional functioning. Neff (1971), in an article entitled "Chemicals and Their Effects on the Adolescent Ego," has described how chemicals, whether self- or medically prescribed, can profoundly alter ego functioning. He indicates that the regressive effects may be transient or prolonged, and goes on to say the following:

> Adolescents are uniquely susceptible to changes in body state and defensive organization as a result of their particularly fluid developmental stage. They seek diverse forms of perceptual experiences to enhance their awareness of themselves. At other times, because of the pressure of internal processes, estrangement and depersonalization can occur. . . . Soporific and somnolent effects, in particular, interfere with certain highly cathected defenses, for example, intellectualization and motoric discharge activities [Neff 1971, p. 108]. . . . The somatic changes in adolescence, the surge of sexuality and aggression, and the increased self-aggrandizement . . . require vigorous defensive adaptational efforts. . . . Not only can the integration of the altered body image and heightened impulses in adolescence be affected by chemicals, but the adaptational function of object relations can be interfered with as well. [Neff 1971, p. 110]

He concludes as follows:

> "Chemicals, whether 'dope' or drugs, can have a profound effect on the ego functioning of the adolescent." [Neff 1971, p. 118]

The use of mind–altering chemicals competes with the development of a transference relationship that could be used constructively in the therapy. Consequences, even of short-term heavy use of many drugs, include distortion in perception, damage to memory, interference with acquiring new learning, and affective lability. Depending upon the drug ingested, there is likely to be an increase in depressive symptoms (alcohol), an increase in suspiciousness and paranoia (crack cocaine, PCP), an increase in aggression (alcohol, methamphetamine), and an increase in lethargy and inability to engage in goal-setting and implementation (marijuana). The aftermath of heavy drug taking may result in a contrasting picture, with symptoms of anxiety (alcohol), agitation (hallucinogens), and marked depression (cocaine). (Doweiko 1990).

Use of these chemicals between or before therapy sessions makes the therapeutic alliance difficult, confusing, and unsatisfying. Patients are likely to be unpredictable in presentation if they are high during sessions, getting high between sessions, or in the process of "rebounding," or withdrawing, from intoxication during sessions. Since research indicates that such drugs as lysergic acid diethylamide (LSD),

PCP, cocaine, and amphetamines induce changes in the brain that far outlast the clinical effects (Talbott 1986), even patients who establish weeks of abstinence may be suffering aftereffects of use that may not be apparent to them or to a casual observer (Hawthorne and Menzel 1983, Niven 1986). The therapist is left puzzled about what part of the affect and relationship is an artifact of the chemicals and what is the therapeutic relationship. During this stage of treatment, it often feels like there is no healthy ego with which to join.

The adolescent's ability to maintain boundaries when high or recently high may well be impaired. The process of substance abuse significantly alters boundary functioning, and boundary inadequacy is widely found in chemically dependent families (Coleman and Colgan 1986). Not only does this have implications for the therapeutic relationship, but it also provides insight into the probable family experiences of those adolescents who have at least one parent or guardian who is chemically dependent (Nielsen 1988).

The Therapeutic Context in Which the Adolescent is Seen

The often involuntary nature of therapy for the adolescent plays an important part in the development of countertransference. Adolescents are often coerced into treatment by parents, courts, schools, or child protective agencies. *Denial,* an inability to perceive the severity of the situation, is a prominent dynamic for most patients with substance abuse problems, whether coerced or not. This allows patients to view themselves as "in control," with no particular problem that requires work. The patient perceives that the therapist wants to take something away—not only a comforting substance, a familiar escape, and a way to ensure peer acceptance, but an avenue to separation, autonomy, adulthood. To counter denial, therapists often experience the impulse to argue, harangue, or exhort, postures that immediately identify them with the parent.

The *scrutiny and demands of the social system* may intensify these difficulties. Often the social system, including the family, schools, court, and social service agencies, expect an immediate cure. Due to the nature of the condition, there are periodic gains and then losses. This may open the therapist to criticism from the family or from other mental health professionals. Acceptance of the possibility of death due to accidents, overdose, and related problems is difficult for the therapist, who may feel personally and professionally threatened by the patient's failure to respond to treatment, especially under the scrutiny of the other caregiving systems. A related problem may be denial on the part of parents and of the social system, which holds that excessive use of drugs is a "rite of passage" for the teen, a transient, age-appropriate activity that will spontaneously remit as maturation and development continue.

The *adolescent's unwillingness to commit to abstinence* becomes another source of countertransference reactions. Most teens maintain the belief that abstinence is unrealistic and simply an idiosyncratic request from an adult. The notion that abstinence is akin to "cruel and unusual punishment" is reinforced by the adolescent's belief that drug use is a requirement for being accepted into the peer group, and by media glamorization and normalization of drug use, especially alcohol. In addition, the common absence of physical addiction as a consequence of the adolescent's use, and a sense that what happens today has little relationship to life in the future, increase the adolescent's entrenched resistance to the idea of abstinence.

If illegal behavior is involved, *ethical issues* may create internal conflicts for the clinician, interfering with the bonding process. The securing and taking of illegal drugs or the use of alcohol by underage adolescents raise ethical dilemmas for the therapist. As the substance abuse problem becomes more severe, the patient's values often change in a negative direction. The adolescent's priorities shift from drug use as a secondary activity to drug use and the securing of drugs as primary and preoccupying activities. The adolescent's relationship with drugs becomes more focused and intense. Relationships with peers or associates are formed for the purpose of obtaining or using drugs. Patterns evolve that are characterized by secretiveness, lying, and manipulation. Lying is seen as the norm and becomes an essential survival method. Interacting with dealers, selling drugs, sharing drugs with other teens or younger children, or colluding in other types of illegal behavior become commonplace.

The therapist who gives prominent focus during sessions to issues of ethics and legality runs the risk of assuming an authoritarian posture that will interfere with the therapeutic alliance and can make successful treatment almost impossible. However, the therapist who fails to address these issues with the teen will be seen as condoning the behavior, and may be left feeling that his posture inadvertently facilitated continued illegal activities. Credibility with parents, service providers, and other adults involved in the treatment can also be lost if it becomes known that the therapist knew of these activities and failed to take a stand.

The "Filters" of the Therapist

Societal and professional filters related to substance abuse. A number of factors related to the life experiences of therapists influence their reactions to patients who are drug dependent and result in "filters," or lenses through which the therapist sees the patient. Among these filters is *societal moralism,* whereby substance abusers are seen as self-indulgent and lacking in self-discipline. Connelly comments that "treaters, like others in the community, may have culturally determined biases toward the substance abuser as one who lacks willpower and does not want to change, or who is antisocial and cannot be treated" (Connelly 1983, p. 154).

A second filter is that of *stereotypes of addiction,* whereby only people in the late stages of addiction are considered to have a problem. Excessive use that is causing damage but is not totally debilitating is defined as "moderate use." Resistance to labeling adolescents as addicted or as problem users is particularly strong in this regard. Googins (1984), describing avoidance of alcoholic patients, identifies a third filter: *nihilism concerning therapy,* a conscious or unconscious belief that there is little hope of success, resulting in clinical behaviors that reflect pessimism and defeatism.

The almost total *lack of professional training* in substance abuse in a number of mental health–related disciplines (Connelly 1983, Faltz and Madover 1988), including psychology, social work, rehabilitation counseling, nursing, psychiatry, pastoral care, and school counseling, provides another important filter. Graduate programs offer few, if any, courses, and agency practice in many settings has not identified substance abuse as an inservice training or clinical supervision priority. In fact, many workers encounter active *agency denial,* in which initial patient or family assessments include no questions about drinking or drug use, case conferences routinely occur without attention to the possibility of substance abuse, and no policies exist to guide workers in referral or treatment planning if substance abuse is diagnosed.

Related to the lack of professional training is a sixth filter, *symptom versus cause*—the split between the mental health and substance abuse fields in their conceptualizations of the etiology of addictions (Googins 1984). Clinicians often bring a psychodynamic framework to their work with substance abuse and become frustrated with the ineffectiveness of this approach. Compounding this may be the worker's *fear of confrontation,* a treatment technique that is often necessary with patients in denial. Lacking professional training and specific strategies for working through denial, many therapists have a history of failed efforts with patients, including protracted power struggles, patient relapse, and worker collusion. Further, clinicians often suffer from a failure to appreciate the long-term nature of addiction (Brown 1985). Unrealistic expectations are imposed, including immediate and unbroken abstinence, and a rapid reinvolvement by the patient in productive activities.

Stereotyped images leading to suspicion of 12-Step programs, such as Alcoholics Anonymous and Narcotics Anonymous, may serve as another filter. Many professionals have preconceived notions of such programs, seeing them as rigid and simplistic, or as unscientific because of their strong emphasis on spirituality, or as the source of a new "addiction" related to frequent or "compulsive" attendance at meetings. Underlying feelings of the therapist that may bolster investment in these stereotypes include the fear of being devalued if patients become active in a "competing" treatment program, and the fear of loss of income if patients turn to 12-Step programs as a major source of support in recovery. Brown (1985) recommends a three-way partnership between the patient, the professional, and the 12-Step program to facilitate and hasten recovery and reduce this sense of competition.

These filters could be conceptualized as contributing to what Giovacchini (1975) calls *homogeneous countertransference*—a reaction that is somewhat predictable given a particular transferential stimulus; in other words, most therapists, under the same circumstances, would be expected to feel or react in the same way. Given the types of cultural and professional conditioning previously described, many therapists will experience countertransference reactions that interfere with their ability to provide supportive and effective treatment. However regrettable this may be, such reactions remain normative for professional practice today.

Next we will consider factors that contribute to *idiosyncratic countertransference*—a reaction that arises from the unique qualities of the therapist's background and particular character makeup. Such reactions may be particularly distressing and are sometimes the result of unresolved conflicts or other psychopathology present in the therapist.

Personal filters related to substance abuse. Perhaps the most common cause of idiosyncratic countertransference in the context of substance abuse is the *therapist's own experience with drinking and drug use.* Connelly (1983) points out that therapists who use alcohol themselves may have difficulty emphasizing the client's need to abstain. On the other hand, therapists who abstain may have a moralistic attitude toward patients' substance abuse. A therapist who has used drugs and was able to control the use without trouble, or who found it easy to reduce the use when problems began, is likely to be impatient and angry with the compulsive nature and psychological dependence of the adolescent's use.

Today's clinician frequently finds himself comparing his own adolescent use of chemicals to the use of his adolescent patients. Important to remember are the significant differences in patterns of use between the youth of twenty and thirty years ago and the youth of today. Two or three decades ago, drugs were less potent, the variety was more limited, substances were less readily available, and drugs were used, at least in part, to make political and social statements. This is in contrast to the faster and more intense "highs" readily available in today's society. The clinician who attempts to relate to today's substance-abusing adolescent based on personal experience may feel confused and alienated. Adolescents are extremely sensitive to the clinician's anxiety (Giovacchini 1975) and may be quick to challenge the clinician about personal use. The clinician may be tempted to disclose his or her history in an attempt to join with the adolescent. This is a risky intervention, however, given the differences in patterns of use and the lack of predictability about how the information may be used. Often adolescents use this disclosure as evidence that chemicals are "not that bad" ("*You* made it even though you used drugs") and see it as hypocrisy that the adult who once used drugs is now trying to keep others away from them.

Another filter-influencing countertransference is the experience of *growing up with an alcoholic or drug-dependent parent,* or *currently being in a close relationship with a chemically dependent person.* Connelly comments:

> Since substance abuse and alcoholism are so common, most treaters will have had first-hand experience with these problems, either personally or with a family member. Treaters' unresolved conflicts about alcoholism make dealing with these issues in patients much more difficult. . . . Experience shows that, when it comes to treating substance abuse, as much time must be spent with staff members' attitudes as with patients' problems. [1983, p. 155]

Many clinicians from chemically dependent families will have recollections of a household dominated by struggles between the alcoholic or drug abuser and other family members who begged, threatened, or ordered the chemically dependent person to stop, or facilitated the use by ignoring it, thereby inadvertently enabling the problem to continue. Depending upon the clinician's childhood role in this family, he may have developed a pattern of diffusing tension and avoiding confrontation at all costs, or perhaps of overfunctioning out of a need to control an environment in which uncontrolled behavior was ever imminent. Therapists from such a background may find that they respond to drug users with feelings of negativity, cynicism, and hopelessness. The therapist may well feel controlled or defeated even in initial interactions with patients. If the patient relapses, self-blame may be the immediate response (Nielsen 1988).

A therapist who is in a personal relationship with a chemically dependent person who is actively using substances may feel emotionally depleted, angry, sad, or judgmental in having to deal with substance-abusing patients on the job. Alternatively, such a therapist may feel hypocritical in advising patients of ways to confront or leave a destructive relationship when they themselves are mired in an enabling partnership.

If the therapist is drug dependent but in denial, this will serve to prevent him from seeing the patient's use as troublesome, since it mirrors the therapist's own use. The therapist's denial would operate in such a way that a thorough assessment would be avoided, a superficial one would be completed, or the diagnosis would be transformed into a psychiatric diagnosis other than substance abuse.

If the therapist is in recovery, as are many of those working in specialized substance abuse treatment programs, there are predictable countertransference issues that arise. The clinician may be intolerant of the patient's need to experiment with controlled use, experience a lack of compassion if relapse occurs, or subscribe to 12-Step programs as the only viable treatment methods. If 12-Step programs made a major contribution to the clinician's recovery and the patient has difficulty using these programs, the clinician's loyalty to the 12-Steps may cause him to harangue the patient and make pessimistic predictions of his fate.

Recovering clinicians may be unwilling to discuss the patient's early childhood experiences, traumatic life events, or the relationship with the therapist, for fear that in doing so they will be manipulated away from the essential abstinence work, thereby increasing the possibility of relapse. Exploring feelings may be equated with providing patients with an excuse to return to the use of drugs. Recovering counselors who lack professional training may show significant personal boundary inadequacy, which can lead to professional boundary violations. For many in the substance abuse field, good training on professional boundaries and boundary violations has been almost completely lacking (Nielsen 1988).

Personal filters related to early "loss of control" experiences. *Interactions with patients that are reminiscent of painful or traumatic early life experiences of the therapist* are an additional source of idiosyncratic countertransference. Interacting with substance-abusing adolescents who seem trapped in a pattern of compulsive behavior, or who repeatedly involve themselves in sexual acting out or sex that is unprotected from the possible spread of sexually transmitted disease, or who have out-of-body experiences or psychotic symptoms as a result of drug use, may be especially likely to stimulate powerful fears of loss of control in the therapist for whom this was an early life issue. And interacting with patients who become withdrawn, depressed, or suicidal may trigger fears of rejection and abandonment for the therapist whose early life was characterized by repeated losses or threats of loss.

The therapist's experiences as an adolescent will also play a role in countertransference. A positive adolescent experience may lend energy and objectivity to the clinical work. A troubled adolescence may leave many unresolved issues. Overidentification is a common pitfall. One therapist found that her patient's drug abuse became a secondary concern as she vicariously relived her unhappy adolescence through the exciting life of her socially popular patient.

CASE EXAMPLE: ANGELA

Angela, age 17, was referred for drug and alcohol evaluation and treatment by a community outreach worker following a confrontation Angela had had with her mother. Angela's mother had been increasingly concerned about her daughter's poor school performance, breaking of curfew, and frequent lying. Angela was the younger of two girls, with one sister 6 years older than she. Angela's parents had divorced when she was 2, and both her father and her mother subsequently remarried. She lived with her mother until she was 12, and then, at her own request, went to live with her father. She returned to her mother's home when she was 14 and entered the local high school.

Although Angela was attractive, warm, and articulate, she was only an average student. She described always hating school because she was ill at ease with her peer group. An ongoing theme was her perception that she was bound to be on the outside of any group of which she longed to be a part. In treatment sessions, she explained her use of drugs as an attempt to find a group to which she could belong. This solution proved unsatisfactory, however, because the more involved she became, the less confident she was that her newfound friends liked her for herself and not because of her willingness to "party" at a moment's notice.

At the time of the evaluation she was clearly dependent on marijuana and LSD and was heavily abusing alcohol. As she engaged in treatment, she readily embraced the need for abstinence from drugs and began a program of recovery that included Narcotics Anonymous (NA) meetings and counseling sessions. Her intention was to continue to try to drink in a limited and safe manner, but she found that she failed at controlling the amount she drank once she began. Further, she was unable to ensure that an evening of drinking would not end with harmful results. After 5 months Angela stopped attending NA meetings because she felt she didn't belong: her drinking and drug history was not as severe as that of many of the young people she met. She was planning to begin college in the fall, and this transition had increased her need to see herself as a "normal person." She was resentful that she would be robbed of a social life if the option of drinking and drugs was gone.

Working with Angela triggered memories in the therapist of a group of teenagers that she had longed to join when she was in high school. Being socially awkward and relatively unattractive, the therapist had remained on the periphery of the group of girls she had tried to emulate. As the therapeutic relationship evolved, the therapist became increasingly aware of her resistance to seeing Angela as addicted, despite the accumulation of evidence that she was indeed addicted. The therapist repeatedly reminded herself that the priority in their sessions was helping Angela accept the diagnosis and establish immediate abstinence from all substances, yet she regularly lost this focus as she vicariously experienced the camaraderie and excitement of adolescence through Angela's stories of weekends at the beach, all-night parties, romance, and intrigue.

In supervision, the therapist was asked to consider whether her work with Angela was being impeded by a desire to have Angela like and approve of her as a way of healing the still-tender wounds of her own painful adolescence. This feedback allowed the therapist the opportunity to more clearly differentiate her needs from Angela's and to establish a clearer position and therapeutic contract with her patient.

Many adolescents look and sound relatively healthy despite an ongoing problem with substances. Those adolescents who are attractive, popular, and generally appealing are at special risk for suffering the effects of therapist overidentification, since the unsuspecting clinician, as well as those individuals with close personal ties to the adolescent, is prone to dismiss the substance abuse as nonproblematic or as "just a phase."

A critical component of clinical work with substance-abusing patients is that "care" be provided for the caregiver to help prevent overidentification, projection, and a range of countertransferential reactions. This can be accomplished through supports such as clinical supervision or consultation with professionals sensitive to issues of substance abuse and countertransference, a peer support group with colleagues involved in similar work, continuing education opportunities that pay specific attention to the indicators of countertransference and methods for working through those feelings, and attendance at Al-Anon meetings. Designed originally for family members of alcoholics, Al-Anon has become an invaluable resource for those who interact closely with others who have substance abuse problems. Many caregivers have found that attending meetings helps them with limit-setting and with maintaining the "loving detachment" necessary to ensure that responsibility and control rests in the hands of the patient.

The Transference and the Personality of the Patient. Countertransference, as it is classically viewed, offers insight about the patient's personality and dynamics that can be useful, if not crucial, in guiding diagnostic thinking, formulation, treatment planning, and methods of intervention. The term *objective countertransference* has been used to indicate that such reactions do not originate in the therapist but are induced by the patient. These can be diagnostic, and with substance-abusing adolescents they may indicate the character structure of the patient underneath the addiction.

Transference is likely to change as the treatment progresses. Initially, the transference with adolescents who are actively drinking and using other drugs involves the patient's viewing the therapist as a threat to his or her continued use. As the therapist successfully joins with the patient and eliminates the substances as an issue around which they are struggling, they can look together at the nature of the relationship between what is happening to the adolescent and the adolescent's use of substances. At this point, the transference will be less distorted by the chemical interference. The possibility exists for the emergence of both more positive and more negative transference, but this transference will be more in keeping with the quality of the actual relationship.

With increasing abstinence and recovery, the personality profile of the adolescent will become clearer, with some adolescents achieving a high level of emotional and social adjustment and others remaining mired in self-defeating patterns and evidencing severe personality problems. Nielsen (1988) and Bratter (1976) describe the more seriously impaired adolescents with whom they have worked as having a crisis orientation that often results from the presence of chemical dependency in the parents or family, with the substance abuse of the adolescent further contributing to this coping style. Reactions include difficulty in identifying sequential steps to be taken to solve a problem, failure to deal with problems until they reach emergency proportions, panic when situations escalate, and a pattern of hysterical and excessive emotional demands on caregivers. These authors see authority issues as characteristic of such adolescents, as a result of an absence of consistent and appropriate limits in the family, leading to a general lack of safety and developmentally appropriate learning. Children grow up not understanding how to use rational rules or how to challenge appropriately those with whom they disagree. In addition, an external locus of control and communication dysfunction are described as common to the adolescent substance-abusing population.

Nielsen (1988) characterizes chemically dependent families as "enmeshed," wherein members are overinvolved with one another and underinvolved with others outside the family. The high rate of physical and sexual abuse among the population seeking treatment attests to the boundary problems in these families. Some estimate the incidence of physical and sexual abuse at 25 to 80 percent (Nielsen 1988, p. 123). According to Nielsen, "A client from an enmeshed system will attempt to both merge with the counselor as well as fight the counselor's attempts at setting boundaries that allow for appropriate connection and appropriate separation. The client is likely to react with shame and rage" (p. 121). Other adolescents, discribed below, will achieve a higher level of emotional and social adjustment.

The following section focuses on the stages of recovery, and proposes that each of the sources of countertransference described earlier is activated differentially, depending upon the stage of recovery. A conceptual framework is presented for viewing the shifts in these various sources of countertransference in relationship to the stages of recovery.

STAGES OF TREATMENT AND RECOVERY, AND EFFECTS ON COUNTERTRANSFERENCE

Brown (1985) offers a valuable conceptualization of the treatment and recovery process in her developmental model of recovery from alcoholism. Although she focuses on alcoholism, the model is equally useful for viewing drug dependency. Beginning at the point when therapy is initiated, she identifies four stages and describes goals and tasks to be accomplished at each stage:

Stage 1: The active drinking (drug dependency) stage

Stage 2: The transitional stage at which the patient is considering that loss of control may exist and that abstinence may be necessary

Stage 3: The early recovery stage, when the patient has made a commitment to abstinence

Stage 4: The ongoing recovery stage

Brown has presented the four stages as a way to view necessary shifts in the role of the therapist and the work of the patient as recovery progresses. However, these stages are also useful for viewing changes in countertransference reactions as recovery progresses, with each stage presenting different challenges and eliciting different responses from the therapist. The four stages serve as the foundation for a framework presented in Table 13–1, which proposes that countertransferencereactions change in relation to the stage of recovery, and that this change is influenced by a shift in the *sources* of countertransference, which are differentially activated at various points in the process. In other words, these stages of recovery dynamically "interact" with the sources of countertransference experienced by the therapist to produce countertransference reactions that shift over time. Identifying the patient's stage of treatment and recovery can predict the likely source and nature of the countertransference that is currently activated, and identifying the source and nature of the countertransference can predict the stage of treatment and recovery of the patient.

Table 13–1: Shifts in Sources of Countertransference in Response to Stage of Recovery

| | Stages of Recovery | | | |
| | 1 | 2 | 3 | 4 |
	Drinking and Drug Use	Transitional	Early Recovery	Ongoing Recovery
Sources of *Countertransference*				
Effects of alcohol and other drugs on the adolescent's functioning	X	X		
The therapeutic context	X	X	X	
The "filters" of the therapist	X	X	X	
The adolescent's personality and the transference			X	X

Adapted from S. Brown. *Treating the Alcoholic: A Developmental Model of Recovery.* Copyright © 1985. New York: John Wiley & Sons. Adapted by permission of John Wiley & Sons.

Earliest contacts with the patient who is actively involved with drinking or drug use activate feelings in the clinician primarily related to three areas: the effects of alcohol and other drugs on the adolescent's functioning, the personal "filters" of the therapist, and the therapeutic setting. The transitional and early abstinence phases activate feelings in the clinician related to the same three sources of countertransference. However, as the adolescent achieves substantial abstinence, is increasingly safe from relapse, and moves into a fuller recovery, these circumstances activate feelings in the clinician related more to the personality of the adolescent and the actual transference—feelings similar to those stimulated by non–substance-abusing clients. If relapse occurs during early abstinence or ongoing recovery, the sources of countertransference related to the *earlier* stages of recovery return as potent dynamics.

It should be noted that Brown's model focuses on work with adults rather than adolescents. While it serves as a useful framework for the concepts discussed here and seems generally consonant with the dynamics of treatment and recovery for adolescents, some variations may exist between the paths of adolescent and adult recovery, which may necessitate an alternate developmental model of recovery. If there is in fact a divergent path for adolescents, it would likely result in a variation in the countertransference responses highlighted here.

Stage 1: Active drinking and abuse of other drugs. At the initiation of the therapeutic relationship, when patients are actively drinking and abusing other drugs, much of their energy goes into maintaining a belief in their ability to control drug use. At this point the therapist's work is highly influenced by the societal and professional "filters," or homogeneous countertransference described earlier—the clinician's attitudes and beliefs about substances, his personal relationship to drugs during adolescence and adulthood, the nature of professional support for substance abuse work in the agency or clinical setting, how the substance abuse was identified (acknowledged by the patient as the presenting problem or discovered by the therapist after intake), the availability and extent of family involvement, and the clinician's comfort with what may be the adolescent's disdain, apathy, or inability to engage in a meaningful process or dialogue.

When parents bring their child for a substance abuse evaluation, it is often upon the recommendation (or requirement) of an outside agency such as a school or juvenile court. Although it is rare that the parents are considering for the first time that their child is involved with drinking and other drugs, the public exposure in the form of a referral brings the issue to a head, penetrating, at least temporarily, the denial system that has allowed the family to avoid confronting the issue directly. When the evaluation process includes the parents and other appropriate family members, their inclusion will increase the range of information and feelings that generate countertransference in the clinician.

It is natural and healthy for parents to be anxious in the face of their child's possible use of alcohol or drugs. It is also common for that anxiety to be expressed as hostility, suspiciousness, and lack of confidence in the evaluator. As the clinician plans how he will present the results of the evaluation, he may feel constrained by anxiety, anger, and concern about the accuracy of the evaluation. These feelings are often related to the clinician's response to the family's defensiveness and need to protect themselves and their child from the shame and guilt associated with a substance abuse problem. The clinician, recognizing the source of his feelings, will be better able to maintain clarity about the extent and severity of the adolescent's relationship to substances and present that feedback in a nonjudgmental and empathic manner.

With clinicians who are inexperienced in working with substance-abusing patients, the need for professional omnipotence may result in a fear of showing ignorance or being seen as not very "hip." This often occurs when adolescents use street slang to talk about drugs and drug-taking activities. The therapist may fail to ask follow-up questions or challenge contradictory statements in spite of being confused. For other therapists, the fear of appearing puritanical may lead to passivity and rationalization concerning the patient's dangerous drug-taking behaviors, thereby "enabling" and colluding with the denial. The therapist's fear of being conned, manipulated, or emotionally exploited may express itself in an artificial demonstration of control through inappropriate or punitive limit-setting or denigration of the patient.

Providing patient education about the progressive nature of alcohol and other drug dependence may serve to empower the patient to take charge of his own treatment and help the clinician manage the impulse to impose ever greater control over the patient's behavior. Information about the progression may also preempt the client's often futile attempts at reducing the frequency and quantity of substance use in an effort to avoid the need for total abstinence. Although education may not appear to have an immediate impact, this process may "plant a seed" that begins to erode denial and may germinate at a later time.

If the patient's drinking and drug use is putting him in day-to-day jeopardy and creating situations of imminent danger, the therapist should undertake what Bean (1986) has described as "handwringing"—

a vivid demonstration of worry and concern on the part of the therapist related to the patient's physical and emotional safety and ability to engage in self-care. This becomes necessary because patients maintain the illusion that they operate normally when intoxicated with alcohol or other drugs, and believe that there is no impairment in judgment, coordination, perception, reaction time, mental acuity, emotional evenness, or medical status. They are often oblivious to the crisis nature of the situation. It becomes essential then for the therapist to provide reality-testing by reflecting a sense of alarm at the circumstances. The degree to which "handwringing" is recommended depends on the urgency of the situation and the therapist's judgment about the patient's ability to respond constructively to a heightening of anxiety.

In the final analysis, therapists working with adolescents who use dangerous and potentially life-threatening drugs must examine their personal values, attitudes, and visceral reactions to these patients. If the therapist recognizes a strong dislike or repulsion for the behavioral manifestations of drug dependence, acknowledgment of these feelings on a personal level and in clinical supervision is necessary if treatment is to be effective. Some clinicians will struggle with feelings of moralism, anger or anxiety, hoping to overcome such feelings, but in the end may realize that they will never be effective with this population.

Stage 2: Transition. The process of alcohol and other drug dependence in adolescents differs from that in adults in that adolescents often become dependent much faster than adults (Schaefer 1987); tend to abuse a wider variety of substances, since they are more willing to use whatever is available; consume substances with more ferocity than adults as a result of needing to conceal their use from adults and to achieve their primary goal of intoxication; and are physically and cognitively more vulnerable to the effect of the chemicals, having spent fewer years of life feeling "normal"—that is, without being high on chemicals. Alcohol and other drugs have often been a best friend, perhaps the only friend, for many drug-dependent adolescents. The clinician, offering the promise of a better life, is competing not only with the adolescent's distorted thinking and feeling states, but also with what the adolescent has learned to trust about the drugs and what they can do for him that no human being and no other experience seems able to do.

Many clinicians fail to remember the profound psychological impact of drugs and the strength of the adolescent's attachment to them. This can be clearly observed in the clinician who is perplexed or annoyed by the adolescent who is not interested in changing his relationship to substances and makes that clear, overtly or covertly, despite numerous negative consequences, drug education sessions, and intense family pressure to abstain. Time spent in this stage may depend upon the severity of the substance abuse problem and resultant psychological and social deterioration. Progress will be partially related to the patient's willingness to experiment with abstinence from all mind-altering drugs.

During the transitional phase, it becomes essential for the therapist to "ally with the client against the substances" (Bean 1987) and to avoid power struggles that pit the therapist against the patient. One method for accomplishing this is acknowledging that early drug use is reinforcing (i.e., that at low doses and with only occasional use, the positive effects operate without an accumulation of negative effects) and that dependence develops subtly and without the conscious awareness or consent of the user. This needs to be done without the implication of condoning continued use. Many teens begin using substances as a way of finding relief from uncomfortable or painful feelings; then psychological dependence gradually develops, "seducing" the adolescent back to behavior that has been renounced. Discussing dependence from this perspective minimizes the self-blame and societal blame that the adolescent brings to the therapy, and allows the treatment to move on to address the here and now.

A further method for allying with the patient against the substances is to establish the causal connection between the adolescent's current pain and deteriorating life circumstances, and his or her use of drugs or alcohol—that is, to identify and explore the pain and to help the patient look at the temporal connection between substance use and its painful consequences. As the patient begins to accept the reality of this relationship, the clinician has more freedom to develop the alliance and use it in the service of designing a viable treatment plan with the patient.

If work with adolescents is carried out in an individual therapy setting, contact with the parents is virtually obligatory. Dynamics that become clear in family assessment and education sessions are likely to create additional countertransference responses. The therapist's contact with parents may result in fantasies of rescuing the adolescent from the parents, leading to guilt at the fantasy of replacing them. And while the therapist's rescue fantasies may sometimes result in positive countertransference, which allows for a high level of emotional investment, the dangers are myriad. These include the likelihood that the therapist will develop intense anger toward the adolescent who resists being rescued; or that he will begin to view the adolescent as a victim, leading to infantilizing or enabling behavior; or that a breach may develop in the therapist's alliance with the parents.

CASE EXAMPLE: LARRY

Larry was a 16-year-old who had been using an assortment of drugs—anything he could get his hands on—since he was 12 years old. Although he presented as an adolescent with a sense of self and an interest in his future, he had poor impulse control, was easily led into risky situations, and was on probation for the second time on charges of breaking and entering. He was easily engaged in treatment and had a great deal to talk about, as did his mother and his stepfather of four years.

Larry was born when his mother was 16. Larry's father was 19 at the time and not prepared to get married or to support either of them. Larry's mother continued to live with her family, finished high school, and took a job as a receptionist for a medical practice. Larry had revolving parent figures and called his grandmother "mother" and his mother by her first name until they moved to their own apartment when he was 5. Larry was 9 when his mother's boyfriend moved in with them, and he was 12 when they married. Larry did not remember the last time he saw his father; he guessed it was when he was 9. He believed that his father lived in Colorado and was an alcoholic. He had never asked for help to contact him but thought he would like his father because they would have a lot in common.

Larry's mother and stepfather were concerned parents who wanted to help Larry even though they felt that he had betrayed them several times. They expressed love for him but were wary and suspicious of him and viewed his antisocial behavior as a threat to their marriage. As treatment progressed, the mother and stepfather disclosed their own drug histories, which had included weekend binges with cocaine and heavy marijuana use. Although their pattern of drug abuse had stopped three years prior to Larry's coming to treatment, during Larry's formative years he was ignored, neglected, and bribed to entertain himself during periods when his parents were either high or in the depressed aftermath of being high. Although the parents were convinced that Larry was unaware of their drug use, the stepfather remembered that Larry had discovered a mirror and straw left under the couch after a cocaine-filled weekend, and Larry's mother recounted many times when she had pushed Larry aside, ignoring his pleas that she play with him, read to him, or engage with him in some concrete way.

The parents looked expectantly to the therapist to cure Larry. However, the therapist, hearing how the parents had been repeatedly oblivious to the needs of this child who they now blamed for disrupting their lives, reacted internally with anger and disdain. The therapist restrained her impulse to ask the parents sarcastically how they expected Larry to cope with his life circumstances when he was provided with no support or guidance outside of a peer group of similarly neglected boys who were eager for and vulnerable to any excitement that might come their way. Having grown up in a verbally abusive family, the therapist had strong feelings about parental roles and responsibilities and could muster little empathy for these parents. Through supervision, the therapist recognized that she was stuck in a position of blaming the parents. This limited her ability to help the parents change their enabling behaviors and be less punitive with Larry about his alcohol and drug use.

Other dangers of this stage are the therapist's need for control over the therapy and for compliance from the patient, leading to an authoritarian, rigid, or demanding posture. The therapist may also inadvertently withdraw personal involvement if it seems that the patient is not moving at a sufficient pace. The therapist's ability to view the patient as conflicted and ill, even though the patient's behavior may be broadcasting the opposite, will go a long way toward reducing polarization in the therapy. It is helpful for the patient to hear the therapist describe the existence of two competing parts of the patient—one that is preoccupied with maintaining use and is repeatedly drawn to recreating the mood swing, and another that wishes for a way out of the dependence. The therapist's accepting and normalizing this ambivalence in a nonjudgmental manner may be crucial to the patient's engagement in the transitional stage of recovery. Continual awareness of this ambivalence allows the therapist to support the part of the patient for whom the drug dependence is ego dystonic, and thereby minimizes the likelihood of emotional distancing and withdrawal on the part of the therapist.

CASE EXAMPLE: KRISTIE

Fifteen-year-old Kristie agreed to inpatient substance abuse treatment because she was frightened by her parent's reaction to discovering her substance abuse problem. Although her parents had been worried about her deteriorating school performance and relationship with them for several months, it was only after a meeting with a guidance counselor that the parents became willing to consider that Kristie's problems had to do with her use of drugs. The initial evaluation revealed that Kristie had been smoking marijuana daily for six months and had been getting drunk almost every weekend for the last year and a half. With this discovery, Kristie's parents were distraught and threatened to tell her grandmother, whom Kristie revered, if she did not agree to treatment.

Kristie experienced her hospital stay as long and trying, and she was discharged with a poor prognosis. She returned home with a treatment plan that included attending ninety meetings of Alcoholics Anonymous (AA) and Narcotics Anonymous (NA) in ninety days, getting a sponsor from one of those programs, participating in individual and family therapy, giving up drug-using friends, and attending an aftercare family group. The parents agreed to attend Al-Anon, a self-help program for families with an alcoholic member.

In individual and family therapy sessions, Kristie said little, was accomplished in her ability to reveal nothing about how she felt or what she wanted for herself, and remained aloof from all attempts to engage her. Initially, the therapist's self-esteem was battered by Kristie's resistance; this was fueled by the therapist's concern that she was inadequate in dealing with this kind of case, and she felt demoralized and enraged. She was fearful that Kristie's condition would worsen under her care, and that she (the therapist) would overlook signs of an impending relapse because she was preoccupied with her own professional impotence.

In supervision, the therapist discovered that she was carrying all of the mounting anxiety that rightfully belonged to Kristie and her family. When the therapist was able to describe to the family that the difficulties with treatment stemmed from the fact that Kristie suffered from a "partially treated addiction" (Bean 1989), she was able to create a more even distribution of anxiety within the therapeutic system. She explained that, although Kristie was maintaining abstinence from drugs, she was failing to undertake the emotional work that provides the foundation for recovery. The therapist proposed that Kristie would be unable to engage in the therapy until her addiction was more "fully treated"—that is, until she could acknowledge that her condition had emotional and interpersonal parameters as well as physical ones. The therapist stated that she was greatly worried for Kristie: precious time to arrest Kristie's downhill slide was being lost, and the odds were that she would probably advance into late-stage addiction.

The therapist's shift allowed the parents to reclaim their anxiety, which enabled them to become decisive. In the following weeks, they significantly reduced their previous enabling behaviors; they stopped fighting between themselves about which one was more lenient, they began to insist that Kristie go to AA and NA meetings, and they began to retract privileges when she failed to follow through on agreed-upon behaviors. Subsequently, Kristie became observably angry with the therapist and her own family—a marked improvement over the Cheshire Cat grin and coy muteness that had previously characterized her behavior. Now therapy could get underway.

Family therapy is a useful modality when working with the substance-abusing adolescent. Like countertransference responses to individuals, countertransference responses to family systems take a variety of forms. Since other members of the family have often established a pattern of excessive drinking and drug use, the therapist may become a lone voice calling for abstinence. This may lead the therapist to feel overresponsible for the adolescent and to dismiss the parents as incompetent and unable to establish consistent limits and act as positive role models. Another common scenario involves anxious, angry parents who alternately minimize the seriousness of the problem, then blame and punish the adolescent as the substance abuse and its attendant crises becomes worse. This marked reversal of posture interferes with developing a viable treatment plan. The therapist finds himself expending tremendous energy to stabilize the *parents* to help them organize in a positive way to help their child. As the parents are unable to sustain a united and objective stance, especially during the bumpy road of the adolescent's early recovery, the therapist can be left feeling disempowered and demoralized.

Stage 3: Early recovery. Brown (1985) views early recovery as spanning the first several months of abstinence, and often extending to as many as eighteen months. The work of early recovery centers around acquiring the emotional and behavioral tools necessary to maintain a drug-free life and integrating the identity of the drug-dependent person, which provides the foundation for the necessary intense commitment to abstinence.

Once the drug use has ceased, some adolescents will demonstrate clear areas of goal orientation and competence, will be positive in their outlook, and will be able to achieve moderate objectives. This is particularly so for those adolescents whose families are not characterized by generations of chemical dependency, and whose family life has some degree of stability and nurturance. Therapists working with adolescents whose recovery curve involves a steady positive progression are prone to their own denial of the severity and aftermath of the drug dependence. Patients, too, view the situation as if there has been a spontaneous remission, believing that they can get on with the rest of their lives as if nothing has happened. They spend sessions focusing on everything—girlfriends and boyfriends, social life, college or career—except the maintenance of abstinence. The therapist is continually forced to refocus on abstinence and behaviors that are or are not being used to reinforce it. Sometimes clinicians collude in the belief that the struggle is over. Other times they fail to confront patient behaviors that might undermine abstinence due to the mistaken fear that talking about the issues will induce relapse.

Another dilemma occurs for the clinician who recommends that the adolescent join a 12-Step program, and then finds that the patient has bonded with his AA or NA sponsor even more closely than with the therapist. The patient may convey the sense that he is getting more from the sponsor than from the therapist, leaving the therapist with feelings of competitiveness and rejection. Therapists should first examine whether they might be perceiving this incorrectly, or whether the patient may be trying to convey a message about the transference or a realistic need to have this type of attachment in early recovery, that is, an active role model, mentor, and identification object. Further, in early abstinence, the first priorities are 12-step program participation and integration of the identity of the substance abuser who has lost control over his substance use. As abstinence progresses into long-term recovery, when a host of earlier unresolved developmental issues may come to the fore, the mental health professional's contribution becomes more valuable and can assume center stage (Brown 1985).

Stage 4: Ongoing recovery. Brown (1985) envisions ongoing recovery as occurring after approximately eighteen months of early recovery work. The focus in this stage involves a movement away from intense focus on abstinence and a broadening of the therapeutic work. Redefining life goals and exploring aspects of identity other than that of a recovering person, establishing close personal relationships, exploring early life events that may have contributed to the development of the drug dependency, and discussing the transference are all appropriate work of the therapy at this point.

In long-term recovery, countertransference resembles "classical" or "idiosyncratic" countertransference. The transference is now less distorted by chemicals, and the patient begins to look more like other adolescents in treatment. The adolescent with a history of drug dependence is likely to carry emotional, behavioral, and cognitive evidence of that condition throughout his life, but his profile now becomes more similar to that of his peers. The therapist is now able to use countertransference as a guide to the therapeutic work because he is now more likely to be reacting to who the patient really is.

There may be remarkable gains once abstinence is achieved and maintained; functioning in behavioral, emotional, academic, familial, and social spheres is likely to improve markedly. Despite these gains, however, the clinician needs to return periodically to the discussion of drugs and the meaning they had for the adolescent, even though the duration of abstinence at this point might exceed a year. The patient's understanding of the function, consequences, and significance of the drug dependence will change as abstinence accumulates and will continue to be a rich area for exploration and insight. For some clients, significant developmental arrests will become apparent. Most often, these adolescents will be children of alcoholic or drug dependent parents, often in families where this chemical dependency is in its second, third or fourth generation. There may be more than one parent who is chemically dependent, and often siblings and other adults in the household are alcohol and drug involved as well.

Relapse remains a possibility. Caregivers need to monitor their tendency to become invested in the client as "recovered" because it will lead to missing clues that relapse is imminent.

CASE EXAMPLE: CARRIE

Carrie was a 13-year-old alcoholic who had completed an outdoor challenge program as part of a broader substance abuse treatment program. She joined AA, got a sponsor, went back to school, and stayed sober for several months. Her mother and sisters were willing to participate in the recommended family treatment but her father, a chronic alcoholic, refused. The family had become less tolerant of his drinking, and the mother was considering telling him to live somewhere else until he too had established a period of abstinence.

Carrie worried about him and blamed family members for the chaos which swirled around him when he was drinking. She had typically served as his protector over the years, developing characteristics of the "hero" or overresponsible child in an alcoholic family. The therapist was convinced that Carrie would resume drinking, given her need to deflect pressure away from her father. Despite the therapist's interpretations and reasoned arguments to Carrie about her need to detach from her sense of overresponsibility, confrontations with the family about their enabling behavior, and appeals to the father to get treatment, nothing happened. Carrie's enmeshment in the family system seemed more powerful than her desire to maintain sobriety. The unconscious need to maintain the homeostasis of a family organized around an actively drinking person emerged as the overshadowing dynamic.

The therapist felt increasingly furious with Carrie and self-righteous about her efforts. When Carrie became less regular in attendance, the therapist did not pursue her or question her absences when she returned. It took intense examination of the therapist's attitudes to reclaim a sense of empathy and compassion for this little girl caught in a dysfunctional family system, the momentum for which existed long before Carrie was born.

If relapse does occur, it can be instructive for client and clinician as a way of understanding high risk situations, and dangers within them, which might previously have been minimized. However, equating relapse with a failure on the part of the client or clinician can block the learning potential of this temporary set-back. Relapse is likely to trigger a host of countertransference reactions including anger, shame and self-blame, and disgust. Often, the sources of countertransference which were so prominent in the drinking and drug abuse phase return as major dynamics to be reckoned with.

The choice of treatment modalities should also be reconsidered if a treatment impasse occurs or countertransference reactions repeatedly interfere with the therapist's comfort in managing the therapy. With individual treatment as the exclusive modality, the likelihood of polarization is increased. Including family therapy or group therapy in the treatment plan is strongly recommended as a way to help the therapist diffuse the transference and acquire a clearer sense of countertransference dynamics.

In concluding this discussion of a framework for viewing shifts in countertransference in relation to stages of recovery, one final point deserves emphasis. The framework can be used as a clinical or supervisory tool to inform client-therapist relationships which appear to be foundering—it may have particular utility for the clinical supervisor attempting to understand confusing or changing therapist reactions to substance abusing adolescents. Identifying the stage of treatment/recovery of the client can predict the likely source and nature of the countertransference which is currently activated, and identifying the source and nature of the countertransference can predict the stage of treatment/recovery of the client.

CONCLUSIONS

We have attempted here to address a gap in the existing literature on countertransference with substance-abusing adults and adolescents. While the literature on countertransference with substance-abusing adults is minimal, the literature on adolescents is almost nonexistent.

Substance-abusing patients commonly generate powerful negative countertransference reactions, due at least in part to societal moralism and the therapist's personal experiences with drinking and drug use and family alcoholism or drug dependence. The developmental issues of adolescence, as well as the pressure from social systems that bring the adolescent to treatment, complicate and intensify the countertransference.

In addition, heavy drinking and drug use profoundly inhibit the cognitive and emotional development of the adolescent, and use of these drugs between or before sessions makes the development of the therapeutic alliance difficult and unsatisfying. As the client progresses along the continuum of recovery, from the stage of active use of alcohol and other drugs through the stage of ongoing recovery, an evolution in the therapist's countertransference occurs, with differing sources and aspects of countertransference coming into play at various stages.

The therapist's focus on the adolescent's impaired control over use and the need for abstinence in the active use, transitional and early recovery phases facilitates the adolescent's ability to establish long-term abstinence and recovery. As the case examples have shown, the therapist's countertransference responses may undermine a successful completion of therapy at any stage of assessment, treatment, and recovery unless those responses are regularly monitored.

REFERENCES

Abbate, S. (1964). Panel report: Child analysis at different developmental stages. *Journal of the American Psychoanalytic Association* 12:135–150.

Abend, S. (1989). Countertransference and psychoanalytic technique. *Psychoanalytic Quarterly* 58:374–395.

Abend, S., Porder, M., and Willick, M. (1983). *Borderline Patients: Psychoanalytic Perspectives.* Madison, CT: International Universities Press.

Abraham, K. (1921). Contribution to a discussion on tic. In *Selected Papers on Psychoanalysis*, pp. 323–325. New York: Basic Books, 1953.

——(1924). A short study on the development of the libido, viewed in the light of mental disorders. In *Selected Papers on Psychoanalysis*, pp. 418–501. New York: Basic Books, 1953.

Adams, P. L. (1970). Dealing with racism in biracial psychiatry. *Journal of the American Academy of Child Psychiatry* 9:33–34.

Alpert, J. (1986). *Psychoanalysis and Women: Contemporary Reappraisals.* Hillsdale, NJ: The Analytic Press.

Altschul, S. (1968). Denial and ego arrest. *Journal of the American Psychoanalytic Association* 16:301–318.

——(1988). *Childhood Bereavement and Its Aftermath.* Madison, CT: International Universities Press.

Alvarez, A. (1983). Problems in the use of the countertransference: getting it across. *Journal of Child Psychotherapy* 9:7–23.

American Psychiatric Association (1980). *Diagnostic and Statistical Manual of Mental Disorders,* 3rd ed. Washington, DC: American Psychiatric Association.

——(1987). *Diagnostic and Statistical Manual of Mental Disorders*, 3rd ed., revised. Washington, DC: American Psychiatric Association.

315

American Psychoanalytic Association Panel (1988). Anorexia nervosa, theory and therapy: a new look at an old problem. *Journal of the American Psychoanalytic Association* 36:153–161.

Anthony, E. (1970). Two contrasting types of adolescent depression and their treatment. *Journal of the American Psychoanalytic Association* 18:841–859.

———(1982). The comparable experience of a child and adult analyst. *Psychoanalytic Study of the Child* 37:339–366. New Haven, CT: Yale University Press.

———(1986). The contributions of child psychoanalysis to psychoanalysis. *Psychoanalytic Study of the Child* 41:61–87. New Haven, CT: Yale University Press.

Anzieu, D. (1986). *Freud's Self-Analysis*, trans. P. Graham. London: Hogarth Press.

Armstrong, J. G., and Roth, D. M. (1989). Attachment and separation difficulties in eating disorders, a preliminary investigation. *International Journal of Eating Disorders* 8:141–155.

Atwood, G., and Stolorow, R. (1984). *Structures of Subjectivity: Explorations in Psychoanalytic Phenomenology*. Hillsdale, NJ: The Analytic Press.

Ausubel, D. P. (1958). *Drug Addiction: Physiological, Psychological, and Sociological Aspects*. New York: Random House.

Bachrach, A., Erwin, W., and Mohr, J. (1965). The control of eating behavior in an anorectic by operant conditioning techniques. In *Case Studies in Behavior Modification*, ed. L. Ullman and L. Krasner, pp. 153–163. New York: Holt, Rinehart and Winston.

Balint, M. (1935). Clinical notes on the theory of the pregenital organizations of the libido. In *Primary Love and Psychoanalytic Technique*, pp. 37–58. New York: Liveright, 1965.

Barbarin, O. A. (1984). Racial themes in psychotherapy with blacks: effects of training on the attitudes of black and white psychiatrists. *American Journal of Social Psychiatry* 4:13–20.

Barchilon, J. (1958). On countertransference cures. *Journal of the American Psychoanalytic Association* 6:222–236.

Basch, M. (1980). *Doing Psychotherapy*. New York: Basic Books.

———(1983). The perception of reality and the disavowal of meaning. *The Annual of Psychoanalysis (Chicago)* 11:125–153.

Bean, M. (1981). Denial and the psychological complications of alcoholism. In *Dynamic Approaches to the Understanding and Treatment of Alcoholism*, ed. M. Bean and N. Zinberg, pp. 55–96. New York: The Free Press.

———(1982). Identifying and managing alcohol problems of adolescents. *Psychosomatics* 23:389–396.

———(1984). Clinical implications of models for recovery from alcoholism. *The Addictive Behaviors* 3:91–104.

———(1986). Personal communication to author.

————(1987). Personal communication to author.

————(1989). Personal communication to author.

Beattie, H. J. (1988). Eating disorders and the mother–daughter relationship. *International Journal of Eating Disorders* 7:453–460.

Beiser, H. (1971). Personality characteristics of child analysts: a comparative study of child analyst students and other students as analysts of adults. *Journal of the American Psychoanalytic Association* 19:654–669.

Bemporad, J. R. (1988). Psychodynamic treatment of depressed adolescents. *Journal of Clinical Psychiatry* 49:26–31.

Bemporad, J. R., and Lee, K. W. (1988). Affective disorders. In *Handbook of Clinical Assessment of Children and Adolescents—Volume II*, eds. C. J. Kestenbaum and D. T. Williams. New York: New York University Press.

Bemporad, J. R., Ratey, J. J., O'Driscoll, G., and Daehler, M. L. (1988). Hysteria, anorexia and the culture of self-denial. *Psychiatry* 51:96–103.

Benjamin, J. (1988). *The Bonds of Love.* New York: Pantheon Books.

Berenson, E. V., Gordon, C., and Herzog, D. B. (1989). The process of recovering from anorexia nervosa. *Journal of the American Academy of Psychoanalysis* 17:103–130.

Berlin, I. N. (1987). Some transference and countertransference issues in the playroom. *Journal of the American Academy of Child and Adolescent Psychiatry* 26:101–107.

Berlin, I. N., Boatman, M. Z., Sheimo, S. L., and Szurek, S. A. (1951). Adolescent alternation of anorexia and obesity. *American Journal of Orthopsychiatry* 21:387–419.

Bernard, V. W. (1953). Psychoanalysis and members of minority groups. *Journal of the American Psychoanalytic Association* 1:256–267.

————(1972). Interracial practice in the midst of change. *American Journal of Psychiatry* 128:978–983.

Bernstein, I. (1957). Indications and goals of child analysis as compared with child therapy. *Journal of the American Psychoanalytic Association* 5:158–163.

Bernstein, I., and Glenn, J. (1978). The child analyst's emotional reactions to his patients. In *Child Analysis and Therapy*, ed. J. Glenn, pp. 375–392. New York: Jason Aronson.

———— (1988). The child and adolescent analyst's emotional reactions to his patients and their parents. *International Review of Psycho-Analysis* 15:225–241.

Bettelheim, B. (1975). The love that is enough: countertransference and ego processes of staff members in therapeutic milieu. In *Tactics and Techniques in Psychoanalytic Therapy*, vol. 2, ed. P. Giovacchini, pp. 251–278. New York: Jason Aronson.

Bick, E. (1968). The experience of the skin in early object relations. *International Journal of Psycho-Analysis* 49:484–486.

Bion, W. R. (1955). Language and the schizophrenic. In *New Directions In*

Psychoanalysis, ed. M. Klein, P. Heinmann, and R. E. Money-Kyrle, pp. 220–237. London: Tavistock.

Birksted-Breen, D. (1989). Working with an anorexic patient. *International Journal of Psycho-Analysis* 70:29–40.

Blake, W. (1973). The influence of race on diagnosis. *Smith College Studies in Social Work* 43:184–192.

Blatt, S. L. (1976). Levels of object representation in anaclitic and introjective depression. *Psychoanalytic Study of the Child* 29:107–158. New York: International Universities Press.

Bleiberg, E. (1987). Stages in the treatment of narcissistic children and adolescents. *Bulletin of the Menninger Clinic* 51:296–313.

Blinder, B., Freedman, D., and Stunkard, A. (1970). Behavior therapy of anorexia nervosa: effectiveness of activity as a reinforcer of weight gain. *American Journal of Psychiatry* 126:1093–1098.

Blos, P. (1967). The second individuation process of adolescence. *Psychoanalytic Study of the Child* 22:162–186. New York: International Universities Press.

———(1972). The epigenesis of the adult neurosis. *Psychoanalytic Study of the Child* 27:106–135. New York: International Universities Press.

———(1979). *The Second Individuation Process of Adolescence: The Adolescent Passage.* New York: International Universities Press.

Blotcky, M., and Looney, J. (1980). A psychotherapeutic approach to silent children. *American Journal of Psychotherapy* 34:487–495.

Bollas, C. (1983). Expressive uses of countertransference. *Contemporary Psychoanalysis* 19:1–34.

Bonier, R. (1982). Staff countertransference in adolescent milieu treatment setting. In *Adolescent Psychiatry* 10:382–390, ed. S. Feinstein and P. Giovacchini. Chicago: University of Chicago Press.

Boris, H. (1984). The problem of anorexia nervosa. *International Journal of Psycho-Analysis* 65:315–322.

Bornstein, B. (1948). Emotional barriers in the understanding and treatment of children. *American Journal of Orthopsychiatry* 18:691–697.

Borowitz, G. (1970). The therapeutic utilization of emotions and attitudes evoked in the caretakers of disturbed children. *British Journal of Medical Psychology* 43:129–139.

Bowlby, J. (1960). Grief and mourning in infancy and early childhood. *Psychoanalytic Study of the Child* 15:9–52. New York: International Universities Press.

Boyer, L. B. (1989). Countertransference and technique in working with the regressed patient, further remarks. *International Journal of Psycho-Analysis* 70:701–714.

Brandell, J. (1988). Narrative and historical truth in child psychotherapy. *Psychoanalytic Psychology* 5:241–257.

Bratter, T. (1973). Treating alienated, unmotivated, drug abusing adolescents. *American Journal of Psychotherapy* 27:585–598.

———(1976). Responsible therapeutic eros: setting limits with self-destructive adolescents who abuse drugs. *The Addiction Therapist* 1:69–78.

———(1985). Special clinical psychotherapeutic concerns for alcoholic and drug addicted individuals. In *Alcoholism and Substance Abuse*, eds. T. Bratter and G. Forest, pp. 523–574. New York: The Free Press.

Breuer, J., and Freud, S. (1895). Studies on hysteria. *Standard Edition* 2:1–307.

Briere, J. (1989). *Therapy for Adults Molested as Children: Beyond Survival*. New York: Springer.

Bromberg, P. M. (1983). The mirror and the mask: On narcissism and psychoanalytic growth. *Contemporary Psychoanalysis* 19:359–387.

Broverman, I. et. al. (1970). Sex role stereotypes and clinical judgments of mental health. *Journal of Consulting and Clinical Psychology* 34:1–7.

Brown, S. (1985). *Treating the Alcoholic: A Developmental Model of Recovery*. New York: John Wiley and Sons.

Bruch, H. (1973). *Eating Disorders: Obesity, Anorexia Nervosa, and the Person Within*. New York: Basic Books.

———(1974). Perils of behavior modification in treatment of anorexia nervosa. *Journal of the American Medical Association* 230:1419–1422.

———(1978). *The Golden Cage: The Enigma of Anorexia Nervosa*. Cambridge, MA: Harvard University Press.

———(1982). Anorexia nervosa, therapy and theory. *The American Journal of Psychiatry* 139:1531–1538.

Brunnquell, D., and Hall, M. (1982). Issues in the psychological care of pediatric oncology patients. *American Journal of Orthopsychiatry* 52:32–44.

Buirski, P., and Buirski, C. (1980). The split transference in the simultaneous treatment of mother and child. *Bulletin of the Menninger Clinic* 44:639–646.

Burke, N. (1991). Starved for words: on the anorexia of language. *Psychoanalytic Psychology* 8:145–168.

Calder, K. (1980). An analyst's self-analysis. *Journal of the American Psychoanalytic Association* 28:5–20.

Calnek, M. (1970). Racial factors in the countertransference: the black therapist and the black client. *American Journal of Orthopsychiatry* 40:39–46.

Carpy, D. V. (1989). Tolerating the countertransference: a mutative process. *International Journal of Psycho-Analysis* 70:287–294.

Casement, P. J. (1986). Countertransference and interpretation. *Contemporary Psychoanalysis* 22:548–559.

Casuso, G. (1965). The relationship between child analysis and the theory and practice of adult psychoanalysis. *Journal of the American Psychoanalytic Association* 13:159–171.

Chatham, M. (1989). *Treatment of the Borderline Personality*. Northvale, NJ: Jason Aronson.

Chatoor, I. (1989). Infantile anorexia nervosa: a developmental disorder of separation and individuation. *Journal of the American Academy of Psychoanalysis* 17:43–64.

Chehrazi, S. (1986). Female psychology: a review. *Journal of the American Psychoanalytic Association* 34:141–162.

Chesler, M., and Barbarin, O. (1987). *Childhood Cancer and the Family*. New York: Brunner/Mazel.

Chesler, P. (1972). *Women and Madness*. New York: Avon Books.

Chethik, M. (1976). Work with parents: treatment of the parent/child relationship. *Journal of the American Academy of Child Psychiatry* 15:453–463.

Chethik, M., and Fast, I. (1970). A function of fantasy in the borderline child. *American Journal of Orthopsychiatry* 40:756–765.

Chethik, M., and Spindler, E. (1971). Technique of treatment and management with the borderline child. In *Healing Through Living*, eds. M. Myer and A. C. C. Blum, pp. 176–189. Springfield, IL: Charles C Thomas.

Chodorow, N. (1978). The reproduction of mothering. In *Psychoanalysis and the Sociology of Gender*. Berkeley: University of California Press.

———(1989). *Feminism and Psychoanalytic Theory*. New Haven, CT: Yale University Press.

Christ, A. (1964). Sexual countertransference problems with a psychotic child. *Journal of Child Psychiatry* 3:298–316.

Cohen, M. (1952). Countertransference and anxiety. *Psychiatry* 15:231–243.

Cohen, R., Cohler, B., and Weissman, S., eds. (1984). *Parenthood: A Psychodynamic Perspective*. New York: The Guilford Press.

Cohler, B. (1976). The significance of the therapist's feelings in the treatment of anorexia nervosa. *Adolescent Psychiatry* 5:352–386, ed. S. Feinstein and P. Giovacchini. New York: Basic Books.

———(1980). Adult developmental psychology and reconstruction in psychoanalysis. In *The Course of Life: Adulthood and the Aging Process* 3:149–200, ed. S. Greenspan and G. Pollock. Washington, DC: U.S. Government Printing Office.

———(1982). Personal narrative and life course. In *Life-Span Development and Behavior*, vol. 4, eds. B. Baltes and O. G. Brim, Jr., pp. 205–241. New York: Academic Press.

———(1991). The life-story and the study of resilience to adversity. *Journal of Narrative and Life-history*, in press.

Coleman, E., and Colgan, P. (1986). Boundary inadequacy in drug dependent families. *Journal of Psychoactive Drugs* 18:21–30.

Coles, P. (1988). Aspects of perversion in anorexic/bulimic disorders. *Psychoanalytic Psychotherapy* 3:137–147.

Colette (1963). *Lettres au Petit Corsaire*. Paris: Flammarion.

Colm, H. (1955). A field theory approach to transference and its particular application to children. *Psychiatry* 18:329–352.

Connelly, J. (1983). Detection and treatment of alcohol and drug abuse. *Bulletin of the Menninger Clinic* 47:145–161.

Coppolillo, H. (1969). A technical consideration in child analysis and child therapy. *Journal of the American Academy of Child Psychiatry* 8:411–435.

Craig, R. (1988). Diagnostic interviewing with drug abusers. *Professional Psychology: Research and Practice* 19:14–20.

Dailey, D. (1980). Are social workers sexist? A replication. *Social Work* 35:46–51.

Davidson, V. (1977). Transference phenomena in the treatment of addictive illness: love and hate in methadone maintenance. In *Psychodynamics of Drug Dependence*, eds. J. D. Blaine and D. A. Julius, NIDA Research Monograph No. 12. Washington, DC: NIDA.

Day, M. (1977). Counter-transference in everyday practice. In *Issues in Psychotherapy*, vol. 1. Boston: Boston Institute for Psychotherapies, Inc.

de Urtubey, L. (1989). Contre-transfert et interpretation freudienne ou kleinienne. In *Revue Francais de Psychanalyse* 53:873–883.

Debray, R. (1987). Le trauma de corps maladie somatique et loberte psychique. *Revue Francaise de Psychanalyse* 51:937–946.

Decker, H. (1991). *Freud, Dora, and Vienna, 1900.* New York: The Free Press.

Deering, C. G. (1987). Developing a therapeutic alliance with the anorexia nervosa client. *Journal of Psychosocial Nursing and Mental Health Services* 25:10–17.

Denis, J. F. (1990). Personality disorders in psychiatry. *Canadian Journal of Psychiatry* 35:208–214.

Deutsch, H. (1926). Occult processes occurring during psychoanalysis. In *Psychoanalysis and the Occult*, ed. G. Devereaux, pp. 133–146. New York: International Universities Press, 1953.

——— (1933). Motherhood and sexuality. *Psychoanalytic Quarterly* 2:476.

——— (1942). Some forms of emotional disturbance and their relationship to schizophrenia. *Psychoanalysis* 11:301–321.

Devereaux, G. (1953). Cultural factors in psychoanalytic therapy. *Journal of the American Psychoanalytic Association* 1:629–655.

Doweiko, H. (1990). *Concepts of Chemical Dependency.* Pacific Grove, CA: Brooks/Cole.

Dresser, I. (1987). The use of transference and countertransference in assessing emotional disturbance in children. *Psychoanalytic Psychotherapy* 1:95–106.

Dunkel, J. and Hatfield, S. (1986). Countertransference issues in working with persons with AIDS. In *Social Work* 31:114–117.

Eissler, K. (1943). Some psychiatric aspects of anorexia nervosa: demonstrated by a case report. *The Psychoanalytic Practice* 1:7–22.

——— (1951). Remarks on the psychoanalysis of Schizophrenia. In *Interna-*

tional Journal of Psycho-Analysis 33:139–156. New York: Liveright Publishing Corporation.

Ekstein, R. (1966). *Children of Time and Space, Of Action and Impulse.* New York: Appleton-Century-Crofts.

————(1983). The adolescent self during the process of termination of treatment: termination, interruption or intermission. In *Adolescent Psychiatry: Developmental and Clinical Studies* 9:125–146, ed. A. Esman, S. Feinstein, V. Looney, A. Schwartzberg, A. Sorosky, and M. Sugar. Chicago: University of Chicago Press.

Ekstein, R., and Cauruth, E. (1964). Certain phenomenological aspects of the countertransference in the treatment of schizophrenic children. *Reiss-Davis Clinic Bulletin* 1:80–88.

Ekstein, R., and Wallerstein, J. (1954). Observations on the psychology of borderline and psychotic children. *Psychoanalytic Study of the Child* 9:344–369. New York: International Universities Press.

Ekstein, R., Wallerstein, J., and Mandelbaum, A. (1959). Countertransference in the residential treatment of children: treatment failure in a child with symbiotic psychosis. *Psychoanalytic Study of the Child* 14:186–218. New York: International Universities Press.

Elson, M. (1986). *Self Psychology in Clinical Social Work.* New York: W. W. Norton.

Epstein, L., and Feiner, A. (1979a). Countertransference: the therapist's contribution to treatment. *Contemporary Psychoanalysis* 15:282–303.

————, eds. (1979b). *Countertransference: The Therapist's Contribution to the Therapeutic Situation.* New York: Jason Aronson.

Erikson, E. H. (1950/63). *Childhood and Society.* New York: W. W. Norton.

————(1959). *Identity and the Life Cycle.* New York: International Universities Press.

Esman, A. (1985). A developmental approach to the psychotherapy of adolescents. In *Adolescent Psychiatry: Developmental and Clinical Studies* 12:119–133, ed. A. Esman, S. Feinstein, V. Looney, A. Schwartzberg, A. Sorosky, and M. Sugar. Chicago, IL: University of Chicago Press.

Faltz, B., and Madover, S. (1988). Treatment of substance abuse in patients with HIV infection. In *AIDS and Substance Abuse.* Haworth, NJ: The Haworth Press.

Feigelson, C. (1974a). A comparison between adult and child analysis. *Journal of the American Psychoanalytic Association* 1:268–284.

————(1974b). Play and child analysis. *Psychoanalytic Study of the Child* 29:21–26. New Haven, CT: Yale University Press.

Feiner, A. H. (1982). Comments on the difficult patient: some transference–countertransference issues. *Contemporary Psychoanalysis* 18:397–411.

Fine, R. (1984). Countertransference reactions to the difficult patient. *Current Issues in Psychoanalytic Practice* 1:7–22.

————(1985). Countertransference and the pleasures of being an analyst. *Current Issues in Psychoanalytic Practice* 2:3–19.

Fischer, N. (1971). An interracial analysis: Transference and countertransference significance. *Journal of the American Psychoanalytic Association* 19:736–745.

————(1989). Anorexia nervosa and unresolved rapprochement conflicts: a case study. *International Journal of Psycho-Analysis* 70:41–54.

Fisher, J. (1976). Are social workers sexist? *Social Work* 21:428–433.

Flarsheim, A. (1975). The therapist's collusion with the patient's wish for suicide. In *Tactics and Techniques in Psychoanalytic Therapy: Countertransference*, vol. 2, ed. P. Giovacchini, pp. 155–195. New York: Jason Aronson.

Fleiss, R. (1942). The metapsychology of the analyst. *Psychoanalytic Quarterly* 11:211–227.

————(1953). Countertransference and counter-identification. *Journal of the American Psychoanalytic Association* 1:268–274.

Fleming, J., and Altschul, S. (1963). Activation of mourning and growth by psychoanalysis. *International Journal of Psycho-Analysis* 44:419–432.

Fraiberg, S. (1969). Libidinal object constancy and mental representation. *Psychoanalytic Study of the Child* 24:9–47. New York: International Universities Press.

————(1980). *Clincial Studies in Infant Mental Health*. New York: Basic Books.

Freud, A. (1926). *The Psychoanalytic Treatment of Children*. London: Imago, 1946.

————(1951). *The Psychoanalytic Treatment of Children*, third trans., N. Proctor. London: Anglo Books.

————(1965). *Normality and Pathology in Childhood*. New York: International Universities Press.

————(1971). The infantile neurosis: genetic and dynamic considerations. *Psychoanalytic Study of the Child* 26:79–90. New Haven, CT: Yale University Press.

————(1978). The role of insight and psychotherapy: introduction to the Anna Freud Hampstead Center Symposium held at the Michigan Psychoanalytic Society, Nov. 1978. In *Psychoanalytic Explorations of Technique: Discourse on the Theory of Therapy*, ed. H. P. Blum. New York: International Universities Press, 1980.

Freud, S. (1895). Project for a scientific psychology. *Standard Edition* 1:295–387.

————(1900). The interpretation of dreams. *Standard Edition* 4/5:1–621.

————(1905a). Three essays on the theory of sexuality. *Standard Edition* 7:130–243.

————(1905b). Fragment of an analysis of a case of hysteria. *Standard Edition* 7:3–112.

——(1909a). Notes upon a case of obsessional neurosis. *Standard Edition* 11:63–138.

——(1909b). Analysis of a phobia in a five year old boy. *Standard Edition* 10:5–152.

——(1909c). Family romances. *Standard Edition* 9:236–241.

——(1910a). Five lectures on psychoanalysis. *Standard Edition* 11:3–55.

——(1910b). Leonardo Da Vinci and a memory of his childhood. *Standard Edition* 11:63–138.

——(1910c). The future prospects of psychoanalytic therapy. *Standard Edition* 11:139–153.

——(1911). Formulations regarding the two principles of mental functioning. *Standard Edition* 12:215–226.

——(1912a). The dynamics of transference. *Standard Edition* 12:99–108.

——(1912b). Recommendations to physicians practicing psychoanalysis. *Standard Edition* 12:111–120.

——(1913a). On beginning the treatment: further recommendations on the technique of psychoanalysis. *Standard Edition* 12:123–144.

——(1913b). The disposition to obsessional neurosis: a contribution to the choice of neurosis. *Standard Edition* 12:313–326.

——(1914a). Remembering, repeating and working through: further recommendations on the technique of psychoanalysis. *Standard Edition* 12:146–156.

——(1914b). On narcissism: an introduction. *Standard Edition* 14:73–104.

——(1915a). Repression. *Standard Edition* 14:143–158.

——(1915b). Observations on transference-love: further recommendations on the technique of psychoanalysis. *Standard Edition* 12:158–171.

——(1915c). The unconscious. *Standard Edition* 14:159–195.

——(1915d). Instincts and their vicissitudes. *Standard Edition* 14:109–140.

——(1915–1917). Introductory lectures on psychoanalysis. *Standard Edition* 15/16.

——(1920a). Group psychology and the analysis of the ego. *Standard Edition* 18:65–144.

——(1920b). Beyond the pleasure principle. *Standard Edition* 18:1–65.

——(1921). Group psychology and the analysis of the ego. *Standard Edition* 18:67–143.

——(1923). The ego and the id. *Standard Edition* 19:1–59.

——(1925). An autobiographical study. *Standard Edition* 20:3–76.

——(1926). Inhibition, symptoms and anxiety. *Standard Edition* 20:75–177.

——(1927a). Civilization and its discontents. *Standard Edition* 21:1–56.

——(1927b). Civilization and its discontents. *Standard Edition* 21:57–146.

——(1937). Analysis terminable and interminable. *Standard Edition* 23:209–254.

——(1938a). An outline of psycho-analysis. *Standard Edition* 23:141–207.

————(1938b). Splitting of the ego in the process of defense. *Standard Edition* 23:271–279.

————(1954). *The Origins of Psychoanalysis: Letters to Wilhelm Fleiss, Drafts and Notes (1887–1902)*. New York: Basic Books.

Friedlander, M. L., and Siegel, S. M. (1990). Separation–individuation difficulties and cognitive–behavioral indicators of eating disorders among college women. *Journal of Counseling Psychology* 37:74–78.

Friedman, L. (1978). Trends in the psychoanalytic theory of treatment. *Psychoanalytic Quarterly* 47:524.

Friedrich, W. N. (1990). *Psychotherapy of Sexually Abused Children and Their Families*. New York: W. W. Norton.

Friend, M. R. (1972). Psychoanalysis of adolescents. In *Handbook of Child Psychoanalysis*, ed. B. B. Wolman, pp. 297–363. New York: VanNostrand Reinhold Co.

Fromm-Reichmann, F. (1950). *Principles of Intensive Psychotherapy*. Chicago: University of Chicago Press.

Furman, E. (1974). *A Child's Parent Dies*. New Haven, CT: Yale University Press.

————(1980). Transference and externalization in latency. *Psychoanalytic Study of the Child* 35:267–284. New Haven, CT: Yale University Press.

Galatzer-Levy, R., and Cohler, B. (1990). The developmental psychology of the self and the changing world view of psychoanalysis. *Annual of Psychoanalysis* 17:1–43.

Ganzarain, R. C., and Buchele, B. J. (1988). *Fugitives of Incest*. Madison, CT: International Universities Press.

Garber, B. (1981). Mourning in children: toward a theoretical synthesis. *Annual of Psychoanalysis* 9:9–19.

————(1984). Parenting responses in divorce and bereavement of a spouse. In *Parenthood: A Psychodynamic Perspective*, ed. R. Cohen, B. Cohler, and S. Weissman. New York: Guilford Press.

————(1988). Some common transference–countertransference issues in the treatment of parent loss. In *Childhood Bereavement and Its Aftermath*, ed. S. Altschul, pp. 145–163. New York: International Universities Press.

Gardner, M. R. (1983). *Self-Inquiry*. Boston: Little-Brown.

Gartner, A. (1985). Countertransference issues in the psychotherapy of adolescents. *Journal of Child and Adolescent Psychotherapy* 2:187–196.

Gartner, A., Marcus, R. N., Halmi, K., and Loranger, A. W. (1989). DSM-III-R personality disorders in patients with eating disorders. *American Journal of Psychiatry* 146:1585–1591.

Gay, P. (1988). *Freud: A Life for Our Time*. New York: W. W. Norton.

Gedo, J. (1976). Freud's self analysis and his scientific ideas. In *Freud: The Fusion of Science and Humanism. The Intellectual History of Psychoanalysis*,

Psychological Issues Monographs 34 and 35, ed. J. Gedo, and G. Pollock, pp. 286–306. New York: International Universities Press.

———(1977). Notes on the psychoanalytic management of archaic transference. *Journal of the American Psychoanalytic Association* 25:787–803.

———(1979). *Beyond Interpretation: Toward a Revised Theory of Psychoanalysis*. New York: International Universities Press.

———(1981). *Advances in Clinical Psychoanalysis*. New York: International Universities Press.

Gedo, J. and Goldberg, A. (1973). *Models of the Mind: A Psychoanalytic Theory*. Chicago: University of Chicago Press.

Geiser, J. R. (1980). The effect of therapists attitudes towards homosexuality on the clinical assessment of the homosexual client. Masters Thesis, Smith College School for Social Work.

Geist, R. (1979). Onset of chronic illness in children and adolescents: psychotherapeutic and consultative intervention. *American Journal of Orthopsychiatry* 49:4–23.

Gill, M. (1982). *Analysis of the Transference. Volume I: Theory and Technique*. New York: International Universities Press.

Gilligan, C. (1982). *In a Different Voice: Psychological Theory and Women's Development*. Cambridge, MA: Harvard University Press.

Giovacchini, P. (1973). The adolescent process and character formation. In *Developmental and Clinical Studies*, ed. S. Feinstein and P. Giovacchini, pp. 269–284. New York: Basic Books.

———(1974). The difficult adolescent patient: countertransference problems. In *Adolescent Psychiatry, Volume 3: Developmental and Clinical Studies*, ed. S. Feinstein and P. Giovacchini, pp. 271–288. New York: Basic Books.

———(1975). Productive procrastination: technical factors in the treatment of the adolescent. In *Adolescent Psychiatry* 4:352–370, ed. S. Feinstein and P. Giovacchini. New York: Basic Books.

———(1979). *The Treatment of Primitive Mental States*. Northvale, NJ: Jason Aronson.

———(1981a). Countertransference and therapeutic turmoil. *Contemporary Psychoanalysis* 17:565–594.

———(1981b). Editor's introduction. In *Adolescent Psychiatry, Volume 6: Developmental and Clinical Studies*, eds. S. Feinstein and P. Giovacchini, pp. 271–288. New York: Basic Books.

———(1985). Countertransference and the severely disturbed adolescent. In *Adolescent Psychiatry, Volume 3: Developmental and Clinical Studies*, ed. S. Feinstein, M. Sugar, A. Esman, V. Looney, A. Schwartzberg, and A. Sorosky, pp. 449–467. Chicago, IL: University of Chicago Press.

———(1986). *Developmental Disorders: The Transitional Space in Mental Breakdown and Creative Integration*. Northvale, NJ: Jason Aronson.

————(1989). *Countertransference: Triumphs and Catastrophes.* Northvale, NJ: Jason Aronson.

Gitelson, M. (1952). The emotional position of the analyst in the psychoanalytic situation. *International Journal of Psycho-Analysis* 33:1–10.

————(1962). The first phase of psychoanalysis. *International Journal of Psycho-Analysis* 43:194.

Glenn, J. (1978). *Child Analysis and Therapy.* New York: Jason Aronson.

————(1986). Freud, Dora and the maid: a study of countertransference. *Journal of the American Psychoanalytic Association* 34:591–606.

Glenn, J., Sabot, L., and Bernstein, I. (1978). The role of the parents in child analysis. In *Child Analysis and Therapy,* ed. J. Glenn, pp. 393–426. Northvale, NJ: Jason Aronson.

Glover, E. (1955). *The Technique of Psychoanalysis.* New York: International Universities Press.

Goldberg, A. (1972). On the incapacity to love: A psychotherapeutic approach to the problem in adolescence. *Archives of General Psychiatry* 26:3–7.

————(1977). Some countertransference phenomena in the analysis of perversions. In *The Annual of Psychoanalysis* 5:105–120. New York: International Universities Press.

————(1978). *The Psychology of the Self: A Casebook,* ed. A. Goldberg. New York: International Universities Press.

Goldberg, E. L., Myers, W. A., and Zeifman, I. (1974). Some observations on three interracial analyses. *International Journal of Psycho-Analysis* 55:495–500.

Golombek, H. (1983). Personality development during adolescence: implications for treatment. In *The Adolescent and Mood Disturbance,* eds. H. Golombek and B. D. Garfinkel. New York: International Universities Press.

Goodsitt, A. (1984). Self psychology and the treatment of anorexia nervosa. In *Handbook of Psychotherapy for Anorexia Nervosa and Bulimia,* ed. D. M. Garner and P. E. Garfinkel, pp. 55–82. New York: Guilford Press.

Googins, B. (1984). Avoidance of the alcoholic client. *Social Work,* March–April, pp. 161–166.

Gordon, C., Berenson, E. V., and Herzog, D. B. (1989). The parents' relationship and the child's illness in anorexia nervosa. *Journal of the American Academy of Psychoanalysis* 17:29–42.

Gorkin, M. (1986). Countertransference in cross-cultural psychotherapy: the example of Jewish therapist and Arab patient. *Psychiatry* 49:69–73.

Gottlieb, B., and Dean, J. (1981). The co-therapy relationship in group treatment of sexually mistreated adolescent girls. In *Sexually Abused Children and Their Families,* eds. P. B. Mrazek and C. H. Kempe, pp. 211–218. New York: Pergamon Press.

Grayer, E. D., and Sax, P. A. (1986). A model for the diagnostic and therapeutic use of countertransference. *Clinical Social Work Journal* 14:295–309.

Greene, L. R., Rosenkrantz, J., and Muth, D. Y. (1986). Borderline defenses and countertransference: research findings and implications. *Psychiatry* 49: 253–264.

Greenson, R. (1960). Empathy and its vicissitudes. *International Journal of Psycho-Analysis* 41:418–424.

———(1965). The working alliance and the transference neurosis. *Psychoanalytic Quarterly* 34:155–181.

Grinberg, L. (1979). Projective counteridentification and countertransference. In *Countertransference: The Therapist's Contribution to the Therapeutic Situation*, ed. L. Epstein and A. Feiner, pp. 169–191. New York: Jason Aronson.

Grinker, R. (1975). Neurosis, psychosis, and the borderline states. In *Comprehensive Textbook of Psychiatry*, eds. A. M. Freedman, H. I. Kaplan, and B. J. Saddock, pp. 845–850. Baltimore, MD: Williams & Wilkins.

Groen, J. J., and Feldman-Toledano, Z. (1966). Educative treatment of patients and parents in anorexia nervosa. *British Journal of Psychiatry* 112:671–681.

Gunderson, J. G., and Kolb, J. E. (1978). Discriminating features of borderline patients. *American Journal of Psychiatry* 135:792–796.

Guttman, S., Jones, R., and Parrish, S. (1980). *Concordance to the Psychological Works of Sigmund Freud*. Boston: G. K. Hall.

Hallston, A., Jr. (1965). Adolescent anorexia nervosa treated by desensitization. *Behavioral Research Therapy* 3:87–91.

Halperin, D., Lauro, G., Miscione, F., Rebhan, J., Schnabolk, J., and Shacter, B. (1981). Countertransference issues in a transitional residential treatment program for troubled adolescents. In *Adolescent Psychiatry* 9:559–577, eds. S. Feinstein and P. Giovacchini. Chicago: University of Chicago Press.

Havens, L. (1976). *Participant Observer*. Northvale, NJ: Jason Aronson.

Hawthorne, W., and Menzel, N. (1983). Youth treatment should be a programming priority. *Alcohol Health and Research World*. Summer 1983.

Heilbrun, C. (1979). *Reinventing Womanhood*. New York: W. W. Norton.

Heimann, P. (1950). On countertransference. *International Journal of Psycho-Analysis* 31:81–84.

Herdieckerhoff, G. (1986). Therapeutic managment of habitual body language. *Zeitschrift Fur Psychosomatische Medizin Und Psychoanalyse* 32:181–195.

Hethrington, E. M. (1972). Effects of father absence on personality development in adolescent daughters. *Developmental Psychology* 77:313–326.

Hoffman, I. (1983). The patient as interpreter of the analyst's experience. *Contemporary Psychoanalysis* 19:389–422.

———(1990). Expressive participation and psychoanalytic discipline. Paper presented at the symposium, Interpersonal Frontiers in Psychoanalytic Practice, November. New York: The William Alanson White Institute.

Holmes, S., Barnhart, C., Cantoni, L., and Reymer, E. (1976). Working with the parent in child abuse cases. In *Differential Diagnosis and Treatment in Social Work*, 2nd ed., ed. F. Turner, pp. 637–650. New York: Free Press.

Horney, K. (1942). *Self-Analysis*. New York: W. W. Norton, 1968.

Hunt, W. and Issachoroff, A. (1977). Heinrich Racher and countertransference theory. *Journal of the American Academy of Psychoanalysis* 5:95–105.

Imhof, J. E. (1979). Addicts, addicts, everywhere: but has anyone seen a person? *Contemporary Drug Problems* 8:289–290.

Imhof, J., Hirsch, R., Terenzi, R. (1983). Countertransferential and attitudinal considerations in the treatment of drug abuse and addiction. *International Journal of the Addictions* 18:491–510.

Issacharoff, A. (1979). Barriers to knowing. In *Countertransference: The Therapist's Contribution to Treatment*, ed. L. Epstein and A. Feiner, pp. 27–43. New York: Jason Aronson.

Jacobson, E. (1961). Adolescent moods and the remodeling of psychic structure in adolescence. *Psychoanalytic Study of the Child* 16:164–183. New York: International Universities Press.

Johnson, C. L., ed. (1990). *Psychodynamic Treatment of Anorexia Nervosa and Bulimia*. New York: Guilford Press.

Judd, D. (1986). Psychotherapeutic work with a 10-year-old girl: with particular reference to the development of her introjective potential. *British Journal of Psychotherapy* 3:27–41.

Kabcenell, R. (1974). On countertransference: the contribution of Berta Bornstein to psychoanalysis. *Psychoanalytic Study of the Child* 29:27–34. New Haven, CT: Yale University Press.

Kanner, L. (1949). Problems of nosology and psychodynamics of early infantile autism. *American Journal of Orthopsychiatry* 19:416–426.

Katz, J. L. (1987). Eating disorder and affective disorder, relatives or merely chance acquaintances? *Comprehensive Psychiatry* 28:220–228.

Kaufman, M., and Heiman, M. (1964). *Evolution of Psychosomatic Concepts: Anorexia Nervosa—A Paradigm*. New York: International Universities Press.

Kellerman, J., ed., (1980). *Psychological Aspects of Childhood Cancer*. Springfield, MA: Charles C. Thomas.

Kernberg, O. (1965). Notes on countertransference. *Journal of the American Psychoanalytic Association* 13:38–56.

———(1966). Structural derivates of object relations. *International Journal of Psycho-Analysis* 47:236–253.

———(1967). Borderline personality organization. *Journal of American Psychoanalytic Association* 15:641–685.

————(1970). A psychoanalytic classification of character pathology. *Journal of American Psychoanalytic Association* 18:800–822.

————(1974a). *Borderline Conditions and Pathological Narcissism*. New York: Jason Aronson.

————(1974b). Further contributions to the treatment of narcissistic personalities. *International Journal of Psycho-Analysis* 55:215–240.

————(1975). *Borderline Conditions and Pathological Narcissism*. New York: Jason Aronson.

————(1976). *Object Relations Theory and Clinical Psychoanalysis*. New York: Jason Aronson.

————(1978). The diagnosis of borderline conditions in adolescence. In *Adolescent Psychiatry, Volume 6: Developmental and Clinical Studies*, ed. S. Feinstein and P. Giovacchini, pp. 298–319. Chicago: University of Chicago Press.

————(1982a). The psychotherapeutic treatment of borderline personalities. In *The American Psychiatric Association Annual Review*, ed. L. Grinspoon, pp. 470–487. Washington, D.C.: American Psychiatric Press.

————(1982b). Self, ego, affects, and drives. *Journal of the American Psychoanalytic Association* 30:893–917.

King, C. H. (1976). Counter-transference and counter-experience in the treatment of violence prone youth. *American Journal of Orthopsychiatry* 46:43–52.

Klein, G. (1976). *Psychoanalytic Theory: An Exploration of Essentials*. New York: International Universities Press.

Klein, M. (1928). *The Psychoanalysis of Children*. New York: Delacorte Press, 1976.

————(1946). Notes on some schizoid mechanisms. *International Journal of Psycho-Analysis* 33:433–438.

Klein, M., Heiman, P., Heiman, S., et al. (1932). *Developments in Psychoanalysis*. London: Hogarth Press, 1952.

Knight, R. (1953). Borderline States. *Bulletin of the Menninger Clinic* 17:1–12.

————(1954). Management and psychotherapy of the borderline schizophrenic. In *Psychoanalytic Psychiatry and Psychology*, volume 1, eds. R. P. Knight and C. R. Freedman, pp. 110–122. New York: International Universities Press.

Kohon, G. (1986). *The British School of Psychoanalysis*. New Haven: Yale University Press.

Kohrman, R. et. al. (1971). Technique of child analysis: problems of countertransference. *International Journal of Psycho-Analysis* 52:487–497.

Kohut, H. (1959). Introspection, empathy, and psychoanalysis. In *The Search for the Self*, ed. P. Ornstein, pp. 205–232. New York: International Universities Press, 1984.

————(1971). *Analysis of the Self: A Systematic Approach to the Psychoanalytic*

Treatment of Narcissistic Personality Disorders. New York: International Universities Press.

———(1976). Creativeness, charisma, group psychology: reflection on the self-analysis of Freud. In *The Search for the Self: Selected Writings of Heinz Kohut, 1950–1978*, vol. 2, ed. P. Ornstein, pp. 793–844. New York: International Universities Press, 1978.

———(1977). *The Restoration of the Self.* New York: International Universities Press.

———(1984). *How Does Psychoanalysis Cure?* Chicago: University of Chicago Press.

Kraft, A., Palombo, J., Mitchell, D., Woods, P., Schmidt, A., and Tucher, N. (1986). Some theoretical considerations on confidential adoption, Part IV: countertransference. *Child and Adolescent Social Work Journal* 3:3–14.

Kramer, S., and Byerley, L. J. (1978). Technique of psychoanalysis of the Latency Child. In *Child Analysis and Therapy*, ed. J. Glenn, pp. 205–236. Northvale, NJ: Jason Aronson.

Krell, H. L. and Okin, R. L. (1984). Countertransference issues in child abuse and neglect cases. *American Journal of Forensic Psychiatry* 5:7–16.

Krieger, M. J., Rosenfeld, A. A., Gordon, A., and Bennett, M. (1980). Problems in the psychotherapy of children with histories of incest. *American Journal of Psychotherapy* 34:81–88.

Kris, E. (1956). On some vicissitudes of insight in psychoanalysis. *International Journal of Psycho-Analysis* 37:445–455.

Kuver, J. (1986). Dynamics of supervision in the treatment of alcoholism. *Alcoholism Treatment Quarterly* 3:125–143.

Lacan, J. (1977). *Ecrits: A Selection.* New York: W. W. Norton.

Lang, P. (1965). Behavior therapy with a case of nervosa anorexia. In *Case Studies in Behavior Modification*, ed. L. Ullman and L. Krasner. New York: Holt, Rinehart and Winston.

Langs, R. (1976). *The Therapeutic Interaction*, vol. 2. New York: Jason Aronson.

Leitenberg, H., Agras, W., and Thomoson, I. (1968). A sequential analysis of the effect of selective positive reinforcement in modifying anorexia nervosa. *Behavioral Research Therapy* 6:211–218.

Lerner, H. (1986). Current developments in the psychoanalytic psychotherapy of anorexia nervosa. *Clincial Psychologist* 39(2):39–43.

Levine, S. and Stevens, R. (1971). Games addicts play. *Psychiatric Quarterly* 45:582–592.

Levinson, V., and Ashenberg-Straussner, S. (1961). Social workers as enablers in the treatment of alcoholics. *Social Casework* 59:14–20.

Little, M. (1951). Countertransference and the patient's response to it. *International Journal of Psycho-Analysis* 32:32–40.

————(1957). "R"—The analyst's response to his patient's needs. *International Journal of Psycho-Analysis* 38:240–254.

Littner, N. (1969). The caseworker's self observations and the child's interpersonal defenses. *Smith College Studies in Social Work* 39:95–117.

Loewald, H. (1979). Reflections on the psychoanalytic process and its therapeutic potential. In *Psychoanalytic Study of the Child* 34:115–167. New Haven: Yale University Press.

Lyon, M. E., and Silber, T. J. (1989). Anorexia nervosa and schizophrenia in an adolescent female. *Journal of Adolescent Health Care* 10:419–420.

Maenchen, A. (1970). On the technique of child analysis in relation to stages of development. In *Psychoanalytic Study of the Child* 25:175–208. New York: International Universities Press.

Mahler, M. (1963). Autism and symbiosis: two extreme disturbances of identity. *International Journal of Psychoanalytic Psychotherapy* 39:77–83.

————(1968). *On Human Symbiosis and the Vicissitudes of Individuation*, vol. 1. New York: International Universities Press.

————(1972). A study of the separation/individuation process and its possible application to borderline phenomena in a psychoanalytic situation. In *Psychoanalytic Study of the Child* 26:403–424. New York: Quadrangle.

Mahler, M., Pine, F., and Bergman, A. (1975). *Psychological Birth of the Human Infant: Symbiosis and Individuation*. New York: Basic Books.

Malcolm, J. (1983). *Psychoanalysis: The Impossible Profession*. New York: Basic Books.

Mandelbaum, A. (1977). The family treatment of the borderline patient. In *Borderline Personality Disorders: The Concept, The Syndrome, The Patient*, ed. P. Hartocollis, pp. 423–428. New York: International Universities Press.

Mann, J. (1973). *Time-Limited Psychotherapy*. Cambridge, MA: Harvard University Press.

Marcus, I. (1980). Countertransference and the psychoanalytic process in children and adolescents. In *Psychoanalytic Study of the Child* 35:285–299. New Haven, CT: Yale University Press.

Marcus, S. (1984). Freud and Dora: story, history, case history. In *Freud and the Culture of Psychoanalysis*, pp. 42–86. New York: W. W. Norton.

Marmor, J. (1982). Changes in psychoanalytic treatment. In *Curative Factors in Dynamic Psychotherapy*, ed. S. Slipp, pp. 60–70. New York: McGraw Hill.

Marshall, R. J. (1979). Countertransference in the psychotherapy of children and adolescents. In *Contemporary Psychoanalysis* 15: 595–629.

Marvasti, J. A. (1985). Fathers who commit incest, jail or treatment? The need for "victim-oriented law." *American Journal of Forensic Psychiatry* 6:8–13.

————(1986). Female sex offenders: incestuous mothers. *American Journal of Forensic Psychiatry* 263–69.

————(1989). Play therapy with sexually abused children. In *Vulnerable Populations: Sexual Abuse Treatment for Children, Adult Survivors, Offenders, and Persons with Mental Retardation*, vol. 2, ed. S. Sgroi. Lexington, MA: Lexington Books.

———(1991). Dysfunctional mothering in survivors of incest. *American Journal of Forensic Psychiatry* 12(4): 39–47.

———(1992). Playgroup therapy with sexually abused children. In *Handbook of Clinical Intervention in Child Sexual Abuse*, revised edition, ed. S. Sgroi (in press). New York: Lexington Books/MacMillan Free Press.

Masterson, J. (1972). *Treatment of the Borderline Adolescent: A Developmental Approach*. New York: Wiley.

McCann L., and Pearlman, L. A. (1990) Vicarious traumatization: the emotional costs of working with survivors. In *The Advisor*, vol. 3. American Professional Society on the Abuse of Children, Fall.

McDougall, J. (1987). Un cuerpo para dos. *Revista de Psicoterapia-psicoanalitica* 2:199–222.

Meeks, J. (1971). *The Fragile Alliance: An Orientation to the Outpatient Psychotherapy of Adolescents*. Baltimore, MD: Williams & Wilkins.

Meissner, W. W. (1985). Adolescent paranoia: transference and countertransference issues. In *Adolescent Psychiatry, Volume 12: Developmental and Clinical Studies*, eds. S. Feinstein, M. Sugar, A. Esman, V. Looney, A. Schwartzberg, and A. Sorosky, pp. 478–508. Chicago, IL: University of Chicago Press.

Mendelson, M. (1974). *Psychoanalytic Concepts of Depression*, 2nd ed. Flushing, NY: Spectrum Publishing.

Middlemore, M. (1941). *The Nursing Couple*. London: Hamish–Hamilton Medical Books.

Miller, J. B. (1971). Children's reactions to the death of a parent: A review of the psychoanalytic literature. *Journal of the American Psychoanalytic Association* 19:697–719.

Milman, D., Bennet, A., and Hanson, M. (1983). Psychological effects of alcohol in children and adolescents. *Alcohol, Health and Research World* 7:50–53.

Mintz, T. (1981). Clinical experience with suicidal adolescents. In *Adolescent Psychiatry* 10:493–496, ed. S. Feinstein and P. Giovacchini. Chicago: University of Chicago Press

Missenard, A. (1989). Contre-transfert et processus analytique: I (countertransference and analytic process: I). *Topique Revue Freudienne* 19(44): 295–315.

Mitchell, J. (1974). *Psychoanalysis and Feminism*. New York: Pantheon.

Mitchell, S. (1988). *Relational Concepts in Psychoanalysis*. Cambridge, MA: Harvard University Press.

———(1991). Wishes, needs, and interpersonal negotiations. *Psychoanalytic Dialogues: A Journal of Relational Perspectives* Vol. I.

Modell, A. (1990). *Other Times, Other Realities: Toward a Theory of Psychoanalytic Treatment.* Cambridge, MA: Harvard University Press.

Money-Kyrle, R. E. (1956). Normal countertransference and some of its deviations. *International Journal of Psycho-Analysis* 37:360–366.

Moore, R. A. (1961). Reaction formation as a countertransference phenomenon in the treatment of alcoholism. *Quarterly Journal of Studies on Alcoholism* 22:481–486.

Morgan, D. W. (1984). Cross-cultural factors in the supervision of psychotherapy. *Psychiatric Forum*, Spring, pp. 61–64.

Mrazek, P. B. (1981). Special problems in the treatment of child sexual abuse. In *Sexually Abused Children and Their Families*, ed. P. B. Mrazek and C. H. Kempe, pp. 159–166. New York: Pergamon Press.

Myers, W. A. (1987). Actions speak louder. In *Psychoanalytic Quarterly* 56:645–666.

Naegle, M. (1983). The nurse and the alcoholic: redefining an historically ambivalent relationship. In, *Journal of Psychiatric Nursing and Mental Health Services* 21:17–23.

Neff, L. (1971). Chemicals and their effects on the adolescent ego. In *Adolescent Psychiatry, vol. I, Development and Clinical Studies*, p. 118. New York: Basic Books.

Neubauer, P. (1980). The role of insight in psychoanalysis. In *Psychoanalytic Exploration of Technique: Discourse on the Theory of Therapy*, ed. H. Blum. New York: International Universities Press.

Newcomb, M. D., and Bentler, P. M. (1989). Substance use and abuse among children and teenagers. *American Psychologist* 44:242–248.

Nielsen, L. (1988). Substance abuse, shame and professional boundaries and ethics: disentangling the issues. In *The Treatment of Shame and Guilt*. Haworth, NJ: The Haworth Press, Inc.

Niven, R. G. (1986). Adolescent drug abuse. *Hospital and Community Psychiatry* 37:596–607.

Notman, M., Khantzian, E., and Koumans, A. (1987). Psychotherapy with the substance-dependent physician: pitfalls and strategies. *American Journal of Psychotherapy* 41:220–230.

Oberndorf, C. P. (1954). Selectivity and option for psychiatry. In *American Journal of Psychiatry* 110:754–758.

Ogden, T. H. (1989). *The Primitive Edge of Experience.* Northvale, NJ: Jason Aronson.

Olden, C. (1953). On adult empathy with children. In *Psychoanalytic Study of the Child* 8:111–126. New York: International Universities Press.

Orbach, S. (1978). *Fat is a Feminist Issue.* New York: Paddington Press.

Ordway, J. A. (1973). Some emotional consequences of racism for whites. In *Racism and Mental Health*, eds. C. V. Willie, B. M. Kramer, and B. S. Brown, pp. 144–147. Pittsburgh: University of Pittsburgh Press.

Palaci, J. (1980). Psychoanalysis of the self and psychotherapy. In *Advances in Self Psychology*, ed. A. Goldberg, pp. 317–347. New York: International Universities Press.

Palazzoli, M. (1963). *Self-starvation: From the Intrapsychic to the Transpersonal Approach to Anorexia Nervosa*. London: Human Context Books.

Palombo, J. (1985). Self psychology and countertransference in the treatment of children. *Child and Adolescent Social Work Journal* 2:36–48.

Pearson, G. (1968). *A Handbook of Child Psychoanalysis: A Guide to the Psychoanalytic Treatment of Children and Adolescents*. New York: Basic Books.

Perkins, M. and Hornsby, L. (1984). Common countertransference issues related to inpatients/residential psychiatric treatment of children. *The Psychiatric Hospital* 15:65–74.

Person, E., and Ovesey, L. (1983). Psychoanalytic theories of gender identity. *Journal of the American Academy of Psychoanalysis* 11:203–226.

Piene, F., Auestad, A., Lang, J., and Leira, T. (1983). Countertransference-transference seen from the point of view of child psychoanalysis. *Scandinavian Psychoanalytic Review* 6:43–57.

Pinderhughes, C. A., and Pinderhughes, E. B. (1982). Cultural issues in psychiatric residency training: perspective of the training directors. In *Cross-cultural Psychiatry*, ed. A. Gaw, pp. 247–284. Littleton, MA: John Wright-PSB Inc.

Pine, F. (1974). On the concept "borderline" in children: a clinical essay. In *Psychoanalytic Study of the Child* 29:341–347. New Haven, CT: Yale University Press.

———(1988). The four psychologies of psychoanalysis and their place in clinical work. *Journal of the American Psychoanalytic Association* 36:571–596.

Piran, N., Lerner, P., Garfinkel, P., Kennedy, S. H., et al. (1988). Personality disorders in anorexic patients. *International Journal of Eating Disorders* 7:589–599.

Pollak, J., and Levy, S. (1989). Countertransference and failure to report child abuse and neglect. *Child Abuse and Neglect* 13:515–522.

Pollock, G. H. (1961). Mourning and adaptation. *International Journal of Psycho-Analysis* 42:344–361.

Polombo, J. (1985). Self psychology and countertransference in the treatment of children. *Child and Adolescent Social Work Journal* 2:36–48.

Poznanski, E. O. (1979). Childhood depression: a psychodynamic approach to the etiology and treatment of depression in children. In *Depression in Children and Adolescents*, eds. A. French and I. Berlin, pp. 46–68. New York: Human Sciences Press.

Proctor, J. (1959). Countertransference phenomena in the treatment of severe character disorders in children and adolescents. In *Dynamics of Psychopa-*

thology in Childhood, eds. L. Jessner and E. Pavenstedt, pp. 293–309. New York: Grune and Stratton.

Racker, H. (1953). The countertransference neurosis. *International Journal of Psycho-Analysis* 34:313–324.

———(1957). The meanings and uses of countertransference. *Psychoanalytic Quarterly* 26:303–357.

———(1968). *Transference and Countertransference*. New York: International Universities Press.

Rando, T. (1984). *Grief, Dying, and Death*. Champaign: Research Press.

Rapaport, D., and Gill, M. (1959). The points of view and assumptions of metapsychology. In *The Collected Papers of David Rapaport*, ed. M. Gill, pp. 795–811. New York: Basic Books.

Raphael, B. (1983). *The Anatomy of Bereavement*. New York: Basic Books.

Ray, O., and Ksir, C. (1990). *Drugs, Society, and Human Behavior*. Boston: Times Mirror/Mosby.

Redl, F. (1963). Psychoanalysis and group psychotherapy: a developmental point of view. *American Journal of Orthopsychiatry* 33:135–147.

Reeves, C. (1979). Transference in the residential treatment of children. *Journal of Child Psychotherapy* 5:25–38.

Reich, A. (1951). On countertransference. *International Journal of Psycho-Analysis* 32:25–31.

———(1960). Further remarks on the countertransference. *International Journal of Psycho-Analysis* 41:389–395.

———(1966). Empathy and countertransference. In *Psychoanalytic Contributions*. New York: International Universities Press, 1973.

Reich, W. (1925). *The Impulsive Character and Other Writings*. New York: New American Library, 1974.

Reichard, S. (1956). A re-examination of "Studies in Hysteria." *Psychoanalytic Quarterly* 25:155–177.

Reik, T. (1948). *Listening with the Third Ear*. New York: Farrar and Straus.

Renik, O. (1986). Countertransference in theory and practice. *Journal of the American Psychoanalytic Association* 34:699–708.

Rinsley, D. B. (1981). Borderline psychopathology: the concepts of Masterson and Rinsley and beyond. *Adolescent Psychiatry* 9:259–274.

Rosen, H. D., and Frank, J. D. (1962). Negroes in psychotherapy. *American Journal of Psychiatry* 119:456–460.

Rosenfeld, A. A., and Newburger, E. H. (1977). Compassion vs. control: conceptual and practical pitfalls in the broadened definition of child abuse. *Journal of the American Medical Association* 237:2086.

Rosenfeld, H. A. (1964). *Psychotic States*. New York: International Universities Press.

Rosenfeld, S. (1965). Some thoughts on the handling of borderline children.

In. *Psychoanalytic Study of the Child* 20:495–517. New York: International Universities Press.

Rosenfeld, S., and Sprince, M. (1963). An attempt to formulate the meaning of the concept borderline. In *Psychoanalytic Study of the Child* 18:603–635. New York: International Universities Press.

Rutter, M. (1971). Parent child separation: psychological effects on the children. *Journal of Child Psychology and Psychiatry* 12:233–260.

Sadow, L., Gedo, J., Miller, J., Pollock, G., Sabshin, M., and Schlessinger, N. (1968). The process of hypothesis change in three early psychoanalytic concepts. In *Freud: The Fusion of Science and Humanism—The Intellectual History of Psychoanalysis*, ed. J. Gedo and G. Pollack. *Psychological Issues* 10, monographs 34 and 35.

Saint-Exupery, A. de (1971). *The Little Prince*. New York: Harcourt, Brace and World.

Sandler, J. (1976). Countertransference and role responsiveness. *International Review of Psycho-Analysis* 3:43–47.

Sandler, J., Kennedy, H. J., and Tyson, R. L. (1980). *The Technique of Child Psychoanalysis: Discussions with Anna Freud*. Cambridge, MA: Harvard University Press.

Schachter, J. S., and Butts, H. F. (1968). Transference and countertransference in interracial analysis. *Journal of the American Psychoanalytic Association* 16:792–808.

Schaefer, D. (1987). *Choices and Consequences: What to Do When a Teenager Uses Alcohol/Drugs*. New York: Johnson Institute.

Schafer, R. (1959). Generative empathy in the treatment situation. *Psychoanalytic Quarterly* 28:117–126.

Schowalter, J. (1986). Countertransference in work with children: review of a neglected concept. *Journal of the American Academy of Child Psychiatry* 25:40–45.

———(1977). The child's reaction to his own terminal illness. In *Loss and Grief*, ed. B. Schoenberg, A. Carr, D. Peretz, and A. Kutscher, pp. 51–69. New York: Columbia University Press.

Schwartz, D., Thompson, M. (1979). Epidemiology of anorexia nervosa. *American Journal of Psychiatry*.

———(1981). Do anorectics get well? Current research and future needs. *American Journal of Psychiatry* 138:319–323.

Schwartz, D., Thompson, M., and Johnson, C. (1982). Anorexia nervosa and bulimia: the socio-cultural context. *International Journal of Eating Disorders* 1:20–36.

Searles, H. (1958). The schizophrenic's vulnerability to the therapist's unconscious processes. *Journal of Nervous and Mental Diseases* 127:247–262.

———(1979). *Countertransference and Related Subjects*. New York: International Universities Press.

Segal, H. (1957). Notes on symbol formation. *International Journal of Psycho-Analysis* 38:391–397.

———(1964). *Introduction to the Work of Melanie Klein.* New York: Basic Books.

Shaffer, D. (1986). Developmental factors in child and adolescent suicide. In *Depression in Young People,* ed. M. Rutter, C. F. Izard, and D. B. Read, pp. 383–396. New York: Guilford Press.

Shane, M. (1979). A developmental approach to working through. *International Journal of Psycho-Analysis* 60:375–382.

———(1980). Countertransference and the developmental orientation and approach. *Psychoanalysis and Contemporary Thought* 3:195–212.

Shapiro, H. and Morris, L. (1971). Placebo effects in medical and psychological therapies. In *Handbook of Psychotherapy and Behavioral Change: Empirical Analysis,* ed. A. Bergin and S. Garfield, pp. 369–410. New York: John Wiley and Sons.

Shapiro, T. (1983). The borderline syndrome in children: a critique. In *The Borderline Child: Approaches to Etiology, Diagnosis and Treatment,* ed. K. Robson, pp. 12–27. New York: McGraw-Hill.

Sharoff, R. L. (1969). Character problems and their relationship to drug abuse. *American Journal of Psychoanalysis* 29:186.

Shectman, G. (1989). Countertransference dilemmas with borderline patients, the contribution of psychological testing. *Bulletin of the Menninger Clinic* 53:310–318.

Sheppy, M. I., Friesen, J. D., and Hakstian, A. R. (1988). Eco-system analysis of anorexia nervosa. *Journal of Adolescence* 11:373–391.

Shneidman, E. (1973). *The Deaths of Man.* New York: Quadrangle/New York Times Book.

———(1978). Some aspects of psychotherapy with dying patients. In *Psychological Care of the Dying Patient,* ed. C. Garfield. New York: McGraw-Hill.

Silver, D. (1983). Psychotherapy of the characterologically difficult patient. *Canadian Journal of Psychiatry* 28:513–521.

Smirnoff, V. (1971). *The Scope of Child Analysis.* New York: International Universities Press.

———(1988). Countertransference, thus lives the analyst. *Jahrbuch der Psychoanalyse* 22:9–35.

Sohlberg, S., Norring, C., Holmgren, S., and Rosmark, B. (1989). Impulsivity and long-term prognosis of psychiatric patients with anorexia. *Journal of Child Psychotherapy* 10:199–215.

Sohn, L. (1985). Anorexic and bulimic states of mind in the psycho-analytic treatment of anorexic/bulimic patients and psychotic patients. *Psychoanalytic Psychotherapy* 1:49–56.

Sourkes, B. (1977). Facilitating family coping with childhood cancer. *Journal of Pediatric Psychology* 2:65–67.

————(1982). *The Deepening Shade: Psychological Aspects of Life-threatening Illness*. Pittsburgh: University of Pittsburgh Press.

————(1990). Witness through time. *Journal of Palliative Care* 6:55–56.

Sours, J. A. (1974). The anorexia nervosa syndrome. *International Journal of Psycho-Analysis* 55:567–576.

Spiegel, J. P. (1976). Cultural aspects of transference and countertransference revisited. *Journal of the American Academy of Psychoanalysis* 4:447–467.

Spinetta, J., and Deasy-Spinetta, P., eds. (1981). *Living with Childhood Cancer*. St. Louis: C. V. Mosby.

Spitz, R. (1946). Anaclitic depression. In *Psychoanalytic Study of the Child* 5:113–117.

Spitzer, R. I., Endicott, J., and Gibbon, M. (1979). Crossing the border into borderline personality and borderline schizophrenia: the development of criteria. *Archives of General Psychiatry* 36:17–24.

Spotnitz, H. (1969). *Modern Psychoanalysis of the Schizophrenic Patient*. New York: Grune and Stratton.

————(1976). *Psychotherapy of Preoedipal Conditions*. Northvale, NJ: Jason Aronson.

————(1979). Narcissistic countertransference. In *Countertransference: The Therapist's Contribution to Treatment*, ed. L. Epstein and A. Feiner, pp. 329–343. New York: Jason Aronson.

Sprince, M. (1984). Early psychic disturbances in anorexic and bulimic patients as reflected in the psychoanalytic process. *Journal of Nervous and Mental Disease* 177:249–258.

Steiger, H., Van der Feen, J., Goldstein, C., and Leichner, P. (1989). Defense styles and parental bonding in eating-disordered women. *International Journal of Eating Disorders* 8:131–140.

Sterba, R. (1934). The fate of the ego in psycho-analytic therapy. *International Journal of Psycho-Analysis* 15:117–126.

Stern, A. (1938). A psychoanalytic investigation of therapy in the borderline neurosis. *Psychoanalytic Quarterly* 7:467–489.

————(1945). A psychoanalytic therapy in the borderline neurosis. *Psychoanalytic Quarterly* 14:190–198.

————(1948). Transference in the borderline neurosis. *Psychoanalytic Quarterly* 17:527–528.

Stern, D. (1985). *The Interpersonal World of the Infant*. New York: Basic Books.

Stolorow, R., and Lachman, F. (1980). *Psychoanalysis of Developmental Arrests: Theory and Treatment*. New York: International Universities Press.

Stone, L. (1954). The widening scope of indications for psychoanalysis. *Journal of the American Psychoanalytic Association* 2:567–594.

————(1961). *The Psychoanalytic Situation*. New York: International Universities Press.

————(1981) Notes on the noninterpretive elements in the psychoanalytic situation and process. In *Transference and its Context*, pp. 153–175. New York: Jason Aronson, 1984.

Stone, M. (1981). Borderline syndrome: a consideration of subtypes and an overview—directions for research. *Psychiatric Clinics of North America* 4:3–24.

Strupp, H. (1975). Comments on Bratter. *Counseling Psychologist* 5:25–26.

Sukosky, D. G., and Marvasti, J. A. (1991). Comparative Overview of child and elder abuse: relevance for the forensic professional. *American Journal of Forensic Psychiatry* 12:23–39.

Sullivan, H. S. (1953). *The Interpersonal Theory of Psychiatry*. New York: W. W. Norton.

Talbott, J. A. (1986). Chronic mentally ill young adults (18–40) with substance abuse problems; a review of relevant literature and creation of a research agenda. In *Task Force on Chronic Mentally Ill Young Adults*, November. University of Maryland.

Tansey, M., and Burke, W. (1989). *Understanding Countertransference*. Hillsdale, NJ: The Analytic Press.

Thoma, H., Kachele, H., and Jiminez, J. P. (1986). La countertransferencia en una perspectiva historico-critica. *Revista de Psicoanalisis* 43:1237–1272.

Thomas, A. (1962) Pseudo-transference reactions due to cultural stereotyping. *American Journal of Orthopsychiatry* 32:894–900.

Thompson, C., Crowley, R., and Tauber, E. (1952). Symposium on countertransference. *Samiska* 6:205–228.

Ticho, G. (1967). On Self-analysis. *International Journal of Psycho-Analysis* 48:308–318.

———(1971). Cultural aspects of transference and countertransference. *Bulletin of the Menninger Clinic* 35:313–334.

Tolpin, M. (1978). Self objects and oedipal objects. In *Psychoanalytic Study of the Child* 33:167–184.

Touhy, A. (1987). Psychoanalytic perspectives on child abuse. *Child and Adolescent Social Work* 4:25–40.

Tower, L. (1956). Countertransference. *Journal of the American Psychoanalytic Association* 4:224–225.

Treadway, D. (1989). *Before It's Too Late: Working with Substance Abuse in the Family*. New York: W. W. Norton & Co.

Trout, M. (1986). *Working Papers on Process In Infant Mental Health Assessment and Intervention*. (Available from The Infant–Parent Institute, 328 N. Neil Street, Champaign, IL 61820).

Tustin, F. (1984). Autistic shapes. Paper presented at Meeting of the Applied Section of the British Psycho-Analytical Society, 25 January, 1984.

Tylim, I. (1978). Narcissistic transference and countertransference in adolescent treatment. In *Psychoanalytic Study of the Child* 33:279–292. New Haven, CT: Yale University Press.

Tyson, P. (1978). Transference and developmental issues in the analysis of a prelatency child. In *Psychoanalytic Study of the Child* 33:213–236.

———(1980). The gender of the analyst in relation to transference and countertransference in prelatency children. In *Psychoanalytic Study of the Child* 35:321–338. New Haven, CT: Yale University Press.

Uphoff, K. (1990). Personal communication.

Vaillant, G. (1981). Dangers of psychotherapy in the treatment of alcoholism. In *Dynamic Approaches to the Understanding and Treatment of Alcoholism*, eds. M. Bean and N. Zinberg. New York: The Free Press.

Van Dam, H. (1966). Problems of transference in child analysis. *Journal of the American Psychoanalytic Association* 14:528–537.

Van Dongen-Melman, J., and Sanders-Woudstra, J. (1986). The fatally ill child and the family. In *Psychiatry*, eds. R. Michels and J. Cavenar. Philadelphia: J. B. Lippincott.

Vaslamatzis, C., Kanellos, P., Tserpe, V., and Verveniotos, S. (1986). Countertransference in short-term dynamic psychotherapy. *Psychotherapy and Psychosomatics* 46:105–109.

Vela, R., Gottlieb, E., and Gottlieb, G. (1983). Borderline syndrome in childhood: a critical review. In *The Borderline Child—Approaches to Etiology, Diagnosis and Treatment*, ed. K. Robson. New York: McGraw Hill.

Wagner, S., Jalmi, K. A., and Mcguire, T. V. (1987). The sense of personal ineffectiveness in patients with eating disorders: one construct or several? *International Journal of Eating Disorders* 6:495–505.

Waksman, J. (1986). The countertransference of the child analyst. *International Review of Psycho-Analysis* 13:405–415.

Wallace, N. L., and Wallace, M. E. (1985). Transference/countertransference issues in the treatment of an acting-out adolescent. In *Adolescent Psychiatry* 12:468–477, eds. C. Feinstein, M. Sugar, A. Esman, J. Looney, A. Schwartzberg, and A. Sorosky.

Wassell-Kuriloff, E., and Rappaport, D. M. (1970). Eating disorders and hostility towards the inner life. *Contemporary Psychotherapy Review* 4:96–104.

Weatherston, D., and Tableman, B. (1989). *Infant Mental Health Services: Supporting Competencies-Reducing Risks*. Lansing, MI: Michigan Department of Mental Health.

Weil, A. M. (1953). Certain severe disturbances of ego development in children. In *Psychoanalytic Study of the Child* 8:271–287. New York: International Universities Press.

Weiner, M. I., and King, J. W. (1977). Self-disclosure by the therapist to the adolescent patient. In *Adolescent Psychiatry, vol. 5: Developmental and Clinical Studies*, eds. S. Feinstein, M. Sugar, A. Esman, V. Looney, A. Schwartzberg, and A. Sorosky, pp. 449–459. Chicago, IL: University of Chicago Press.

Weisman, A. (1977). The psychiatrist and the inexorable. In *New Meanings of Death*, ed. H. Feifel. New York: McGraw Hill.

Weiss, S. (1964). Parameters in child analysis. *Journal of the American Psychoanalytic Association* 12:587–599.

Weiss, S., Fineberg, H., Gelman, R., and Kohrman, R. (1966). Technique of child analysis: problems of the opening phase. *Journal of Child Psychiatry* 7:639–662.

Weller, E. B., and Weller, R.A. (1990). Depressive disorders in children and adolescents. In *Psychiatric Disorders in Children and Adolescents*, ed. B. Garfinkel, G. Carlson, and E. B. Weller, pp. 3–20. Philadelphia: W. B. Saunders.

West, M. (1979). The influence of social class on diagnosis. Master's thesis, Smith College School for Social Work (unpublished).

Wheeler, K., and Malmquist, J. (1987). Treatment approaches in adolescent chemical dependency. *The Pediatric Clinics of North America* 34:437–447.

Winnicott, D. W., ed. (1945). Primitive emotional development. In *Collected Papers: Through Pediatrics to Psychoanalysis*, pp. 145–156. New York: Basic Books, 1958.

———(1949). Hate in the counter-transference. In *International Journal of Psycho-Analysis* 30:69–75.

———ed., (1953). Transitional objects and transitional phenomena. In *Collected Papers: Through Pediatrics to Psychoanalysis*, pp. 229–242. New York: Basic Books.

———(1958). *Collected Papers: Through Pediatrics to Psychoanalysis*. New York: Basic Books.

———(1960). The theory of the parent–infant relationship. *International Journal of Psycho-Analysis* 41:585–595.

———(1962a). Ego integration. In *The Maturational Process and the Facilitating Environment*, ed. D. W. Winnicott, pp. 53–56. New York: Basic Books, 1965.

———(1962b). Providing for the child in health and crisis. In *The Maturational Process and the Facilitating Environment*, ed. D. W. Winnicott, pp. 63–72. New York: Basic Books, 1965.

———(1962c). Dependence in infant-care, in child-care, and in the psychoanalytic setting. *International Journal of Psycho-Analysis* 44:339–344.

———(1963). Psychiatric disorder in terms of infantile maturational processes. In *The Maturational Process and the Facilitating Environment*, ed. D. W. Winnicott, pp. 230–241. New York: Basic Books, 1965.

———(1969). The use of an object. *International Journal of Psycho-Analysis* 50:711–716.

———(1986). *Holding and Interpretation: Fragment of an Analysis*. London: Hogarth Press.

Wolf, E. (1972). *Technique of child analysis: Problems of Countertransference*, report of paper delivered to the Chicago Analytic Society.

———(1988). *Treating the Self: Elements of Clinical Self Psychology*. New York: Guilford Press.

Wooley, S. C. (1990). Uses of countertransference in the treatment of eating disorders: a gender perspective. In *Psychodynamic Treatment of Anorexia Nervosa and Bulimia*, ed. C. L. Johnson. New York: Guilford Press.

Worden, W. (1982). *Grief Counseling and Grief Therapy: A Handbook for the Mental Health Practitioner*. New York: Springer.

Wright, B. (1986). An approach to infant-parent psychotherapy. *Infant Mental Health Journal* 4:247–263.

Wurmser, L. (1972). Drug abuse: nemesis of psychiatry. *American Scholar* 41:393–407.

Yandell, W. (1962). Therapeutic problems related to the expression of sexual drives in children. In *Clinical Studies in Childhood Psychoses*, ed. S. Szurek and I. Berlin, pp. 498–508. New York: Brunner/Mazel, 1973.

Yorke, C. (1970). A critical review of some psychoanalytic literature on drug addiction. *British Journal of Medical Psychology* 43:151–159.

Zelman, G. L. (1990). Child abuse reporting and failure to report among mandated reporters. *Journal of Interpersonal Violence* 5:3–22.

Zerbe, D. (1986). Countertransference, resistance and frame management in the psychotherapy of a 15-year-old anorexic and her mother. *Clinical Social Work Journal* 14:213–223.

Zetzel, E. (1956/1970). The concept of transference. In E. Zetzel, *The Capacity for Emotional Growth*, pp. 168–181. New York: International Universities Press.

———, ed. (1958a). Therapeutic alliance in the analysis of hysteria. In *The Capacity for Emotional Growth*, pp. 182–196. New York: International Universities Press, 1970.

———(1958b). The analytic situation and the analytic process. In *The Capacity for Emotional Growth*, pp. 197–215. New York: International Universities Press, 1970.

———, ed. (1965). A developmental model and the theory of therapy. In *The Capacity for Emotional Growth*, pp. 266–271. New York: International Universities Press, 1970.

Zetzel, E., and Meissner, W. (1973). *Basic Concepts of Psychoanalytic Psychiatry*. New York: Basic Books.

Zinner, J., and Shapiro, E. (1972). Projective identifications as a mode of perception and behavior in families of adolescents. *International Journal of Psycho-Analysis* 53:523–529.

INDEX